# A CASEBOOK
# IN ABNORMAL PSYCHOLOGY

2

# Contributors

Robin F. Apple
*Stanford University School of Medicine*

W. Stewart Agras, M.D.
*Stanford University School of Medicine*

Nancy Andreasen, M.D., Ph.D.
*University of Iowa School of Medicine*

Russell Barkley, Ph.D.
*University of Massachusetts School of Medicine*

David Barlow, Ph.D.
*Boston University*

Fred Berlin, M.D.
*Independent practice*

Bruce Bongar, Ph.D.
*Pacific Graduate School*

Timothy A. Brown
*Center for Stress and Anxiety Disorders*

Gwenyth Edwards
*University of Massachusetts School of Medicine*

Albert Ellis, Ph.D.
*Independent practice*

Richard P. Halgin, Ph.D.
*University of Massachusetts at Amherst*

Gerald Hurowitz
*Columbia University College of Physicians and Surgeons*

Helen Singer Kaplan, M.D., Ph.D. (deceased)
*New York Hospital–Cornell Medical Center*

Donald F. Klein
*Columbia University College of Physicians and Surgeons*

Richard Kluft, M.D.
*Institute of Pennsylvania Hospital*

Donald Meichenbaum, Ph.D.
*University of Waterloo*

Theodore Millon, Ph.D.
*Independent practice*

Marc Schuckit, M.D.
*University of California San Diego*

Gail S. Steketee, Ph.D.
*Boston University*

Susan Krauss Whitbourne
*University of Massachusetts at Amherst*

Thomas Widiger, Ph.D.
*University of Kentucky*

Judy M. Zarit
*Pennsylvania State University*

Steven Zarit, Ph.D.
*Pennsylvania State University*

# A CASEBOOK IN ABNORMAL PSYCHOLOGY

## FROM *THE FILES OF EXPERTS*

*EDITED BY*

**Richard P. Halgin**
*University of Massachusetts at Amherst*

**Susan Krauss Whitbourne**
*University of Massachusetts at Amherst*

*New York   Oxford*
OXFORD UNIVERSITY PRESS
1998

Oxford University Press

Oxford   New York
Athens   Auckland   Bangkok   Bogota   Bombay
Buenos Aires   Calcutta   Cape Town   Dar es Salaam
Delhi   Florence   Hong Kong   Istanbul   Karachi
Kuala Lumpur   Madras   Madrid   Melbourne
Mexico City   Nairobi   Paris   Singapore
Taipei   Tokyo   Toronto   Warsaw

and associated companies in
Berlin   Ibadan

Published by Oxford University Press, Inc.
198 Madison Avenue, New York, New York 10016

Oxford is a registered trademark of Oxford University Press

**Library of Congress Cataloging-in-Publication Data**

A casebook in abnormal psychology: From the files of experts / edited
by Richard P. Halgin, Susan Krauss Whitbourne.
p.   cm.
Includes bibliographical references and index.
Whitbourne, Susan Krauss.
ISBN 0-19-509298-8 (pbk.)
1. Psychology, Pathological—Case studies.   2. Psychotherapy—Case
studies.   I. Halgin, Richard P.
IN PROCESS
616.89—dc21                                                           97-9227
                                                                      CIP

1  3  5  7  9  8  6  4  2

Printed in the United States of America
on acid-free paper

# Contents

# A CASEBOOK
# IN ABNORMAL PSYCHOLOGY

# 1 | The Therapeutic Process

*Richard P. Halgin and
Susan Krauss Whitbourne*

Relationships, the core of human existence, are experienced in countless ways in our lives. Those that promote positive growth are typically loving, teaching, or caring connections with other people. In this book, you will enter the world of professionals who have devoted much of their lives to the task of helping to foster positive change in individuals suffering from psychological disorders. You will learn about some of the relationships in which these mental health experts have touched the lives of troubled people. You will also read about the ways in which these troubled individuals have, in turn, affected the clinicians who treated them.

All the professionals whose case studies you will read in this book are internationally regarded as leaders in the field of psychiatry and psychology. They share stories from their files that bring to life the complexities of diagnosis and treatment of a disorder in their area of expertise. They tell the stories of their clients (referred to by some as patients) in a way that brings the clinical process to life.

## THE THERAPY RELATIONSHIP

When thinking about psychotherapy, some people conjure an image of a process in which one person "does something" to another person. That is, a therapist "treats" a client by applying certain psychological techniques. What is missing from this view is the reciprocity, or mutual impact, that each person in the dyad has on the other. In therapeutic relationships, caregivers can also be affected in profound ways by those who come to them for help. On a broader level, therapists may find that working with clients stimulates them to develop or refine their theories, research approaches, and scholarly writings. Even the most prominent of experts may be affected in significant ways by those who turn to them for help. As we explore the intricacies of the therapy relationship, we will look separately at the qualities of the helpseekers and the helpers, and then explore the fascinating interaction between the two.

## Who Are the Helpseekers?

Who are these people who seek out the wisdom of helping professionals? To tackle this question, it is important to have an understanding of the different views that professionals have of this relationship. Some clinicians, particularly those who adhere to a medical model of psychiatry, prefer to view the help-seeker as a "patient"—literally, a person who is suffering and in need of a health professional's attention. Although the term may imply that the patient is a passive recipient of care, this is not what is meant by clinicians who favor this term. Clinicians who use the term "patient" regard their relationship as a professional bond that is deeply rooted in mutual trust. The doctor's relationship to a patient is regarded as involving a sacred obligation similar to that which characterizes the work of a priest or minister. Other clinicians prefer to view the help-seeker as a "client" who enters a relationship with a professional who is being paid for services; in this view, the clinician is a consultant who takes more of a collaborative stance with the person seeking help. Interestingly enough, some clinicians use the terms interchangeably, depending on the context; perhaps they see *patients* at the hospital and *clients* in the office of their private practice. Although this debate may seem to be a matter of semantics, it is an important issue for some clinicians.

The most essential point to consider, regardless of terminology preference, is that psychotherapy involves an intense relationship. The concept of a partnership captures the spirit of two people journeying toward some goal. Along this route, each of the participants will change, and in the best of situations each will grow. For the sake of simplicity, and because the term "client" is used in most of the cases in this book, we refer to helpseekers as clients in this chapter.

## Who Are the Helpers?

Who are the people who provide guidance, wisdom, and care for these troubled helpseekers? Optimally, clinicians are astute observers of human nature who have developed expertise in listening to the concerns and problems of people and in recommending interventions that are aimed at reducing distress and alleviating pain. There are many types of clinicians, and they approach their work in a variety of ways, based on their training and orientation. Some are psychiatrists, or medical doctors, whose initial training was that of a physician with a subsequent specialization in the field of psychiatry. Others are clinical psychologists whose post-college training has been in a graduate program in psychology. Social workers comprise a third segment of the mental health field; these professionals obtain their training in graduate schools of social work. You will read cases by specialists in each of these three fields. Interestingly, it is not their clinical practice alone that has brought them international renown, although they are gifted clinicians. Their prominence has evolved from the research and scholarship they have published in books and prestigious journals. In their case studies, they draw from both their clinical experience and their scientific expertise in telling the stories of their work with clients.

## THE CASE STUDY

This book is a compilation of some of the most compelling case histories you will ever read. They are the ones that have stood out in the minds of the contributors for very special reasons. Some have been turning points in the careers of the contributors. Others epitomize the theoretical and clinical approach of the contributors. To prepare you for reading these stories, we feel it is helpful to share the elements of a well-developed case study, elements you will find in each of these chapters.

Customarily, a case study is the clinician's description of the client's presenting problem, assessment of the client, and intervention. Those are the basics, but for this volume we have asked contributors to go beyond the essentials of the usual case study in which the clinician speaks only about the client. We have asked these clinicians to put their narratives in the first person, to reflect on their thoughts about the case, their strategies in approaching the case, and the struggles they encountered along the way. What has emerged in this process is a unique collection of the innermost thoughts and reactions of the contemporary world's experts. This is a wonderful privilege, usually provided only to other professionals.

In these cases, the clinicians begin their stories by giving us a snapshot of the initial presentation of the clients. The initial presentation helps the reader imagine how these individuals appeared at the point of the first encounter—their appearance, notable behaviors, and manner of speaking. The clinicians draw our attention to some of the clues which they perceived to be key to the development of their diagnostic hypotheses. Next, you will read about the history of these clients—the past and recent life events that give some insight into how the client developed the disorder.

### The Diagnostic System

Following the introductory material, the contributors present their diagnoses using the technical terms that are common in the field. These diagnostic terms are derived from a formal list that is published by the American Psychiatric Association in its *Diagnostic and Statistical Manual of Mental Disorders*, currently in its fourth edition. This volume, which was published in 1994, is more commonly known as *DSM-IV*.

In the *DSM-IV* each psychological disorder appears on one or both of two "axes," or dimensions, known as Axis I and Axis II. The three remaining axes are used to provide objective indicators of a client's physical health (Axis III), extent of stressful life circumstances (Axis IV), and overall degree of functioning (Axis V). Let's take a closer look at each of these dimensions, or axes.

### Axis I: Clinical Disorders

The major disorders that form the focus of clinical treatment are designated on Axis I. Included on Axis I, for example, are anxiety disorders, dissociative disorders, sexual disorders, mood disorders, schizophrenia, and so on. These disorders share the common feature that they are, in a sense, like illnesses that arise at some point in the individual's life and overwhelm or overshadow the individual's underlying personality or cognitive functioning.

### Axis II: Personality Disorders and Mental Retardation

In contrast to Axis I disorders, the disorders on Axis II are considered to be part of the underlying "fabric" of the individual's disposition or intellectual capacity. Personality disorders represent enduring, inflexible, and maladaptive personality traits that cause the individual to experience feelings of distress or to suffer from considerable impairment in the ability to carry out the everyday tasks of life. Although this book does not include a case involving mental retardation, such a diagnosis would be specified on Axis II and would represent an enduring disorder of intellectual functioning. In this book, you will read about two personality disorders—one involving borderline personality disorder, and the other antisocial personality disorder.

Clients may receive diagnoses on both Axis I and Axis II, and this is the case for a number of the individuals described in this casebook. As you will see in your reading of these cases, clients with multiple diagnoses present especially difficult treatment challenges for clinicians.

### Axis III: General Medical Conditions

Clinicians document medical conditions on Axis III, which is based on a medical classification system. Some of the medical conditions that can interact in important ways with psychological disorders include chronic diseases such as arthritis, multiple sclerosis, respiratory dysfunction, cancer, cardiovascular diseases, asthma, and diabetes. Terminal illnesses such as cancer or AIDS present particular psychological difficulties that may become the basis of a psychological disorder. The documented existence of a physical disorder is a crucial piece of information that the clinician must have because it means that a major facet of the client's life is being affected by something outside the psychological realm.

*Axis IV: Psychosocial and Environmental Problems*

On Axis IV, the clinician documents events or pressures that may affect the diagnosis, treatment, or outcome of a client's psychological disorder. Stressful events such as job loss, an automobile accident, or the break-up of a long-term relationship can interact with psychological disorders in significant ways. For the most part, the life events on Axis IV are negative in nature. However, "positive" life events, such as a job promotion, might cause problems for an individual because of the increased stresses associated with the position and should be taken into account when developing a comprehensive diagnostic picture.

*Axis V: Global Assessment of Functioning*

The full *DSM-IV* diagnosis is completed when the clinician arrives at an overall judgment on Axis V, which indicates a client's psychological, social, and occupational functioning. The Global Assessment of Functioning (GAF) scale provided on Axis V rates the individual's overall level of psychological health, ranging from a high rating of 100, indicating good functioning in all areas, to a low rating of 1, indicating a markedly serious level of functioning, possibly including suicidal acts. Clinicians use the GAF ratings both to assess the client's prognosis, or chances of improvement, and the seriousness of the client's current symptoms.

## Case Formulation

As you will see when you read the diagnoses assigned to the clients in this volume, very limited information and understanding is communicated by the shorthand phrases of the *DSM-IV* diagnoses. Because even people with the same diagnosis have different characteristics, and the contributing factors to each individual's psychological problem are unique, it is important for clinicians to try to understand the complex set of issues that coalesce in causing and maintaining psychological disturbance. A case formulation transforms the diagnosis from a set of code numbers to a rich descriptive narrative about the client's personal history, and helps the clinician in designing a treatment plan that is attentive to the client's symptoms, unique past experiences, and potential for growth.

Once the stage has been set for understanding the client's history and diagnosis, the clinician describes the course of treatment and the outcome of the case. It is here that you will learn about the events which unfolded in the helping relationship. Even the experts must confront and manage the ups and downs involved in trying to bring about change in a person whose life has been seriously disrupted by psychological disorder. Although most of the cases provide cause for optimism, you will certainly be struck by the fact that clinicians, even world-renowned experts, face a formidable set of challenges. You will see that "success" in psychotherapy is sometimes elusive, and may be measured in different ways.

## EMPIRICAL CONTRIBUTIONS TO UNDERSTANDING AND TREATMENT OF THE DISORDER

The case studies, compelling as they are, only tell part of the story. The contributors to this volume have provided us with insights into how their cases have become woven into their scholarly work. We asked them to explain how their research and theoretical views contributed to their understanding of these clients. They provide an insider's look into the development of their approach, and they explain how their research and treatment of similar clients over the course of years led to the formulation of their system of understanding psychological disorder.

The excitement of looking into the minds of these world-famous clinicians will become evident as you read these cases. In addition to witnessing the therapeutic processes of experts, you will also be privy to understanding how their clinical models have been informed by their scholarship, and how their research and theory have evolved from these clinical endeavors.

# PERSONALITY DISORDERS

A personality disorder involves a longlasting maladaptive pattern of inner experience and behavior, manifested in the ways that a person thinks, feels, relates to other people, and controls impulses. This longlasting pattern is a rigid aspect of the individual and pervades most aspects of the person's life. People with personality disorders are likely to suffer from intense inner distress or encounter problems in many spheres of life.

Personality disorders are usually apparent by the early adult years and over time, these difficulties become part of the very fabric of the individual's being. Inner conflicts and problems relating to other people become more and more entrenched. It's not surprising that many clinicians find these psychotherapy with individuals to be so challenging.

# 2

## About the Author

*Theodore Millon, PhD., DSc, is Professor, Department of Psychiatry, Harvard Medical School, Professor of Psychology, University of Miami, and Dean, Institute for Advanced Studies of Personology and Psychopathology. He has served as President of the International Society for the Study of Personality Disorders and was founding editor of the* Journal of Personality Disorders. *Author of numerous books, notably* Disorders of Personality, *2nd edition (Wiley, 1996),* Personality and Psychopathology *(Wiley, 1996),* Toward a New Personology: An Evolutionary Model *(Wiley, 1990), he has also published numerous other books, chapters, and articles. Professor Millon is perhaps best known for his diagnostic clinical inventories, namely the* Millon Clinical Multiaxial Inventory (MCMI), *the* Millon Adolescent Clinical Inventory (MACI), *and the forthcoming* Millon Behavioral Medicine Consult (MBMC), *each published by NCS Assessments. A widely respected lecturer, Professor Millon has given talks throughout the European continent, in Asia, as well as in over 250 universities and regional workshops in the United States. His forthcoming book on Synergistic Psychotherapy represents his culminating ideas regarding the most effective and successful approaches to the treatment of both Axis I and Axis II mental disorders.*

# Ann: My First Case of Borderline Personality Disorder

**About**

**the**

**Disorder**

Borderline personality disorder, a condition that is both complex and fascinating, causes inner torment for the individual as well as tension and exasperation in relationships. Sparking many interpersonal difficulties is the style used by these individuals in order to frantically avoid real or imagined abandonment; even a brief departure by a loved one may set off depression and rage. It is not surprising, then, that relationships tend to be unstable and pathologically intense, characterized by sudden shifts between idealization and devaluation of others. These individuals tend to be perplexed about their own identity; they may be confused about their direction in life and other central features of their personality. Their impulsivity may create self-damaging or possibly fatal problems; for example, they may recklessly engage in promiscuity, dangerous driving, or binge eating. Attempts to injure themselves may be so extreme that suicide is considered or attempted; some individuals do not go so far as to threaten their own life, but they injure themselves by cutting or burning. Instability of mood results in emotionality that causes them to feel anxious, irritable, and unhappy. They commonly describe feelings of emptiness, which are intensified by boredom that propels them to take action to fill a distressing sense of void. When provoked, even by something unimportant, their expression of rage may overpower others. Lastly, they may become so upset that, at times, they develop psychotic-like symptoms such as paranoid thinking or feelings of unreality or dissociation.

Imagine how challenging it is to treat someone who is so unpredictable. In Dr. Milion's words, they "run through the whole gamut of emotions in therapy, and their erratic and frequently threatening behaviors stir many therapists in response to them."—*Eds.*

9

## THE CASE OF ANN

It was in the mid-1960s that I first stumbled across a young women who, upon retrospection, clearly fit one of the several variants of what we now term the borderline personality. What follows not only summarizes my recollections, but the several formulations of the construct as I have thought and written about them subsequently.

### Initial Presentation

I was somewhat discomforted in returning a call to June. She had been a patient over a nine-month period a little less than a decade or so earlier. Troubled though June appeared to be, her voice and tone were somewhat different than when she was upset in the prior period. After the usual brief pleasantries and family inquiries, June began to tell me about her concerns regarding her daughter Ann, the eldest child of her three children, the youngest being a son now a resident in surgery at a nearby medical center, the middle child a student in a nearby college. I had seen both June and her husband, as well as her children, perhaps six to eight times some years earlier when her daughter Ann was about 9 or 10 years of age, once for a brief period of family therapy, and once just a few years ago, shortly following the death of June's husband, a well-known and respected surgeon in the community.

June began by reporting that Ann was in trouble at college, a prestigious New England university. She was a junior, having dropped out for a couple of semesters owing to prior difficulties. Ann had graduated as the class salutatorian from a local private high school, this despite, as June put it, her erratic emotional behaviors, notably her extensive involvement in drugs, a prior period of life-threatening anorexia, and an aborted two-month pregnancy. Ann was being sent home by the university Dean of Students "to pull herself together" and to be treated for her ostensive psychosomatic problems. June sounded more and more distraught as she recounted concerns over the phone, noting patterns of behavior that were increasingly similar to aspects of her own troubled past. As the phone conversation progressed, June unburdened herself of her own continuing fears and erratic emotions, but also of her periodic bouts with alcohol, which had been a major element of her earlier difficulties. An appointment was made to see June the next day, to be followed by an appointment to see Ann as soon as possible thereafter. Canceling her own appointment, June appeared with Ann the following week. Much to my surprise, Ann had returned from the university the night before with a young professor of English at the university with whom she was having an extended affair. The young man mentioned in passing that he felt quite responsible for many of Ann's current problems and that he was largely unaware that Ann had difficulties going back a decade or more.

Little did I know or think about it at the time, but Ann turned out to be the first genuinely "borderline" patient I had seen professionally. As her history unfolded, it became increasingly clear that her pattern of symptoms and behaviors, though clearly stirred by drugs, reflected many of the central and deeper features of what came to be labeled borderline personality disorder in the DSM-III.

When Ann first was seen, she appeared depressed, contrite, and self-condemning; she knew that the problems she had been experiencing were not merely psychosomatic, as had just been diagnosed by a college physician, that she caused difficulties with both her current and past boyfriends, that she precipitated complications with their friends, and that she periodically became very depressed, if not "crazy." This self-deprecation did not last long; almost immediately after placing the burden of responsibility on her own shoulders, she reversed her course, and began to complain about her boyfriend, her parents, her college chums, her neighborhood, and so on. Once she spilled out her hostility toward everyone and everything, she recanted, became conscience-smitten and self-accusing again.

## Case History

The first item Ann referred to when discussing her past was her belief that she was an unwanted child, that her parents decided not to divorce at the time so as to make her "legitimate." Her parents remained married, though, as she stated, it was a "living hell much of my life." In her first two years, Ann was "clung to" by her mother, receiving a superabundance of love and attention. "It seems as if my mother and I must have stuck together to protect ourselves from my father." Apparently, parental bickering characterized home life from the first day of their marriage; Ann's father remained antagonistic to her from the very beginning, since Ann represented the "cause" of his misery.

The protection and affection that Ann received from her mother in her first two years was substantially reduced with the advent of a sister's birth; Mother's attention turned to the new infant and Ann felt abandoned and vulnerable. She recalled the next several years as ones in which she tried desperately to please her mother, to distract her from her sister and recapture her affection and protection. This "worked at times." But as often as not, Ann's mother was annoyed with her for demanding more than she was able to provide.

By the time a third child appeared on the scene, parental conflicts were especially acute, and Ann was all the more demanding of support and attention as a means of assuaging her increasing anxieties. It was not long after that she began to hear the same comment from her mother that she had heard all too often from her father: "You're the cause of this miserable marriage." Mother would feel pangs of guilt following these outbursts, and would bend over backwards for brief periods to be kind and affectionate. But these moments of affection and love were infrequent; more common were long periods of rejection or indifference.

Ann never was sure what her mother's attitude would be toward her, nor what she could do to elicit her love and attention. Thus, at times when she attempted to be helpful, she gained her mother's appreciation and affection; at other times when Mother felt tired, distraught or preoccupied with her own problems, the same behavior would evoke hostile criticism. It was during these mid-teen years that Ann became anorexic. Though the disorder was extremely distressing to June, Ann appeared to regain weight and resume normal eating habits within one year.

Ann hated her sister "with a vengeance," but feared to express this hostility most of the time. Every now and then, as she put it, she would "let go," tease her unmercifully or physically attack her. Rather interestingly, following these assaults, Ann would "feel terrible" and be contrite, becoming nurturant and protective of her sister. She quickly recognized in therapy that her behavior with her sister paralleled that of her mother's toward Ann. And, in time, Ann observed that this vacillating and ambivalent pattern served as the prototype for her relationships with most people.

Until college, Ann's peer relationships were not notably unusual, although she reported never having been a member of the "in group"; she had her share of friends nevertheless, especially when they would "share" drugs. Ann attended an all-girls prep school where she experienced repeated problems in social relationships. She had a sequence of ill-fated girl friendships; for example, during her first two years, she had four different roommates. Typically, Ann would become "very close" to her roommate; after a short period, usually less than a semester, she would become disillusioned with her friend, noting faults and finding her disloyal; eventually, Ann would become "blue," then "nasty" and hostile.

Before Ann met her current boyfriend, during the first semester of her junior year in college, she decided to move into a single room in her dormitory; though not a total isolate, she rarely mingled socially with the other girls. The new courtship had its trying moments. Ann was inordinately jealous of his "mature friends," and feared he would leave her for someone more desirable. Quite often, she would threaten to break off the romance so as not to be hurt should it progress further; this threat served to "bring him back" to her.

Ann's current relationship mirrored many of the elements she experienced and observed in her childhood. She was submissive and affectionate, then sickly, demanding, and intimidating of her boyfriends, a pattern not unlike the one she saw her mother use to control her father. Ann's partner spent much of his energies trying to placate her, but "Ann is never content." During the nine months of their cohabitation, she seemed satisfied only when they first moved to a new location. But these "bright weeks" dimmed quickly, and the same difficulties reemerged. This time, however, her boyfriend would have "none of this," and refused to budge. Ann again began to experience her physical symptoms, to withdraw affection, vent anger, and vacillate in her moods.

For the first time, Ann began to show bipolar features, as evidenced in rapid shifts between irritable excitement and depressive withdrawal; similarly, aspects of her thought processes became somewhat disorganized. She also began to evidence suspicion regarding the motives of her beau, overdramatizing her emotional difficulties, all signifying, as I viewed it, her deep "cry for help."

Somewhat updated, the following clinical report on Ann was based on an early form of the MCMI; it was written to inform and guide her family physician.

---

This young woman exhibits marked dependency needs, deep and variable moods, and impulsive, angry outbursts. Ann anxiously seeks reassurance from others and is especially vulnerable to fear of separation from those who provide support, despite her frequent attempts to undo their efforts to be helpful. Dependency fears may compel her to be alternately overly compliant, profoundly gloomy, and irrationally argumentative and negativistic. Almost seeking to court undeserved blame and criticism, Ann may appear to find circumstances to anchor her feeling that she deserves to suffer.

She strives at times to be submissive and cooperative, but her behavior has become increasingly unpredictable, irritable, and pessimistic. She often seeks to induce guilt in others for failing her, as she sees it. Repeatedly struggling to express attitudes contrary to her feelings, she may exhibit conflicting emotions simultaneously toward others and herself, most notably love, rage, and guilt. Also notable may be her confusion over her self-image, her highly variable energy levels, easy fatigability, and her irregular sleep-wake cycle.

Ann is particularly sensitive to external pressure and demands, and she may vacillate between being socially agreeable, sullen, self-pitying, irritably aggressive, and contrite. She may make irrational and bitter complaints about the lack of care expressed by others and about being treated unfairly. This behavior keeps others on edge, never knowing if she will react to them in a cooperative or a sulky manner. Although she may make efforts to be obliging and submissive to others, she has learned to anticipate disillusioning relationships, and she often creates the expected disappointment by constantly questioning and doubting the genuine interest and support shown by others. Self-destructive acts and suicidal gestures may be employed to gain attention. These irritable testing maneuvers may exasperate and alienate those on whom she depends. When threatened by separation and disapproval, Ann may express guilt, remorse, and self-condemnation in the hope of regaining support, reassurance, and sympathy.

Beyond her helplessness and clinging behavior, Ann may exhibit an irritable argumentativeness. Recognizing that others may have grown weary of this behavior, she may alternate between voicing gloomy self-deprecation, being apologetic and repentant, and being petulant and bitter. A struggle between dependent acquiescence and assertive independence constantly intrudes into most relationships. Her inability to regulate her emotional controls, her feeling of being misunderstood, and her erratic moodiness contribute to innumerable wrangles and conflicts with others and to persistent tension, resentfulness, and depression.

---

## Diagnosis

Retrospectively analyzed, I would currently assign the following designations according to the *DSM-IV*.

| | |
|---|---|
| Axis I: | • Polysubstance dependence |
| | • Dysthymic disorder |
| | • Somatization disorder |
| Axis II: | • Borderline personality disorder |
| Axis III: | • None |
| Axis IV: | • Partner relational problem |
| Axis V: | • GAF = 55 (current) |

## Case Formulation

Acting erratically, vacillating from one course to another, attempting to achieve incompatible goals, Ann scatters her efforts and dilutes her effectiveness. Caught in her own crosscurrents, she cannot commit herself to one clear direction, swinging indecisively back and forth, performing ineffectually, and experiencing a sense of paralyzing inertia or exhaustion. In addition to the wasteful nature of her ambivalence, she actively impedes her own progress toward conflict resolution and goal attainment. Thus, she frequently undoes what good she previously had done. Driven by contrary feelings, she retracts her "kind words" to others and replaces them with harshness; further, she undermines achievements she struggled so hard to attain. In short, her ambivalence often robs her of what few steps she secured toward progress. This inconstant "blowing hot and cold" behavior precipitates others into reacting in a parallel capricious and inconsistent manner. By prompting these reactions, she recreates the very conditions of her childhood that fostered the development of her unstable behaviors in the first place. Most people weary of her sulking and stubborn unpredictability. Others are frequently goaded into exasperation and confusion when their persistent efforts to placate her negativism so frequently meet with failure. Eventually, everyone is likely to express both anger and disaffection, reactions that serve only to intensify her dismay and anxiety.

Not only does Ann precipitate real difficulties through her behaviors, but she often perceives and anticipates difficulties where none in fact exist. She has learned from past experience (the birth of her sister) that "good things don't last," that positive feelings and attitudes from those whom she sought love will end abruptly and capriciously, and be followed by disappointment, anger, and rejection. Rather than be disillusioned and embittered, rather than allowing herself to be led down the "primrose path" to suffer the humiliation and pain of having her hopes dashed again, she believes it would be better to put a halt to illusory gratifications and to the futility and heartache of short-lived pleasures. Protectively, then, she refuses to wait for others to make the turnabout. Instead, she "jumps the gun," pulls back when things are going well, and thereby cuts off experiences that may have proven gratifying had they been completed. The anticipation of being set back and left in the lurch prompts Ann into a self-fulfilling prophecy. By her own hand, she defeats her chance to experience events that could have promoted change and growth. By cutting off the good will of others and by upsetting their pleasurable anticipations, Ann gains the perverse and negative gratification of venting hostility and anger. These acts, however, prove to be pyrrhic victories; not only do they sabotage her chances for rewarding experiences, but they inevitably provoke counter-hostility from others and increased guilt and anxiety for herself. Her defensive action has instigated responses that perpetuate earlier difficulties, setting into motion a vicious circle in which she feels further discontent and disappointment.

Despite her ambivalence, Ann operates on the premise that she can overcome past disappointments and capture, in full measure, the love and attention she only partially gained in childhood. Unfortunately, Ann's search for complete fulfillment can no longer be achieved since she now possesses needs that are in fundamental opposition to one another; for example, she both wants and does not want the love of those she depends upon. Despite this ambivalence, Ann enters new relationships as if a perfect and idyllic state could be achieved. She goes through the act of seeking a consistent and true source of love, one that will not betray her as her parents and others have in the past. She ventures into new relationships with enthusiasm and blind optimism; this time, all will go well. Despite this optimism, Ann remains unsure of the trust she really could place in others. Mindful of past betrayals and disappointments, she begins to test her newfound "loves" to see if they are loyal and faithful. She may intentionally irritate others, frustrate them, and then withdraw, all in an effort to check whether they will prove as fickle and insubstantial as the others. Soon these testing operations exhaust the partner's patience; annoyance, exasperation, and hostility follow. Ann quickly becomes disenchanted; the "idol" has proved to be marred and imperfect; and she is once more disillusioned and embittered. To vent her resentment at having been naive, Ann usually turns against her "betrayers," disavows and recoils from the affections she had shown, and thereby completes the *vicious* circle. These experiences recur repeatedly, and with each recurrence, Ann further reinforces her pessimistic anticipations. In their efforts to overcome past disillusionment, Ann throws herself into new ventures that will inevitably lead to further disillusion.

Ann's habitual negativism may occasionally cross the line of reason, break out of control and drive her into rages in which she may distort reality, make excessive demands of others, and attack those who she believes have trapped her or forced her into intolerable conflicts. However, following these outbursts, Ann will usually turn her hostility inward, be remorseful, plead forgiveness, and promise "to behave" and "make up" for her unpleasant and "miserable past." One need not be too astute to recognize that these resolutions will likely be short-lived.

As noted, Ann has always resented her dependence on others and often expresses venom toward those she has turned to for security, love, and esteem. She is indecisive and oscillates between apologetic submission, on the one hand, and stubborn resistance and contrariness on the other. She is unable to "get hold of herself," unable to find an enduring or even comfortable niche with others. Although expressing her discontent in an erratic and changeable manner, she has become more inward-turning, and most typically expresses her anger in an intropunitive way. Failures to evoke needed emotional support have led to periods of somatization and depression. At times high-strung and moody, straining to express attitudes contrary to her inner feelings of tension, anger, and dejection, she is overly sensitive to the moods and expectations of others. Whereas in earlier years she successfully learned to be alert to signs of potential hostility and rejection, in recent years, this ability has diminished appreciably. The pattern of adapting her behaviors to comply with the desires of others had been a central coping element of her lifestyle. Not only have these efforts become less and less successful over time, but they have also resulted in a growing sense of personal unworthiness and social inadequacy. Anger has become increasingly intropunitive rather than extrapunitive. She decreasingly expresses her antagonisms and resentments openly and directly. More and more we see a depressive, self-abnegating tone to her verbal and emotional expressions. Although abrupt outbreaks of contrary feelings occasionally emerge, for the most part we now observe an increasingly self-destructive and self-depreciating pattern of behaviors and attitudes. The possibilities of suicide are now almost always present.

## Course of Treatment

Although Ann stayed in treatment for nearly a year, the experience was not a happy or successful one. She frequently left sessions quite upset, unable to express why she was so troubled and confused. During these months, her capacity to orient her life deteriorated. When her boyfriend returned to his teaching responsibilities, she became more depressed and socially withdrawn. Medications were introduced, the very earliest of anti-depressants, but they did little to halt her slide. Therapy drifted in this agitated and depressive state as I concluded that I could do nothing further for her. I referred her to a psychiatrist who hospitalized her at an excellent institution where she stayed for close to two years.

Ann found the entire experience of therapy to be very trying and largely unsuccessful. She felt abandoned by me, bewildered by hospitalization, and miserable when returning home. Despite her deteriorated condition, she continued to be focused on scholarly achievement. She graduated from a local university, entered graduate school, completed a Ph.D., and is now teaching at a community college. Following hospital discharge, she became involved in a therapy group of mine, which she found to be less stressful than individual therapy, staying active and involved for several years before I left the area for another university position.

Ann showed significant improvement over the several years of group treatment, but failed to regain the level of functioning in close relationships that she desired. Dealing with her grief surrounding the death of both her mother and father and the uncertainties that created in her life occupied much of the discussions in the group, but together with the therapist and fellow group members she was able to make useful inroads into the pattern of self-loathing, irritable acting-out, and the despair that had dominated so much of her life.

Group therapy was not smooth going, by any means. Highly unpleasant emotional actions characterized many sessions. These outbursts were dramatic departures from her more usual state, triggered usually by something said that reactivated her sensitivity to being abandoned. Sometimes they would be expressed after a session, but more typically her reaction would occur in the middle of the meeting when Ann would become either mute or resentful, often sitting in silence for the remainder of the session or leaving in tears before it was over. Interim phone calls to me would sometimes create a measure of relief-usually after our discussion uncovered some incidental or unintentional comment that had served to precipitate her anger or dismay, comments that stimulated her fear of being rejected or abandoned. Subsequent clarification of what her fellow group members meant and reassurances about the therapist's commitment to her usually proved sufficient to assuage her feelings, but, on other occasions, no relief was produced and Ann would go for days in a dysphoric state. At times, these events seriously interfered with her willingness to continue her therapy sessions.

Within several months after I transferred the group to another therapist, Ann regressed into the same pattern she exhibited periodically with me. She would become upset about something said by a group member, or more often, the therapist. She would then become noncommunicative, or resentfully angry, or tearfully withdraw from the meeting, followed by an emotionally charged telephone call until the issue was calmly, if temporarily, resolved. She invariably sought out the therapist to mediate between herself and the "offending" group member; this was almost always done outside the group session, mirroring a pattern that Ann had "arranged" in her family of origin, that is, forcing one parent, usually her mother, to serve as the intermediary between her and her father. What the new therapist found himself doing was reworking, with transient success, the interplay of manipulations within Ann's family of origin. Over time, Ann reached the point where she could deal directly with "insensitive" group members, but only with the support of the therapist. Only with repeated assurances and while talking through incidents of possible abandonment, that is, being reassured that neither therapist nor group members would abandon her if she acted out, was Ann able to begin to ride through these rough moments.

## Outcome of the Case

Progress in therapy was desultory, with numerous steps forward and almost as many back. Carry-over to Ann's life outside of therapy was even slower. Nevertheless, and despite numerous disappointments in her social life, her vocational efforts were reasonably successful. She achieved tenure and published two books, one highly biographical. She acquired a few friends, traveled during vacation periods, although she would at times become overwhelmed with the possibility that a personal or social misadventure might occur, leading her to cancel her plans rather abruptly. Nevertheless, over many more years, Ann gradually increased her social contacts and improved the quality of her life. She broadened her range of largely casual acquaintances and learned to moderate her excess sensitivity to potential abandonment. She is still working full time as a college professor, although her inability to establish a long-term intimate relationship is a continuous source of unhappiness in her life.

It is not clear why progress with this borderline was as slow and limited as it has been. Ann is a highly intelligent and generally competent woman. Although she has difficulty in dealing with her insecurities, especially in new relationships, she became a supportive group member to those she came to trust. Ann was at her best in relating to others in distress. Surprisingly, she handled her parents' declining health and death with care and dignity. Their role in engendering her original difficulties seemed to fade, although its residuals continued to plague her, despite all the efforts that individual and group therapy offered to her.

# EMPIRICAL CONTRIBUTIONS TO UNDERSTANDING BORDERLINE PERSONALITY DISORDER

In the past two decades, there have been persuasive reports suggesting a high incidence of abuse during childhood in the history of borderline patients[1,2,3,4] Although sexual abuse appears the most prominent of the abusive triad, it is clear that both verbal and physical abuse may play a role as well. Some investigators[5] have seen an overlap between posttraumatic stress disorder and borderline personalities, noting that it is not only abuse which generates the psychic discordance that can give rise to borderline processes. Other investigators suggest that borderline patients experience their parents as emotionally neglectful rather than overtly abusive.[4]

The results of empirical studies seeking to verify the preceding hypotheses indicate a mixed and complex picture in the pathogenic background of the borderline personality. For example, although childhood sexual abuse appears to be relatively common in borderline patients, not all borderlines have a history of such abuse, and many nonborderlines, as well as nonpatients, also have such histories. It is evident that there are a number of pathways that lead to the development of borderline pathology, some experiencing abuse, neglect, parental loss, and so on. The possible mechanisms of abuse or trauma require an explication of several interacting forces including such secondary elements as feelings of betrayal, shame, and guilt, as well as stigmatization and powerlessness.

Broad and pervasive sociocultural forces may also play a significant role in the development of many borderline personality patterns. This is likely to be found where a society's values and practices are fluid and inconsistent, such as appears increasingly prominent in current Western societies, notably the United States. Under these circumstances its residents are likely to evolve deficits in psychic solidity and stability, especially as they affect the processes which develop during the *adolescent* stage; It is here that the coordination and synthesis of thought and feeling must take place, the failure of which results in the psychic schisms and vacillations that typify the borderline personality structure. An amorphous cultural state, so characteristic of our modern times, is clearly mirrored in the interpersonal vacillations and affective instabilities that characterize the borderline personality. Central to our recent culture have been the increased pace of social change and the growing pervasiveness of ambiguous and discordant customs which children are expected to follow. Under the cumulative impact of rapid industrialization, immigration, mobility, technology, and mass communication, there has been a steady erosion of traditional values and standards. Instead of a simple and coherent body of practices and beliefs, children find themselves confronted with constantly shifting styles and increasingly questioned norms whose durability is uncertain and precarious.[6]

No longer do youngsters find the certainties and absolutes which guided earlier generations. The complexity and diversity of everyday experience play havoc with simple "archaic" beliefs, and render them useless as instruments to deal with contemporary realities. Lacking a coherent view of life, maturing youngsters find themselves groping and bewildered, swinging from one set of principles and models to another, unable to find stability either in their relationships or in the flux of events; each of these elements are core characteristics of the borderline disorder.

Few times in history have so many children faced the tasks of life without the aid of accepted and durable traditions. Not only does the strain of making choices among discordant standards and goals beset them at every turn, but these competing beliefs and divergent demands also prevent them from developing either internal stability or external consistency. And no less problematic in generating such disjoined psychic structures is the escalation of emotionally capricious and interpersonally discordant role models.

The fabric of traditional and organized societies not only comprises standards designed to indoctrinate and inculcate the young, but it also provides "insurance," if you will, backups to compensate and repair system defects and failures. Extended families, church leaders, schoolteachers, and neighbors provide nurturance and role models so that children experiencing troubling parental relationships can find a means of support and affection, enabling them to be receptive to society's established body of norms and values. Youngsters subject to any of the diffusing and divisive forces so typical in the developmental background of borderlines must find one or another of these culturally sanctioned sources of surrogate modeling and sustenance to give structure and direction to their emerging capacities and impulses. Without such bolstering, maturing potentials are likely to become diffuse and scattered. Without admired and stable roles to emulate, such youngsters are left to their own devices to master the complexities of their varied and changing worlds, to control the intense aggressive and sexual urges which well up within them, to channel their fantasies, and to pursue their goals. Many borderlines become victims of their own growth, unable to discipline their impulses or find acceptable means for expressing their desires. Scattered and unguided, intracortically discordant, they are unable to fashion a clear or integrated sense of personal identity, a consistent direction for feelings and attitudes, a coherent purpose to their existence.

## EMPIRICAL CONTRIBUTIONS TO TREATMENT OF BORDERLINE PERSONALITY DISORDER

Borderlines are notoriously difficult patients for therapists. They run through the whole gamut of emotions in therapy, and their erratic and frequently threatening behaviors stir many therapists to respond to them.[7] Since the risk of burn-out is so high, therapists should limit the number of borderline patients in their caseload, if possible. This having been said, however, it should be noted that therapy working with a borderline can prove to be a gratifying experience, this despite my experience with Ann. Unlike working with some personalities, such as antisocials or schizotypals, with whom the therapist can hope at best only for modestly increased levels of adaptive behavior, I have found that borderlines are much more amenable to personality change and reorganization. Many borderlines have a range of highly developed social skills, along with the intrinsic motivation to restrain contrary and troublesome impulses. Therapeutic gains can lead to extended periods of productive functioning and interpersonal harmony in the borderline's life, and can provide the therapist with both an unusual, if not satisfying, relationship, as well as the opportunity to see therapeutic goals realized, as they were in part with Ann.

Before I attempt to gauge a borderline's prognostic picture and recommend a remedial course of therapy, I make sure to remember that borderlines, despite their common defining characteristics, are frequently more severe variants of other personality disorders, notably the negativistic, depressive, histrionic, avoidant, and antisocial. As a result, I have found them to be even less homogeneous a classification than other personality disorder categories. Some are well compensated; most are not. Some are bolstered by supportive families, while others face destructive environmental conditions. Despite symptom commonalities, these differences in the clinical picture must be attended to closely in order to produce effective remedial intervention.

Despite changes in the borderline diagnostic conceptions and definitions over time,[7] one aspect has remained stable: therapists, including myself, have many difficulties dealing with borderline patients. Despite the near inevitability of therapist frustrations, the importance of a solid alliance between therapist and patient cannot be overestimated. More than other personality disorders, borderlines have erratic interpersonal relationships that take a great toll on their lives, and that will be mirrored in their relationship with a therapist, as seen so clearly with Ann. These patients' strong positive and negative reactions and their rapidly fluctuating attitudes toward a therapist can evoke powerful countertransference responses. The patient may have bouts with therapist idealization and devaluation, threats of legal repercussions, suicidality, self-harm, and other uncontrollable behaviors, each of which may evoke empathy, anger, frustration, fear, as well as feelings of inadequacy.

Benjamin[8] sees this interactional pattern as deriving from the patient's long history and expectation of abandonment, and as a recent consequence of therapist burn-out after prolonged but failed attempts to effect significant therapeutic changes. It is when the patient realizes that the therapist will never be able to provide enough nurturance that desperate and extreme behaviors, such as suicidal gestures, may cause the therapist to begin to withdraw. The borderline in turn accuses the therapist of not caring, and often "ends" therapy in a dangerous and dramatic way. At times, the therapist is held responsible or even threatened with lawsuits. If the patient decides to return to treatment, the therapist may have lost enthusiasm but may fear legal repercussions or charges of professional irresponsibility. The vicious cycle for continued failure is now set. Another possible pattern that I have encountered is one in which the patient starts to get better but fears that improvements will lead to being "kicked out" of therapy. At this realization, the patient will therefore preemptively regress.

In the course of either of these troublesome sequences, I have occasionally experienced a blurring of my personal boundaries, an invasion of my privacy that has left me at a loss as what to do. Borderlines often do not hesitate to intrude into the therapist's space. A number have asked me out for lunch, called me at home at off hours, or used abusive tactics to manipulate and "set me up." Although I have not had this experience, I know other therapists whose patients plead for inappropriate intimacies and then turn the tables and accuse the therapist of taking advantage of his or her more powerful position. These difficulties should be avoided as much as possible by making it clear at the beginning of therapy that the goal of treatment is to foster independence, and that limits will have to be set in order to aid its achievement. This does not imply that the therapist should refuse to help or provide support in a crisis, but rather that help should also support the goal of strength-building; long hand-holding phone calls and special arrangements are replaced with a supportive but brief reminder of treatment goals, contracts, and gains in therapeutic work. In short, clear limits should be set in the first few sessions. Then the therapist should be as responsive and supportive as possible *within* those clear limits. A failure to be responsive will lead to accusations of abandonment and hypocrisy; overstepping agreed-upon boundaries will lead to further testing of the therapist by the patient. Some potential clients may decide from the beginning that they need a therapist to provide a more nurturant position.

If the patient accepts the therapist's terms, the two can begin working on building an alliance. A good therapeutic relationship can take quite some time to develop. Much can be gained therapeutically as the borderline realizes that not all individuals are dangerous and that not all self-disclosure necessarily leads to being judged unacceptable and worthy of abandonment. Beck and Freeman[9] note that the patient's difficulty trusting the therapist cannot be resolved quickly and easily. Explicit acknowledgment of the patient's difficulty with trust, special care to communicate clearly, assertively, and honestly, and especially the maintenance of congruity between verbal and nonverbal cues by the therapist can all help. The importance of a basic attempt to behave in a trustworthy manner cannot be overestimated. While it may not be appropriate for the therapist to flood the patient with information regarding his or her reactions, any strong emotions that the therapist fails to contain should be partially acknowledged, lest the patient find reason to mistrust the therapist.

Many borderlines are uncomfortable with intimacy (due to their basic mistrust of others) and can become quite anxious in therapy if their boundaries are overstepped. It is suggested by Beck and Freeman[9] that the therapist solicit the patient's feedback regarding how to make therapy more comfortable. Many borderlines experience greater comfort with the intimacy involved in the therapeutic process if they feel they have some control over the pace and the topics discussed in therapy sessions.

### Notes

1. Walsh, F. (1977). The family of the borderline patient. In R. Grinker & B. Werble (Eds.), *The borderline patient* (pp. 149–177). New York: Jason Aronson.

2. Herman, J.L., Perry, J.C., & van der Kolk, B.A. (1989). *Childhood trauma in borderline personality disorder.* New York: Guilford.

3. Perry, J.C., & Herman, J.L. (1993). Trauma and defense in the ideology of borderline personality disorder. In J. Paris (Ed.), *Borderline personality disorder. Ideology and treatment.* Washington, DC: American Psychiatric Press.

4. Paris, J. (1994). *Borderline personality disorder. A multidimensional approach.* Washington DC: American Psychiatric Press.

5. Kroll, J. (1993). *PTSD/Borderlines in therapy.* New York: Norton.

6. Millon, T. (1987). On the genesis and prevalence of the borderline personality disorder: A social learning thesis. *Journal of Personality Disorders,* 1, 354–372.

7. Millon, T., & Davis, R. (1995). *Disorders of personality: DSM-IV and beyond.* New York: Wiley.

8. Benjamin, L.S. (1993). *Interpersonal diagnosis and treatment of personality disorders.* New York: Guilford.

9. Beck, A.T., & Freeman, A. (1990). *Cognitive therapy of personality disorders.* New York: Guilford.

# 3

## About the Author

*Thomas Widiger is a Professor of Psychology at the University of Kentucky. He received his Ph.D. from Miami University in 1981, and completed his internship at Cornell University Medical Center in 1982. He has been an active researcher as well as clinician. He is currently on the editorial boards of nine journals, is a member of the National Institute of Mental Health clinical psychopathology review committee, and was a member of the American Psychiatric Association's Task Force that developed DSM-IV. He is an Honorary Fellow of the American Psychiatric Association. He is also actively involved with the Kentucky State Board of Psychology, providing investigations of complaints of ethical violations, supervision of psychologists on probation, and assessments of psychologists resuming clinical responsibilities after suspension. His private clinical practice is confined largely to the treatment of personality disorders, which keeps him busy (as he believes that few persons lack clinically significant maladaptive personality traits) and frustrated (as maladaptive personality traits are among the most difficult to treat).*

# Murray: A Challenging Case of Antisocial Personality Disorder

**About the Disorder**

The classic picture of antisocial personality disorder includes a number of criminal behaviors and psychopathic traits. Individuals with this disorder show a pervasive disregard for the rights of others, which is commonly so extreme that others are harmed or placed in jeopardy. Even in childhood, these individuals can be recognized by their conduct disordered behavior, which may include stealing, truancy, running away from home, lying, firesetting, breaking and entering, physical cruelty to people and animals, sexual assault, and mugging.

By age 15, the pattern is deeply engrained and evident in a number of behaviors. Individuals may be arrested repeatedly because of failure to abide by social norms or to obey the law. Deceitfulness may be evident in their repeated lying. They are prone to impulsive actions, possibly making serious, life-altering decisions on the spur of the moment rather than through careful evaluation. Irritability often degenerates into aggressive behavior, such as physical abuse of others. Disregard for others may be manifested in reckless behavior in which others are placed at risk. Irresponsibility typically permeates most aspects of life, and may be evident in financial carelessness, unreliability in fulfilling work duties, and inattention to family needs.

Especially striking is the lack of remorse that people with antisocial personality disorder feel for their transgressions. These individuals seem disturbingly capable of moving on without a moment's thought to the pain they may have caused. Callousness can be so extreme that they minimize consequences, rationalize their actions, or blame their victims.

As Dr. Widiger notes, of all personality disorders, the antisocial type is the most resistant to change. Individuals with this disorder often do not realize that they have a problem. Even when such clients stay in therapy, which is unusual, the therapist may continue to question the sincerity of their desire to change.—Eds.

25

## THE CASE OF MURRAY

### Initial Presentation

Murray stopped by my office to see if we could "meet for a few times." I thought he wanted to discuss some research or clinical issues; but soon I soon realized that he was seeking psychotherapy.

I was a bit reluctant. Murray was a graduate student within the Counseling Psychology program, and I was a professor within the Clinical Psychology program. There was very little interaction across the programs and it was unlikely that I would ever be involved in his academic work, but there was certainly the potential for confidentiality and dual relationship problems to arise.[1] Murray, however, appeared to be very sincere and forthright, and was certainly quite likable. I must admit, though, that his charm was also somewhat manipulative. I don't know if my initial willingness to see him was not influenced, at least in part, by his flattery and engaging charm.

I discovered later that Murray had not been honest regarding his reasons for seeking therapy. He told me that he was seeking "personal growth" and better self-awareness. When, in fact, he had been compelled by his advisor to seek help because of a number of incidents. For example, he had become sexually involved with an undergraduate who was enrolled in a course for which he was a teaching assistant, he had used a fellowship award to purchase a "hog" (a high-powered motorcycle), he often became very intoxicated at parties, and he had a rather glib and superficial attitude toward his work. He had not failed any courses, but his achievements were sporadic.

### Case History

Murray was born in Detroit, Michigan, to an upper-class family. His father was a physician, his mother a model. The marriage, however, was quite unstable. There were many fights, often involving his mother's use of drugs and his father's sexual affairs. His parents were divorced when Murray was fifteen, precipitated by the arrest of his father for the sexual abuse of Murray's younger sister. His father left, but there was no real improvement in stability. He recalled how his mother, in a drugged state, would often bring men home.

The university admissions committee was only partially aware of this history. Murray told them about his emotional pain and trauma, and how he had suffered for a long time from nightmares and crying spells from which he had recovered through the support and guidance of a counseling psychologist at his high school.

However, during the course of his therapy, Murray presented a more complete history. He was disciplined by a juvenile court at the age of 12 for killing a neighbor's cat by taping a powerful firecracker to its body. He began using drugs at the age of 14. He laughed as he described his many shoplifting and burglary exploits, and eventually acknowledged that he had also had sex with his younger sister. This occurred after she had confided in him about the abuse by their father. She was seeking Murray's support and protection, which he used to his own advantage: "She didn't always like it, but it was harmless compared to what my dad did."

Murray, however, was also very bright, and he obtained an undergraduate scholarship to attend a prominent university. He failed to report the antisocial behavior in his application, but he justified the omission by indicating that to do so would have simply have eliminated him from consideration. "Why shoot yourself, and, besides, what they don't know won't hurt them." In college, Murray at first majored in creative writing, but he eventually switched to psychology. He found the psychology literature to be very intriguing. He had always been "good with people," being able to sense a person's concerns and insecurities. He felt that psychology would help him "further develop" this talent.

Murray knew that he would need three letters of recommendation to enter graduate school and therefore "cultivated the favors" of two research faculty and one clinician. He assisted the faculty in their experiments, going well beyond their requests. For example, he reviewed articles concerning the studies, particularly those papers written by his supervisors. They were very impressed with Murray's intelligence, motivation, and dedication. To obtain a letter from a clinician, he became a volunteer at an adolescent drug dependency treatment program, and appeared to work very well with the patients, readily establishing rapport. He again impressed his supervisor with his "considerable interest" in the treatment program, suggested not only by his close involvement with the patients, but also by his invaluable assistance with a new software program.

His computer skills also proved to be useful in his application to graduate school, as he applied to many different programs. He was quite open and forthright with some programs, but none of these made him an offer. It was his impression that a greater degree of deception resulted in a greater degree of success.

Murray was initially very successful in graduate school, finding coursework to be "demanding but not insurmountable." He was also very popular. He organized many parties, and soon became involved with a female student within the School Psychology program. The relationship ended poorly, though, and she was so upset that she left the program. Relationships also became strained with other students (e.g., some students became annoyed when it was discovered that he had purchased abstracts and notes from a senior student).

## Diagnosis

| | |
|---|---|
| Axis I: | • Alcohol abuse. |
| Axis II: | • Antisocial personality disorder. |
| Axis III: | • Herpes (by report) |
| Axis IV: | • Educational problems |
| Axis V: | • GAF = 69 (current) |

These diagnoses are based in part on information obtained during and after the course of treatment. For example, at the onset of treatment, I was unaware of the Herpes.

A diagnosis of alcohol abuse is made if the person exhibits a maladaptive pattern of use leading to clinically significant impairment, as manifested, for example, by a recurrent use in situations in which it is physically hazardous, such as driving an automobile.[2] Murray would recurrently become very intoxicated at bars and parties, and then drive home. He had never been charged for driving under the influence, but he was perhaps simply lucky. His occasional attempts to limit or restrain his drinking often failed. He continued to drink at parties despite being told that his behavior was inappropriate for a graduate student in counseling psychology.

A diagnosis of antisocial personality disorder (ASPD) requires evidence of a childhood conduct disorder.[2] "Evidence" could technically fall below the threshold of the presence of the disorder but, in my opinion, Murray did indeed have a conduct disorder during childhood. He had (at least) been repeatedly physically cruel to animals, broken into homes, stolen items of a nontrivial value from stores, and repeatedly abused his younger sister.

A *DSM-IV* diagnosis of ASPD also requires the presence of three or more adult criteria.[2] Some of the traits were known to me when Murray entered treatment (e.g., irresponsibility with respect to work). Others became evident during the course of treatment. His reckless disregard for the safety of himself and others was apparent from his drinking and sexual behavior. For example, he had contracted Herpes from a prostitute and rarely informed subsequent sexual partners.

His girlfriend in the School Psychology Program had contracted Herpes from Murray. She was apparently very ashamed and embarrassed, but Murray expressed little concern: "She's a big girl, and needs to grow up and take care of herself." His lack of remorse was readily apparent in many of his relationships with women. Murray was physically attractive, bright, and potentially successful, and he used these attributes to seduce women he met at bars or within classes. Many of these women justifiably felt used, abandoned, or mistreated, but Murray was unsympathetic. He was only troubled by the harm they might cause him with their accusations. He at times expressed to them considerable pain or guilt, but he would acknowledge to me ("man to man") that he was only doing this "to make them feel better."

## Case Formulation

Murray does not present as a prototypical example of antisocial personality disorder. He lacks some of the common features, such as overt criminal activity and physical aggression. However, he did have some of the traits that I consider to be central to the disorder, such as deceitfulness, disregard for the feelings and rights of others, lack of empathy, superficial and glib charm, and lack of feelings of guilt, shame, or remorse.

In some respects, Murray was functioning at a relatively high level, and certainly higher than is usually seen in persons with mental disorders. He had been very successful in college and was on the way toward obtaining a professional degree. Yet, his achievements were due in part to his intelligence and socioeconomic background compensating for his antisocial traits. In addition, his success was superficial and fragile. He could manipulate and deceive many persons, but his success depended on the failure of others to eventually discover his manipulations and falsehoods.

He considered himself to be very successful with women, but he was only successful in obtaining sex. He conquered many women, but he had never developed a meaningful or sustained relationship, nor perhaps was this likely to occur given his impairments in empathy, sympathy, and remorse.

Murray may have also have been reaching the limits of his professional success. His undergraduate achievements were excellent, due in part to his intelligence and charm overcoming his irresponsibility. However, his limitations were more apparent with the greater demands and closer monitoring of graduate school. His clinical work was not discussed in our treatment because of confidentiality issues and the possible confusion of my role as his therapist rather than his supervisor. But he would at times reveal a lack of empathy, a lack of appreciation for ethical issues, and poor judgment. For example, he once acknowledged having drinks at a bar with an ex-patient who had been in treatment for a paraphilia. Murray did not seem to appreciate the boundary confusions of a therapist and a "drinking buddy."

## Course of Treatment

Personality disorders are among the most difficult to treat, and ASPD is the most resistant to change. Murray, like many persons with ASPD, did not consider himself as having any significant problems. My initial goal was to help him appreciate the maladaptivity of his behaviors. My approach was neutral, nonjudgmental, supportive, and empathic. A more confrontational style is often recommended (and usually more effective) in the treatment of persons with ASPD, but this was unlikely to be successful in this situation. It was important to first establish a rapport and trust, which could be difficult in this case, as I could be perceived by him as a voice or arm of the faculty rather than as his therapist.

Murray gradually acknowledged the maladaptivity of his irresponsibility and recklessness, and the faculty became less concerned regarding his performance. However, it was not clear if the apparent improvements in his judgment and conscientiousness were just temporary changes in order to successfully complete the graduate program. He may have been learning how to con the faculty (and me).

He continued to offer rationalizations and excuses for his current and past behaviors. He was very adept at understanding the pathology of others, but not himself. He eventually acknowledged that he did not really feel traumatized by his past, and in fact enjoyed his antisocial behavior, including the sexual abuse of his sister.

Some of Murray's admissions to me might seem surprising, but many persons with ASPD are proud of their successful exploitations and deceits. They may enjoy recounting how they successfully conned, humiliated, or victimized someone. At times it appeared that Murray did not really appreciate the significance of his behavior, or he seemed to believe that I might share in the amusement of his exploits. For example, he might begin a story of a successful exploitation, deception, or humiliation by saying "let me tell you about . . . , this is really funny." One might say that he not only lacked empathy for his victims, but also for his therapist.

Hervey Cleckley, an early and very influential clinical researcher, suggested that psychopaths have a "semantic dementia," which the more current psychopathy researcher Robert Hare describes as an inability to appreciate the significance or meaning of emotional language.[3] In other words, they just don't get it. Murray understood the importance that such feelings had for *other* persons. He was very skilled at using and manipulating this "weakness," as he once described it, but he could not really experience such feelings for himself.

There was little improvement during treatment concerning his lack of empathy. He acknowledged that he had never had a sustained relationship with a woman, but he felt that it would not be difficult once he wanted to have one. He had "dumped" many women who had wanted a serious relationship; if he ever changed his mind, then such a woman should be readily available. He did not consider his lack of concern for their feelings to be his problem. However, Murray eventually began to appreciate that this lack of empathy could be problematic as a therapist. He often felt that he really didn't care that much about the problems of his patients, other than a desire to be successful as a therapist. At times he felt that this disinterest reflected an objectivity or neutrality that was absent in persons who he felt became too emotionally involved with their patients.

Murray's duplicity and manipulativeness became more evident as therapy progressed, and at times contaminated the treatment. For example, during one session he revealed that a fellow student, a person he identified, might be sexually involved with a faculty member. It was apparent that he hoped to somehow cause trouble for these persons by leaking this damaging information to me. During a social function, another student, who did not know Murray was in treatment with me, revealed that Murray had suggested that I had revealed confidential information concerning a patient to him. Protection of confidentiality and appropriate professional boundaries are sensitive and important concerns when providing therapy for any patient, but they are especially problematic for students within a graduate program.[1] Murray was not only insensitive to these issues; he appeared to disregard and perhaps even exploit them. I subsequently obtained an ongoing consultation from a colleague who did not have any professional relationship with Murray or with the counseling program. I wanted this consultation not only for a discussion of ethical issues, but also for a consideration of countertransference issues that might develop in response to his antisocial behavior. I was becoming concerned that I might also be victimized by Murray, and I did not want my fears or irritation to undermine my effort to be his therapist.

Murray eventually grew to question his motivation for graduate school. He realized that he did not really value or enjoy the psychotherapy, deciding he preferred a career in science and research, although this was not realistic given his current training. He was also disheartened by the "lack" of money that was being earned by prior graduates. He wondered if he was better suited for medicine or law. He left the program and terminated treatment after completing his thesis.

### Outcome of the Case

Murray did not maintain contact with me after leaving treatment. I did hear from a colleague that he had requested a letter of recommendation for law school, but did not follow up when it became apparent that this letter would acknowledge a number of concerns. There was a rumor that he had been charged with statutory rape, but many questionable stories concerning his behavior during graduate school grew in their exaggeration and embellishment after he left.

## EMPIRICAL CONTRIBUTIONS TO UNDERSTANDING ASPD

ASPD is one of the most harmful and destructive mental disorders. ASPD is of substantial concern to clinicians because it is the most difficult of the personality disorders to treat, and its presence will invariably undermine the treatment of any comorbid mental disorders. ASPD should also be of concern to the general public because they are more victimized by this disorder than the persons with the disorder. It is not surprising, then, that ASPD is the personality disorder that is most heavily researched.[4]

The American Psychiatric Association[2] estimates a prevalence rate of 3% of males and 1% of females with ASPD. However, the rate may be as high as 4% of the general population—with 1% of females and 7% of males.[5] ASPD occurs more often in lower socioeconomic populations and urban settings, which may reflect both an effect and a cause of the disorder. Persons with ASPD are likely to drift toward a lower socioeconomic level, and the tough, harsh environment of an impoverished and high-crime-rate district will in turn facilitate its development. The prevalence of ASPD may be as high as 50% of male prison inmates, although some have argued that a more accurate estimate is "only" 20%.[3,5] The emphasis given in its diagnosis to overt acts of criminality, delinquency, and irresponsibility may contribute to an overdiagnosis of ASPD within prison settings and to an underdiagnosis within more legitimate professions, such as business, law, and politics.[3–7] For example, clinicians may fail to recognize the more successful psychopath, or the person for whom such psychopathic traits as deception, manipulation, and exploitation have contributed to a success within a particular profession. I chose to present Murray in part because he illustrates this more successful psychopath.

There does appear to be a gradual decrease in the severity of the disorder as the person ages. This will be especially evident in the criminal, aggressive, and impulsive behaviors. This mellowing with age may reflect a gradual response to the costs of the antisocial lifestyle. However, it is also important to note that persons with ASPD, including Murray, may never develop substantial empathy or a strong sense of moral responsibility. They may become more realistic and controlled, but they may continue to be egocentric, unempathic, manipulative, and deceptive.[8]

There does not appear to be a specific etiology for the development of ASPD. Instead, there appear to be a multitude of contributing factors (biological, psychological, and social) that interact in different ways across different persons. There is considerable support from twin, family, and adoption studies for a genetic disposition toward ASPD,[9] but ASPD is not itself inherited. The phenotypic traits that are correlated with the transmitted genotype(s) are unclear, and may include tendencies toward impulsivity, antagonism, or low anxiousness.[4]

A variety of pathological mechanisms have been studied, including low baseline levels of arousal, premorbid attention-deficit hyperactivity disorder, deficits in the processing of emotional cues, impairment in passive avoidance learning, neuropsychological deficits, and deficits in behavioral inhibition,[3,9] but none have been shown to be highly sensitive or specific to the disorder, nor have these mechanisms been able to account for a substantial proportion of the antisocial behavior.

There is equal support for the contribution of a variety of family, peer, cultural, and other environmental factors. Modeling by parental figures; excessively cruel, lenient, or erratic parental discipline; and a tough, harsh environment in which feelings of empathy and warmth are discouraged and tough-mindedness, aggression, and exploitation are rewarded, have all been associated with ASPD.[10] Many cases will involve an interaction of dispositional temperaments and environmental factors. For example, the development of feelings of guilt, empathy, conscience, and remorse may not occur naturally. They may require a capacity for normal anxiousness and attentional self-regulation. Normal levels of anxiousness will facilitate the internalization of a moral conscience by associating distress and anxiety with the social mores modeled and reinforced by the parents, and the temperament of self-regulation may be necessary to modulate impulses so they become socially acceptable.[4] Parents could have a child who lacks adequate levels of anxiousness or self-regulation to respond effectively to their discipline, or their modeling and discipline may be inadequate relative to the temperament of the child or to the environment outside of the home in which the child must also function.

## EMPIRICAL CONTRIBUTIONS TO THE TREATMENT OF ASPD

I had no illusions of achieving a significant change in the personality of Murray. My goals in his treatment were to develop his awareness of the maladaptivity of his behavior pattern, to facilitate a motivation to change, to modulate some of the facets of the disorder, and to (jointly) assess his future plans and goals.

In my opinion, no personality is without some degree of maladaptivity.[11,12] Personality is, by definition, the tendency to respond consistently across situations. All persons will have some situations in which their personality is problematic and maladaptive. Most of us seek friends, colleagues, roles, and jobs that provide a good match for or complement our dispositional tendencies. As a result, we often fail to recognize the limitations of our personality because we stay largely within situations for which we are well suited (or at least stay out of situations for which we are poorly suited).

Persons with clinically significant personality disorders are not as successful in finding their niche in life. They may need help modulating the more severe facets of their personality (e.g., reducing the impulsivity or aggression of persons with ASPD) or finding relationships, roles, and careers for which they are best suited. The treatment of Murray was successful in helping him recognize that he was not well suited for a career in counseling psychology. However, it is possible that I simply passed the buck to another profession that will suffer the consequences of his antisocial tendencies.

It would be naive to attempt to treat ASPD significantly through traditional outpatient therapy.[3,13] Outpatient therapy is rarely successful, although it can be helpful in addressing a current crisis or interpersonal conflict. Community residential and wilderness programs will likely be more effective.[4] These programs have the advantages of a firm structure, removal from the existing environment, and close involvement throughout each day. A common feature is the use of intense confrontation by peers. The tendency to rationalize irresponsibility, to minimize the consequences of acts, and to manipulate others needs to be confronted on an immediate and daily basis. Rapport, trust, and respect may also be more readily obtained by a peer than by a professional clinician from a different economic, ethnic, age, and cultural background. However, it is not yet clear whether the effects of residential and wilderness programs are sustained for a significant period of time after the person leaves. It is conceivable that ASPD could be reversed through an environment that is as intense and sustained as the environment in which the person was raised, but no such environment is realistically available.

Persons with ASPD are difficult to treat in part because they often fail to recognize or appreciate the maladaptivity of their disorder. They might even argue that they are better adjusted than the average person because they are not burdened by the negative affects that trouble the rest of us. A prognostic indicator is the ability to establish rapport or a meaningful and sincere relationship.[14] Factors to consider in assessing this potential are demographic similarities between the therapist and patient, the quality of the patient's prior relationships, and the initial attitudes or feelings of the patient and therapist toward each other. Rapport can be difficult to obtain not only for the person with ASPD, but also for the therapist. It is not unusual for clinicians to have suppressed or even overt feelings of resentment, animosity, or distaste for persons with a history of abusive and exploitative behaviors. However, these feelings will undermine one's ability to relate effectively. Persons with ASPD can themselves be rejected, exploited, or victimized by clinicians expressing a desire to seek retribution for their own past victimization. These countertransference issues should be monitored and explored throughout treatment.

On the other hand, therapists must also be careful not to commit the opposite error of being overly trusting and naive. Persons with ASPD are very good at obtaining forgiveness that provides them with the opportunity to further exploit and victimize. It is not difficult to be seduced by a compelling portrayal of contrition, remorse, and insight that is not in fact sustained. Persons with ASPD can appear to be involved and responsive, when in fact they are only manipulating you to curry a favor or to avoid some penalty. It is regrettable, but true, that they are as likely to con their therapist and fellow patients as any of their prior victims.

## Notes

1. American Psychological Association. (1992). Ethical principles of psychologists and code of conduct. *American Psychologist, 47,* 1597–1611.

2. American Psychiatric Association. (1994). *Diagnostic and statistical manual of mental disorders* (4th ed.). Washington, DC: Author.

3. Hare, R.D. (1993). *Without conscience: The disturbing world of the psychopaths among us.* New York: Pocket Books.

4. Widiger, T.A., & Hicklin, J. (1995). Antisocial personality disorder. In P. Wilner (Ed.), Psychiatry (Chapt. 23, pp. 1–13). Philadelphia, J.B. Lippincott.

5. Robins, L.N., Tipp, J., & Przybeck, T. (1991). Antisocial personality. In L.N. Robins & D.A. Regier (Eds.), *Psychiatric disorders in America* (pp. 258–290). New York: Free Press.

6. Sutker, P.B. (1994). Psychopathy: Traditional and clinical antisocial concepts. In D.C. Fowles, P.B. Sutker, & S.H. Goodman (Eds.), *Progress in experimental personality and psychopathology research* (pp. 73–120). New York: Springer.

7. Widiger, T.A., & Corbitt, E.M. (1993). Antisocial personality disorder: Proposals for *DSM-IV. Journal of Personality Disorders, 7,* 63–77.

8. Harpur, T.J., & Hare, R.D. (1994). Assessment of psychopathy as a function of age. *Journal of Abnormal Psychology, 103,* 604–609.

9. Sutker, P.B., Bugg, F., & West J.A. (1993). Antisocial personality disorder. In P.B. Sutker & H.E. Adams (Eds.), *Comprehensive handbook of psychopathology* (2nd ed., pp. 337–369). New York: Plenum.

10. Dodge, K.A. (1993). Social-cognitive mechanisms in the development of conduct disorder and depression. *Annual Review of Psychology, 44,* 559–584.

11. Widiger, T.A. (1993). The *DSM-III-R* categorical personality disorder diagnoses: A critique and an alternative. *Psychological Inquiry, 4,* 75–90.

12. Widiger, T.A., & Corbitt, E.M. (1994). Normal versus abnormal personality from the perspective of the *DSM.* In S. Strack & M. Lorr (Eds.), *Differentiating normal and abnormal personality* (pp. 158–175). New York: Springer.

13. Stone, M.H. (1993). *Abnormalities of personality: Within and beyond the realm of treatment.* New York: Norton.

14. Gerstley, L.J., McLellan, A.T., Alterman, A.I., & Woody, G. (1989). Ability to form an alliance with the therapist: A possible marker of prognosis for patients with antisocial personality disorder. *American Journal of Psychiatry, 46,* 508–512.

## Recommended Readings

The following are texts I would recommend highly for persons who wish to read further on issues discussed within this chapter.

Hare, R.D. (1993). *Without conscience: The disturbing world of the psychopaths among us.* New York: Pocket Books. Dr. Robert Hare has conducted the most influential research on the traditional concept of psychopathy. His effort to differentiate the normal criminal from the psychopath has been particularly instructive.

Stone, M.H. (1993). *Abnormalities of personality. Within and beyond the realm of treatment.* New York: Norton. Dr. Stone is an insightful, successful, and talented clinician, a highly respected researcher, and brilliant theorist. This text is the best I have seen on the treatment of personality disorders.

Widiger, T.A., Mangine, S., Corbitt, E.M., Ellis, C., & Thomas, G. (1995). *Personality disorder interview—IV: A semistructured interview for the assessment of personality disorders.* Odessa, FL: Psychological Assessment Resources. If you are interested in additional reading on the diagnosis of personality disorders, I would recommend the text that accompanies this semistructured interview. It provides an extensive summary of the history and rationale for each of the 94 DSM-IV personality disorder diagnostic criteria, a detailed discussion of their assessment, and overviews of many issues relevant to the diagnosis of personality disorders.

Fowles, D.C., Sutker, P., & Goodman, S.H. (Eds.). (1994). *Progress in experimental personality and psychopathology research.* New York: Springer. This edited text provides an excellent overview of many of the issues being explored in the current research on antisocial personality disorder, including pathological mechanisms, childhood development, biological correlates, gender differences, and diagnosis.

Costa, P.T., & Widiger, T.A. (Eds.). (1994). *Personality disorders and the five-factor model of personality.* Washington, DC: American Psychological Association. This edited text provides an excellent overview of an alternative perspective on the *DSM-IV* personality disorders which I believe will (or should) ultimately supplant the categorical distinctions provided within *DSM-IV.* It considers the *DSM-IV* personality disorders to represent maladaptive variants of personality traits that are present in all of us.

# PART II

# ANXIETY DISORDERS

➤ Chapter 4: Panic Disorder
➤ Chapter 5: Obsessive-Compulsive Disorder
➤ Chapter 6: Post-traumatic Stress Disorder

People who suffer from anxiety disorders experience a range of unpleasant and disturbing feelings, thoughts, and sensations related to the prospect that something terrible will happen to them. Feeling powerless in the face of imagined impending danger, their only recourse is to try to prepare themselves for the worst or find ways of avoiding the situations they fear. Their anxiety can be so intense, irrational, and incapacitating that they are unable to function in everyday life. Fortunately, within recent years effective interventions have been developed which make it possible for clients and clinicians alike to feel some degree of hope about the prospects for change.

# 4

**About**

**the**

**Authors**

*David H. Barlow received his Ph.D. from the University of Vermont in 1969 and has published over 300 articles and chapters and over 20 books, mostly in the areas of anxiety disorders, sexual problems, and clinical research methodology. Books include "Anxiety and its disorders: The nature and treatment of anxiety and panic, New York: Guilford Press (1988) and, most recently, Barlow, D.H. (1993, Ed.),* Clinical handbook of psychological disorders, 2nd edition. *New York: Guilford Press and Barlow, D.H. & Durand, V.M. (1995).* Abnormal psychology: An integrative approach. *Pacific Grove CA: Brooks/Cole.*

*Currently, Dr. Barlow is Professor of Psychology and Director of Clinical Training Programs and Director of the Center for Anxiety and Related Disorders at Boston University. He is Past-President of the Division of Clinical Psychology of the American Psychological Association and Past-President of the Association for the Advancement of Behavior Therapy.*

*Timothy A. Brown is Associate Director of the Center for Anxiety and Related Disorders and Research Associate Professor at Boston University. He has published numerous scientific articles and chapters in the area of anxiety disorders. He has been a consultant to the National Institute of Mental Health on the evaluation of psychosocial and pharmacological treatments of anxiety disorders, and he has served as a consultant to large-scale projects focusing on the assessment and diagnosis of the anxiety disorders and using DSM-IV. He was a member of the DSM-IV Anxiety Disorders Advisory Committee for generalized anxiety disorder and mixed anxiety depression.*

# Eric: A Case Example of Panic Disorder with Agoraphobia

**About the Disorder**

People with panic disorders experience episodes of emotional terror combined with a range of overwhelming and frightening bodily sensations. These panic attacks have a sudden onset and usually reach a peak within a ten-minute period. During these attacks, these people may fear that they are dying, going "crazy," or losing control, as they struggle with terrifying physical symptoms such as shortness of breath, dizziness, hot flashes or chills, numbness, and tightness in the chest.

People with panic disorders learn to avoid places where they fear they may be trapped and unable to obtain help. Seemingly harmless places such as elevators, crowded stores, or movie theaters may be seen as ominous environments to be avoided at all costs. When this avoidance becomes extreme, the individual is said to have developed panic disorder with agoraphobia. Because people with this disorder become so fearful of panic attacks, they develop idiosyncratic personal styles and behaviors in order to avoid threatening situations. Like the case described by Drs. Barlow and Brown, they may engage in safety behaviors that they think will protect them from harm. For example, they may refuse to leave the house unless they are accompanied by someone who knows about their disorder.

Central to the treatment of panic disorder with agoraphobia is coming to an understanding of how the individual "thinks." As you will see in the case of Eric, Dr. Brown conducted a thorough analysis of Eric's irrational and anxiety-provoking cognitions. As these thoughts were identified, Dr. Brown helped Eric to see them as maladaptive and dysfunctional. This painstaking process helped Eric to escape from the real threat in his life—the torment of his anxiety disorder.—*Eds.*

## APPROACHES TO PDA (BARLOW)

The history of psychosocial approaches to panic disorder with agoraphobia (PDA) is, in itself, an interesting case study in the development of psychotherapy. As late as the 1960s, there were no proven effective treatments for PDA. Traditional psychotherapy aimed at uncovering possibly unconscious conflicts had little effect on the various components of panic disorder with agoraphobia. In retrospect, it is not surprising that "talk therapy" conducted in the sanctity of the therapist's office would affect phobias, since Sigmund Freud himself had pointed out at the end of the last century that progress would never be made until the patient begins to face up to his or her irrational fears in the situation in which they occur.

Nevertheless, psychotherapists did not heed Freud's advice until the 1960s, when several British psychologists and psychiatrists began encouraging individuals with agoraphobia to venture away from their homes or the clinic along routes that were very difficult for them. This would include increasingly crowded situations such as busy streets and shopping malls where escape would be difficult if they experienced a panic attack. However, they cautioned their patients to avoid experiencing any anxiety during this exercise and to turn back if this occurred.[1]

During the rest of the decade of the 1960s, clinicians began to take a more active role with their patients, often by asking them to engage in various exercises outside of the therapist's office. It wasn't long before we discovered that individuals with phobias, including agoraphobia, must not only confront their feared situations, but should also actually *experience* anxiety during these exercises for it to do any good.[2] In fact, under conditions where these experiences could be discussed with a therapist, it seemed to be useful for patients to experience what would sometimes be substantial anxiety. It wasn't long before we discovered that one of the most important therapeutic components in the treatment of phobias including agoraphobia was to practice exposing oneself to feared situations in a systematic way under the therapeutic direction.[2] By the late 1970s and 1980s, this was a widely accepted treatment for agoraphobia.

Another substantial component of this complex and debilitating problem, in addition to phobic behavior, is the presence of unexpected panic attacks, as we will see in the case of Eric. These sudden experiences of terror and impending doom with the accompanying physical symptoms are unique because they often occur in situations where there is absolutely nothing of be afraid of. This further frightens the patient, who then believes that he or she must be dying or losing their mind. In the 1960s, Donald Klein, along with other biological psychiatrists, discovered that certain drugs designed for use in treating depression could also be helpful in treating panic attacks. Subsequent evidence proved him correct,[3] and we now know that a variety of drugs have some therapeutic benefit for patients with PDA.

Thus, in the 1980s we were faced with a state of affairs in which we were treating panic attacks with drugs, and agoraphobic avoidance with psychological exposure-based procedures. During the early 1980s, clinical experience in our anxiety disorders research center convinced us that patients with panic disorder were avoiding more than shopping malls, public transportation, and other contexts more typical of agoraphobia. They were also very frightened of, and avoided, if possible, their own bodily sensations such as a racing heart, perspiration, muscle aches and pains due to exertion, and so on. Further evaluation revealed that the reason these patients were avoiding their own physical sensations was because it made them think that they were beginning to have another panic attack, which was one of the worst things that could happen to them in their own minds. In other words, an increase in heart rate, or the early sensations of perspiration would "trigger" a deep-seated fear that they were going to have a panic attack, even if the increases in heart rate were due to exercise, or the perspiration to entering a hot, stuffy room. Often these individuals were not aware of the connection between their physical sensations and their subsequent fear and anxiety. For many patients, any emotional expression, such as the feelings of excitement at a sporting event or the tingles of horror while watching a scary movie, would be enough to trigger this fear, and they would assiduously avoid sporting events and scary movies.

Realizing this, we felt that we might be able to develop a treatment for panic attacks in which patients would be systematically exposed to their own bodily sensations in a therapeutic context so that they might eventually learn at an emotional level that there was nothing to fear. During these exposure exercises, we could also work on changing the automatic emotional thoughts of dying, going crazy, and so on, that accompany panic attacks. We felt that these procedures might greatly reduce subsequent panic attacks, which seem to be triggered by bodily sensations. Thus, we developed a psychosocial treatment for panic disorder that targets panic attacks directly, which will be illustrated in the case described here. This case highlights the interaction of clinical observations and clinical research, both of which are necessary in the development of new and effective psychosocial treatments for specific mental disorders.

## THE CASE OF ERIC (BROWN)

### Initial Presentation

On a Monday morning in late April, I met with Eric Morse for the first time. Eric had heard about our clinic from his family doctor. As is customary at our clinic, our first meeting was devoted entirely to assessment. Specifically, in this meeting I administered the Anxiety Disorders Interview Schedule for *DSM-IV* (ADIS-IV),[4] a semi-structured clinical interview that we have developed to assist in diagnosing anxiety disorders and related conditions (e.g., mood disorders), as well as to assist in providing clinical information that is valuable in treatment planning (e.g., the specific types of situations avoided due to panic attacks; the person's fears associated with the panic, such as dying, going crazy, etc.). Prior to administering the ADIS-IV, I spent several minutes with Eric to get an overview of his presenting complaints and life situation.

## Case History

Eric was a 45-year-old Caucasian male who was married with three sons (ages 3 to 15). Although well-educated and successful (he was a high school principal), Eric stated that he had been experiencing difficulties with panic attacks since the early 1980s. He related that the period between 1981 and 1987 was a particularly rough time for him because, as a method of trying to cope with panic attacks of increasing frequency and intensity, he relied on alcohol. In fact, he was drinking a case of beer per day! Fortunately, with the assistance of therapists at a local community mental health center and a brief hospital stay, Eric's alcohol dependence ended quite abruptly in 1988. However, at that time, Eric was prescribed a high dose of Xanax (4 mg per day, with an extra mg if needed) which he was continuing to use at the time of our initial treatment sessions. Xanax (the brand name for alprazolam) is a high-potency benzodiazepine that is frequently prescribed for the treatment of panic disorder. In addition to the Xanax, Eric had been treated on a regular basis with psychotherapy by a clinical social worker for several years (1988 to 1993). He regarded his work with this social worker to be quite valuable because he was able to learn more about the nature of panic attacks as well as learn a number of skills to cope with the attacks (e.g., distraction, snapping a rubber band on the wrist, and self-statements such as "This will pass"). However, approximately eight months prior to our initial session, Eric had his last session with this social worker when she had left the Albany area. In the interim, he had relied on self-help books that he read regularly. Unfortunately, he found these books of limited value in furthering his recovery.

## Diagnosis

As we proceeded through the ADIS-IV interview, I was able to learn a great deal more about Eric's difficulties that later would be very helpful in our treatment sessions. Eric stated that currently he experienced two to five panic attacks per month. The physical sensations that accompanied his typical panic attack included depersonalization (a sensation of being detached from or being an outside observer of one's thoughts or body), dizziness/unsteady feelings, sweating, accelerated heart rate, hot flushes, and trembling. While the majority of Eric's panic attacks had now become associated with specific situations (that is, they tended to occur more in some situations than in others or, in *DSM-IV* terms, the panics were "situationally predisposed"), he reported that he still occasionally had panic attacks that he experienced as totally "out of the blue." Eric reported that, while he was only having a few panic attacks per month on average, he was experiencing a high level of anxiety every day, focused on the possibility that he might have another panic attack at any time. Indeed, Eric had developed extensive apprehension or avoidance of a variety of situations. These situations included driving (particularly long distances or interstate driving), air travel, elevators, wide open spaces (e.g., empty parking lots), taking long walks alone, movie theaters, church, and being out of town. Because I knew that it would be very important in treatment later on, I attempted to determine exactly what Eric was afraid of regarding what might happen if he were to experience a panic attack in these situations. He recalled that during the time when his panic attacks were most severe (1981 to 1987), he thought they must have a physical cause; specifically, that the panic attacks were symptoms of heart disease that his doctors had failed to identify. At present, however, he pointed out that he was not concerned about dying or having a physical disease because his doctors had persuaded him that he was fine. Rather, he was now most afraid of losing control by either passing out or by losing control of his arms and legs and falling over. In fact, Eric reported the latter as a *symptom* of his typical panic attack (i.e., involuntary arm and leg movement), but at the time I recall thinking that this "symptom" actually might be one of Eric's *responses* to (coping mechanism) his panic attacks. Nevertheless, this fear of passing out/falling over/losing control of limbs appeared to occur in most situations where he experienced apprehension and avoidance—for example, driving (losing control of the car and crashing), church, elevators, and wide open spaces (falling over and drawing attention to himself).[5]

In gathering more information during our assessment session that might be useful in treatment, I asked Eric if there were specific things that he carried with him or things he did in response to a panic attack that either: (a) helped him to feel more comfortable in difficult situations or (b) seemed to decrease the likelihood that a feared consequence (e.g., fainting) would occur. Through this questioning, I was able to identify the following "safety behaviors" and "safety signals": 24-hour access to Xanax bottle, driving to the side of the road, holding onto stationary objects, and remaining near walls. As I previously noted, while Eric believed that his panic attacks occasionally caused him to lose control of his arms, and legs, which made him fall to the floor, I did not regard this as a symptom of his attacks. Instead, I viewed this as another form of safety behavior, the reasons for which I will discuss shortly.

After completing the Panic Disorder and Agoraphobia sections, I administered the remaining portions of the ADIS-IV which address the other *DSM-IV* anxiety disorders, mood disorders, somatoform disorders, substance use disorders, and which screen for the presence of other syndromes (e.g., psychotic). Interestingly, other than a past diagnosis of Alcohol Dependence, Eric did not present with any other diagnoses, with the exception of some symptoms of recurrent worry about several areas (e.g., job performance, children's well-being), characteristic of a generalized anxiety disorder; however, I regarded these symptoms as either "subclinical" (which means insufficiently severe to be considered as part of a clinical problem) or better accounted for by the panic disorder, and thus I did not assign generalized anxiety disorder as an additional diagnosis. The reason that this lack of comorbidity (presence of more than one diagnosis in the same person) is relevant is that our clinic and other research settings around the world, have found that anxiety disorders rarely present in isolation. For example, we have recently found that, of patients with a principal *DSM-III-R* diagnosis of panic disorder with agoraphobia, the percentage receiving at least one additional diagnosis at the time of the assessment is 51% to 72%.[6]

Therefore, my five-axis *DSM-IV* diagnosis for Eric was as follows:

| | |
|---|---|
| Axis I: | • Panic disorder with agoraphobia |
| Axis II: | • No diagnosis on Axis II |
| Axis III: | • None |
| Axis IV: | • Stressful work schedule |
| Axis V: | • GAF = 58 (current) |

## Case Formulation

As you can see, much important information was collected during this initial assessment session. Not only did I obtain the necessary information to make a *DSM-IV* diagnosis, but I attempted to collect information on issues and factors that might be currently important in developing an appropriate treatment for Eric. This included information on current panic attack symptoms, the number of situations avoided, such as shopping malls or public transportation for fear that a panic attack may occur (agoraphobic situations), the types of automatic or emotional thoughts that occur during panic attacks, such as thoughts that one is going to die or go crazy. In addition, I gathered information on levels of anticipatory anxiety—in other words, anxiety focused on upcoming activities and situations which in and of itself can be very debilitating and unpleasant. Finally, information was collected on safety behaviors or safety signals, things that patients may carry with them, or things they may do to give them a little security and comfort. In other words, these are ways with which the patient copes with frightening situations, even if these coping procedures are irrational. In the case of Eric, carrying around a bottle of Xanax, even if he never took one, or driving to the side of the road and stopping, as well as remaining near walls while walking, all seemed to be safety behaviors.

This information is important because it is related to the causes of panic disorder with agoraphobia as well as what keeps it going or maintains it.[7] What seems to happen is that someone will experience a burst of fear (the fight/flight response) at an inappropriate or unexpected time. The emotion of fear is perfectly normal in and of itself. The problem occurs when there is nothing to be afraid of. Having experienced this initial burst of fear, perhaps because the individual is under some stress at the time, it is very likely that the patient will develop anxiety over the possibility of having additional bursts of fear or additional panic attacks. It often reaches the point, as noted above, that almost any physical sensation might signal to the patient the beginning of the next attack, and he or she will begin experiencing feelings of losing control. In other words, the patient will experience a slight elevation in heart rate and think, "Oh my God, this is the beginning of another panic attack and I'm not going to be able to deal with it and, if someone doesn't come and save me, I might die right here on the spot."

A central goal in our treatment therefore is to help the patients gain a sense of control over their panic attacks and to teach them that panic attacks in and of themselves are harmless and most likely just the normal emotion of fear occurring inappropriately. To do this, we don't focus treatment directly on the panic attack itself, but rather we focus on the bodily sensations that often trigger the attack, as well as the automatic and often catastrophic thoughts that accompany the attack. Thus, it is important to find out what these thoughts are, as well as the types of situations that the patients avoid and the reasons why. For example, in the case of Eric, I discovered that he was avoiding drinking caffeinated beverages as well as vigorous exercise. When questioned, Eric had not really made the connection, but after a while decided that it was probably because these activities might provoke a panic attack. Internal bodily sensations such as a racing heart and feelings of heat or dizziness are sometimes called "interoceptive" sensations. Avoidance of these sensations is called "interoceptive avoidance." The types of therapeutic exposure that we use for these sensations is called "interoceptive exposure." The ways in which we do this are described below.

I was also very careful to identify all of the safety signals or safety behaviors. For example, each time Eric experienced a bad panic attack while alone, he would fall to the ground, which he felt was a consequence of the panic attack. However, I was struck by the fact that this never occurred outside a situation in which falling to the ground would be acceptable to Eric; that is, even though he had experienced many severe panic attacks in public places, he was able to prevent himself from falling to the ground or from moving his arms and legs in an "uncontrollable" fashion. If he could not escape the situation in a public place, he would often find somewhere to sit down or something to lean against. Almost every panic attack that had been associated with falling had occurred at home. Thus, these actions (falling to the ground, sitting down, leaning against something) seemed to be safety behaviors that were Eric's attempts to cope with the attack by preventing the feared consequence of passing out or collapsing physically. Although Eric used them to reduce his anxiety, these behaviors were causing Eric's anxiety to persist over time because they prevented him from disproving his prediction that he would faint, and in many respects these behaviors supported his belief that a panic attack could result in fainting or falling.

## Course of Treatment

In addition to obtaining more information about Eric's symptoms (e.g., interoceptive avoidance), I spent a good portion of our first treatment session providing him with information on the nature of anxiety and panic and an overview and rationale of the treatment program, which would involve cognitive restructuring, situational exposure, and interoceptive exposure.[8] At the end of our first session, I provided Eric with self-monitoring forms to record his daily levels of anxiety, depression, fear of panic, and panic attack frequency.

In the next session, Eric and I developed two Fear and Avoidance Hierarchies (FAHs): one for agoraphobic situations, and a preliminary one for interoceptive activities (more activities were added when we reached this component of the treatment program). Each item on these FAHs was very specific with regard to the situation/activity, the duration, and other relevant information (e.g., alone vs. accompanied, time of day). For example, one item on Eric's situational FAH was "Drive up the Northway to Exit #10, alone, after dark." The items on both FAHs were arranged in a hierarchical fashion (from least to most difficult) based on his fear and avoidance ratings for each item. To measure his progress, I had Eric provide new fear and avoidance ratings on both FAHs at the beginning of all subsequent sessions. At the end of this session, Eric and I selected one item toward the bottom of his situational FAH to practice two to three times before our next meeting.

In the third session, I discussed the principles and best methods of conducting situational exposure and informed Eric that, at the end of each session from here on out, we would select an item off his FAH for him to perform a few times as between-session practice. Also starting in this session, I began to focus on the cognitive therapy component of the treatment program. After discussing the nature of automatic thoughts, Eric and I talked about the best way to identify cognitions that contributed to his anxiety and panic. I noted that patients, as well as therapists who are just learning the panic control treatment program, often have difficulty identifying the feared predictions that are *most responsible* for their anxiety in a particular situation. In other words, patients may focus on cognitions that are too general in nature either because of insufficient self-questioning or because of the tendency to avoid thinking about their feared predictions because focusing on these thoughts may increase anxiety. For instance, a patient may identify and attempt to counter the prediction that "If I panic in a situation that is unsafe, the panic attack will persist for hours or maybe days," rather than go a step or two further by asking, "What do I fear will occur if I experience a panic attack that does not subside in this situation?" As a guideline in this process, I told Eric that he can be sure that he has identified an important cognition when another person would experience a similar level of anxiety if they were to have this same thought about a given situation or sensation. After rehearsing methods of identifying automatic thoughts, I described two basic forms of anxiety-producing cognitions: *probability overestimation* which involves overestimating the likelihood of a negative outcome of panic (e.g., Eric's prediction that a panic attack may result in losing control of the car and crashing), and *catastrophic thinking,* which involves the perception that if a negative outcome were to occur, it would be "catastrophic" or beyond the person's ability to cope (e.g., if Eric were to collapse due to a panic attack in church, he perceived the social consequences to be insufferable because of others' harsh judgments of him as weak or sick).

In this and subsequent sessions, I guided Eric on the most effective manner of challenging his feared predictions. As with many other patients, Eric tended to be a bit too global in countering his anxiety cognitions; for example, he would counter his fear of passing out by simply telling himself "I have never passed out before." In challenging feared predictions, I often instruct patients to consider a "trial lawyer" analogy (i.e., to "convict" a thought as being invalid, you must provide the "jury" with sufficient evidence). Moreover, before assisting patients in identifying evidence that disconfirms their feared predictions, I find it very useful to have the patient provide all of the evidence they can think of that *supports* the validity of their feared prediction (the "defense"). Thus, as part of processing patients' feared predictions associated with their panic attacks, it is important not only to assist them in countering their cognition (the "prosecution") but also to assist them in challenging the evidence that they believe might support the validity of their feared prediction. This provides a much more thorough processing of feared predictions and also reduces patients' tendency to "counter their counterarguments." As part of the cognitive therapy component of the program, Eric was provided self-monitoring forms to record his anxiety-producing cognitions and his attempts at challenging these beliefs as they occurred between sessions. In addition to checking his other self-monitoring forms, the review of these materials became an indispensable part of each session (usually right at the beginning of each meeting) because it guided the discussion of what had occurred in the preceding week and the ways in which Eric could "fine tune" his skills to become increasingly effective.

After introducing prediction testing as part of cognitive therapy (discussed later), Eric and I began the interoceptive exposure component of the program. After reviewing the rationale of this component, I typically ask the patient to do a number of sensation-producing activities in-session as a way of identifying potential exercises. These activities include things like breathing through a small straw for two minutes, running in place for a minute, and hyperventilating for a minute. As I went through 10 to 12 activities with Eric, I identified several that would be useful as future interoceptive exposures (based on Eric's report of moderate-to-high anxiety and similarity to natural panic).

This was particularly true for the exercise of spinning in a chair for one minute. Roughly 20 seconds into the exercise, Eric stopped and abruptly developed a full-blown panic attack. Though he was too shaken to speak to me, I could see that he was about to fall from his chair to the floor. I viewed this as an important opportunity in treatment, so in a firm voice, I instructed Eric to stand up quickly. He seemed to respond to me without thinking, but the next thing he knew he was standing in front of me, with blinking eyes and a face beaded in sweat. Because I noticed that he had spread his feet far apart (to stabilize himself), I instructed him to place his feet together. Much to his amazement, Eric informed me that his panic attack had subsided.

Ultimately, this turned out to be one of the more important moments in Eric's treatment, for the following reasons: (a) it provided him with strong disconfirming evidence that a panic attack will cause him to fall to the floor; (b) it suggested to him that when he had fallen to floor during the panic, he had basically *chosen* to fall as a way of coping with the panic (e.g., he had "beaten the panic to the punch" by falling to the floor in a more controlled way before the panic caused him to fall in a way that could be harmful [e.g., hitting his head on the floor]); and (c) it demonstrated how the use of safety behaviors, which he used to cope with or reduce anxiety, may actually increase or prolong his anxiety (in the case of falling to the floor, this behavior prevented Eric from learning that a panic attack would never result in his passing out or falling over; in fact, this behavior usually increased his anxiety because he misinterpreted his voluntary drop to the floor as a consequence of some of his panic attacks).

Because several of the interoceptive activities produced high levels of anxiety, I incorporated prediction testing into Eric's in- and between-session exposure exercises. For example, in a later session, Eric and I planned to do several exposure trials of chair spinning. Prior to the first trial, I obtained Eric's predictions regarding the consequences of spinning as well as his rating of the accuracy/likelihood of his prediction. Eric predicted that there was a 50% chance that the first trial of chair spinning would cause him to fall to the floor and cause his limbs to jerk uncontrollably. I recorded his predictions and we began the first trial. Once again, Eric stopped the trial prematurely because the spinning elicited a panic attack, one of stronger intensity than the first one. As before, I noticed that Eric was beginning to head for the floor so I instructed him to do what I had told him to do several weeks back when we had first began interoceptive exposure (chair spinning was at the top of Eric's hierarchy of interoceptive activities so it had taken us several sessions to arrive at this exercise). Again, Eric complied with my order by request standing with his feet close together. As had occurred the first time, his panic attack subsided quickly. We compared Eric's predictions about the first trial to the actual consequences of the trial. After obtaining his predictions of the second trial (his perceived chance of falling had dropped to 15%), he spun himself in the chair again.

Because the next several trials also produced high levels of anxiety, I continued to have Eric test his concern about falling by performing actions that would seriously challenge this prediction. Set up as a prediction test, I asked Eric do things after each chair spinning trial that he predicted would *increase* the likelihood of falling (e.g., standing with feet together and arms spread apart, standing on one leg, standing while bending forward). Each time, his feared prediction was disconfirmed by the outcome of the trial. By the end of this session, his anxiety had dropped from an "8+" on the first trial (using a 0–8 scale) to a 2. As with other interoceptive exercises, I assigned chair spinning as between-session practice, to be performed in a graduated manner (with regard to duration, alone vs. having wife in house, etc.). Later in the stages of interoceptive exposure, Eric completed practices involving more "naturalistic" activities (such as drinking caffeinated beverages). These types of exercises were also helpful in Eric's treatment because they exposed him to sensations that were less predictable with regard to their intensity and duration, and hence these sensations were more similar to naturally occurring anxiety.

I relied heavily on prediction testing as a method of challenging Eric's anxiety-producing cognitions, not only in tandem with interoceptive exposure, but as a way to challenge thoughts associated with anxiety due to the anticipation of scheduled situational exposure practices and events that came up naturally (e.g., attending his wife's office party). This technique was also a helpful adjunct in the later stages of situational exposure when I had Eric enter these difficult situations without access to his safety behaviors (e.g., take elevator 20 floors while standing in the center of the elevator; drive up 10 exits of the Northway, alone, leaving Xanax bottle at home). Also, I incorporated prediction testing in Eric's practices where situational and interoceptive exposure were combined (e.g., drink two cans of caffeinated soda before interstate driving).

### Outcome of the case

At the point where Eric was engaging in these combined exposures regularly without difficulty and with negligible anticipatory anxiety, I was confident that he could independently apply the techniques of treatment to eliminate or reduce the symptoms that remained (e.g., air travel continued to be feared moderately, given that he did not have the opportunity to practice this item). After the fifteenth session, Eric and I met on a monthly basis for five more sessions. By our final session, Eric's problems were nearly resolved (he had some lingering apprehension of one or two activities; also, on an infrequent basis, he experienced a limited symptom attack that was usually associated with life stress). Of note, during the course of our monthly sessions, Eric had tapered his Xanax use to 1mg per day (from his origin 4mg/day), with the assistance of his prescribing physician. Six months after our last session, Eric telephoned to inform me that he was both panic- and Xanax-free.

## EMPIRICAL CONTRIBUTIONS TO UNDERSTANDING PANIC DISORDER (BARLOW)

When the existence of panic disorder with agoraphobia was first determined to be a separate identifiable disorder back in the 1970s, we tended to concentrate on the occurrence of panic attacks and how often they occurred. This was because many investigators in the field, such as Donald Klein, a biological psychiatrist, thought that panic attacks were the central feature of panic disorder and almost certainly had a direct biological cause involving some sort of brain dysfunction. Thus, treating and eliminating panic attacks, according to this thinking, became the central objective, and the preferred treatments were drugs. And yet, based on our work and that of others, we have learned that there were many individuals in the general population who experienced unexpected and uncued panic attacks.[9] Yet many of these people who reported panic attacks did not develop symptoms that met diagnostic criteria for panic disorder. These people were described as having "nonclinical panic." On the basis of studies of people with nonclinical panic, it appeared to us that anxiety over the possibility of having additional panic attacks was a major feature that distinguished patients with panic disorder from persons with nonclinical panic.[7,10] That is, some individuals with panic attacks would focus anxiously on the next attack and start dreading it; others wouldn't. As discussed earlier, this anxiety appears to be driven by cognitive distortions regarding the consequences of panic (e.g., "I'm going to have a heart attack and die"), as well as beliefs about the inability to control the panic and its associated symptoms.

There is now also a wealth of data showing that panic disorder is associated with an excessive sensitivity to bodily sensations. Researchers have discovered this by adapting traditional paradigms from cognitive psychology. To give one basic example, patients with panic disorder are often slower on the Stroop task, compared to persons without panic disorder. The Stroop task requires the individual to name the color of words rather than read the word itself. For instance, the word "coronary" might be presented on a computer screen in the color of blue, and the subject would be required to say "blue." What we and others have found is that persons with panic disorder are significantly slower in naming the colors of words with themes of physical threat than are persons without panic disorder, even though they are not necessarily aware of this process.[11] What seems to happen is that these cues or words grab the attention of the patients, thereby interfering for a brief time with the task at hand of naming the color.

Strong evidence for the role of anxiety focused on physical sensations in panic disorder has been generated from studies involving various biological challenges, such as sodium lactate injections or inhalation of carbon dioxide-$(CO_2)$-enriched air. In these "challenge" paradigms, individuals with or without panic disorder are expected to react differently when exposed to these biological procedures. For example, in a large study that my colleagues and I recently completed, we found that patients with panic disorder responded with significantly higher anxiety (or panic) to a 15-minute trial involving the inhalation of 5.5% $CO_2$-enriched air, relative to patients with other anxiety disorders and persons with no emotional disorder.[12] Findings from these studies are interesting to consider with regard to the reasons why patients with panic disorder are more reactive to these challenges than patients with other anxiety disorders. From the perspective of the biological investigator, these findings are often regarded as strong evidence that panic attacks in panic disorder represent a brain or biochemical dysfunction which can be activated via $CO_2$ inhalation, injection of sodium lactate or yohimbine, and so on.[13]

Yet several studies exist which we believe provide convincing evidence that patients' response to these challenges are influenced mainly by psychological factors. In one study, patients with panic disorder and patients with social phobia underwent a biological challenge involving the inhalation of a strong 50% $CO_2$ mixture.[14] Half of each group received information on exactly what physical sensations to expect; the other half received general instructions that did not include information on the sensations to expect. Whereas this pre-trial instructional manipulation had no effect on social phobics' response to challenge, patients with panic disorder who had been provided an explanation of the pending $CO_2$ trial responded with sensations of lower intensity, fewer catastrophic cognitions, and regarded the experience as less similar to natural panic than did patients who had been provided minimal information. In another study of this nature, we had 20 patients with panic disorder undergo a 15-minute trial in which they inhaled 5.5% $CO_2$-enriched air.[15] All 20 patients were told that if a light in front of them was illuminated during the trial, they could manipulate a dial attached to their chair which would decrease the amount of $CO_2$ that they were receiving (in fact, the dial was not actually connected to the flow of $CO_2$). For 10 patients, the light was illuminated; thus, during the entire trial these patients had an "illusion of control." For the other 10 patients, the light was never illuminated. Despite the fact that all patients received the full $CO_2$ mixture, patients in the "illusion of control" condition responded with significantly less anxiety and less intense sensations, reported fewer catastrophic cognitions, reported the experience as less similar to natural panic, and were less likely to report panicking, than patients who did not think they were in control of $CO_2$ administration. These and other studies[16] led us to conclude that strong evidence exists that anxiety focused on future panic and the sensations associated with panic combine as a strong force in maintaining panic disorder. Consequently, the factors linked to this anxious apprehension about panic (e.g., feared predictions of the consequences of panic, interoceptive and situational avoidance, reliance of safety signals and safety behaviors) reflect important targets for treatment, as illustrated in the treatment of Eric.

## EMPIRICAL CONTRIBUTIONS TO TREATMENT OF PANIC DISORDER (BARLOW, BROWN)

As in the treatment of other anxiety disorders, at the heart of the cognitive–behavioral treatment of panic disorder is the systematic exposure to anxiety-provoking cues, whether they be external (e.g., shopping malls) or internal (e.g., somatic sensations such as dizziness).[17] Although more research is required to provide a definitive answer to this issue, exposure-based treatment is most effective in the treatment of panic disorder if it is applied in conjunction with cognitive restructuring.[18] In addition to dimensions discussed earlier in this chapter, research has suggested the following as other aspects of maximally effective exposure, whether it be situational or interoceptive.[19] First, it is important that the exposure triggers a notable level of anxiety in the initial trials. A significant increase in anxiety upon exposure can be regarded by the clinician as a sign that the patient's "fear structure" has been activated. In the absence of this anxiety increase, the clinician should be concerned that either exposure is of little therapeutic benefit or that the patient is covertly engaging in some behavior to lessen the impact of the activity. For example, if Eric reported that chair-spinning produced no anxiety, I would have concluded that this interoceptive exercise was either: (a) of minimal relevance (e.g., dizziness had not developed into a feared somatic cue) or (b) was relevant but the manner in which the exercise was conducted prevented Eric's fear response from being fully triggered, which could be due to a number of factors including failure to evoke the sensation in sufficient intensity, the situational context in which the sensation was produced (e.g., my office may have been viewed as a "safe place"), or patient behavior such as distraction or use of a safety behavior. Regarding the role of distraction, Eric was struck by the fact that my treatment approach required him to *focus* on his panic-related symptoms and cognitions rather than to distract from these cues as he had been informed to do in his prior therapies (e.g., snap a rubber band on his wrist). Early on in therapy, it was important for me to ensure that Eric understood the rationale behind this so that he could begin to drop certain behavioral tendencies that had been instilled in him over the years.

A second important component of therapeutic exposure is to arrange for the exposure to be of sufficient duration to allow for some anxiety reduction to occur on a given trial. Occasionally, patients and therapists will terminate an exposure trial at the point where a panic attack or high anxiety is experienced. However, to foster maximal emotional processing, it is important that the person be exposed to the feared stimuli long enough for habituation (anxiety reduction) to occur. For instance, in the case presented here, I instructed Eric to complete several additional trials of chair spinning even though he had just experienced a severe panic attack. Had we discontinued the exercise at the point of his panic, Eric would not have experienced a decrease in anxiety over the sensations associated with chair-spinning; in fact, I expect that he would have been more apprehensive of this exercise in the future. As mentioned earlier, the integration of the techniques of cognitive therapy with situational and interoceptive exposure is very helpful, particularly with the use of prediction testing. In using this technique, it is helpful for patients to gauge the success of their situational and interoceptive exposure by whether or not their feared predictions occurred as the result of the exposure, and not in terms of how they felt during the practice.

Finally, research has shown that successful emotional processing is indicated by between-trials habituation, that is, the patient's peak anxiety response should decrease over several exposure trials. In preparing patients for what to expect over the course of treatment, I say to patients that they should anticipate that, if we were to plot their clinical response on a graph, the line indicating symptom reduction would not be a straight line but rather a jagged line denoting symptom decreases and periodic symptom increases, but nonetheless sloping down in the direction of symptom remission. In my experience, this characterizes the clinical response of most treatment responders. I tell patients this to try to prevent catastrophic interpretations of any temporary setbacks they may experience during treatment, as well as to instruct them that they can exploit these brief symptomatic periods to their long-term advantage (e.g., if I drive up the Northway in my current state of near panic, this will *really* test my concern that anxiety will cause me to lose control of the car). However, if clinicians do not observe between-session decreases in anxiety for a given activity, they should closely examine the potential role of such factors as firmly held beliefs regarding the potential consequences of panic in that activity, overt or covert behaviors performed by the patient during exposure (e.g., distraction, safety behaviors), as well as the manner in which the exposure is structured (e.g., is the exposure of sufficient duration?). I am a firm believer that, if possible, it is helpful for patients not only to drop any safety behaviors that they may use to cope with anxiety in feared situations, but to *do the opposite* of what they would normally do to feel safe.

To illustrate, in the treatment of Eric, he was asked to stand up (and in later trials, stand on one leg while leaning over) at times when he was certain the panic was going to cause him to fall over. Practices in which the patient brings sensations on voluntarily in a feared situation could be considered as another example of doing the opposite. Because these "actions may speak louder than the words," such exercises may be quite effective in providing the patient with strong disconfirming evidence for any persisting beliefs. (Also, these beliefs may be responsible for why the clinician has not observed an appreciable decrease in anxiety despite repeated exposure trials.) Occasionally, interventions of this nature might be regarded by some as a bit colorful (or peculiar). One male patient with panic disorder misinterpreted his panic as evidence that he may commit an uncontrolled, aggressive act such as stabbing a family member or throwing his infant child down a flight of stairs. This patient entered one session in a state of near panic, believing that he was going to become aggressive at any moment. About five minutes later, the therapist was successful at coaxing this patient to press the sharp blade of his office scissors to his neck (he did not have a knife in his office) while telling the therapist repeatedly, "You bastard, I'm going to drive this blade through your neck!" This impromptu exposure practice (which lasted about 15 minutes, until the patient's anxiety had decreased from an 8 to a 1 on a 0–8 scale), later proved to be a significant turning point in the patient's response to treatment. This case example underscores the potential therapeutic effect of conducting these prediction tests "doing the opposite" exposures at times when the patient is in a state of high anticipatory anxiety (because if the feared consequences do not occur under these conditions, then this provides the patient with strong evidence of their unlikelihood).[20]

Although psychosocial treatments that target panic attacks directly are relatively new, many research studies now exist that attest to their effectiveness, perhaps even more effective than pharmacotherapy.[21] For example, focusing on long-term outcome, in a major outcome study comparing the effectiveness of cognitive therapy, imipramine, and applied relaxation, David Clark and colleagues found that a significantly greater percentage of patients who received cognitive therapy were classified as panic-free (85%) at 15-month follow-up than patients in the other two treatment conditions (60% and 47% for imipramine and applied relaxation, respectively).[22] Similarly, the percentage of patients who met "high endstate functioning criteria" at 15-month follow-up was significantly higher in the cognitive therapy condition (70%) than for imipramine (45%) and applied relaxation (32%) ("high endstate" was defined as no panic attacks in the month before the assessment plus a clinical severity rating of 2 or less on a 0–8 scale of distress/impairment). These findings are quite similar to those obtained from our research center, where we examined the long-term efficacy of our panic control treatment.[23] Specifically, 86.7% of patients completing treatment were classified as panic-free at 24-month follow-up; 53.3% met criteria for high endstate functioning (using criteria similar to those used by Clark and colleagues). Although these findings are quite encouraging, particularly in comparison to results of long-term outcome studies of drug treatments, these data also indicate the need for us to develop even more powerful treatments for panic disorder, because many patients are not cured and some don't improve at all.

In addition, our research has shown that the method by which treatment outcome has been evaluated may somewhat overestimate the efficacy of psychosocial and drug treatments of panic disorder.[24] This is because treatment outcome has been assessed by determining the patient's functioning at the time of the evaluation. Particularly in the case of long-term outcome evaluation, this "snap shot" approach fails to consider the patient's functioning over the entire course of time since treatment has ended (e.g., between the time of treatment termination and follow-up evaluation, did any relapses occur? was additional treatment sought?). This issue is very relevant in determining treatment outcome of panic disorder, a disturbance whose natural course is characterized by marked fluctuations in symptoms.

It is very important for the researcher and clinician to identify and account for potential predictors of treatment outcome (e.g., the presence of additional diagnoses such as major depression, severity of the panic disorder).[24,25] Although no one predictor has been *consistently* found to be strongly associated with treatment outcome, researchers have been quite interested in the question of whether concurrent use of psychotropic medications (especially the high-potency benzodiazepines such as Xanax) may be linked to a poorer response to psychosocial treatments of panic disorder. One reason why use of medication has been thought to potentially interfere with psychosocial treatment is that the drug might prevent the evocation of anxiety necessary for emotional processing to occur. However, if medications do have a negative impact on treatment, we feel that this phenomenon could be psychologically mediated. Specifically, the use of medication during treatment could reduce the ability of some patients to credit any positive changes in their symptoms to the efficacy of therapy and their competency in applying newly learned techniques. If this is so, then these patients may not garner a personal sense of control over their symptoms, which conceptually is a central maintaining factor of panic disorder and hence is an important goal of psychosocial treatment. As with other potential predictors such as comorbid depression and severity of the panic disorder, there is some evidence for the association of concurrent medication use and poorer treatment outcome.[24] Nevertheless, these findings are inconsistent and often very weak, and thus, no conclusive statement can be made.

Of note, Eric was on a very high dosage of Xanax (4 to 5 mg per day) during treatment. Although we cannot conclude much on the basis of one case alone, in my view his medication use did not affect the course of treatment other than to later set the occasion for a Xanax discontinuation schedule (which, for some patients, can be quite lengthy and associated with the reemergence of symptoms).

Finally, while I have spent some of this last section discussing an agenda for further research aimed at the reconciliation of less encouraging results, allow me to conclude by underscoring the fact that the psychosocial treatment of panic disorder is one of our profession's "success stories." Indeed, tangible evidence of this assertion is reflected by the fact that a recent conference sponsored by the National Institute of Mental Health recommended this intervention, along with certain drugs, as the treatment of choice for panic disorder. We hope, the next few years will witness advances leading to even more powerful treatments.

## Notes

1. Meyer, V., & Gelder, M.G. (1963). Behaviour therapy and phobic disorders. *British Journal of Psychiatry, 109,* 19 28.

2. Agras, W.S., Leitenberg, H., & Barlow, D.H. (1968). Social reinforcement in the modification of agoraphobia. *Archives of General Psychiatry, 19,* 423–427.

3. Zitrin, C.M., Klein, D.F., Woerner, M.G., & Ross, D.C. (1983). Treatment of phobias: I. Comparison of imipramine hydrochloride and placebo. *Archives of General Psychiatry, 40,* 125–138.

4. Brown, T.A., Di Nardo, P.A., & Barlow, D.H. (1994). *Anxiety Disorders Interview Schedule for DSM-IV (ADIS-IV).* Albany, NY: Graywind Publications.

5. As is the case with most patients with panic disorder, Eric reported other cognitive distortions besides those relating to fainting or falling. We have opted to focus on these cognitions in this chapter because of space limitations and the fact that these misperceptions were strongly associated with the patient's anticipatory anxiety and agoraphobic avoidance.

6. Moras, K., Di Nardo, P.A., Brown, T.A., & Barlow, D.H. (1994). *Comorbidity, functional impairment, and depression among the DSM-III-R anxiety disorders.* Unpublished manuscript.

7. Barlow, D.H. (1988). *Anxiety and its disorders: The nature and treatment of anxiety and panic.* New York: Guilford Press.

8. Craske, M.G., & Barlow, D.H. (1993). Panic disorder and agoraphobia. In D.H. Barlow (Ed.), *Clinical handbook of psychological disorders: A step-by-step treatment manual* (2nd ed., pp. 1–47). New York: Guilford Press.

9. Norton, G.R., Cox, B.J., & Malan, J. (1992). Nonclinical panickers: A review. *Clinical Psychology Review, 12,* 121–139.

10. Telch, M.J., Lucas, J.A., & Nelson, P. (1989). Nonclinical panic in college stu-

dents: An investigation of prevalence and symptomatology. *Journal of Abnormal Psychology, 98,* 300–306.

11. McNally, R.J., Riemann, B.C., & Kim, E. (1990). Selective processing of threat cues in panic disorder. *Behaviour Research and Therapy, 28,* 407–412.

12. Rapee, R.M., Brown, T.A., Antony, M.M., & Barlow, D.H. (1992). Response to hyperventilation and inhalation of 5.5% carbon dioxide-enriched air across the *DSM-III-R* anxiety disorders. *Journal of Abnormal Psychology, 101,* 538–552.

13. Klein, D.F. (1993). False suffocation alarms, spontaneous panics, and related conditions. *Archives of General Psychiatry, 50,* 306–317.

14. Rapee, R.M., Mattick, R., & Murrell, E. (1986). Cognitive mediation in the affective component of spontaneous panic attacks. *Journal of Behavior Therapy and Experimental Psychiatry, 17,* 243–253.

15. Sanderson, W.C., Rapee, R.M., & Barlow, D.H. (1989). The influence of an illusion of control on panic attacks induced via inhalation of 5.5% carbon dioxide-enriched air. *Archives of General Psychiatry, 46,* 157–162.

16. Ehlers, A., Margraf, J., Roth, W.T., Taylor, C.B., & Birbaumer, N. (1988). Anxiety induced by false heart rate feedback in patients with panic disorder. *Behaviour Research and Therapy, 26,* 1–11.

17. Brown, T.A., Hertz, R.M., & Barlow, D.H. (1992). New developments in cognitive–behavioral treatment of anxiety disorders. In A. Tasman & M.B. Riba (Eds.), *American Psychiatric Press review of psychiatry* (Vol. 11, pp. 285–306). Washington, DC: American Psychiatric Press.

18. Michelson L.K., & Marchione, K. (1991). Behavioral, cognitive, and pharmacological treatments of panic disorder with agoraphobia: Critique and synthesis. *Journal of Consulting and Clinical Psychology, 59,* 100–114.

19. Foa, E.B., & Kozak, M.J. (1986). Emotional processing of fear: Exposure to corrective information. *Psychological Bulletin, 99,* 20–35.

20. These illustrations may provide the reader with the sense that, in many cases, the most significant strides in treatment occur as the result of one interoceptive or situational exposure trial. However, these procedures must usually be carried out in a repeated, systematic fashion in order to be efficacious.

21. Brown, T.A., & Barlow, D.H. (1992). Long-term clinical outcome following cognitive–behavioral treatment of panic disorder and panic disorder with agoraphobia. In P.H. Wilson (Ed.), *Principles and practice of relapse prevention* (pp. 191–212). New York: Guilford Press.

22. Clark, D.M., Salkovskis, P.M., Hackmann, A., Middleton, H., Anastasiades, P., & Gelder, M. (1994). A comparison of cognitive therapy, applied relaxation, and imipramine in the treatment of panic disorder. *British Journal of Psychiatry, 164,* 759–769.

23. Craske, M.G., Brown, T.A., & Barlow, D.H. (1991). Behavioral treatment of panic disorder: A two-year follow-up. *Behavior Therapy, 22,* 289–304.

24. Brown, T.A., & Barlow, D.H. (1995). Long-term outcome in cognitive-behavioral treatment of panic disorder: Clinical predictors and alternative strategies for assessment. *Journal of Consulting and Clinical Psychology, 63,* 754–765.

25. Brown, T.A., Antony, M.M., & Barlow, D.H. (1995). Diagnostic comorbidity in panic disorder: Effect on treatment outcome and course of comorbid diagnoses following treatment. *Journal of Consulting and Clinical Psychology, 63,* 408–418.

## Recommended Readings

Barlow DH (1988). *Anxiety and its disorders: The nature and treatment of anxiety and panic.* New York: Guilford Press.

Barlow DH, & Craske, MG (1994). *Mastery of your anxiety and panic II.* Albany, NY: Graywind Publications.

Clark DM (1986). A cognitive approach to panic. *Behaviour Research and Therapy, 24,* 461–470.

Craske MG, & Barlow, DH (1993). Panic disorder and agoraphobia. In D.H. Barlow (Ed.), *Clinical handbook of psychological disorders: A step-by-step treatment manual* (2nd ed., pp. 1–47). New York: Guilford Press.

# 5

**About**

**the**

**Author**

*Gail Steketee,* Ph.D., *is a Professor and Associate Dean of Academic Affairs at Boston University's School of Social Work. She received her undergraduate degree from Harvard University and her masters and doctorate degrees from Bryn Mawr Graduate School of Social Work and Social Research. Dr. Steketee trained with Joseph Wolpe, M.D. and Edna Foa, Ph.D., at Temple University Department of Psychiatry. Currently, she collaborates on several research projects focused on the treatment of obsessive-compulsive disorder (OCD) and other anxiety disorders. Her ongoing research on family roles in behavioral treatment outcome for OCD and agoraphobia is sponsored by the National Institute of Mental Health. Other research interests include assessment of cognitions and other traits in OCD and anxiety disorders, and group and multiple family group treatment for OCD. She has published extensively in these and related areas, including two books, one for OCD sufferers and their families,* When Once in Not Enough, *New Harbinger Press, 1990 and one for practicing clinicians interested in learning behavioral treatment* Treatment of Obsessive Compulsive Disorder, *Guilford Press, 1993.*

# Judy: A Compelling Case of Obsessive-CompulsiveDisorder

**About**

**the**

**Disorder**

Obsesive-compulsive disorder (OCD) is a disorder in which the experience of anxiety seems to be very different from that seen in panic disorder. People with OCD also feel inner torture, but find other ways to reduce their suffering. Unfortunately, their attempt at a solution brings about its own set of problems—the development of obsessions and compulsions. An obsession is an unwanted thought, word, phrase, or image that persistently and repeatedly comes into a person's min/ and causes distress. A compulsion is a repetitive behavior/ ritual that occurs in response to uncontrollable urges to t action. In some cases these compulsive behaviors and ob sive thoughts disrupt the person's life to the point whe or she cannot engage in even the simplest of daily ro The obsessive thoughts and compulsive behaviors seer ple with the disorder are inconsistent with their / wishes, values, and personal style. The symptoms consuming, irrational, and distracting but the indi able to suppress them.

It might be difficult to imagine how some could ever regain normal functioning. How/ treatable condition. Many symptoms may be havioral interventions. As Dr. Steketee poir of Judy, the use of medication is not alwa may be an option for clients who are una' on a behavioral regimen. Although not / such positive outcomes as Judy's, we c etee's "model" case about the compo ment for this debilitating condition.

Like m
sympton
pear wit
present
worsened
riage. She
dren, and
husband's i
"do things

# THE CASE OF JUDY

## Initial Presentation

Judy called me several years ago seeking an appointment for anxiety problems that she believed were obsessive. She heard that I specialized in this disorder and hoped I might be able to help her. At the time of our first appointment, she was 32 years old and had given birth three months before to her second child. She complained of increasing problems with checking faucets, light switches, and buttons on her children's clothing, among other things. She also engaged in several types of magical rituals because certain numbers, clothing, and activities had become connected in her mind to the devil and to bad outcomes for people she knew. These rituals would stop her in her tracks in the middle of ordinary activities until she could correct the idea. She had managed, she thought, to keep her children from realizing that she behaved oddly at times, but she could not hide it from her husband. Although she felt he was generally supportive, he was frustrated by her behavior and its interference with daily life. Judy felt that this bizarre behavior had gone on long enough, and she was particularly worried about its effect on her children.

Judy struck me as a reasonably bright, very earnest, and hard-working mother and wife who was a bit overwhelmed with a new child and financial pressures. Her efforts to establish a part-time career as a freelance video producer appeared to add to her stress. She was dressed casually, although she was obviously anxious about my opinion of her and her situation. As she described her situation and her frustration in trying unsuccessfully to control her anxiety and her "ridiculous" behavior, I liked her immediately. Although she was not a particularly attractive woman, she was very engaging and appeared very motivated to correct an obviously upsetting problem. I sometimes find it difficult to respond empathically to clients who speak in superlatives about their troubles, hoping to impress me so I will come to the rescue. By contrast, Judy described her situation and her feelings simply, without exaggeration. Her concerns about herself and about the effects of her problems on her family seemed very appropriate and matched my own values.

## Case History

Like many who develop OCD, Judy could not precisely date the first onset of symptoms, but recalled some examples at the age of nine that seemed to disappear with time, and were not present during her teens. She believed that her adult symptoms began at age 25 or 26 before she met her husband, but grew with the several stressors that accompanied their courtship and marriage. She had difficulty adapting to the role of stepmother to partly grown children. She was very concerned about the family's financial stability since her husband's income as an artist was unstable and never large. She tried hard to "do right" to prevent problems in their relationship, and found herself going to the synagogue to meditate to gain strength before visiting his apartment when his children were there. Interestingly, magical rituals that had begun at this time virtually disappeared at age 27, only to resurface again at age 29, possibly connected with her pregnancy with their first child, a girl. She also later recalled that her aging dog died at that time, after she had a strong premonition about his death.

Judy's early history was far from enjoyable. She and her two older brothers grew up in an upper-middle-class family in which her physician father and housewife mother did not hide the unhappiness in their marriage. Both were away frequently, and her mother had several affairs. Neither parent spent much time with Judy, attended her school events, or gave her gifts. Later in treatment, Judy recalled having considerable trouble learning in school; she now believes she had a significant learning disability that went unrecognized by her teachers or parents. During her teenage years, her father began to mock her appearance and manners, calling her a "loser." She recalled his singling her out at family events to focus on her flaws. It was not clear how Judy came to know that her father was dependent on barbiturates. She cried during the session when recalling that when she was 22, her brothers confronted him about his drug addiction, leading to a stormy argument after which she went to tell him she loved him. He accepted her overture and finally told her he loved her as well. After this incident, the harassment stopped and they developed a good relationship until he died four years later of a self-inflicted drug overdose. She felt angry at him for depriving her so soon of this more positive experience with him. Judy's relationship with her mother had improved considerably in recent years, although Judy still found her self-centered. Judy had good relationships with both brothers, though she felt closer to the youngest, perhaps because the older one resembled her father. Her mother and both brothers lived in distant states, so she saw them rarely, but kept up phone contact. Interestingly, Judy describes all of her family members as highly anxious, with some evidence of depression in her father and one brother.

Judy had been quite popular and sociable at school in her early teens and had dated several boys. However, by age 17 she felt self-conscious in the wake of her father's constant criticism. At college she engaged in few social activities and was lonely. After graduation she worked, and although her social life became more active, cocaine use led to feelings of confusion, fear, and out-of-body experiences. At 24, for several days she experienced some very odd sensations, in which she felt very distant from people around her, as if she was not really present, even though she could see and hear everything that went on around her. These appeared to be dissociative states and possible panic attacks which lasted for three to four days, so that she feared she was losing her mind. She sought psychotherapy at this time and continued this until she was 28, observing that it helped her greatly to understand and, perhaps more important, to express her feelings. She could not clarify whether or how the dissociative state was related to the onset of OCD symptoms, and this remains a mystery.

Of particular interest in Judy's case is her religious background because several of her obsessive symptoms centered on Satan and demons. She attended a reformed Jewish Saturday school, where she developed a strong sense of Jewish cultural identity. She viewed God as all-knowing and punitive, fixing on the idea that if she made a mistake, he would punish her. Paradoxically, she felt that this belief coincided with her fear of her father's criticism and did not reflect what she was taught or really felt: that if there was a God, he would not be like that. Nonetheless, her fear persisted that punishment would follow mistakes or bad thoughts or behavior.

## Diagnosis

Judy's *DSM-IV* diagnosis was:

| | |
|---|---|
| Axis I: | • Obsessive compulsive disorder |
| Axis II: | • No diagnosis, dependent and avoidant traits |
| Axis III: | • None |
| Axis IV: | • Economic problems (inadequate finances) |
| | • Occupational problems (underemployed) |
| Axis V: | • GAF = 68 |

Judy met all criteria on Axis I of the *DSM-IV* (at the time, *DSM-III-R*) for obsessive compulsive disorder. She had recurrent thoughts that were intrusive, inappropriate, and anxiety-provoking. These obsessions were focused almost entirely on fears that bad luck would happen to people she knew and especially to her children unless she intervened. The bad luck was associated with the numbers 3 and 13; reading or hearing about the Devil, demons, Satan, black magic, and voodoo; religious rules she didn't believe in against cooking meat with milk and shopping on the sabbath; superstitious ideas such as stepping on cracks; passing funeral homes and cemeteries; saying something negative about someone; and having a good time.

To reduce her fears of bad consequences if these events occurred, she engaged in multiple rituals that could be summarized as repeating, undoing, and checking. Any of the obsessive cues would trigger repetitions of actions that she was doing at the time, such as dressing and redressing. She also tried to "right the wrong" by doing such things as saying "Amen" when passing a gravestone or stopping all activity until the clock passed beyond 13 minutes before or after the hour. Whenever she left the house, she performed checking rituals to ensure that she would not be responsible for a fire or harm that might come to the cat. These typically included checking each room several times in sequence looking for the cat and making sure that nothing could fall on her, and checking the stove and heaters to be sure they were off and nothing was near them that could catch on fire.

Consistent with DSM criteria for OCD, Judy felt that her symptoms were senseless and unreasonable, and reported spending well over an hour a day either obsessing or doing rituals. She was most anxious to rid herself of these thoughts and behaviors since they interferred with ordinary activities in maintaining the household and particularly in dressing and playing with the children.

Although I did not conduct a formal interview regarding other possible concurrent diagnoses, I do not believe Judy would have met criteria for any that affected her daily living. Her moderately depressed mood might have been diagnosed by some as dysthymia, though not by me. Her mood appeared to be fully explained by her anxiety symptoms and her circumstances as a mother of small children with a low income. I was convinced that improvement in her OCD symptoms would lift her low mood, at least in part. I also observed no Axis II conditions and no personality traits that could be considered prognostic of a poor outcome. Although Judy met criteria for a few traits associated with dependent personality disorder and with avoidant personality disorder, these did not appear prominent styles of behavior likely to interfere with the conduct of therapy or its outcome. Since this is often not the case, I felt fortunate to be treating such a motivated and generally stable young woman.

Judy reported no medical conditions relevant to Axis III. Several stressors impinged on her life, classifiable on Axis IV as economic problems, occupational problems, and other stressors. These included the very low family income, the inability to find satisfactory part-time work in her field, and the recent birth of her second child. Otherwise, relationships with her husband, family, and friends were generally good. On Axis V, her functioning would be assessed as moderately high, in the range of 70, since, although they were upsetting, her symptoms interfered only mildly in her roles as wife, mother, friend, and worker.

## Case Formulation

In many ways, I thought Judy's situation was very hopeful. She was highly motivated, and by her own assessment, she saw her symptoms as unreasonable behaviors that might eventually have a negative effect on her children. She had a generally supportive husband, healthy children, good social skills, an engaging personality, and a reasonable outlook regarding her symptoms and life situation. Although sometimes dysphoric, she did not evidence the serious depression that some patients develop as a consequence of debilitating OCD. However, although her life circumstances were generally positive, her self-esteem had suffered considerably in the wake of her parents' disinterest and criticism during childhood. This was evident in a tendency to denigrate some (though not all) of her accomplishments and to expect negative outcomes.

On the Maudsley Obsessional-Compulsive Inventory (MOCI), Judy scored 14 out of 30, indicating substantial symptoms that were mainly focused on magical efforts to control potential negative events or outcomes, and rituals of extensive checking and repeating actions. The nature of her symptoms seemed tied to her childhood experiences of being unable to please her parents or prevent herself from being harshly criticized and neglected. She expected her efforts to lead to negative outcomes and wanted to prevent these from harming her children. The excessive responsibility Judy voiced is evident in many patients with OCD,[1] and was also consistent with her primary role at that time of caretaker and manager of the household. Since Judy's freelance work was so sporadic, she couldn't derive much satisfaction and identity from it. She expressed doubts about her capacity as a mother, despite strong evidence that her caretaking of her own children was very attentive and considerably superior to that of her parents. Overall, then, Judy displayed somewhat low self-esteem, compounded by her lack of control over her obsessions and compulsions.

To address both the OCD symptoms and low self-image, I proposed that we engage in weekly therapy sessions using a behavioral homework program that included exposure to her obsessive thoughts and gradual blocking of the rituals associated with each thought, along with rational evaluation of some of her attitudes about herself and her behavior in her everyday life. Judy readily agreed to this plan, and for financial reasons, we planned to meet for one hour a week for the first two months and then to reduce the time to half-hour sessions for as long as needed. Such a plan differs from my usual practice of beginning with two or even three sessions a week for a few weeks and then reducing the time as the client needs less support between sessions to do homework and symptoms reduce in frequency and intensity.[2]

## Course of Treatment

The first several treatment sessions were concentrated on identifying all of the obsessive ideas that she experienced and the rituals that accompanied them. Judy kept a log of OCD symptoms for one week, and from this and her description of her symptoms, we jointly constructed a hierarchy of increasingly disturbing obsessive situations and the rituals that followed them. She arranged these by the level of anxiety she would feel if prevented from ritualizing, using a scale from 0 (no discomfort) to 100 (panic, terror). The following situations were selected for exposure in order of easier to harder: Fastening the snaps on the children's clothes, dressing herself, turning on lights and faucets, having angry thoughts about her step children, stepping on cracks, going up and down stairs with bad thoughts about acquaintances, leaving the car or the house without checking, saying or writing the numbers 3 or 13 or combinations of numbers that add to these, doing activities at 13 of or 13 after the hour, cooking cheese with chicken, shopping on Saturday, driving by and walking by funeral homes and cemeteries, going into an occult shop, reading about devils and demons, writing and saying the words "devil," "demon," and "satan." At each step of the list, Judy agreed not to use any ritual (checking, repeating) that would relieve anxiety.

Judy's progress through this list was generally steady, with a few snags as would be typical of most motivated clients. She kept appointments and found that she did best if she signed a contract each week regarding her homework assignment. We each kept a copy and reviewed her progress at the next session. She progressed successfully through dressing her children and herself, checking lights and faucets, avoiding checking the house and car locks, the number 3, and retracing steps when a bad idea occurred to her about someone else. Much as I tried to get her to stop rituals altogether and provided several possible strategies for doing so, she was never able to control her rituals completely. However, she did reduce them by about 80%. She struggled quite a bit with the number 13 and its association with the clock, taking several weeks to get this under control, but accomplishing it about 10 weeks into treatment. Despite continuing to perform rituals at a low rate, overall she made good progress. A hiatus in therapy occurred because of financial problems, but Judy began again about four months later, having lost a little ground, but by no means all of it. We then went together to visit a cemetery and a funeral home, and soon thereafter, an occult shop where she purchased a few small items she associated with the devil.

Judy found this exercise very difficult. The idea that her children would die if she were not "good" surfaced with a vengeance and required considerable discussion that led to her reviewing events surrounding her father's death. This seemed to help her to struggle harder with rituals designed to prevent harm to her children, although it took another two months to gain about 80% control of most of the magical rituals. However, she continued to have considerable difficulty deliberately exposing herself to words associated with the devil. With concerted effort, she began to serve devil's food cake, deviled eggs, and so forth, and to keep papers with the words "devil" and "satan" in her drawers and appointment book. She felt it would be too embarrassing to put these on her refrigerator as I proposed, so I backed off from this request.

## Outcome of The Case

Judy's treatment continued weekly for four more months, at which point she requested spacing sessions every other week. By then she felt that all obsessions and rituals were under good control, except for the devil and the number 13. Her behavior with these remaining items was improved, but not yet under complete control. I asked her to complete a second questionnaire (MOCI), which showed mild symptoms with a score of 6 out of 30. For another three years, we continued with sessions every two to three weeks, discussing progress on OCD symptoms and occasionally making written contracts for the first few minutes. Increasingly, we reverted to discussions of Judy's career, her marriage, which continued to be generally good, and the birth of her third child. Visits became more sporadic, leading to a one year hiatus, followed by appointments every three to four weeks, with periodic gaps of two to three months for another two years. During this time, Judy's symptoms remained stable and at a mild level.

She was unable to eliminate them entirely, perhaps because, despite her best intentions, it sometimes seemed easier after having ideas about the devil to give in to urges to ritualize than to resist them.

I last saw Judy for a single brief appointment a year ago. She was turning 40 and felt stressed by an attraction to another man and by concerns about her husband's lack of sexual interest in her, though she realized that their 15-year age difference might be a contributing factor. She had more free lance video work and was proud of several professional accomplishments, including one show in which her work was featured. She reported that the same obsessive thoughts continued to occur occasionally, but that she rarely engaged in rituals. Overall, she felt she was 80% to 90% improved compared to when she first came for treatment eight years before. She realized that although she continued to struggle to some extent with some obsessive ideas, she did not feel burdened by this. Because Judy had never gained complete control over the "devil" rituals, I had always worried that she might lose the gains she made without my contin- ued encouragement, since my colleagues and I had observed in our research that clients with only partial gains at the end of treatment tended to do poorly at follow-up.[3] However, Judy had already demonstrated that she did not need my help during the months of no treatment, so it seemed clear that I had little cause for concern. I was certainly very pleased with her progress and the evident improvement in her self-esteem, and encouraged her to keep up occasional ex- posures to feared situations and call if needed.

## EMPIRICAL CONTRIBUTIONS TO UNDERSTANDING OCD

Judy exhibited an excessive fear of criticism and sensitivity to making mistakes that my colleagues and I have previously found common among individuals with OCD.[4] These also figured prominently in her obsessions and rituals, in that she feared being responsible for harm to her family if she failed to carry out her magical rituals. She also thought she would be punished for making the dog or cat angry whenever the light caught the animal's iris, making it appear red, and she was particularly worried about being considered selfish. Interestingly, as of- ten as I have observed guilt to be a predominant component of the emotions of clients with OCD like Judy, our research has only partly confirmed this and only with volunteers who had mild OCD symptoms.[5] Were I to treat Judy again, I would be very interested to see whether her concerns about offending others and her exaggerated sense of responsibility would respond to a cognitive treat- ment that engaged her in challenging and testing her assumptions. Research from the Netherlands suggests that cognitive therapies have been successful in reducing OCD symptoms.[6] I have recently advocated rigorous scientific testing of such methods with OCD after we have first identified the types of beliefs and attitudes that particularly characterize this disorder and would be appro- priate targets for cognitive therapy.[7]

Judy also displayed a few mental rituals that I believe require careful assessment to avoid missing these often subtle efforts to neutralize obsessive anxiety.[8] Judy's took the form of a silent "Amen" when passing cemetaries and commutation of any numbers adding to 13 by mentally substituting other numbers. During the course of therapy, it is important to be sure that mental rituals are not intruding while clients are confronting obsessive thoughts or situations, because these rituals can undermine the benefits of prolonged exposure.[9] Fortunately, Judy did not exhibit overvalued beliefs in her power to prevent bad events, because my colleagues have found these to predict poor outcome.[10] However, like many clients with OCD, she lost some perspective when in the grip of an obsession, and worried that if she really did have such powers and didn't exercise them, the price of harming her family was too high to pay. This type of thinking is quite common and does not seem to have a negative effect on treatment outcome, though clients must struggle hard to force themselves to do exposure in the face of these ideas.

Judy was fortunate to have a generally supportive husband who did not view her OCD symptoms as significant detriments to their family life. Indeed, in my view, Judy functioned quite well as a wife and mother despite her fears. For several years, I have been very interested in why some patients do well in therapy and hold onto their gains, whereas others appear to lose ground quickly after treatment ends. One possibility is adverse family influences on OCD, in cases where the therapist's support during intensive treatment is replaced by critical and occasionally hostile or intrusive family members. My preliminary research on this topic indicated that unpleasant interchanges with angry relatives, who thought that patients could really stop ritualizing if only they tried hard enough, were indeed associated with a relapse in OCD symptoms.[11] I have recently repeated this research using more trustworthy measures of family interactions and a larger sample of OCD clients. Our very preliminary and as yet unpublished results suggest that familial criticism may be associated with loss of gains after therapy, but I am not yet confident of this finding, since we have not yet followed up all of the treatment participants in the study. In any case, it seemed clear to me that, in Judy's case, I did not need to be concerned about negative family interactions adversely affecting her ability to rid herself of OCD symptoms.

Judy's main environmental concerns were financial, as she worried very understandably about how to provide her family with adequate housing and good educational experiences. As might be expected, low income is a predictor of worse outcome from behavior therapy.[12] However, in Judy's case, her financial concerns did not appear so severe that I was concerned about her ability to concentrate on the treatment and homework. Like many other clients, she also worried about whether her symptoms could be passed on to her children. This is a difficult question for therapists to address because there is evidence that OCD "runs in families," although not necessarily more often than other disorders of anxiety and depression. In a recent study, we found that some personality traits, such as risk avoidance and perfectionism, were more common in parents of people with mild OCD symptoms than among parents of people without these symptoms.[13] However, these findings do not indicate whether or not OCD symptoms will be passed on to children. My usual response to queries from parents with OCD is that the best way to try to ensure that their children are not adversely affected is to work hard in treatment and reduce their own symptoms, as well as any underlying attitudes that seem to feed their obsessive fears.

## EMPIRICAL CONTRIBUTIONS TO TREATMENT OF OCD

As noted in the case report, Judy's treatment contained both exposure to feared obsessions and prevention of rituals that accompanied the obsessions. My colleagues and I have demonstrated the need for both of these elements of behavioral treatment in order to reduce both types of symptoms. It is quite clear that exposure directly reduces obsessive anxiety, whereas prevention of responses controls rituals.[14] In Judy's case, I chose not to use imagined exposure, though we have found this intervention helpful for clients whose obsessive ideas center on fears of disastrous consequences.[15] Although this was true of Judy's obsessions, since she feared harm to her children or others, her thoughts contained few specifics, and she rarely reported having vivid images of negative outcomes. It seemed that the direct exposure was producing anxiety as expected and provided sufficient exposure, so that imagining feared consequences would add little to her level of anxiety.

My own and others' research has provided confusing information about the role of depressed mood as a predictor of poor outcome for OCD. Initially, it appeared to interfere with reduction of anxiety during and between exposure sessions, thereby rendering treatment less effective.[16] However, in another more recent study, I found no connection of depressed mood to a poor treatment response, and others have reported similar findings.[17] Needless to say, this left me more than a little confused about just what role depression plays during therapy. I hoped that my most recent study might shed some further light on the problem. In doing preliminary (and I stress "preliminary") analyses, we observed that clients with a diagnosis of major depression, but not those with dysthymia, had a somewhat poorer immediate and six-month outcome after behavioral treatment. Perhaps it is only severe depression that affects clients' ability to benefit from exposure treatment. In Judy's case, since she showed no evidence of major depression, but experienced only occasional and mild dysthymia, there seemed no cause for concern and, in retrospect, I believe this was justified. Likewise, I saw no reason to consider antidepressant medication for Judy. Our previous research has shown that, even for clients who have substantial depressed mood, a common antidepressant medication like imipramine reduced depression, but had little effect on OCD symptoms. Most important, adding medication to behavioral treatment did not lead to any more improvement than using behavior therapy alone.[18]

The medications that have been demonstrated to be most effective for OCD are those that affect the serotonin system, reducing both depressed mood and OCD symptoms. Since these serotonergic medications also have not been demonstrated to add to the benefits achieved by exposure and response prevention, I saw no reason to encourage Judy to take any medication at all. I should note, however, that clients who have difficulty engaging in exposure treatment because their anxiety or depressed mood is extremely high often *do* benefit from taking serotonergic medications prior to behavioral treatment.[19]

## COMMENT

Judy's case is somewhat unusual in that there were no significant comorbid diagnoses or severe adverse effects on her functioning. In this regard, Judy appeared to be a better "survivor" than her background and symptoms might have warranted. Her "survivor" instincts also served her well during therapy: she attended sessions faithfully, made her contracts, and did her homework as best she could. In short, she was my idea of a model patient in a treatment that was far from ideal, since I saw her far less frequently than is desirable and could not convince her to give up rituals altogether, even for a short while. Such clients warm therapists' hearts, but also indicate that our research-generated treatment protocols can be bent considerably and still deliver good effect for certain clients, though undoubtedly not in all cases.

### Notes

1. For a discussion of the role of excessive responsibility in OCD, see Salkovskis, P.M. (1989). Cognitive-behavioural factors and the persistence of intrusive thoughts in obsessive problems. *Behaviour Research and Therapy, 27,* 677–682.

2. Such more-intensive treatment plans are described in my book for clinicians, which is listed among the recommended readings at the end of this chapter.

3. Foa, E.B., Steketee, G., Grayson, J.B., & Doppelt, H.G. (1983). Treatment of obsessive compulsives: When do we fail? In E.B. Foa & P.M.G. Emmelkamp (Eds.), *Failures in behavior therapy.* (pp. 10–34). New York: Wiley.

4. Turner, R.M., Steketee, G., & Foa, E.B. (1979). Fear of criticism in washers, checkers and phobics. *Behaviour Research and Therapy, 17,* 79–81.

5. We failed to find guilt more prominent in OCD than other psychiatric disorders in Steketee, G., Quay, S., & White, K. (1991). Religion, guilt and obsessive compulsive disorder. *Journal of Anxiety Disorders, 5,* 359–367. Guilt did distinguish volunteers with OCD symptoms from those without in Frost, R.O., Steketee, T.G., Cohn, L., & Griess, K. (1994). Personality traits in subclinical and non-obsessive compulsive volunteers and their parents. *Behaviour Research and Therapy, 32,* 47–56.

6. Emmelkamp, P.M.G., & Beens, H. (1991). Cognitive therapy with obsessive-compulsive disorder: A comparative evaluation. *Behaviour Research and Therapy, 29,* 293–300.

7. Steketee, G. (1993). *Treatment of obsessive compulsive disorder.* New York: Guilford Press.

8. Ibid.

9. Ibid.

10. See Foa, E.B. (1979). Failure in treating obsessive-cumpulsives. *Behavior Research and Therapy, 17,* 169–176.

11. Steketee, G. (1993). Social support as a predictor of follow-up outcome following treatment for OCD. *Journal of Behavioural Psychotherapy, 21,* 81–95.

12. Steketee, G., Kozak, M. J., & Foa, E. B. (1985, September). *Predictors of outcome for obsessive compulsives treated with exposure and response preventions.* Paper presented at the annual meeting of the European Association for Behavior Therapy, Munich, West Germany.

13. Frost, R.O., Steketee, T.G., Cohn, L., & Griess, K. (1994). Personality traits in subclinical and non-obsessive compulsive volunteers and their parents. *Behaviour Research and Therapy, 32,* 47–56.

14. Two of our studies have provided evidence that directly substantiates the need for both types of therapy: Steketee, G., Foa, E.B., & Grayson, J.B. (1982). Recent advances in the treatment of obsessive-compulsives. *Archives of General Psychiatry, 39,* 1365–1371; Foa, E.B., Steketee, G., Grayson, J., Turner, R.M., & Latimer, P.R. (1984). Deliberate exposure and blocking of obsessive-compulsive rituals: Immediate and long term effects. *Behavior Therapy, 15,* 450–472.

15. Foa, E.B., Steketee, G., Turner, R.M., & Fischer, S.C. (1980). Effects of imaginal exposure to feared disasters in obsessive-compulsive checkers. *Behavior Research and Therapy, 18,* 449–455.

16. Foa, E.B., Grayson, J.B., Steketee, G., Doppelt, H., Turner, R.M., & Latimer, P. (1983). Success and failure in the behavioral treatment of obsessive-compulsives. *Journal of Consulting and Clinical Psychology, 51,* 287–297.

17. Steketee, G. (1988). Intra- and interpersonal characteristics predictive of long-term outcome following behavioral treatment of obsessive compulsive disorder. In H. Wittchen & I. Hand (Eds.), *Treatments of panic and phobias* (pp. 221–232). New York: Springer-Verlag.

18. Foa, E.B., Kozak, M.J., Steketee, G., & McCarthy, P.R. (1992). Treatment of depressive and obsessive compulsive symptoms in OCD by imipramine and behavior therapy. *British Journal of Clinical Psychology, 31,* 279–292.

19. Steketee, G. (1995). Behavioral assessment and treatment planning with obsessive compulsive disorder: The state of the art. *Behavior Therapy, 25,* 613–633.

## Recommended Readings

### Books for Professionals

Beech, H.R. (Ed.). (1974). *Obsessional states.* London: Methuen. Although somewhat dated, several chapters in this volume contain excellent insights into the nature of this disorder.

Jenike, M.A., Baer, L., & Minichiello, W.E. (Eds.). (1990). *Obsessive-compulsive disorders: Theory and management.* Chicago: Year Book Medical. An excellent collection of chapters on all aspects of this disorder, including biological theories and treatments.

Mavissakalian, M., Turner, S.M., & Michelson, L. (Ed.). (1985). *Obsessive-compulsive disorder: Psychological and pharmacological treatment.* New York: Plenum. One of the few books to contain any material on psychodynamic theories about OCD. Good summary chapters on various topics.

Pato, M.T., & Zohar, J. (Eds.). (1990). *Current treatments of obsessive-compulsive disorder.* Washington, DC: American Psychiatric Press. Useful chapters, including one on family factors in OCD.

Rachman, S.J., & Hodgson, R.J. (1980). *Obsessions and compulsions.* Englewood Cliffs, NJ: Prentice Hall. Although an older volume, this book keeps disappearing from my office, probably because Rachman and colleagues' work on this disorder is seminal in the field.

Steketee, G. (1993). *Treatment of obsessive compulsive disorder.* New York: Guilford Press. What can I say? I did my best to capture the assessment and behavioral treatment process for clinicians.

Turner, S.M., & Beidel, D.C. (1988). *Treating obsessive-compulsive disorder.* New York: Pergamon. A good short volume describing treatment.

Zohar, J., Insel, T., & Rasmussen, S. (Eds.). (1991). *The psychobiology of obsessive-compulsive disorder.* New York: Springer. Good coverage of the research knowledge about biological aspects of OCD.

## Books for OCD Sufferers and Their Families

Baer, L. (1991). *Getting control.* Lexington, MA: Little, Brown & Co. A self-help book that many sufferers have liked greatly.

De Silva, P., & Rachman, S. (1992). *Obsessive compulsive disorder: The facts.* Oxford: Oxford University Press. More informational than self-help.

Foa, E.B., & Wilson, R. (1991). *Stop obsessing!* New York: Bantam. Clear behavioral self-help strategies with additional coping skills.

Neziroglu, F., & Yaryura-Tobias, Y.A. (1990). *Over and over again: Understanding obsessive-compulsive disorder.* Lexington, MA: Lexington Books. Also more informational than self-help, but offers some strategies for managing symptoms.

Steketee, G., & White, K. (1990). *When once is not enough.* Oakland, CA: New Harbinger Press. I can only say that we have had many compliments on this book.

# 6

*Donald Meichenbaum, Ph.D., is one of the founders of Cognitive Behaviour Modification (CBM), and his book* Cognitive Behaviour Modification: An Integrative Approach *is considered a classic in the field. He has also authored* Coping With Stress. Stress Inoculation Training *(Allyn & Bacon, 1985),* A Clinical Handbook for Assessing and Treating Adults with Post-traumatic Stress Disorders *(Institute Press, 1994); co-authored* Pain and Behavioural Medicine *(Guilford Press, 1983) and* Facilitating Treatment Adherence: A Practitioner's Guidebook *(Plenum, 1987); and co-edited* Stress Reduction and Prevention *(Plenum, 1983) and* The Unconscious Reconsidered *(Wiley, 1984). He was Associate Editor of* Cognitive Therapy and Research *from its inception, and is on the editorial boards of a dozen journals. He is editor of the Plenum Press series on Stress and Coping. He is currently Professor of Psychology at the University of Waterloo, Waterloo, Ontario, Canada and a clinical psychologist in private practice.*

*In a survey reported in the* American Psychologist. *North American clinicians voted Dr. Meichenbaum one of the ten most influential psychotherapists of the century.*

# Sheila and Karen: Two Cases of Post-traumatic Stress Disorder

**About**

**the**

**Disorder**

Imagine the unimaginable. You are the victim of a horrific trauma—a robbery, an assault, a life-threatening disaster, or a shattering personal loss. Besides the terror of the experience itself, people who have suffered a trauma may face months or even years of having to relive their nightmare. Post-traumatic stress disorder (PTSD) can develop in people who witness a life-threatening or otherwise terrifying event that causes them to respond with intense feelings of helplessness or horror. They re-experience the traumatic event in thoughts and dreams that are filled with disturbing recollections of what happened. For some, the disturbance feels so real that they act and feel as if the traumatic event were recurring by experiencing flashbacks, nightmares, and accompanying strong distressing feelings. Reminders of the trauma, either in their own thoughts or in the environment, evoke intense levels of psychological or physiological distress. Avoidance is another component of this disorder. People with PTSD go to great lengths to avoid anything that reminds them of the trauma. Numbness may characterize their reactions to everyday life situations, perhaps even to the point where they seem to be dissociated from their surroundings. They may feel an increased level of arousal and hypervigilance that causes them to have trouble sleeping, relaxing, concentrating, and controlling their emotions. Generally speaking, the greater the trauma, the greater the risk of developing PTSD, and the more severe the traumatic exposure, the more severe will be the individual's symptoms.

As difficult as it might seem to repair the damaged lives of traumatized individuals, Dr. Meichenbaum shows us how a collaborative and compassionate approach can enable clients to see their symptoms in a different and adaptive light.—*Eds.*

## INDIVIDUALS AND TRAUMA

Conducting psychotherapy is "bloody hard work" and at the same time one of the most challenging and rewarding experiences I have been privileged to engage in. Part of what makes it so much hard work is that the entire time I am seeing a client I am constantly talking to myself. Now, don't get me wrong; my internal speech is conducted covertly. Moreover, as will become apparent, at times I even talk to the client. While actively listening to the client, I am continually thinking about what I am hearing and seeing, and what to say and do next. In my head is a branching decision tree of options that reflect my knowledge of the clinical literature, as well as all the sensitivity, and whatever perspicacity, I can bring to bear. This chapter is the story of what goes on in a clinician's head when he or she is trying to help clients who have been "victimized" by traumatic events.

Approximately some 40% to 60% of the psychiatric population have a history of "victimization" due to intentional human design (e.g., physical and/or sexual abuse, domestic violence, criminal victimization such as robberies, rape, and the like).[1] Such victimization may come in different forms. Sometimes traumatic events are short term in duration, isolated events (e.g., some natural disasters, rape, car accidents), even though the emotional aftermath and behavioral sequelae may last a long time. In contrast, a second class of traumatic events may be more sustained and reflect a repeated ordeal over a prolonged period of time, as in the instance of combat, physical and sexual abuse, or being victimized in the Holocaust.

While most individuals who experience such traumatic events demonstrate remarkable resilience and courage in negotiating their lives with style and grace, some 20% to 40% evidence psychiatric disturbances. As Bonnie Green, a noted investigator of traumatized individuals, observed, approximately three out of four of the general population in the United States have been exposed to some event in their lives that would meet the criteria of a trauma, but only one out of four of these individuals will develop a full blown post-traumatic stress disorder (PTSD).[2] What distinguishes those individuals who develop PTSD from those who do not develop PTSD? And what can be done to help those in need? Consider the following two cases and the challenging and rewarding enterprise of psychotherapy.

## TWO CASES

### Case 1: Sheila

A school teacher, Sheila sought treatment for the classic symptoms of PTSD. She was remarkably distraught and suicidal. She had difficulty sleeping; had repetitive "flashbacks" that she felt just came out of nowhere. These intrusive disturbing thoughts seemed "to visit" her, as she described them. She avoided all social contact, feeling detached, as if constantly living a bad dream. "Tell me this is all unreal. I don't deserve to live!" The slightest noise, such as a car backfiring, a dropped dish, or the sudden unexpected barking of a dog, would trigger a racing heart, sweating, and other signs of anxiety. Uncontrollable agitation, sadness, and anger became her constant companions. Even the rare moments of comfort and pleasure that her dearest friends tried to provide would lead Sheila to feel distress and discomfort since she felt she did not deserve to enjoy life. This is what she repeatedly told her husband, until their separation some three weeks before she entered treatment. "I am just a glob of misery. My life is a personal tragedy," Sheila observed in the initial session.

What event could lead this attractive, talented, loving mother and wife to such a depressing clinical picture? What led her to seek treatment was indeed horrific, but not all that uncommon. Some 12 months earlier her husband, Dennis, was out of town on one of his frequent business trips and Sheila was home alone with her only daughter, 10-year-old Lisa. In the middle of the night, Sheila awoke to hear a strange noise, and later discovered that someone had broken into her home and rummaged through the first floor, taking her purse with her house keys and some liquor. While no one was harmed, Sheila's sense of safety, her beliefs about living in a protected area, and her uncontrollable resultant fear, had "shattered" her beliefs and the assumptions that she held so dear.[3] Immediately after the robbery, Sheila took a number of steps to protect herself and her daughter—an alarm system, bolted door locks, changing the locks on all her doors, installing bars on the basement windows, purchasing a guard dog, and at the suggestion of Dennis, even obtaining a gun that she kept in her night table.

It was now some six months since the initial robbery when "the incident" occurred, as Sheila described it. Once again, her husband Dennis was out of town, and in the middle of the night Sheila awoke to a strange noise that startled and frightened her. She thought someone was breaking into her home once again. But this time the noise was not confined to the first floor. "Could it be the robber again? Is he coming up the stairs? Where is Lisa?" Panic set in. Was Sheila dreaming this or was it real? It was stormy outside and the approaching noise inside was getting louder and louder. In fear, she reached into the night table and took up the gun and yelled out, "Who's there?" As she rose to go into her daughter's room with gun in hand, Sheila's bedroom door flew open and in the collision the gun went off. Sheila had pulled the trigger. . . . "No! No! What have I done?" she yelled. The bullet shattered her daughter's brain all over the bedroom door. It was not the robber, it was Lisa, and Sheila had killed her. Words cannot adequately describe the aftermath. For instance, in a dissociative state, Sheila tried to revive her daughter, but to no avail. Sheila sat immobilized in a pool of Lisa's blood. She was found by Dennis the next day, still sitting alone caressing Lisa's limp body.

It is bad enough when something happens to your child, but when you feel personally responsible for the injury or loss, especially for a loss that was preventable, then your life is a "personal tragedy."

Put yourself in my shoes as the therapist. What would you do? What could you say to Sheila? What are your treatment options? Sheila was suffering from a major grief reaction, accompanied by the following classic features of PTSD:[4]

*Persistent reexperiencing* of "the incident" in the form of recurrent and intrusive distressing recollections. Like Rod Steiger in the *The Pawnbroker* or Robin Williams in *The Fisher King*, Sheila was stuck, emotionally frozen in time at that horrific moment when her "world ended" as she knew it. "Only if-, Had I only-," "How could I?", "What if?"—each effort at contrafactual thinking was an attempt to undo what was not reversible. "Only if life had a reverse gear," Sheila would lament in quiet despair.

*Avoidance behavior* of any reminders related to the incident. "I couldn't go back to teach and watch the other 10-year-girls laugh and play. I could not face them. I pine for all the things we had together and for the loss of what will never be available in the future. Dennis felt guilty for insisting that I have a gun and now our marriage has fallen apart."

*Increased arousal* as manifested in not sleeping, being irritable, outbursts of anger, difficulty concentrating, memory lapses and hypervigilance, the latter because the robber was still at large. "I don't know what is real anymore and what is unreal. Suicide may be the only escape, my last hope. Don't you think so, Dr. Meichenbaum?"

As a reader, what is going through your mind as you hear Sheila's story? Can you hear her voice, feel her pain, understand her despair? My life is a "glob of misery," Sheila bemoaned.

Before we address the clinical treatment options for Sheila, let me introduce Karen who also sought help, ostensibly because she had also been a victim of a robbery at work.

## Case 2: Karen

*Dr. Meichenbaum:*    Karen, tell me what brings you to therapy.

*Karen:*    I have been robbed and I am having difficulty handling this. I am going through a challenging separation from my husband. I have been sexually abused as a child, and I am having difficulty with my teenage daughter who is rebelling and leaving home.

Wow, that is quite an opening statement! Just in case you, the therapist, did not have anything to talk about that session. Such an enumeration of stressors could keep any therapist busy for a long while. Once again, put yourself in my shoes as the therapist. What do you say next? Where do you begin? Where do you focus your clinical efforts?

Oh, I am asking this question of the wrong person,—namely, you the reader. Instead, I should be asking this question of the client, Karen. When in doubt, ask the client where you should begin and what we should focus on. In this way, the therapist can empower and enable the client, especially someone who has a history of victimization experiences. Whenever possible, nurture a collaborative stance and give the client choices.

> *Dr. Meichenbaum:*   Of these several issues that you raise, Karen, with regard to the robbery, your separation from your husband, the child sexual abuse, and the difficulties with your daughter, where do you think we should begin?
>
> *Karen:*   Well, I think the robbery is the main thing. I was doing okay before that. But the robbery opened a whole can of worms. I want to close this chapter and write a new chapter.

As Karen answered my question and told me her story, a number of things went through my mind.

1.  Should therapy focus on the robbery and its impact? Was her life threatened? Did she experience or witness injuries or deaths? How did she respond at the time of the robbery and afterward? How did the police, fellow office-workers, and her boss react? Is she avoiding work, thus putting her job in jeopardy? Does she evidence PTSD symptoms?

2.  Should therapy focus on the dangers of Karen separating from her husband? Women are most at risk when they are in the process of separating from their spouses. Is Karen safe? Does she have an escape plan in place, if necessary? In addition to the marital distress, is there evidence of physical abuse or domestic violence? Was there psychological intimidation that accompanied the marital distress? As Karen noted, she was told by her husband that "she was a nothing, a doormat, a whore, and the scum of the earth." Karen observed that there was nothing she could do right to please her husband. Is Karen still repeating to herself the degrading messages that she received from her husband? Has she taken on the "voices" of her "perpetrators" (robber, husband, victimizer of sexual abuse)?

But in spite of this intimidation, Karen was able to sever her relationship with her abusive husband. How did she go about doing this? When did she do this? Did she break up after the robbery? If so, then the robbery did not steal her courage and resourcefulness to take care of herself and to develop a "voice" of her own, to begin to write a new chapter. Is there anything that she did to handle the relationship with her husband that she could use in handling the aftermath of the robbery?

3.  Sexual abuse since childhood places Karen in a select group. Approximately one in four women have experienced abuse before the age of 18.[5] In her case, like many others, the child sexual abuse was perpetrated by her stepfather, the average duration of abuse being four years. In Karen's case, the abuse went on for eight years, from ages 6 to 14. Moreover, Karen had just learned that her

stepfather had also sexually abused her daughter. There seems to be no end to the story of victimization, and now a sense of guilt and responsibility about what had happened to her daughter took hold. Like many other sexually victimized individuals, Karen had a fourfold increase for a lifetime risk of a psychiatric disorder and a threefold risk for substance abuse. These areas needed further investigation. But the assessment and treatment plan also needed to identify Karen's strengths and resilience. As the radio commentator Paul Harvey says, "There is a need to hear the rest of the story." Half of the victims of child sexual abuse evidence remarkable courage and resilience, increased sensitivity and self-reliance.[6] One is not condemned by one's past, but can be an "architect" of one's future; one can co-construct in therapy a different narrative, a new chapter.

But what were the blocks, obstacles, beliefs, and interpersonal patterns of relating that got in the way of Karen achieving her goals? Karen reported that as a result of her victimization experiences she would "stuff her feelings" and not allow others to know how she felt. In therapy we explored the "impact," the "toll," and the "price" of her stuffing her feelings. The answers to these questions and concerns were not addressed in the abstract, but were considered experientially and emotionally in the therapy session. Moreover, Karen came to see that "stuffing her feelings" made sense and "worked," given what she had been through. It was a survival skill. One of her problems was that she was "stuck" doing something that worked in the past, but that was no longer adaptive. If "stuffing feelings" had had such a debilitating effect, then what could she do about it? It was not a big step for Karen to conclude that maybe she should *not* stuff her feelings. The therapist and Karen then considered what this meant behaviorally and explored how she could go about alternative ways of dealing with her emotions. Also, in therapy she explored the impact of the early childhood victimization from her stepfather and the absence of support from her mother, and how these events influence the choices she now makes in interpersonal relationships. What has she learned from the experiences of her life that are worth salvaging, and what should be left in the past?

## Case Evaluations

The diagnosis of both cases is as follows:

| | |
|---|---|
| Axis I: | • Post-traumatic stress disorder: Chronic type |
| Axis II: | • No diagnosis |
| Axis III: | • None |
| Axis IV: | • Victim of criminal act |
| Axis V: | • GAF = 50 (current) |

Imagine being the therapist for Sheila and Karen and seeing them in back to back sessions. Both had remarkable stories to tell, both were contemplating suicide to escape from life, to escape from themselves. Both met the diagnostic criteria of experiencing PTSD, chronic type, which lasts three months or longer, as well as experiencing a major severe depressive disorder with accompanying feelings of guilt, blame, and shame. There was no evidence of personality disorder (Axis II), nor complicating medical conditions (Axis III). In terms of psychosocial and environmental problems (Axis IV), they both experienced stressors that resulted from crimes and in both instances the perpetrators were still at large, representing further continual stressors. These events took a toll as reflected in their levels of global functioning (Axis V), each receiving GAF scores in the 40 to 50 range with current suicidal ideation and serious impairment in social and occupational functioning. For instance, Karen, like Sheila, could not return to work following the robbery. In addition, the robbery for Karen elicited a number of prior prolonged stressors ("opened a can of worms") tied to a history of child sexual abuse and spouse abuse. In contrast, for Sheila the extreme stressor was short term, but it also resulted in intense fear, helplessness, horror, personal threat, and even a death.

Given this diagnostic profile, let us consider what could be done therapeutically in each case. In formulating the treatment options, several guiding principles that derive from the literature were followed. A brief consideration of these principles will make the treatment plan that was chosen more understandable.

## PRINCIPLES UNDERLYING THE TREATMENT PLAN

---

"Give sorrow words: the grief that does not speak whispers the o'er fraught heart and bids it break." (Shakespeare's *Macbeth*)

---

As Shakespeare observed, having traumatized individuals put their experiences into words, either oral or written, is a critical feature of the "healing" process. This hypothesis was confirmed by Pennebaker and his colleagues.[7] They found that traumatized individuals who had an opportunity to share their victimizing experiences improved their long-term adjustment, and even their physical health, as evident in immune functioning, lowered autonomic nervous system activity, and reduced visits to the physician. Harvey and his colleagues[8] reported that the nature of the accounts offered by individuals who experienced traumatic events correlates with the level of their adjustment. Victim/survivors who provide well-developed accounts are more likely to develop a perspective on events, became more hopeful about the future, and develop "closure" regarding events. When people fail to talk about a traumatic experience, they tend to live with it, dream about it, ruminate about it, in an unresolved fashion. But putting these images and their accompanying emotions into language, they become more organized (less fragmented), understood, and resolved. Some of the ways people who have experienced traumas get "stuck" are catalogued by Meichenbaum and Fitzpatrick.[9] These include:

(a) continually making unfavorable comparisons between life as it is and as it might have been had the distressed event not occurred, and pining for the past and the loss of the future,

(b) seeing themselves as "victims" with little expectation or hope that things will change or improve,

(c) engaging in "undoing" thinking such as "Only if," "If I only had," "What if?" and continually trying to answer "why" questions for which there are no satisfactory answers (recall the biblical figure Job in the Old Testament),

(d) failing to find any meaning or anything worth salvaging from their survivorship,

(e) dwelling on the negative implications of stressful events,

(f) seeing themselves as continually at risk or vulnerable to future stressful events and remaining hypervigiliant to potential threats,

(g) feeling unable to control the symptoms of distress (intrusive ideation, psychic numbing, hyperarousal), and

(h) feeling alone in this effort to cope.

In psychotherapy, clients must feel safe enough to tell their stories at their own pace. There is a need to establish a "therapeutic alliance" whereby the client's feelings can be openly expressed, "normalized," and "validated." Clients can come to recognize that what they are experiencing is a "normal reaction to an abnormal situation."

Other key features of the therapy plan, as described by Meichenbaum[5] in a therapist manual for treating clients with PTSD, include the following:

1. The need to establish a safe, nuturant, compassionate, nonjudgmental, trusting, therapeutic setting in which clients can not only tell their stories of what happened, but also consider what they did to cope and survive.

2. As a part of the "normalization process," clients are encouraged to view their presenting behavior (symptoms) in a more "positive" light (e.g., intrusive ideation is their attempt to make sense of what happened; denial and numbing are ways to pace themselves in dealing with only so much distress at one time, a form of taking a "time out"; dissociative behaviors were ways to "safeguard" themselves when feeling overwhelmed). In short, instead of looking upon these behaviors as signs that they are going "crazy," they are viewed as attempts to cope with and handle a stressful event that almost anyone would find distressing. In some ways, they may be continuing to use these same coping techniques when they may no longer be required (that is, they are "stuck"). For instance,

the Vietnam veteran suffering from PTSD who evidences hypervigilance may come to see himself as continually being on "sentry duty," even when it is no longer necessary. "What worked in 'Nam may not be adaptive Stateside." In this way, the distress process is reconceptualized and feelings of hope are interjected into the therapy process.

3. Therapy helps clients disaggregate global, often metaphoric descriptions of their problems (e.g., "I am a glob of misery") into more specific, concrete, behaviorally prospective problem-solving terms (e.g., "I have a series of problems in three areas which include X, Y, and Z"). While recognizing and acknowledging the sense of despair and pain, there is a need to help clients discover solutions to their "problems."

4. Change comes not only from increased awareness and reframing, but also from behavioral acts. There is a need to enlist clients in a collaborative process in which they become their own therapist, a "personal scientist" collecting data by means of self-monitoring ("keeping track") and by means of conducting "homework assignments" and performing "personal experiments." Traumatic events, as in the cases of Sheila and Karen, may lead to avoidance behavior that interferes with their level of functioning. There is a need for clients, with the support of the therapist and social support from others, to confront, gradually and in vivo, the very fears they hold. They need to test the limits of how they will respond when re-entering the stressful situation. They need to view their self-statements and beliefs as "hypotheses" worthy of testing, rather than as "absolutistic assertions." The therapist works with clients to insure that they have the intrapersonal and interpersonal skills to perform these "personal experiments." For example, the therapist may educate clients in a Socratic fashion about PTSD, as well as help them develop coping skills (e.g., relaxation techniques, problem solving, and assertiveness skills). These skills may be taught using behavioral and imaginable rehearsal procedures and practice in real situations. As noted, such treatment may be conducted for individuals, couples, and groups.

5. There is a need for clients and therapist to consider the potential barriers, obstacles, blocks in the form of feelings (fears, guilt, depression) and beliefs ("I'm a doormat, a whore") that get in the way of implementing change and mustering hope. Note that clients often provide some avenues of change, as Karen noted when she said, "I want to write a new chapter." Psychotherapists can use the client's metaphor and ascertain where Karen has already begun this rewriting process as reflected in her efforts to end an abusive relationship with her spouse, by her decision to enter therapy, by her initial efforts to heal the "wounds" with her estranged daughter. "If she wants to write another new chapter, she has come to the right place, because this is what I do, as a therapist. I help people discover the chapters they have already written and possible new chapters yet to be written." I often use a time line with the clients, helping them examine both the occurrence of stressors, but also the strengths, courage, resilience, and signs of recovery.

I sometimes ask clients the rhetorical question: *Why would I work with people who have had very bad things happen to them?* . . . . One of the answers that I have come to is that I see myself as being privileged to bear witness to and act as an archivist, recording the strength, courage, and resilience of the human spirit. I have been continually impressed with what people do to survive; what they do to salvage something from their survivorship that is worth saving, and sharing this with others."

The "art" of psychotherapy is to work with the client's metaphors (e.g., the "chapter" metaphor) and "unpack" them in ways that foster change. In addition, the therapist can select other metaphors that are well suited to the specific client. If you, the reader, do not like the "archivist" metaphor, then see Meichenbaum,[6] who enumerates alternative metaphors that can be used.

Clients often enter treatment with an "internal dialogue" of helplessness and hopelessness, and accompanying feelings of victimization resulting from their thoughts, feelings, circumstances, or other people. Generally clients feel demoralized. Over the course of the treatment, there is a need to help clients alter what they say to themselves and others about their situation and their abilities to handle them. But changes in internal dialogue cannot be "willed." Such changes in internal dialogue more readily follow from the outcomes of "personal experiments" that clients perform. A critical aspect of therapy is to insure that clients perform such "experiments," and moreover, take the results ("data") from their "experiments" as evidence to alter ("unfreeze") the beliefs about themselves and the world. The therapist needs to insure that clients do not discount nor dismiss the "data." Moreover, clients need to take credit, ownership, and responsibility for the changes they have brought about. The therapist works with clients in exploring where else (in what other situations) the clients can use these skills. The therapist may ask the client, "Do you ever find yourself out there asking yourself the kinds of questions that we ask each other here in therapy.[10] In what ways have you changed? . . . Now that you have begun to make some progress with regard to achieving your goals, what advice, if any, might you have for others who have had a similar experience? . . . What have you learned from this experience that you can share with others?"

In the case of clients who have been "victimized," there is also a need to help them find a "personal mission," so they can transform their pain and loss into something worth salvaging, sharing, and remembering, as illustrated in the treatment plan for Sheila described below.

6. Given that psychotherapy is a learning process, there is a high likelihood that clients will re-experience symptoms, have setbacks, lapses, especially on anniversary dates of the trauma. Relapse prevention training is designed to help clients anticipate, accept, and cope with possible lapses (e.g., recurrent flashbacks, bouts of depression, anxiety, self-doubt), so these do not escalate into full-blown relapses. It is not that clients have lapses, but what they say to themselves about such lapses that is critical in determining whether the improvements will be maintained and generalized across settings and over time. Psycho-

therapists do not leave this process to chance, but strategically and collaboratively help clients to work on these elements of change.

Let us consider how these principles were implemented in the treatment plans with Sheila and Karen. Then we will consider briefly the "state of the art" in treating clients with PTSD. Remember we left Sheila and Karen wallowing in despair, experiencing extreme distress.

## Treatment of Sheila

The treatment strategy for Sheila involved the following.

(*a*) Listening to her story and reviewing the circumstances of what happened in detail, so she could come to see the circumstance and information available to her *at the time* of the fatal shooting. It was highlighted that "hindsight is always more accurate."

(*b*) Understanding Sheila's loss by asking her to talk about her daughter. In fact, at the suggestion of the therapist, Sheila brought into therapy a family picture album to review Lisa's life with the therapist. "What was so special about Lisa? What was so special about their relationship?" Sheila noted that Lisa was "wise beyond her years." Reviewing the picture album also helped Sheila move beyond the recollection of the shooting incident. The review "pulled for" positive memories.

(*c*) Sheila was then asked, "What do you think Lisa saw in you, and in your relationship?" Following their discussion, the therapist asked Sheila, "If Lisa, who was so wise beyond her years, were here now if she were curled up in your arms looking up at your loving and caring eyes, what advice, if any, would she offer to help you with your pain, to help you deal with your grief, and your immense guilt?" With support of the therapist, Sheila was able to generate a variety of suggestions.

Note that it would have been easy for the therapist to provide Sheila with these suggestions. The literature on behavior change indicates, however, that suggestions for change are more effective and influential if they come from the client, especially if the client can provide self-explanations about why such change would be helpful and useful.[11] Instead of the therapist being what I have come to call a "surrogate frontal lobe" for his or her clients, the therapist can empower and enable clients by providing conditions in which they themselves can come up with the suggestions for change.

At this point the therapist commented, "I can now more readily understand what you meant when you said your daughter Lisa was so special and 'wise beyond her years.'" Sheila and the therapist then explored how she could follow through on the suggestions that her daughter might have offered. Moreover, the question was raised that if Sheila did commit suicide, what would happen to the memory of her daughter Lisa? Who would know of her special gifts? Did

Sheila owe it to the memory of her daughter to follow through on the proposed suggestions? . . . "Where should *we* begin? (Note: the term we is used to foster a sense of collaboration.) . . . What are the possible obstacles or barriers that might get in the way of you following through on the proposed suggestions? . . . If these barriers (feelings of despair, depression, anger, guilt) should reoccur, what could you do to anticipate and handle them?"

(*d*) Finally, as Sheila began to make progress, she eventually developed a "mission" which was designed to educate parents about the dangers of keeping guns in the home. Sheila became very knowledgeable about the incidence of accidental deaths in the home that resulted from shootings. She kept a scrapbook of news clipping of such shootings, made a slide show, videotapes, and brochures, and established an educational foundation in her daughter's name.

Nothing could replace what Sheila lost, but from her pain came something worth salvaging. While her PTSD symptoms subsided, her "pain" was never gone. Nevertheless, Sheila was able to use her many teaching skills to serve others and the memory of Lisa. As the adage goes, "One shall never forget!" The goal of treatment was *not* to go beyond memory, but to move toward more memory. Sheila spent a lifetime creating a healing ritual. Psychotherapy helped her to undertake this personal journey.

### Treatment of Karen

The treatment of Karen was more multifaceted and directly addressed her PTSD symptoms of flashbacks, intrusive ideation, panic attacks, avoidance behaviors, and depression, as well her interpersonal difficulties with her husband and daughter. The sexual abuse represented "unfinished business" that was also addressed in therapy. The general treatment plan was to first treat the client's presenting symptoms and any signs of comorbidity (dual diagnosis of accompanying clinical problems such as addictive behaviors), before dealing with the emerging memories of early childhood abuse. The effort to deal with traumatic memories was followed by an attempt to reconnect and restore familial and social functioning. The final termination phase of treatment permitted Karen to consolidate changes, engage in relapse prevention, and allow for planning for the future. Let us briefly consider each of these phases. (See Herman's fine book *Trauma and recovery* (1992) for a description of these varied phases of intervention.)

#### Phase I. Initial Phase of Treatment

The treatment goals included establishing a therapeutic alliance; encouraging Karen to tell her "story" at her own pace; collaboratively establishing treatment goals (short-term, intermediate, and long-term); ensuring the client's safety and addressing practical needs first; conducting assessments—both psychological and physical; assessing the client's strengths; educating the client about PTSD and accompanying difficulties; normalizing, validating, and reframing the client's symptoms; and engendering hope.

### Phase II. Address Clients' Presenting Symptoms/Behaviors

The primary treatment objective of this phase is to reduce symptoms and provide relief by teaching the client various coping skills. Psychotropic medication may provide a useful adjunctive treatment designed to address specific symptoms (e.g., sleep disturbance, depression, irritability). In Karen's case, medication was provided to help her sleep. This improvement made her more amenable to psychotherapeutic interventions.

Karen was most distressed by the flashbacks concerning the robbery. Following some initial discussion about the nature of flashbacks, she was asked to keep track of those events that seemed to trigger flashbacks, how she could "notice," "catch," and "interrupt" herself when she was beginning to have a flashback and accompanying panic attack. It was critical that Karen learn how to control the hyperventilation (rapid inhaling and exhaling) that exacerbated her panic attack, as well as learn ways to control her accompanying "catastrophizing" ideation. Sometimes, when she would have a flashback of the robbery and feel anxious, she would begin to dwell on the traumatic memories of abuse, or as she described it, "I'm having a time-slide." Recall that Karen noted how the robbery had "opened a can of worms." When these memories, these flashbacks occurred, Karen would, as she described it, begin to "space out" (dissociate). There was a need to help Karen "get grounded" and develop other coping skills including reducing exposure to triggers, "catch" ruminations faster, control hyperarousal, engage in regularly scheduled activities, and learn ways to bring herself back to the present. She learned to label such time-slides by saying "I'm having a flashback" and then use a variety of coping self-statements. Moreover, Karen learned ways to change the memory, especially of her abusive childhood. Instead of working to actively "avoid" or "combat" the memory, the client and therapist explored whether Karen could learn something important from the memory so she could "integrate" it and move beyond these events.

Psychotherapists have developed a variety of imagery-based and group-based interventions to help clients alter the impact of their distressing memories. One technique is called Direct Therapy Exposure. In this procedure, clients are asked to replay a traumatic scene imaginarily, as if it were happening right now. The client describes the scene in some detail. This account is tape recorded, and the distressed traumatized client is given an opportunity to replay the recorded account as well. In this way, the "emotional sting" tied to the traumatic event can be reduced. "It is like peeling off the outer layers of an onion, layer by layer, until you get to the stinking core, so it doesn't stink anymore."[12] "It is like watching a scary movie, over and over again, so it's no longer threatening." Another feature of treatment was Karen's need to confront her avoidance behavior in order to go back to work. Thus, she was encouraged and challenged to gradually overcome her fears one step at a time by re-entering the feared setting.

Another way to address her feelings about the incest was to help her tell her "story," and then use imagery techniques to alter the account. Karen told the story of what happened, but this time told the story from the viewpoint of the young "victimized" Karen. The "adult" Karen could now go back in imagery to comfort the "child," Karen, and if she wished, alter the scene in some way that would be comforting.

Another by-product of the child sexual abuse was the core beliefs that Karen developed. A variety of cognitive restructuring techniques were used to help her reconsider the implications, the "if . . . then" rules, that have come to guide her behavior as a result of victimization. She could now begin to take steps to change her patterns of relating and her beliefs about herself.

Throughout treatment, Karen's "sense of safety" was continually monitored, given the potential threat from her recently separated spouse. While anger was the dominant mood with reference to her husband, guilt was the major emotion defining her relationship with her daughter. The therapy eventually moved into a phase where both Karen and her daughter were seen together. They decided that the best "revenge" for what happened to them was "to live their lives well." In therapy, Karen and her daughter were able to detail ("operationalize") what it meant to "live their lives well." Relapse prevention—and having the clients take credit for the changes that they brought about—constituted a concluding phase to treatment.

Many other treatment options are available to psychotherapists working with PTSD clients. At this point, there is little empirical data to guide these important clinical decisions. In many areas of the clinical enterprise, research can be called upon to inform clinicians. For instance, effective cognitive-behavioral treatment procedures have been developed for clients with anxiety and depressive disorders.[13]

PTSD represents the cutting edge, the new frontier, for treatment outcome research. It should be noted that at this time there is *not* sufficient evidence to suggest the superiority of one form of treatment for PTSD over any other, nor an appreciation of how the various treatment components can be combined most effectively. For instance, Solomon and her colleagues noted that there have been only six double-blind pharmacotherapy studies and six randomized control studies of psychotherapy techniques with PTSD clients.[14] This is a meager foundation upon which to make important clinical decisions. Such uncertainty is surely enough to make a clinician talk to himself or herself. But this is where we began, and perhaps a good place to stop.

The need for systematic evaluation of alternative treatments is critical. In the interim, all the clinician can do is follow some general principles of behavioral change and keep abreast and open-minded about treatment options. When in doubt, the therapist should respectfully explore treatment options with the client. As a result, not only will the therapist learn to talk to himself or herself differently, but so will the client. What more can we ask for?

*Notes*

1. Herman, J.L. (1992). *Trauma and recovery.* New York: Basic Books.
2. Green, B.L. (1994). Psychosocial research in traumatic stress: An update. *Journal of Traumatic Stress, 7,* 341–362.
3. Janoff-Bulman, R. (1992). *Shattered assumptions: Towards a new psychology of trauma.* New York: Free Press.
4. American Psychiatric Association. (1994). *Diagnostic and Statistical Manual of Mental Disorders* (4th ed.). Washington, DC: Author.
5. Russell, D.E. (1984). *Sexual exploitation: Rape, child sexual abuse and sexual harrassment.* Beverly Hills, CA: Sage.
6. Meichenbaum, D. (1994). *A Clinical handbook for assessing and treating adults with post traumatic stress disorder.* Waterloo, ON: Institute Press.
7. Pennebaker, J.W. (1990). *Opening up: The healing power of confiding in others.* New York: Avon.
8. Harvey, J.H., Weber, A.L., & Orbuch, T.L. (1990). *Interpersonal accounts: A social psychological perspective.* Oxford, England: Basil Blackwell.
9. Meichenbaum, D., & Fitzpatrick, D. (1993). A constructivist narrative perspective on stress and coping: Stress inoculation applications. In L Goldberger & S. Breznitz (Eds.). *Handbook of stress* (pp. 706–723). New York: Free Press.
10. Tomm, K. (1985). Circular interviewing: A multifaceted clinical tool. In D. Campbell & R. Draper (Eds.), *Applications of systematic field therapy.* New York: Grune & Stratton.
11. Meichenbaum, D., & Turk, D. (1987). *Facilitating treatment adherence: A Practitioner's Guidebook.* New York: Plenum.
12. Rothbaum, B.O., & Fox, E.B. (1993). Cognitive-behavioral treatment of post traumatic stress disorder. In P.A. Saigh (Ed.), *Post traumatic stress disorder.* New York: Pergamon.
13. Hollon, S.D., & Beck, A.T. (1993). Cognitive and cognitive-behavioral therapies. In S.L. Garfield & A.E. Bergin (Eds.), *Handbook of psychotherapy and behavior change.* New York: Wiley.
14. Solomon, S.D., Gerrity, E.T., & Muff, A.M. (1992). Efficacy of treatments for post traumatic stress disorder: An empirical review. *Journal of American Medical Association, 268,* 633–638.

*Recommended Readings*

Freedy, J.R., & Hobfoll, S.E. (Eds.). (1994). *Traumatic stress: Theory and practice.* New York: Plenum.
Herman, J.L. (1992). *Trauma and recovery.* New York: Basic Books.
Meichenbaum, D. (1994). *Clinical handbook on post traumatic stress disorder.* Waterloo, ON: Institute Press.
Terr, L. (1990). *Too scared to cry.* New York: Basic Books.
Wilson, J., & Raphael, B. (Eds.). (1993). *International handbook of traumatic stress disorders.* New York: Plenum.

# PART III

# DISSOCIATIVE IDENTITY DISORDER

➤ Chapter 7: Dissociative Identity Disorder

Dissociative disorders are among the most intriguing human conditions, affecting the very essence of the "self" in which people lose a fundamental sense of who they are. People with dissociative disorders experience anxiety or conflict so severe that part of their personality becomes separated from the rest of conscious functioning. They may experience a temporary alteration of consciousness including loss of personal identity, decreased awareness of personal surroundings, and odd bodily movements. The dissociative disorders have been the subject of fiction and nonfiction accounts in which the main character develops amnesia, goes into a fugue state, or develops multiple personalities. The chapter in this section focuses on a case of multiple personalities, a condition now referred to as dissociative identity disorder.

# 7

**About**

**the**

**Author**

*Richard P. Kluft,* M.D., *is a psychiatrist and psychoanalyst in private practice in Bala Cynwyd, Pennsylvania. He is a Clinical Professor of Psychiatry at Temple University School of Medicine, a Visiting Lecturer on Psychiatry at Harvard Medical School, and on the faculty of the Philadelphia Psychoanalytic Institute. Dr. Kluft majored in English at Princeton University before he graduated from Harvard Medical School. He did his psychiatry residency at the University of Pennsylvania and his psychoanalytic training at the Philadelphia Psychoanalytic Institute. From 1989 to 1996 he was Director of the Dissociative Disorders Program at The Institute of Pennsylvania Hospital. Dr. Kluft has been studying dissociative identity disorder and the consequences of child abuse for over 25 years. He has published over 200 scientific articles and book chapters and edited or co-edited four books, including* Clinical Perspectives on Multiple Personality Disorder *(American Psychiatric Press, 1993) with Catherine G. Fine, Ph.D. He is Editor-in-Chief of* Dissociation. *The recipient of many awards, Dr. Kluft has been elected a Fellow of the American Psychiatric Association, the American Society of Clinical Hypnosis, the International Society for the Study of Dissociation, and the Society for Clinical and Experimental Hypnosis. He has been president of the International Society for the Study of Dissociation and the American Society of Clinical Hypnosis.*

# Joe: A Case of Dissociative Identity Disorder

**About**

**The**

**Disorder**

The experience of different personalities residing within one person has captivated the interest of the public for centuries. In the psychiatric literature, the stories of Eve and Sybil brought to light the psychological underpinnings of this fascinating condition.

Most people have come to know cases such as Eve's and Sybil's as instances of "multiple personality disorder." In recent years, this term has been replaced by "dissociative identity disorder," reflecting an understanding that the essence of the condition involves the experience of dissociation or the fragmentation of one's self into many. The core self is referred to as the "host," and the selves are referred to as "alters." Each alter is a consistent and enduring pattern of perceiving, relating to, and thinking about the environment and the self. At different times, one of these identities or personality states takes control of the person's behavior; what is even more striking is the fact that the person is unable to recall important personal information that could be explained by ordinary forgetfulness.

How would a therapist go about reconstructing a personality that has been so radically divided? Dr. Kluft shares his multifaceted strategy, involving nine phases in which the therapist and client work as a "team" to restore or bring about a sense of integration among the alters. In this process, the therapist responds to the separate selves almost as if they are separate individuals rather than as manifestations of one person.—Eds.

## THE CASE OF JOE

### Initial Presentation

Over the telephone, Joe's voice sounded hollow, demoralized, and defeated. Joe was a psychologist with a private practice in an affluent suburb. At one time he had a drug and alcohol problem, but he became deeply involved in AA and had been sober now for five years. He told me that he had just returned from a month in a residential treatment program for depression and codependency problems to find his wife, Louisa, not only unwilling to support his efforts to straighten himself out, but determined to divorce him. Earlier that day he and Louisa had seen her therapist, Dr. Knowles. Louisa had confronted Joe about his emotional inaccessibility and angry outbursts. He protested she was exaggerating. She accused him of a number of childish pursuits and immature behaviors that puzzled him—he didn't recall them at all. In turn, he protested her sexual withdrawal and lack of support. He claimed he had made great efforts to change, including going to the residential treatment program, risking his professional reputation.

Dr. Knowles confirmed that Louisa wanted a divorce. She reviewed Joe's hospital report. In addition to the depression, a dissociative disorder had been suspected. She recommended that he see me for an evaluation. The only way she could reconcile the different perspectives she had heard from Louisa and from Joe would be if one or both were self-deceived or lying, or if Joe suffered a dissociative disorder.

I arranged an appointment and got Joe's permission to talk to Louisa's therapist. Louisa had given Dr. Knowles permission to talk me. Dr. Knowles told me that Louisa depicted Joe as a raging maniac who usually acted as if he did not recall or would not admit his outbursts. He often hid away in his home office playing with toys for hours on end, and frequently snuggled up to her as if he were a child begging to be mothered. The next day he would act as if these events had not occurred, and became perplexed or resentful if he was confronted. During his hospital stay, Joe had complained of a sudden headache during a group therapy sessions and abruptly began to behave like a mischievous youngster. Half an hour passed before he reverted to adult behavior, amnesic for the childlike period of time.

Although I had never met Joe, I recognized him from professional lectures we had both attended. A tall, beefy man, he walked with a stoop and had the facial expression of a dejected basset hound. He was badly shaken. I deferred a formal assessment, encouraging him to tell his story in his own way. Joe openly admitted that he was seriously considering suicide, but believed he could promise to remain safe, and would be able to call me if he were losing control of his self-destructive urges. After the previous day's devastating confrontations, he had gone back to his office and tried to continue with his scheduled patients. He persevered, but found himself becoming exhausted in a new and distressing way. "It's like I'm dragging my anchor. I am not my usual self." When he looked in the mirror, he had trouble recognizing himself.

Joe was overwhelmed and befuddled. There were problems in the marriage, but he had believed they were minor. He was looking forward to starting a family, a step he and Louisa had deferred in order to pursue their careers. He said that as we spoke movers were taking Louisa's belongings to an apartment she had rented while he was away. He recognized that he had looked to her for nurture, support, and help in making even minor decisions. His characteristic intellectuality, controllingness, and perfectionism were pronounced, but they were not able to contain his strong emotions. Hurt, despair, and anger permeated his words. I experienced him as an abandoned child. I had to work to remind myself I was interviewing a 38-year-old psychologist with the build of an out-of-shape football lineman.

## Case History

Joe described himself as an alcoholic from a family of alcoholics. His physician father, his mother's brother (a Catholic priest), and one older brother had been very heavy drinkers. His father was deceased. His uncle became sober after being forced into treatment. His brother was dying of cirrhosis. Although Joe had been in therapy and 12-step programs for years, problems with alcohol and other substances had been their focus.

Joe's father had been a workaholic physician with little time for him; when not working, he drank himself into oblivion in the privacy of his den. His mother was a weak, ineffectual, and dependent woman who was totally dedicated to religion. She avoided conflict and controversy. Joe had been the second of three sons and had a younger sister. He cried when he mentioned her. Remote and preoccupied, his parents were more concerned with the appearance rather than the fact of a happy family. Joe's brothers ran wild, especially Nick, the oldest. Nick bullied Joe and Billy, the third brother, mercilessly and, for the most part, without parental intervention.

I asked more about Nick's bullying. Joe's lips quivered and he slipped into a trancelike state. His eyes at first appeared to be fixed and staring, and then they closed. His right hand made writing gestures. I asked if he would like to write, and he nodded. I placed a pen in his hand and a pad on a clipboard on his lap. His right hand began to move. In contrast to the penmanship on a form of he had filled out, it was backhand and cramped. The hand wrote: "Stupid doesn't know. Nick rammed it up his ass." I asked if there was more to be said. The hand wrote: "His mouth, too. Don't tell Stupid."

Soon Joe opened his eyes and rubbed his forehead, complaining of a headache. Without acknowledging the missing time, he went on to tell me that between ages 11 and 14 he had been sexually molested by the organist of his church. He complained of nightmares of sexual molestation by his priest uncle, but doubted that they represented memories. As he spoke, his headache worsened.

I learned that Joe's memory was a problem area. "My life history is a series of chunks," he said. Joe had little recall prior to age six; he had many missing episodes and blank periods thereafter. For example, he had no recall of his high school graduation. Not only were there missing blocks of time, but Joe was forever double-scheduling his clients, forgetting to do things he had promised to do, arriving late for crucial appointments, going blank in conversations, and becoming confused as to whether or not he had actually done what he planned to do. Family and friends teased him for being an "absentminded professor."

Among the things I asked Joe about in that first interview was whether he heard voices inside his head, a common experience for many patients with dissociative disorders. Joe admitted he heard several voices inwardly, including a very harsh and critical voice and a childish voice. He admitted that often he heard himself saying things he had no intention of saying, and that often his voice sounded different when this occurred. In addition, Joe admitted he was prone to outburst of rage, but maintained that when they occurred he not only had not willed them, but also had the experience of watching himself say the angry words while he could only observe, mortified and aghast, unable to believe that this was happening without his volition. He revealed that when he "saw" himself behave in this way, he saw himself as different in appearance and manner from his usual self. When I pursued this, he said that the image he had of himself at those times was a combination of himself and his brother Nick.[1]

## Diagnosis

In Joe's next two visits, I completed a formal mental status and psychiatric history. In view of his dissociative response to my inquiry about his brother Nick, I backed away from pursuing topics I considered scale potentially destabilizing. I also administered a Dissociative Experiences Scale (DES)[2] and a Hypnotic Induction Profile (HIP).[3] The DES score was 43, in the range of patients with dissociative identity disorder (DID).[4] The HIP score suggested extreme hypnotizability, a characteristic of DID patients. Joe ruefully admitted that after he had been sexually abused, he had sexually abused his younger sister for a period of time. He blamed himself for his sister's being "a mess." He sometimes became so guilty that he considered suicide. Also, on several occasions, I observed Joe's voice and demeanor change briefly to being very rageful or being childlike. This suggested the intrusion of alter states—that is, other identities or personalities.[5]

Joe and I discussed the possibility that he might suffer a dissociative disorder in addition to his depression, current misery, and the residua of childhood exploitation. He decided to go forward with treatment, and in the fourth visit, abruptly became childlike and tearful. "I hurt! I hurt!" he wailed. When I asked him to tell me what hurt him, he looked at me with a mixture of pain and mischief on his face, and said, "I'm not Big Stupid, you know." "Who is Big Stupid?" I asked. "Joe. Dumb Joe. He doesn't know anything."

"Why do you hurt?" I asked. "Nick. Nick is bad. He hurt me." I was about to inquire further when Joe's voice and demeanor changed abruptly. A harsh voice spoke: "That little rat isn't supposed to talk. Wait till I fix him. Ha! I can hear him wailing already."[6] Later, Joe would recall only a "blank spot," and complained of a headache.

By this time, I did not have much doubt that Joe, a Ph.D., suburban psychologist, and newly separated husband, was suffering a major dissociative disorder with the structure and form of DID, formerly known as multiple personality disorder (MPD). Because Joe functioned well, held an academic appointment, and enjoyed an excellent professional reputation, I inferred that his condition was usually quite covert. Perhaps his month of intense inpatient therapy had unsettled his defenses. Perhaps by stimulating and gratifying his wish to be nurtured and cared for, other alters, eager to be loved, had become more active. Perhaps when he returned home in this state, his wife's decision to leave him placed further burdens upon him, and his condition became more overt. It is not unusual for DID to be clandestine, a "psychopathology of hiddenness."[7] It seemed plausible, even likely, that the brief out-of-character behaviors that his wife had described, the ones Joe could not recall, were manifestations of the intrusions of the other identities or personalities.

My overall diagnostic impression, based on four sessions, the DES, the HIP, and my study of Joe's hospital records, was as follows:

Axis I:
- Dissociative identity disorder (formerly multiple personality disorder)
- Major depressive disorder, recurrent, severe without psychotic features
- Polysubstance dependence, by history

Axis II:
- Personality disorder not otherwise specified, with predominantly dependent and obsessive compulsive features

Axis III:
- No diagnosis made

Axis IV:
- Problems with primary support group

Axis V:
- GAF = 65 (highest level in the current year)
- GAF = 45 (current level)

## Case Formulation

My formulation was that Joe was a basically high-functioning professional with significant problems in interpersonal and intimate relationships whose intelligence and obsessional style overlay and usually suppressed and contained a major dissociative disorder, which only intermittently became overt. I hypothesized that Joe had been an overtly dissociative child whose condition went unrecognized, and that as he matured and was no longer an easy victim, and as he was removed from the circumstances that exposed him to abusers in an ongoing manner, his dissociative defenses were no longer called upon as frequently, and his condition became much more subtle. He was able to conduct his life without manifesting discrete multiple personality phenomena in a decompensated and chaotic manner. The advent of his depression compromised his adaptation and the effectiveness of his nondissociative coping, and psychotherapy had begun to stir up the buried ghosts of his past. Even though he had always retained memory of some aspects of his abuse, additional traumatic material had been mobilized, and the aching painful aloneness of his childhood intruded into his contemporary life with greater urgency. Under those circumstances, his dissociation became more overt, first in the hospital and then in my initial sessions with him. I hypothesized that since he did not appear to have much affect associated with his maltreatment, it was likely that strong feeling was also dissociated, and that as we turned over the rocks and encountered what had been hidden, the emergence of a post-traumatic stress disorder with a delayed onset would be likely.

### Course of Treatment

Joe and I agreed to meet twice weekly. He needed continuity and support with regard to his current crisis. He also needed an intense enough treatment so that we would be able to address the past as well as the present crisis in his life. Less frequent appointments might leave Joe unsupported, burdened by traumatic material, and unable to contend with the problematic behavior of the alters; we hoped to avoid a deterioration in function. We hoped to avoid such consequences. I arranged for Joe's sessions to be buffered from his own professional activities by periods of at least two hours. I also stipulated that Joe arrange to be supervised by a colleague whom he informed of his condition, and who could serve as an ombudsman for the safety of Joe's patients. Although it is rare for patients such as Joe to behave badly in their professional lives, such incidents are not unknown. They are more likely to overidentify with their trauma patients or to avoid or collude with them to avoid approaching painful material that their patients need to address. I decided to continue Joe's antidepressant regimen. I could not be sure if his depression was another disorder that required its own treatment, or if it was due to the alter's inner misery. I planned to reassess the need for psychopharmacology sequentially.

My first goals with Joe were to make him feel safe and supported in the therapy.[8] We had to collaborate so that neither current circumstances, the dissociative disorder, nor the impact of the past slipped out of focus. If Joe started with a here-and-now issue, I made sure to ask if the personalities had any urgent concerns, and reserved time for them if they did. If alters pressed to pursue a theme, I insisted that we keep in touch with here-and-now issues as well. I explained that important issues had to be brought up early, so that we could both address issues and restabilize matters. Whenever possible, you want the DID patient to leave a session with a sense of mastery and control, rather than feeling splattered and blown away by the material. I always insist on following my "rule of thirds"—if you can't get into the painful work you planned to do in the first third of the session, so you can work on it the remainder of the first third and the second third, reserving the final third to process the material and restabilize the patient, then don't proceed with the painful work.

When Joe had settled into therapy and weathered his wife's leaving, I spent a series of sessions teaching him how to contain strong affect, shut down flashbacks and spontaneous abreactions, and deal with distressed alters. There were no plans for taking legal action on the basis of any material that might emerge, so I felt comfortable in using and teaching hypnotic techniques.[9] I taught Joe how to enter trance rapidly. Then I helped him to create and envision with self-hypnosis the image of a rheostat that controlled the intensity of his feelings, and to turn both positive and negative affects "up" or "down." I taught him how to imagine physical or emotional pain becoming moist and liquid, circulating it to a point in the body, and leaving him. We developed "safe place" images for all alters, so that they could escape from pain or stress without creating additional alters or "spacing out." I taught Joe to bring on and dispel flashbacks of painful events, so that his contemporary life would not be held hostage by the past. I helped the alters accept the idea of being "put to sleep" between sessions, lest they remain in pain for long periods of time, lest alters with poor judgment, inappropriate impulses, or precarious control imperil Joe's life and well-being, and lest the pain of an alter involved in trauma work "leak" into the awareness of the others and disrupt function. Intrusions of traumatic material were addressed briefly, and then shut down.[10]

This phase of the therapy required three months. Thus far, I had taken pains to avoid focusing work on the trauma of the alters. Instead, I got to know them, built alliances with them, explained the therapy to them, and persuaded them to contract for safety and against self-sabotage.[11]

The self-sabotage caused by the alters' wishes and agendas was worrisome, because Joe's alters were masters of psychological guerilla warfare. For example, the "younger" alter that referred to Joe as "Big Stupid" proved to be one of the two nurture-craving "child" alters that had come out in group therapy during his hospital stay, played with toys in his study, and tried to snuggle up to his estranged wife, whom they saw as a mother figure. When this alter realized that Joe's wife was not going to return, it mounted a campaign of inner orders and complaints, heard as hallucinations, entreating Joe to find a new woman right away. Joe was not inclined to socialize, and his libido was nil. Furthermore, he was terrified a woman would reject him or hurt him again. This alter urged him to break boundaries with his attractive female clients, and wanted all therapy sessions with me to be dedicated to mobilizing Joe to date. When I supported a delay in socialization, this alter expressed its displeasure by taking over at the wheel when Joe was en route to a session, and drove hundreds of miles before it relinquished control, effectively cancelling the appointment.

Another alter, whose anger came through at times, was preoccupied with fantasies of revenge on Joe's estranged wife. Its anger was readily displaced onto those who displeased Joe in his daily life. Joe came to sessions mortified by events in which he had felt like a hapless observer while this alter, whose periods of dominance Joe often recalled with the sense of having watched them as if they were a movie, poured out its wrath on a series of salespersons and managed care reviewers by whom it felt offended. It, too, drove irresponsibly. Enraged by a trucker it felt was following too closely, the alter "stood on the brakes" to discourage the trucker. The trucker was unable to stop his rig, and totaled Joe's car. Joe sustained broken ribs and facial injuries. Finally, the alters agreed to contain themselves between appointments and restrict their emergences to home and to sessions. With few exceptions, they kept their promises for the rest of the treatment.

Now I began to map the system of the alters. I had Joe write his name on a piece of paper, and encouraged the other alters to do so, or to speak inwardly and instruct Joe or another alter to put their names where they felt they should be, near the names of those to whom they felt most close.[12] Those without names were to put down a descriptive word or phrase instead. Those who did not want to reveal anything about themselves were to write a line or dash. There were over 30 alters. Most had a description rather than a name. For example, the younger alter was "the Little One," one angry alter was "the volcano," while another angry alter I had encountered was named "Nick," after the brother who allegedly abused him.

A basic group of alters was active in the here and now. It consisted of Joe, "the Little One," "the volcano," Nick, and "the Professor." The latter was a wise overseer and advisor, who spoke in a stilted and affected tone. Though he was mocked and derided, he was obeyed. The Professor was a barely disguised imitation of Joe's father when he had a little to drink and became friendly, but stuffy and philosophical, but before he had still more to drink and degenerated into incoherence. The Little One gave voice to Joe's frustrated wishes for nurturance and love, expressing Joe's urgent wishes for affection from his emotionally unavailable mother. This alter also expressed the wish to be accepted and gratified sexually, which had, unfortunately, been directed in an exploitive manner toward his younger sister. The alter "Billy," based on Joe's younger brother, retained an idealized view of the abusers and the parents, and voiced doubts that any mistreatment had ever occurred. A larger group of alters had minimal activity in Joe's daily life, but constituted an intricate inner world that often impinged on the alters that conducted life. In this inner world they were associated with colorful symbols that represented Joe's personal metaphors and imagery for containing painful traumas behind dissociative barriers. For example, Joe depicted his painful anal rapes by his brother Nick as locked in a vault of incredible strength and durability. Once therapy prepared him to experience the door as opening, we encountered a triad of alters that contained his emotional response to these experiences and the physical pain he experienced during these assaults. Most alters were related to abuse by Nick and the priest uncle, whose abuse of Nick apparently precipitated Nick's abuse of his siblings.

When I had commitments from all known alters that safety would be maintained, and that containment strategies would be used when requested, I asked Joe to listen inwardly as I asked the alters for their suggestions about how they felt the treatment might go forward. This enhanced the therapeutic alliance and facilitated discovering what areas the various alters regarded with trepidation, reluctance, and defiance. I tried to anticipate difficulties and negotiate solutions to problems in advance, rather than to plunge forward and find myself in the middle of a crisis.

A characteristic pattern emerged in the treatment. After I helped one group of alters to abreact their experiences and dealt with Joe's absorbing what they knew, they generally experienced spontaneous integration or requested that I use hypnosis to let them join one another, and then Joe. Then I would work through with Joe what he had absorbed and might need to abreact further with the newly reconstituted Joe into which the alters had integrated.[13] Typically, we would then have a few sessions in which Joe ruminated over whether he would need to work on any more trauma, or whether he could conclude that "enough was enough." We would focus on the here-and-now concerns, the often importunate demands of Nick and the Little One, and Billy's stout denial. Then Joe would get severe headaches or other body pains related to hidden material, to which were added first contentless nightmares, and then traumatic nightmares of additional abuse scenarios. We would begin their exploration, only to encounter dire warnings from the Professor that we should not proceed. Typically, my dialogue with the Professor would lead to both the warning that the next material might destroy Joe, and to constructive suggestions as to how to proceed with caution. Then the Professor would describe the imagery that represented the obstructions to be overcome, and we would agree on a plan of action. For example, in dealing with a layer of material described as covered over with 12 feet of cement, we developed the imagery of drilling a very small channel through the concrete and placing a pipe ending in a very specially made valve in that channel. In such a manner, only the smallest amount of the toxic contents would be released at any moment in time. This imagery comforted the alter system. I noted that for a person who had been violated many times over, the imagery to a certain extent recapitulated forceful penetration. However, insofar as I could determine, it had no adverse impact on Joe.

As we explored a good many abuse scenarios, Joe abreacted them, worked through their implications, grieved their consequences, and improved gradually. In the course of treatment Joe's brother Nick, whose alcoholism had led to serious liver disease (cirrhosis), sickened and died. Joe went to his bedside, not only because of his affection for Nick, but also hoping Nick would make some confession or apology. Nick did not, although he alluded vaguely to mistreatment by the priest uncle and refused to see the uncle when he came to visit.

However, in the family discussions that followed between Joe, his sister, Billy, his other (younger) brother, and his mother, he became aware that both of his siblings alluded to sexual mistreatment by Nick. In addition, when Joe spoke about his suspicions that Nick had been abused by his uncle, Joe's mother sighed and did not defend her brother. Privately, his mother told Joe that if he, too, had been abused, he did not have to tell her. She rapidly reconstituted her denial, but several months later, however, when they were discussing the sister's difficulties, she became tearful, and said she was sad that so much had happened that she regretted, but had felt helpless to prevent.

Joe concluded that his mother knew at least some of what had occurred.

He tried to apologize to his sister. She offered no forgiveness, but volunteered that anyone who had been abused as Joe had been would have been "screwed up" by it. She had come upon Nick raping Joe anally, and had been intimidated into silence. Joe began to get undisguised traumatic nightmares in which his mother, father, and sister had come upon him being abused by Nick or his uncle. Most poignantly, he recovered a memory of his father weeping as he repaired an injury Joe had suffered due to sexual mistreatment from Nick. His father drank himself to sleep thereafter. Joe had always wondered how he got the scars this event seemed to explain.

We discussed the possible inaccuracy of recalled materials, and the chance that some of these scenarios were suggested by our work and what Joe was learning from his family. Joe wondered whether they were accurate in whole or in part. However, it was clear that he had been traumatized and that working with these materials was closely associated with his making substantial clinical improvements. Although Joe found dealing with traumatic issues unnerving and frequently tried to convince himself that nothing had ever befallen him (despite his longstanding conscious memory to the contrary), he was gratified by his general clinical improvement. His memory improved, and his concentration sharpened. He began to value and enjoy a more free-flowing and less inhibited emotional responsivity to life. He liked the person he was becoming. His depression diminished. He mourned and accepted the loss of his wife, weathered their nasty divorce, became a more gregarious individual with a variety of interests he could share with others, and ultimately began to date.[14]

Joe had integrated many of his alters; most of those still separate had begun to fade and coalesce when he brought to therapy a dream that he was sure was important, but which left him puzzled. In the dream, Joe was the engineer of a freight train that was returning from its outbound journey. The passage home was fraught with difficulties and challenges. The rails were covered with ice and snow. Progress was slow and uncertain. As Joe looked behind to check on the box cars behind him, he was shocked to find they were no longer there. As he turned back, he found that he was no longer the engineer of the train. Instead, he and his mother were seated in luxurious comfort in the back of a limousine. He knocked on the opaque window that separated him from the driver. When the window was opened, he discovered the driver was his brother Billy. He instructed Billy to turn back and find the missing boxcars, but Billy's efforts to do so were half-hearted and lackadaisical.

Joe initially had no associations to the dream. When I asked other alters, Billy, instead of speaking inwardly, took over and made an impassioned plea for banishing all knowledge of the painful past from awareness, and making a "fresh and happy start." Modeled on Joe's younger brother, Billy embodied Joe's wish to be untouched by trauma and was based on Joe's (innaccurate) fantasy that Billy had been spared from all mistreatment. Joe, Billy, the Professor, and some other alters contributed to understanding the dream.

Joe was conflicted about whether to finally own his traumas and integrate within himself awarenesses and of what had caused him the most pain, shame, and self-hatred. His life prior to therapy was the journey out; his recovery of the past was the therapy, the treacherous, torturous, and frequently humiliating return trip to where he had already been. He would like to leave his past and the encapsulated memories of it (the boxcars) behind, and share his mother's bland denial and the relative comfort associated with that stance (the limousine). Billy attempted, in his own way, to actualize this wish. Billy's less than vigorous efforts to find the missing portions of the train expressed Joe's ambivalence about integrating his view of himself as damaged by his past with his urgent longings to create a more palatable, sanitized, and comforting autobiography and identity.

As we explored the dream and its implications over a series of sessions, Joe "bit the bullet." After a month of worsening depression, he began to move forward dramatically. The painful efforts that surrounded our dealing with the dream were a turning point. The remaining alters that were related to encapsulating memories of past traumas integrated smoothly after abreactive work. Finally Nick, the angry "volcano," and Billy joined. The Little One integrated only after Joe was dating successfully. Then came the day that the Professor told me that his work was over. He requested help integrating with hypnotic imagery and suggestions, and blended easily. I used hypnosis to check whether there was any residual or recurrent dividedness.[15] After three months without signs of separateness, I was confident that Joe had achieved integration.[16] He had been in treatment for two and one-half years.[17]

Integration leaves a patient with "single personality disorder," and work must be done to solidify the integration and other gains, to address residual problems, and to manage life without pathological dissociation. Joe continued in twice a week treatment for three more months, twice a week alternating with once a week for three months, and then once a week for a year. There were many false and painful steps on Joe's route to the sort of life he wanted for himself, but he was determined to have a committed relationship with a ferocity that recalled the yearnings that had driven the Little One. Within a year of his integration, Joe had begun to see an attractive colleague who herself had come through a painful divorce. Their relationship began in a mutually guarded and apprehensive atmosphere. In session after session Joe chuckled bitterly over a weary old joke: "How do porcupines make love?" "Very, very, carefully." As we dealt with the frequently intense conflict between Joe's hunger for a relationship and his fear of being hurt, Joe finally was able to take the risks necessary to express both his loving feelings and his concerns. His affection was returned, and two years after his integration Joe remarried.

## Outcome of Treatment

I tend to follow up integrated DID patients even after formal therapy comes to an end. I do sequential reassessments both for research purposes and for prophylaxis. When Joe stops in every six months or so, he shows me the most recent pictures of his two young children, and I ask questions to ascertain whether there has been a recurrence of dissociative difficulties.[18] Joe "graduated" from regular therapy five years ago, and has had no recurrence of dissociative symptoms or depression. He retains his sobriety and continues to attend AA. So far, so good. He gives all the appearance of being a normal, relatively happy mental health professional. The only trace of his previous difficulties is his exquisite, but slowly diminishing fear of rejection whenever he and his wife have more than a minor disagreement. I still get an occasional telephone call when this happens, and Joe cries wolf. We have talked about his doing more work about this, but Joe has never called more than twice a year with this kind of worry. He tells me, "Don't take it personally, Dr. Kluft, but I'm just plain sick of therapy." To which I respond, "Well, Joe, there's a lot of that going around."

## Empirical Contributions to Understanding Dissociative Identity Disorder

Traditionally, DID has been considered rare and dramatic in its manifestations. Therefore, it was considered unnecessary to include DID in routine differential diagnostic thinking because one would encounter DID so infrequently, and unnecessary to undertake systematic steps to determine its presence because it was assumed the flamboyant nature of its symptoms would make the diagnostic signs and symptoms evident to one and all if they were present. Furthermore, because of widespread concern that the condition was iatrogenic, that is, caused by the therapist's interventions, many declined to ask questions that might elicit signs, lest efforts to make the diagnosis create it.[19]

When I began to discover large numbers of DID patients in the early 1970s, I honored the prevailing wisdom and avoided direct inquiries about DID phenomena. However, I rapidly found that the prevailing wisdom was inconsistent with clinical reality. For example, as I followed DID patients over time, I observed that the majority spent most of their lives disguising rather than flaunting their DID. The florid picture long considered classic DID was, in fact, uncharacteristic. To better understand the presentation of DID over time, I began to do both periodic and serendipitous follow-up assessments of patients I had diagnosed with DID. Between 1976 and 1984, I recruited 210 patients into an ongoing project. Some were in treatment with me, some with others, and some went untreated.[20]

I discovered that although 6% of DID patients have consistently florid and public symptoms, 94% have a more covert presentation. Twenty percent of DID patients have a consistent overt DID adaptation, but 70% of that 20% contrive to pass for unified. Of the 80% that did not have an ongoing overt DID manifestation, most became overt only intermittently, usually in the face of stressful life circumstances or major inner turmoil.

I became convinced that the so-called "classic" picture of DID was in fact overgeneralized from the most obvious 6% of the DID population, and proposed that covert presentations were the true classic manifestation. I urged the consideration of DID in all differential diagnoses and adoption of a new "searching image" for DID based on the natural history of DID. DID was not rare. Maintaining the traditional classic picture guaranteed significant delay in recognizing most DID patients.[20] In fact, the year after I published my findings, Frank Putnam and his colleagues[21] demonstrated that the average DID patient spends 6.8 years in the mental-health-care delivery system with symptoms referrable to DID before the DID is appropriately diagnosed. By 1995, a number of studies had screened populations for DID with reliable instruments, demonstrating my contention that DID is far from uncommon, and had shown that previously undiagnosed DID can be found in about 3% to 5% of psychiatric inpatients.[22]

DID must be considered in every differential diagnosis. Systematic efforts to identify DID patients are justified and appropriate. I see no reason to use one method rather than another always, but I am convinced that diagnostic efforts should actually attempt to assess findings that are characteristic of DID. Only a small minority (15%) of DID patients will declare their conditions as blatantly as Joe did.

DID should be suspected whenever there is reason to suspect alternating separate identities and amnesia. Many conditions will have these features, but fall short of the diagnostic criteria for DID. These will be classified as dissociative disorder not otherwise specified (DDNOS); their treatment is very much like the treatment of DID.

Many strategies are available for approaching the diagnosis of DID. For example, several findings are characteristics DID. While these findings are not diagnostic, they indicate the possibility that DID or a DID-like disorder is present. Pursuing these signs may lead to diagnostic charity. First collected by George Greaves, and expanded by myself and others, these signs remain relevant.[23] They are: (1) prior treatment failure; (2) three or more prior diagnoses; (3) concurrent psychiatric and somatic symptoms; (4) fluctuating symptoms and levels of function; (5) severe headaches or other pain syndromes; (6) time distortion, time lapses, or frank amnesia; (7) being told of forgotten behaviors; (8) others noting observable changes; (9) the discovery of objects, productions, or handwriting in one's possession that one cannot account for or recognize; (10) the hearing of voices—80% experienced as within the head—that are experienced as separate, urging the patient to some activity; (11) the patient's use of "we" in a collective sense or making self-referential statements in the third person; (12) eliciting other entities through hypnosis or drug-facilitated interviews; (13) a history of child abuse; and (14) an inability to recall childhood events from the years 6 to 11. It is important to appreciate that not all apparent evidence of separate self phenomena elicited with the help of hypnosis or other methods is cause for diagnosing DID.

In an actual interview, the DID patient may provide several indications of his or her condition, transparently or subtly. These include brief switchlike phenomena; fluctuations of behavior, facial expression, and personal style; and problems with memory. Recently, Richard Loewenstein[24] reasoned that if one regarded the often bewildering spectrum of signs and symptoms the DID patient is likely to show as DID's basic appearance rather than an impediment to diagnosis, a special mental status examination could be developed to assess them systematically. His protocol asks about (1) indications of the DID process at work, such as differences in behavior, linguistic signs, and switches; (2) signs of the patient's high hypnotic potential, such as intense involvement in an activity to the exclusion of responding to other stimuli, accepting mutually contradictory perceptions without apparent confusion or distress at their incongruity: (3) amnesia; (4) symptoms that appear physical but are without medical foundations (somatoform symptoms); (5) signs of posttraumatic stress; and (6) signs of depression.

While in the past most expert DID clinicians explored suggestive symptoms over time, and gradually were able to ascertain the presence of alters or witness a spontaneous switch to another alter or identity, the clinician of today is likely to follow the model described by Putnam in 1989,[25] in which one asks to meet an alter directly, usually in connection with a puzzling event known to have occurred, but for which the patient has no recall.

For example, I might have used the childlike behavior Joe demonstrated in his hospital group therapy as a focus, and asked, "I wonder if I could talk to the part of the mind that came out in the group therapy and appeared to be much younger than Joe?" Conversely, I might have asked, "I am told that at times there are angry outbursts for which Joe has no memory. Could I speak to the part of the mind that comes out at those moments?" Critics of such approaches fear that alter formation is encouraged by such inquiries. Although they are indeed potentially suggestive, they are also extremely productive. Therefore, the clinician who fears the condition can be iatrogenic avoids such inquiries, while the clinician who assumes that the complex disremembered behavior might be a product of an aspect of the mind that is not currently accessible proceeds with the exploration.

Many modern clinicians became interested in DID after structured diagnostic instruments had become available, or prefer, when working with a controversial condition, to use standard and reliable techniques. Two structured clinical interviews have been developed. They play an expanding role in DID research, and practice as well. Colin Ross[26] developed the Dissociative Disorders Interview Schedule (DDIS). This instrument asks a series of questions that allow the interviewee to endorse the signs and symptoms of DID and many other disorders. Marlene Steinberg[27] developed the Structured Clinical Interview for *DSM-IV* Dissociative Disorders (SCID-D), a semi-structured interview that allows the clinician considerable latitude in following up the patient's initial responses. It allows the interviewer to gain a very detailed picture of the patient's experience of dissociative phenomena. The DDIS is easier to administer, but the SCID-D elicits more clinically useful information.

I usually approach the diagnosis of DID with a series of questions based on my own clinical experience and research findings. Many items from an old structured interview of mine are included in the SCID-D, so I find it user-friendly when I elect to use a more standardized approach. With regard to differential diagnosis, I have found that most often when the signs of DID are present, so is DID. I am aware that patient's expectations, what they have read and seen, and the impact of prior therapies are among the many influences that may affect the clinical picture, but this is inevitable in a society in which information about DID is widely disseminated.[28] I rarely see a patient who has not had previous therapy experiences. Occasionally, I will uncover a DID "wannabe" who believes or wants to believe he or she has DID and represents himself or herself as having it without a conscious intention to deceive me, because he or she is genuinely self-deceived. I do encounter individuals who are faking DID for one reason or another. Differentiating them from true DID is usually not a difficult matter.[29]

## EMPIRICAL CONTRIBUTIONS TO THE TREATMENT OF DID

DID is a dissociative post-traumatic stress disorder. The treatment of DID is a posttraumatic therapy. As Herman noted,[30] such therapies are triphasic. A phase of safety is followed by a phase of remembrance and mourning, which in turn is followed by a phase of reconnection.

I have brought over 160 DID and DDNOS patients to integration. My work is based on my own experience rather than the recommendations of others. In my account of Joe's treatment, I tried to make the structure and plan of the treatment easy to appreciate. You should be able to find the stages and major observations I describe below explicitly or implicitly in the preceding account.

The treatment of DID has nine steps or phases: (1) establishing the therapy; (2) preliminary interventions; (3) history gathering and mapping; (4) metabolism of the trauma; (5) moving toward integration/resolution; (6) integration and resolution; (7) learning new coping skills; (8) solidification of gains and working through; and (9) follow-up.[31] The first through third steps parallel Herman's phase of safety, the fourth is her phase of remembrance and mourning, and the fifth through ninth constitute her final phase of reconnection.

In *establishing the therapy,* I work to create an atmosphere of safety in which the patient can feel "held" by our relationship, by my understanding of him or her, and by my ability to contain his or her painful memories, troublesome feelings, shame, and guilt. I am not referring to physical holding. I try to explain how we will work together, explain the nature of the treatment, and offer, more by what I do than what I say, hope and reassurance.

The phase of *preliminary interventions* has been a particular focus of my efforts to improve the treatment of DID.[8] The patient and I have to become a team before we can approach traumatic material and pursue integration. I try to provide the patient with the tools to undergo the therapy and to reach recovery. I work to access the alters that are readily accessible, and try to establish contracts against self-harm, suicide, leaving treatment, and any other dysfunctional behavior the patient is willing to curtail. I make an outreach to the alters to let them know the treatment is for all of them, and invite their participation. I try to get the alters to talk together instead of "doing their things," encouraging communication as a replacement for sequences of actions by them. I work to offer as much symptomatic relief as I can, by environmental interventions, by inteceding in the inner battles among the alters, by using medication, and by using hypnotic techniques to contain upsetting materials, away from the alters who play a vital role in everyday functioning. I use hypnosis first on minimal symptoms, and then to address more substantial ones. I try to teach the patient to "shut down" discomforts, abreactions, flashbacks, and other painful symptoms until they can be addressed in session. Such efforts are never completely successful, but can play a major role in helping the DID patient cope and prevent decompensation. Joe, for expample, did not miss a single day of work in the course of the entire therapy, although his ability to contain his symptoms was far from perfect.

Only after the patient is fortified and better able to cope do I move into a phase of *history gathering and mapping.* These efforts build on the achievements of what has already been accomplished, because I cannot bringing my patient into the misery of the past without being reasonably sure we can deal with whatever comes up without its "blowing the patient away." I do a mapping and try to take a history from each alter, or at least a spokesperson for each group of alters. I learn whether alters are going to be punished for making revelations. If there is a chance of this, I work with those who threaten to punish rather than those whose efforts will be followed by self-injury or worse. I would rather work for months to negotiate a safe arrangement than press through and have an injury occur that might have been avoided. Even though I try to get the history in the manner of a reconnaissance, planning to go back for the detail in the next phase, after I have a picture of what the patient and I are up against, it is virtually inevitable that some spontaneous abreaction will begin and require attention. With the tools developed in the first two phases, reconnoitering is a safer enterprise.

Having the map of the system and the basic outlines of the alters' histories, I can plan an approach to the traumatic material. For example, without having mapped Joe, and learning that most of the alters were related to abuses by Nick and the priest uncle, I might have begun to work with the material surrounding the choirmaster, only to have simultaneously triggered issues in 20-plus alters I did not know were there, with unfortunate and overwhelming consequences. Informed as I was, I put to sleep the alters associated with Nick and the uncle with hypnosis while we addressed the choirmaster abuses, giving Joe a known amount of material to grapple with, and preventing an avalanche of spontaneous abreactions related to analogous abuses.

In *metabolizing the trauma,* we isolated the alter whose issues were being treated, so that its misery would not infiltrate the system, and then introduced it and its concerns to an alter that was very close to it, or to Joe. Then I would help the close alter or Joe deal with its feelings about the material, reabreacting it if necessary. Often spontaneous integration would occur when this work was complete, or I would be asked to help with hypnotic suggestion.

When I help a patient work through trauma. I often use fractionated abreactions, a technique I developed[32] in order to help patients deal with awful experiences in a stepwise fashion. For example, Joe mastered the rheostat technique, with which I helped him face material first with 5% of the emotional pain, and then more, increasing intensity step-wise up to the full impact. We divided some episodes into blocks of time, and worked on them one block at a time. In others, we blocked out the physical pain of an abuse until emotional pain had been dealt with. For some episodes we combined all the above, so that at first Joe had to face no more than five-second blocks at only a small percentage of maximum intensity and only in the domain of emotional pain.

*Moving toward integration/resolution* involves working through the recovered materials across alters, and moving them toward greater cooperation, communication, mutual awareness, mutual identification, and empathy for one another. It also may require dealing with alters' fantasies that integration means death. I had alters spend time together, and do tasks together, all pre-integration exercises. For example, I had the Professor and the little one attend professional lectures together, trusting that better impulse control and more age-appropriate interests would change the little one favorably, and that the little one's affectivity would help the professor become less remote and aloof. This was quite successful.

Many alters spontaneously integrated, while others requested or seemed to require the help of imagery and suggestion. This phase of *integration/resolution* is often occurring for some alters when other have not yet begun to work on their materials. Some DID patients will not work toward integration, and with others it becomes clear that work with alleged traumata is so unsafe that approaching integration is not practical, either for a period of time or at all. In such situations, therapy attempts a resolution, which is a more felicitous arrangement among the alters to work together more smoothly, without disrupting life. My research shows that integration is the preferable strategy when it is possible.

*Learning new coping skills* involves the patient's acquiring learning new ways of dealing with the world without using dysfunctional dissociative defenses. At this stage, I find I am often in the role of a coach drilling my patient on the fundamentals of dealing with the world. With Joe, this was a brief phase. His basic social skills and interpersonal "savvy" were very good. However, we did focus on Joe's learning how to "hang in there" with strong emotions in situations that previously might have caused him to switch, or come under the influence of alters who did not emerge, but might influence his actual behavior.

*Solidification of gains and working through* often involves still more coaching, in the context of exploring the residual impact of the patient's past upon his or her current functioning. Often this involves work in the transference. For example, it was only in this phase of the therapy that Joe began to work through longstanding resentments against authority that previously had been inaccessible because the dynamics of his reactions involved many alters, and work with those alters in isolation had not resolved the issue.

I describe the final phase as *follow-up* rather than termination. Many DID patients are so demoralized that they do not expect to get well, and the most many of them hope for is consolation and support in their misery. Consequently, they react with fear to the idea of integration, because this means the end of therapy and the loss of the therapist. Many of my colleagues report that DID patients refuse to integrate lest therapy come to an end, and evidence new alters or relapses occurring in a manner that suggests they were designed to preserve the relationship to the therapist. Consequently, I took the stance that therapy would, at an appropriate time, be tapered in its frequency, bypassing the issue of its coming to an end. Joe continues to see me twice a year, and feels that this is useful in monitoring the state of his integration and improvement.

My follow-up studies offer an optimistic prognosis for the DID patients who achieve and maintain integration.[33] Notwithstanding the fact that some DID patients are virtually untreatable, and some have protracted and chaotic therapies, a sizeable proportion simply get well and go on about their lives. Despite its frequent difficulty and demandingness, work with DID patients remains one of the most gratifying areas of my psychotherapeutic practice.

## Notes

1. Alters intruding into one another's thinking, feeling, and behavior create a family of what are called "passive influence experiences," leaving the alter who had experienced the intrusion in the bewildering position of having thought, felt, said, or behaved in a manner that it must acknowledge, but for which it has little or no sense of volition or ownership (Kluft, 1987a, 1991b; Loewenstein, 1991).

2. Bernstein and Putnam published the DES (Dissociative Experiences Scale) in 1986. It has become a major instrument for exploring dissociation.

3. The Hypnotic Induction Profile (Spiegel & Spiegel, 1987) is useful for assessing hypnotizability in a clinical context because it is rapid and easy to administer.

4. Recently, Carlson (nee Bernstein) and her coworkers (1993) have recommended that for screening purposes a score of 30 or more be used, because about 17% of patients with 30 or more will have DID, while only 1% with scores below are likely to have it.

5. The intrusion of alters into one another's experience is discussed in Kluft (1987a, 1991b).

6. The inner world of the personalities often recapitulates or caricatures the patient's perception of the object relationships that prevailed during mistreatment (Kluft, Braun, & Sachs, 1984).

7. An observation by Thomas Gutheil, quoted in Kluft (1985a).

8. For a detailed discussion of the opening phases of the treatment of DID, see Kluft (1993a).

9. Because hypnotically retrieved information may not be reliable, courts may hold that virtually all of a hypnotized person's memory may be suspect. Hypnosis should be withheld if it might interfere with a patient's credibility in court or legal rights.

10. For a detailed description of the techniques, consult Kluft (1988, 1989, 1992, 1994).

11. This overall approach, shutting down traumatic material, major conflicts, and troublesome alters until the patient has mastered ways to contain and moderated it, is one of my most important contributions to the treatment of DID. See Kluft (1988, 1989, 1993a), and Fine (1991). For a discussion of contracting, see Braun (1986).

12. This approach to mapping was developed by Catherine G. Fine, Ph.D. (1991).

13. For a discussion of the pathways patients pursue toward integration, see Kluft (1993b).

14. For a discussion of controversies surrounding the accuracy of reported memories from many perspectives, see Applebaum, Uyehara, and Elin (1997).

15. Special protocols to check the state of integration and monitor the therapy of DID patients are described in Kluft (1985b).

16. Most relapses into dividedness occur in the first three months after apparent integration (Kluft, 1986).

17. Covert and high-functioning DID patients may integrate far more rapidly than more overt and impaired DID patients with more turmoil in their lives and more comorbid psychopathology.

18. Unfortunately, DID patients tend to deny, be unaware of, or are too ashamed to voluntarily report the first signs of relapse. Inquiry is necessary (Kluft, 1984).

19. This is discussed in detail in Kluft (1991b).

20. Kluft (1985) demonstrated how the symptoms of DID patients wax and wane over time, and showed that it is essential to adapt diagnostic strategies to take into consideration the natural history of the disorder.

21. The classic study by Putnam, Guroff, Silberman, Barban, and Post (1986) demonstrated that DID patients are routinely misdiagnosed and established a baseline picture of DID phenomenology.

22. Three studies—Saxe et al. (1993), Ross et al. (1991), and Boon and Draijer (1993)—found that if one eliminates known DID patients, there remains a large reservoir of undiagnosed DID patients not in remote and underserved areas, but in our premier hospital units in academic settings. Many other studies have since made similar findings.

23. Greaves' contribution was made in a classic article in 1980. Putnam (1989) expanded the list, which Kluft (1991a) augmented further.

24. Loewenstein's interview is richly illustrated with typical DID responses to its inquiries. See Loewenstein (1991).

25. Frank Putnam's 1989 text, *The Diagnosis and Treatment of Multiple Personality Disorder* is generally regarded as the best "first book" in the DID field, because it coaches the reader through difficult interventions and helps the reader understand how to apply its recommendations.

26. The DDIS of Colin Ross (1989) is widely used in research.

27. The SCID-D of Marlene Steinberg (1993) is an excellent diagnostic tool, and an expeditious way to appreciate how the patient experiences his or her symptoms on a daily basis.

28. The assembly of a presentation from inner and socially available cues is discussed in Kluft (1995).

29. The differentiation of true from malingered DID is an area of acrimonious controversy. For opposing points of view, see Kluft (1987b) and Orne, Dinges, and Orne (1984).

30. Judith Herman's (1992) lucid exposition of the underlying pattern of treatment of the traumatized, probably was first articulated by Pierre Janet.

31. See Kluft (1991a).

32. I first described fractionated abreactions in an article on treating older patients with DID (1988), and elaborated it elsewhere (1995b). Catherine G. Fine has also described this technique (1991).

33. My research (Kluft, 1984, 1986, 1993c) indicates that stable integration is possible, and that the likelihood of relapse decreases over time. In approximate terms, 19 of 20 DID patients who hold integration for 27 months will never relapse into overt DID, and 3 of 4 will not resort, even under stress, to the use of dysfunctional dissociative defenses.

## References

Appelbaum, P.S., Uyehara, L., & Elin, M. (Eds.). (1997). *Trauma and memory: Clinical and legal consequences.* New York: Oxford.

Bernstein, E., & Putnam, F.W. (1986). Development, reliability, and validity of a dissociation scale. *Journal of Nervous and Mental Disease, 174,* 727–735.

Boon, S., & Draijer, N. (1993). *Multiple personality disorder in the Netherlands: A study on reliability and validity of a diagnosis.* Amsterdam: Swets & Zeitlinger.

Braun, B.G. (1986). Issues in the psychotherapy of multiple personality disorder. In B.G. Braun (Ed.), *Treatment of multiple personality disorder* (pp. 1–28). Washington, DC: American Psychiatric Press.

Carlson, E.B., Putnam, F.W., Ross, C.A., Torem, M., Coons, P.M., Dill, D., Loewenstein, R.J., & Braun, B.G. (1993). Validity of the dissociative experiences scale in screening for multiple personality disorder: A multicenter study. *American Journal of Psychiatry, 150,* 1030–1036.

Fine, C.G. (1991). Treatment stabilization and crisis prevention: Pacing the therapy of the multiple personality disorder patient. *Psychiatric Clinics of North America, 14,* 661–675.

Greaves, G.B. (1980). Multiple personality: 165 years after Mary Reynolds. *Journal of Nervous and Mental Disease, 168,* 577–596.

Herman, J.L. (1992). *Trauma and recovery.* New York: Basic Books.

Kluft, R.P. (1984). Treatment of multiple personality: A study of 33 cases. *Psychiatric Clinics of North America. 7,* 9–29.

Kluft, R.P. (1985a). The natural history of multiple personality disorder. In R.P. Kluft (Ed.), *Childhood antecedents of multiple personality* (pp. 197–238). Washington, DC: American Psychiatric Press.

Kluft, R.P. (1985b). Using hypnotic inquiry protocols to monitor treatment progress and stability in multiple personality disorder. *American Journal of Clinical Hypnosis. 28,* 63–75.

Kluft, R.P. (1986). Personality unification in multiple personality disorder (MPD): A follow-up study. In B.G. Braun (Ed.), *The treatment of multiple personality disorder* (pp. 29–60). Washington, DC: American Psychiatric Press.

Kluft, R.P. (1987a). First-rank symptoms as a diagnostic clue to multiple personality disorder. *American Journal of Psychiatry. 144,* 293–298.

Kluft, R.P. (1987b). The simulation and dissimulation of multiple personality disorder. *American Journal of Clinical Hypnosis. 30,* 104–118.

Kluft, R.P. (1988). On treating the older patient with multiple personality disorder: 'Race againt time' or 'make haste slowly'? *American Journal of Clinical Hypnosis, 30,* 257–266.

Kluft, R.P. (1989). Playing for time: Temporizing techniques in the treatment of multiple personality disorder. *American Journal of Clinical Hypnosis. 32,* 90–98.

Kluft, R.P. (1991a). Multiple personality disorder. In *American Psychiatric Press review of psychiatry* (Vol. 10, pp. 161–188). Washington, DC: American Psychiatric Press.

Kluft, R.P. (1991b). Clinical presentations of multiple personality disorder. *Psychiatric Clinics of North America. 14,* 605–629.

Kluft, R.P. (1992). Hypnosis with multiple personality disorder. *American Journal of Preventive Psychiatry and Neurology. 3,* 19–27.

Kluft, R.P. (1993a). The initial stages of psychotherapy in the treatment of multiple personality disorder. *Dissociation. 6,* 145–161.

Kluft, R.P. (1993b). The treatment of dissociative disorder patients: An overview of discoveries, successes, and failures. *Dissociation. 6,* 87–101.

Kluft, R.P. (1993c). Clinical approaches to the integration of personalities. In R.P. Kluft & C.G. Fine (Eds.), *Clinical perspectives on multiple personality disorder* (pp. 101–133). Washington, DC: American Psychiatric Press.

Kluft, R.P. (1994). Applications of hypnotic interventions. *Hypnos. 21,* 205–223.

Kluft, R.P. (1995a). Current controversies surrounding dissociative identity disorder. In L.M. Cohen, J.N. Berzoff, & M.R. Elin (Eds.), *Dissociative identity disorder: Theoretical and treatment controversies* (pp. 347–377). Northvale, NJ: Jason Aronson.

Kluft, R.P. (in press). The management of abreactions. In B. Cohen & J. Turkus (Eds.), *Multiple personality disorder: Continuum of care.* Northvale, NJ: Jason Aronson.

Kluft, R.P., Braun, B.G., & Sachs, R.G. (1984). Multiple personality, intrafamilial abuse, and family psychiatry. *International Journal of Family Psychiatry. 5,* 283–301.

Loewenstein, R.J. (1991). An office mental status examination for complex chronic dissociative symptoms and multiple personality disorder. *Psychiatric Clinics of North America. 14,* 567–604.

Orne, M.T., Dinges, D., & Orne, E.C. (1984). On the differential diagnosis of multiple personality in the forensic context. *International Journal of Clinical and Experimental Hypnosis. 32,* 118–167.

Putnam, F.W. (1989). *The diagnosis and treatment of multiple personality disorder.* New York: Guilford.

Putnam, F.W., Guroff, L., Silberman, E.K., Barban, L., & Post, R. (1986). The clinical phemomenology of multiple personality disorder: Review of 100 recent cases. *Journal of Clinical Psychiatry, 47,* 385–393.

Ross, C.A. (1989). *Multiple personality disorder: Diagnosis, clinical features, and treatment.* New York: Wiley.

Ross, C.A., Anderson, G.A., Fleisher, W.P., & Norton, G.R. (1991). The frequency of multiple personality disorder among psychiatric inpatients. *American Journal of Psychiatry. 148,* 1717–1720.

Saxe, G., van der Kolk, B.A., Berkowitz, R., Chinman, G., Hall, K., Lieberg, G., & Schwartz, J. (1993). Dissociative disorders in psychiatric inpatients. *American Journal of Psychiatry, 150,* 1037–1042.

Spiegel, H., & Spiegel, D. (1987). *Trance and treatment: Clinical uses of hypnosis.* Washington, DC: American Psychiatric Press.

Steinberg, M. (1993). *Structured clinical interview for DSM-IV dissociative disorders (SCID-D).* Washington, DC: American Psychiatric Press.

## Recommended Readings

Braun, B.G. (Ed.). Multiple personality. *Psychiatric Clinics of North America.* 7(1). (Special issue of a journal with many classic articles)

Braun, B.G. (1986). *Treatment of multiple personality disorder.* Washington, DC: American Psychiatric Press.

Cohen, B.M., Giller, E., & "W," L. (1991). *Multiple personality disorder from the inside out.* Lutherville, MD: Sidran Press.

Cohen, L.M., Berzoff, J.N., & Elin, M.R. (1995). *Dissociative identity disorder.* Northvale, NJ: Jason Aronson.

Kluft, R.P. (Ed.). (1985). *Childhood antecedents of multiple personality.* Washington, DC: American Psychiatric Press.

Kluft, R.P. (1991). Multiple personality disorder. In *American Psychiatric Press review of psychiatry Vol. 10* (pp. 161–188). Washington, DC: American Psychiatric Press.

Kluft, R.P., & Fine, C.G. (1993). *Clinical perspectives on multiple personality disorder.* Washington, DC: American Psychiatric Press.

Loewenstein, R.J. (Ed.). (1991). Multiple personality disorder. *Psychiatric Clinics of North America.* 14(3). (special issue of a journal with many classical articles)

Putnam, F.W. (1989). *The diagnosis and treatment of multiple personality disorder.* New York: Guilford.

Ross, C.A. (1997). *Dissociative identity disorder: Diagnosis, clinical features, and treatment of multiple personality.* New York: Wiley.

van der Hart, O. (Ed.). (1993). "The Amsterdam Papers." *Dissociation,* 6(2–3). (Special issue of the journal with many classic articles).

# SEXUAL DISORDERS

Sexuality is an inherent part of human nature and there are many variations in the way it is expressed. Deciding at what point a person's sexuality becomes disordered is therefore no easy task. When clinicians diagnose a sexual disorder, they base their determination on evidence that a person's sexual behavior results in either personal distress or harm to others. This part contains cases about two very different types of sexual disorders. The first, pedophilia, involves horrific violations of vulnerable children and has become the focus of national alarm. By contrast, sexual dysfunctions do not cause harm to other people but result in a very private and personal form of torment.

# 8

## About

## the

## Author

*Fred S. Berlin, M.D., Ph.D. was educated at a variety of centers, including McGill University in Canada and the Maudsley Institute in England, and currently is an Associate Professor in the Department of Psychiatry and Behavioral Sciences at The Johns Hopkins University School of Medicine, as well as attending physician at The Johns Hopkins Hospital and the Director of the National Institute for the Study, Prevention and Treatment of Sexual Trauma.*

*As a consequence of his work with sexual disorders, Dr. Berlin has been invited to give numerous professional presentations. He has addressed a White House Conference on Childhood Sexual Abuse; the Juvenile Justice Subcommittee of the United States Senate; a Committee of the United States Department of Justice; a Special Conference sponsored by the New York Academy of Sciences; and Colleges of Judges in several states. He has also provided consultation to the National Conference of Catholic Bishops and the European Parliament.*

*Dr. Berlin has performed peer reviews for numerous professional journals including the* Journal of the American Medical Association *and the* American Journal of Psychiatry. *His scholarly works can be found in such journals as the* British Journal of Psychiatry. *He has been the recipient of a contract from the National Institute of Mental Health to prepare an annotated bibliography on sex offender etiology and treatment, and of a grant from the Guggenheim Foundation to study the activity of brain neurotransmitters during sexual arousal. He has done grant reviews for the National Institute of Mental Health.*

# Hal, Driven by an Invisible Force: A Case of Pedophilia

**About**

**the**

**Disorder**

Pedophilia fits into the general category of sexual disorders known as paraphilias, in which the afflicted individual experiences recurrent, intense sexual urges and sexually arousing fantasies generally involving (1) nonhuman objects, (2) the suffering or humiliation of oneself or one's partner, or (3) children or other nonconsenting persons. In cases of pedophilia, an adult (aged 16 or over) has sexual urges toward children. Although all pedophiles are attracted to children, there is a great deal of variability in their sexual phenomenology and behavior. Some do not act out their impulses, but have disturbing fantasies and inclinations to molest children.

Dr. Berlin's case of Hal illustrates one particular form of pedophilia in which a man is sexually attracted exclusively to boys. There is little question that the behavior of a pedophile is unacceptable. As Dr. Berlin points out in the case of Hal, however, it is important to keep in mind that pedophilia is a very complex disorder in which a person may feel driven to engage in behaviors in a way that feels out of his control.

The treatment of pedophilia can involve several different approaches. In the past, some had come to believe that the likelihood of change was disappointingly small. As Dr. Berlin points out, recently published results suggest a much greater promise of success.—*Eds.*

## INITIAL PRESENTATION: THE CASE OF HAL

My God must have still been in heaven back then. The sky was blue; the wispy clouds white. My Grandmother Ritt and Uncle Pep were both still alive. There was a sense of invincibility and timelessness. Not knowing that Utopia was impossible, back then as a child I had found it: health, a good home, a loving family. My future patients, the sex offenders, many of whom were childhood victims at that time, were being watched over by a lesser God.

Hal was a sex offender. When I first met him, I recall thinking about how different in some ways his childhood had been from my own. Our first meeting was on a Wednesday morning. I am certain of that because for years Wednesday mornings had been set aside for evaluating new patients. I have forgotten which year it was, as there have been so many patients. It must have been at least ten years ago. In spite of the elapsed time, Hal still writes to me periodically. Although at times I am slow to respond, I always write back. Today Hal is inmate #85405.

At the time that we first met, Hal was free on bond, having been arrested in conjunction with a federal government "sting" operation. Having corresponded through the mail with a man who he believed shared in common with him a sexual orientation directed toward prepubescent boys, Hal had described in detailed written letters his affectionate, romantic, and erotic yearnings.

A powerful, burly, yet gentle man, at age 35 Hal had believed for years that he was alone in experiencing such attractions. Having come upon an advertisement in a magazine purchased at an erotic book store, Hal had begun to correspond in response to it, believing that finally he had met another person who through his own life experiences could empathize and understand.

In writing (unbeknownst to him to an agent of the Postal Service) Hal spoke graphically about his yearnings, describing as well both loneliness and despair. He wrote about trying to satisfy society's expectations by dating women, even though he had never felt any romantic or sexual attractions toward any of them. But he was not homosexual.

Hal yearned for a "soulmate" with whom he could share companionship, affection, intimacy and sexual expression. In at least one or two instances he had felt such love, and in his mind at least he had shared it with another. Even though those relationships had been over for quite some time, like anyone hurt in love, he still grieved. However, others would surely not empathize with his pain. To the contrary, were they to find out they would more likely cast stones.

The attractions that Hal had felt had been affectionate, romantic, sincere, and sexual. The tragedy of it all had been that in each instance those feelings had been experienced in the context of a relationship with a 12-year-old boy.

The day after I first met Hal I received a phone call from his brother. Hal, the "child molester," had a family who loved him. Matt, an older brother, was five years his senior. Perplexed and confused, how was he going to explain to the rest of the family why Hal had acted as he had? Could we help him? Was there a cure? Would he be sent to prison? When would the horrible newspaper stories about his wicked brother, stories that were embarrassing and traumatizing the entire family, ever come to an end?

Hal's brother, and the rest of his family, though confused and hurt, expressed the hope that he could be successfully treated. Hal's attorney called a few days later, also asking for guidance. Hal had admitted in writing to attractions and interactions with children.

Though I spoke with the family and with the attorney about matters of treatment, I knew all too well that society would view Hal's conduct as a criminal justice rather than a psychiatric matter. People were understandably frightened, angry, and upset. They had every right to want to protect innocent children. Society was not likely to view his condition, nor the condition of others like him, from a public health perspective. I knew even then that Hal would be going to prison and probably for a very long time.

Though pedophilia is considered to be a psychiatric disorder, and rightfully so, I had come to learn over the years that Hal and others like him would nevertheless be treated much like the bank robber, the purse snatcher, or the common thief. Hal had misbehaved in a very serious fashion. Perhaps through punishment he would learn a lesson, mend his immoral ways, and reform.

In working with such patients, I had come to wonder how it was that jail was supposed to punish away a pedophilic orientation. How was jail going to enhance Hal's capacity to successfully resist acting upon unacceptable erotic cravings? Prison officials would not be held accountable if they provided no treatment for pedophilia. Therefore, they would not necessarily feel an obligation to do so.

As a physician, it was not my role to decide whether or not Hal should be incarcerated. However, as a physician I was convinced that his pedophilic disorder could not be punished away. He was not, after all, simply a defiant person who had somehow chosen to experience an alternative sexual orientation. In terms of character, temperament, concern for others, and personality, I found Hal to be a kind and decent man. How could someone so kind and decent have become a "molester" of children?

## Case History

Hal had been born into a good family. True, his father had often been away during his early formative years, but this had been necessary as his job with the railroad required him to travel. Hal had two older brothers and one younger sister. They appeared to be a happy, well-adjusted family.

Schooling had been somewhat difficult for Hal in the beginning, as he had suffered from mild dyslexia. This subsequently improved considerably with specialized tutoring and he successfully completed high school, and later on college. At no time was he a disciplinary or behavioral problem. He was well liked by both schoolmates and teachers.

After graduating from college, Hal entered the military for four years, subsequently receiving a good conduct discharge. After that, he had obtained steady employment as an accountant.

When Hal had been approximately eight years old, he and some of his male friends had begun playing a game called "show and tell." He could not remember who first thought of this game, but it involved the boys showing each other their genitals. Hal and a friend named Ed, who was two years his senior, played this "game" often, progressing to a point where they would fondle one another, sometimes engaging in mutual masturbation. Ed moved away when Hal was approximately 11 years old.

In reviewing his childhood history, Hal recalled that at the age of 12 or 13 some of his male friends began talking about "panty raids," and about obtaining female undergarments. He had had no such interest. However, he did recall feelings of arousal in gym class when viewing the genitals of other young boys in the locker room. At times, he would have to consciously distract himself to keep from developing an embarrassing erection.

At about the same time, he began to worry that perhaps he was "gay." Having heard cruel comments about "gays," he kept his fear to himself. But by two years later, at the age of 14, he was pretty much convinced that he must be "gay." Yet as he grew older, the age of males toward whom he was attracted did not grow older with him. By the time he was 18, Hal secretly knew that he was still strongly attracted to prepubescent males.

Hal dared to discuss this with no one. To all who knew him, he seemed quite normal and functional. However, he rarely dated. Privately his self-esteem was shattered because of what he had come to realize about himself. He carried within him an awful secret. Succumbing to the urge to masturbate to fantasies about boys almost daily, all the while fervently wishing that they could be about women, by age 18 his pedophilic orientation was already well established.

Several additional years would pass before he actually began acting on such urges. Finally, when an opportunity presented itself, rationalizing that because he cared so much about the youngster in question no harm would ensue, he participated for the first time in a sexual liaison with a 12-year-old male.

### Diagnosis

The differential diagnosis in this case was clear from the beginning. Hal was in no way whatsoever generally antisocial. He was not criminally motivated in his makeup. He had consistently shown respect for authority and adherence to society's mores in all other aspects of his life. He did not appear to manifest a malicious disregard for the well-being of others.

True, he had engaged in sexual contacts with youngsters. However, in reviewing his background, and the "victim impact statements" made by two youngsters, I had become convinced that he had genuine concern and affection for them.

In my judgment, the intensity of Hal's emotional needs had blurred his objectivity, allowing him to engage in rationalization, minimization, and denial. It was my impression that he honestly did not believe at the time that he entered treatment that his actions had caused harm.

One could easily have become angry with him for failing to see what seemed so obvious to others right from the start. However, the perceptions of others are not colored by the presence of intense pedophilic cravings. Hal would need to be helped through treatment to appreciate the true potential gravity of his actions. I felt that getting angry at him for not having come sooner to such an appreciation on his own would be analagous to becoming angry at a blind man for not seeing.

Later on, when Hal began to appreciate the implications of his actions more objectively, he showed grief, sorrow, guilt, and remorse. I diagnosed Hal on each of the five major axes as follows:

| | |
|---|---|
| Axis I: | • Pedophilia. Same sex, exclusive type (no attraction to adults or girls) |
| | • Ego dystonic (his pedophilic urges were in conflict with the dictates of his conscience) |
| Axis II: | • Developmental reading disorder (dyslexia), by history |
| Axis III: | • None (no significant physical ailments) |
| Axis IV: | • Severity of psychosocial stressors. Mild (2) during the year preceding evalution. Extreme (5) at the time of assessment. |
| Axis V: | • GAF = 50 (serious impairment in social/ sexual functioning) |

Hal had the exclusive form of homosexual pedophilia. He was attracted exclusively to boys, not to men, girls, or to women. In the non exclusive form of pedophilia, there is some attraction to adults as well. However, having the capacity to be sexual with an adult does not erase pedophilic cravings. Treatment is ordinarily needed both for the exclusive and for the non exclusive forms of pedophilia.

## Case Formulation

How was it that Hal developed pedophilia in the first place? This is a type of question that has frequently gone unasked. Historically and traditionally, society has regarded such matters more as issues of morality than science. Righteous people are attracted to age-comparable members of the opposite gender. Other attractions are moral perversions.

Some have speculated that certain irresponsible adults turn to children because they can be more easily manipulated and controlled and more readily seduced. Personally, I would find approaching a child sexually to be far more awkward and uncomfortable than approaching an adult. Furthermore, as a heterosexual adult, I have never felt tempted to approach a child sexually.

A primary issue that needs to be explained in pedophilia is how thoughts about children have come to acquire the capacity to elicit erotic arousal in the afflicted individual. Most men in thinking about children do not get an erection.

The issue can be broadened even further. What factors determine in each of us the nature of our own romantic and sexual orientations? Why am I attracted to women and not men? Why is the homosexual person attracted to members of the same, rather than the opposite gender? Why is Hal attracted sexually and romantically to boys?

Sexual orientation is not the product of a volitional decision. As a youngster, Hal did not ponder his choices, reflecting about whether he wanted to grow into an adult who would be attracted either to women, men, girls, or boys. In growing up, Hal discovered that he was afflicted with a homosexual pedophilic orientation. This is indeed a sad and tragic affliction.

Hal had initially become sexually active as an 8-year old boy with a 10-year old-male. Was this just harmless childhood curiosity and experimentation, or did Hal inadvertently develop an enduring attraction to boys as a consequence of those actions? Empirically, we still know so little about the role of early life experiences in helping to shape subsequent psychosexual development. It is believed that in some instances a boy may be at heightened risk of developing pedophilia if he has been either sexually abused, or if his normal curiosity about sex has been overzealously suppressed.

Could biology have played a role? Research has suggested a possible functional brain abnormality in pedophilia.[1] Hal suffered from dyslexia as a child. Dyslexia is more prevalent in males than females. Language is stored somewhat differently in the brains of males, in part because of exposure to high levels of testosterone in utero. Is it possible that Hal's brain responded abnormally during utero to the early influences of androgenizing hormones in a way that contributed both to his dyslexia and to his pedophilia?

Of course, this is purely speculative. What is certain is that through no fault of his own, Hal is afflicted with a pedophilic disorder. In the absence of that affliction he would have posed no threat whatsoever to children. In the absense of that affliction, he would not have become the man he is today, Inmate #85405.

## Course of Treatment

Although Hal has continued to correspond with me periodically over the past ten years, we were only able to work together formally in treatment for several weeks. It was during that time that Hal first met a number of other men who also had pedophilia. An esprit de corps quickly developed between him and the others as years of secretly held fears and desires were discussed openly for the first time. Even today, Hal still cherishes having had that experience.

It was in group therapy sessions that Hal finally began to appreciate more clearly the full implications of his actions. He began to develop insights regarding the sequence of events that had led up to his improper sexual behaviors. He worked hard at developing strategies for preventing future relapses. He also began taking antiandrogenic medication in an effort to reduce the intensity of his pedophilic cravings.[2] His family remained loyal and caring, offering to house and to supervise him in the event that this would be helpful.

## Outcome of the Case

When a judge pronounces sentence, he or she is ordinarily expected to address and weigh at least five issues: (1) retribution, (2) deterrence, (3) incapacitation (incarceration), (4) restitution, and (5) rehabilitation. Over the past several years many states have established mandatory sentencing requirements regarding childhood sexual abuse. Understandably, the public is insisting that children be protected.

The emphasis in sentencing has moved away from rehabilitation (even though prisons are often still referred to as correctional facilities), and toward punishment. Psychiatric explanations are often cynically dismissed as either excuses or as irrelevant. It is the victim's rights that must be considered, not the offenders. Offenders need to learn a lesson—do not do the crime if you cannot do the time. This is so even though U.S. Justice Department data have documented lower rates of criminal recidivism among sex offenders than among the perpetrators of other serious criminal acts.[3]

I testified at Hal's sentencing hearing. I did not make any recommendations to the court about sentencing. As a physician, I did not see that as my role. Rather, I tried to provide information about pedophilia that I hoped would be helpful.

However, concerns about treatment and about Hal clearly were not going to rule the day. He had admitted in writing to fondling two 12-year-old boys, and to a long history of recurrent fantasies and sexual desires about boys in general. He was sentenced to 25 years without parole. The judge expressed the hope that he would receive treatment while incarcerated, though he had no means of assuring that he would. For his part, Hal seemed somewhat shaken in his faith. In a letter written shortly after his sentencing he stated "I depend upon a God I cannot see. I pray to a God who may not be."

Over a century ago, the eminent British psychiatrist Sir Henry Maudsley wrote the following in an essay entitled "Responsibility in Mental Disease": "If the law cannot adjust the measure of punishment to the actual degree of responsibility . . . that is no reason why we should shut our eyes to the facts; it is still our duty to place them on the record in the confident assurance that a time will come when men will be able to deal more wisely with them."[4] It is not clear to me more than a hundred years later that time has yet arrived with respect to pedophilia.

## THEORETICAL AND CONCEPTUAL CONTRIBUTIONS TO UNDERSTANDING PEDOPHILIA

Psychiatrists consider pedophilia to be a mental disorder. Ethicists consider sexual relationships between adults and young children to be wrong. So do I.

Perhaps one can accept that Hal did not choose to be afflicted with pedophilia. Who would ever choose that? It may be that his objectivity became clouded because of the nature and intensity of his affective cravings. That can be a difficult cross to bear. Nevertheless, it was his responsibility not to act on his attractions. In acting, he sinned. Bad acts should not be excused.

So put, the matter has been defined morally. If Hal was fully capable of controlling his actions, but simply chose to do otherwise, why speak of disorder and treatment?

Society assumes, and it is just an assumption, that individuals are ordinarily fully capable of conforming their conduct to the requirements of law. Failing such an assumption, the common thief could argue that he had been driven by an overpowering compulsion to steal. Treatment would be in order, not punishment.

One could argue that Hal did what he did because it felt good. Empirically, when a behavior feels good, it can be difficult to resist. Urinating, when one urgently has to go, feels good. However, in responding to the disquieting urge to do so, one is not simply having fun. Rather, one is responding to a powerful, biologically based drive. When it comes to behaviors enacted in response to powerful biological drives, can free will sometimes be compromised?

God or nature has instilled within each one of us a number of powerful biological drives. Without food, the hungry man would die. Without sexual behavior, the human race would die. It is important to eat and it is important to have sex.

Having consumed a full meal, satiety ensues. However, in time, the desire to eat again will surely return. So it is with sex. Both eating and mating are driven behaviors. At any given moment, in response to the circumstances at hand, one may do neither. Over the longer haul, in some manner, we will all repeatedly do both. But a volitional decision to go through life either without food or sex will be opposed by powerful biological forces.

We all have these appetites for sex and food. Americans are currently spending billions of dollars per year trying to change their eating behaviors, often without success. New Year's resolutions about dieting seem so assuredly attainable when made just after a big holiday meal. The idea of dieting, which requires no more than simply changing one's own behavior (just eat less), seems so easy in the absence of hunger.

Did Hal simply choose to misbehave? Are the hundreds of thousands of persons who fail each year to successfully diet simply choosing to overeat? In observing such individuals, that might seem to be so. After all, the overeater premeditatedly walks to the refrigerator or to the cookie jar. The food does not come to him. Furthermore, he may do so sneakily, embarrassed because wife or sister has been told of his dieting. On the surface at least, such sneaky premeditated behavior looks fully volitional.

Internally, after overeating, the would-be dieter often vows to himself "never again." He does so with sincerity and conviction. It is the return of hunger, so invisible and unobservable to others, and in a sense so vague even to himself, that in time often overcomes resolve. It is those unseen cravings that may drive him once again to repeat the cycle.

That, however, is overeating. That is not sex. That certainly has nothing to do with sex involving children and nothing to do with Hal. Overeaters, by sustaining their obesity, may victimize themselves. They do not directly victimize others. They certainly do not victimize innocent children. Why should we believe Hal, who in seeking treatment, insisted that he too had become weakened in his resolve to resist the repeated insistent cravings of his pedophilic appetite? In making such a claim, was he not just trying "to beat the rap"? As a moral person, could not Hal have relieved himself of sexual tensions by masturbating, instead of acting upon his pedophilic cravings?

It is true that masturbation can often temporarily decrease sexual desire. On the other hand, for some it may also whet subsequent sexual appetite. In either case, recurrent masturbation does not necessarily facilitate celibacy. If a primary purpose of sex is to assure survival of the human species, then nature would not ordinarily want masturbation to prevent subsequent sexual acts with others. In some instances, frequency of masturbation may serve as a marker regarding intensity of sexual drive. For Hal, going home and masturbating would not have constituted successful self-treatment.

The psychologist Patrick Carnes has recently coined the term "sexual addiction."[5] Research that I and others have conducted at The Johns Hopkins Hospital, using PET scan technology, has demonstrated that internally produced opiates (endorphins) are released in the brain during erotic arousal.[6] This release of opiates may help to account for the driven, even addictive-like quality sometimes associated with human sexuality.

Biologically, this may be one of nature's ways of assuring a repeated interest in sex as a means of sustaining the human species. However, in a given individual at the extreme end of the continuum, being too driven or too "addicted" could become counterproductive.

In describing the paraphilias more than a hundred years ago, Kraft-Ebing used the word "craving."[7] I prefer the term "driven." The point is that all sexual behavior has the force of a powerful biological drive behind it. That drive recurrently craves satiation. When that powerful force becomes "aimed," to use Sig-

mund Freud's term, in the wrong direction (e.g., toward children), proper professional treatment may be necessary to assist the afflicted individual.[8] In my
judgment, Hal was such an afflicted individual. I did not then, nor do I now,
view him as a bad person who had simply chosen to misbehave.

## EMPIRICAL CONTRIBUTIONS TO TREATMENT OF PEDOPHILIA

Several types of treatment have been proposed to try to help individuals like
Hal. Ultimately, empirical research will need to demonstrate which methods, if
any, are best. Pedophilia is not curable. However, like alcoholism, it can be
successfully treated.

My colleagues and I have published five-year follow-up outcome data docu-
menting less than an 8% recidivism rate among a cohort of over 400 men treated
for pedophilia.[9] More than 92% of men in this study did not recidivate. The
treatment of choice was group therapy, combined in some cases with antiandrogenic ("sex-drive lowering") medications.

Group therapy confronts the denial and rationalizations, the so-called cognitive distortions, that are an expected component of pedophilia prior to treatment. They are expected because when satisfying a craving brings pleasure, it is
often difficult to admit to oneself that satisfaction of that craving needs to be
inhibited. Group therapy provides a supportive mileau conducive to frank discussion. Various relapse-prevention strategies are taught and recommended.
There is ongoing problem-solving, and an effort is made to develop a family-
and community-based social support system. Hal's family may not have been
part of the problem. Perhaps they could have been part of the solution.

In my judgment, traditional psychodynamic therapies are not the treatment
of choice for pedophilia. Most psychodynamic approaches make use of introspection as a therapeutic method designed to uncover the "underlying cause." If
the cause of pedophilia is rooted in biology, introspection will likely not find it.
That may require specialized chromosomal testing or sophisticated analyses of
brain chemistry.

Development of insight regarding one's own strengths and vulnerabilities
can often lead to personal growth. However, a well-adjusted person who has
better insight regarding himself and regarding possible early life contributors to
his pedophilic disorder, who still succumbs to recurrent sexual cravings for children, does not represent a success in treatment. Knowing why one is hungry,
whether for food or for children, neither lowers that hunger nor heightens one's
ability to resist succumbing. There is little empirical evidence that insight-ori-
ented therapies are generally effective in treating pedophilia.

What about behavior therapy? Most behavior therapists assume that sexual
orientation, including a pedophilic orientation, has been learned. More important, it is often assumed that through learning, erotic arousal patterns, including pedophilic patterns, can be altered.

Dogs, classically conditioned to salivate to a bell, quickly learn not to do so when the bell is no longer paired with food. Young ducklings who have learned through "imprinting" to follow their mothers cannot easily, if at all, unlearn that behavior. Some learned behavior is not easily unlearned. It is as if it has been permanently "stamped-in". To the extent that sexual orientation is learned, it may be by "imprinting" rather than by classical conditioning.

I find it very difficult to believe that I could learn to be erotically attracted to boys or that my attraction to women could somehow be deconditioned. Would Hal find changing his sexual orientation to be any more readily achievable?

In the laboratory, using a variety of behavior therapy techniques, short-term changes in erotic arousal patterns have been achieved. Using the penile plethysmograph to measure erections, behavior therapy has proven itself capable of heightening erotic arousal to adults in men with pedophilia, and of extinguishing, at least as measured in the lab, erotic arousal to children. Behavior therapists have not yet documented that such changes in the laboratory lead to enduring long-term behavioral changes in the community. For this reason, I had not recommended such treatment to Hal.

Therapeutic interventions that lower testosterone have been associated with low rates of sexual recidivism. In one Danish study, surgical removal of the testes was used to lower testosterone in more than 900 men, many of whom had pedophilia.[10] There was a 30-year follow-up period with more than 3,000 follow-up examinations. The recidivism rate in that study was less than 3%. Other studies have replicated these positive findings.

Like surgery, various medications are also capable of lowering testosterone. Such "sex-drive lowering" medications can contribute to low rates of redicidivism, when used as an adjunct to group therapy, in the treatment of pedophilia.[11,12] Hal had begun such treatment just prior to entering prison.

Pharmacological treatment aside, sometimes therapy simply involves providing a lifeline. Hal has been in prison for about ten years. He will be required to remain there for another fifteen. He will then be released. He last wrote to me about three months ago. I haven't made the time yet to write him back. Work gets pretty hectic, and I am often very slow to respond. There are other patients just like Hal, and newer more immediate responsibilities. Time has a way of doing that. However, I think about Hal occasionally, especially on sunny days when the sky is blue and the wispy clouds white. In time, I will write him back. Inmate #85405 deserves no less.

### Notes

1. Gaffney, G.R. & Berlin, F.S. (1984). Is there hypothalamic-pituitary-gonadal dysfunction in pedophilia? *British Journal of Psychiatry, 145.* 657–660.

2. Berlin, F.S., & Meineke, C.F. (1981). Treatment of Sex Offenders with Antiandrogenic Medication: Conceptualization, Review of Treatment Modalities and Preliminary Findings. *American Journal of Psychiatry, 138,* 601–607.

3. Greenfeld, L.A. (1997). Sex Offenses and Offenders (NLJ-163342), U.S. Department of Justice, National Criminal Justice Reference Service.

4. Restak, R.M. (1988): *The Mind* (p. 314). New York, Bantam Books.

5. Carnes, P. (1983). *The Sexual Addiction,* Minneapolis: Compcare.

6. Frost, J.J., Mayberg, H.S., Berlin, F.S., et al. (1986). Alterations in brain opiate receptor binding in man following arousal using C-11 Carefentinil and positron emission tomography. Proceedings of the 33rd Annual Meeting of the Society of Nuclear Medicine. *Journal of Nuclear Medicine, 27*(6), 1027.

7. Kraft-Ebing, R. (1965). *Psychopathia sexualis,* New York: Bell Publishing.

8. Freud, S. (rpt. 1977). The sexual aberrations in *Three essays on the theory of sexuality* (pp. 45–87). New York: Penguin Books.

9. Berlin, F.S., Hunt, W.P., Malin, H.M., Dyer, A., Lehne, G.K., & Dean, S. (1991). A five year plus followup survey of criminal recidivism within a treated cohort of 406 pedophiles, 111 exhibitionists, and 109 sexual aggressives: Issues and outcome. *American Journal of Forensic Psychiatry, 12* (3), 5–28.

10. Sturup, G.K. (1968). Treating the "untreatable" chronic criminals at Herstedvester. Baltimore, Johns Hopkins Press.

11. McConaghy, N. (1993). *Sexual behavior: Problems and management* (pp. 357–359). New York, Plenum. Press.

12. Berlin, F.S. (1997). "Chemical Castration" for sex offenders. *The New England Journal of Medicine, 336,* 1030.

## Recommended Readings

Abel, G.G., Gore, D.K., Holland, C.L., et al. (1989). The measurement of the cognitive distortions of child molesters. *Annals of Sexual Research, 2,* 135–153.

Berlin, F.S. (1983). Sex offenders: A biomedical perspective and a status report on biomedical treatment. In J.G. Greer & J.R. Stuart (Eds.), *The sexual aggressor: Current perspectives in treatment* (pp. 83–123). New York: Van Nostrand Reinhold.

Berlin, F.S. (1993). Theories on the physical causality of homosexuality. In R.E. Smith (Ed.), *Proceedings of the 1993 Bishops Workshop "Communicating the Catholic Vision of Life* (pp. 58–70). Braintree. MA: The Pope John Paul XXIII, Medical-Moral Research and Education Center.

Berlin, F.S. & Krout, E. (1986). Pedophilia: Diagnostic concepts, treatment and ethical considerations. *American Journal of Forensic Psychiatry, 7*(1), 13–30.

Bradford, J.M.W. (1988). Organic treatment for the male sexual offender. *Annals of the New York Academy of Sciences. 528,* 193–202.

Freund, K. (1980). Therapeutic sex drive reduction. *Acta Psychiatrica Scandinavica, 287,* 5–38.

Marshall, W.L., Laws, D.R., & Barbaree, H.E. (Eds.). (1990). *Handbook of sexual assault: Issues, theories and treatment of the offender.* New York: Plenum.

Money, J. (1980). *Love and love sickness. The science of sex, gender differences, and pair bonding.* Baltimore, MD: Johns Hopkins University Press.

Money, J. & Lamacz, M. (1989). *Vandalized love maps.* Buffalo, NY: Promethius Books.

Pithers, W.D., Martin, G.R., & Cumming, G.F. (1989). Vermont treatment program for sexual aggressors. In D.R. Laws (Ed.), *Relapse prevention for sex offenders* (pp. 292–310). New York: Guilford Press.

# 9

*Helen Singer Kaplan (1929–1995) was an internationally respected a leader and educator in the field of sex therapy. Doctor Kaplan was founder and for 25 years director of New York Hospital-Cornell Medical Center's acclaimed Human Sexuality Program—the first such program to be affiliated with a medical college in the United States.*

*Dr. Kaplan was renowned for her visionary insights on both theoretical and practical aspects of sex therapy, and she revolutionized the way sexual dysfunction was regarded in the twentieth century. She authored more than 100 articles on both general psychiatry and sex therapy, and a dozen books, including* The New Sex Therapy *(Brunner/Mazel 1974) and* The Real Truth About Women and AIDS *(Her last publication in 1995 was* The Sexual Desire Disorders: Dysfunction of Regulation of Sexual Motivation, *Brunner/Mazel).*

*Dr. Kaplan's scholarly contributions to general psychiatry were less well known, but equally influential. As assistant to the editors of the* Comprehensive Textbook of Psychiatry, *she wrote and edited major portions of this authoritative text.*

# Ernie: A Complicated Case of Premature Ejaculation

**About**

**the**

**Disorder**

Sexual dysfunctions involve an aberration or abnormality in an individual's sexual responsiveness and reactions. They are associated with the desire, arousal, and orgasm phases of the sexual response cycle. In cases of low sexual desire, the individual lacks interest in sexual activity. People with arousal dysfunctions desire sexual intimacy, but are frustrated by their body's failure to cooperate. In disorders involving orgasmic dysfunction, the individual is unable to experience the pleasure normally associated with sexual release. Yet other sexual dysfunctions are the result of the experience of pain rather than pleasure during a sexual encounter. In this chapter, Dr. Kaplan tells us about a man who suffers from premature ejaculation, a condition in this third group of sexual dysfunctions.

Although some sexual dysfunctions can be successfully treated by a circumscribed behavioral intervention, most sexual problems are multifaceted and require an approach that incorporates attention to relational and intrapsychic factors. These problems may interfere with the progress of more behaviorally oriented treatments aimed at alleviating the symptoms.

Dr. Kaplan shares the frustration involved in overcoming the relational problems that Ernie and his partner encountered during treatment. Fortunately, as this case illustrates, when the clinician is determined and patient, there is cause for optimism.—*Eds.*

Ernie, a tall, nice-looking, conservatively dressed man in his early forties, consulted me because of his severe premature ejaculations (PE). The patient was very unhappy. He told me that he was ejaculating "in less than one minute," and that his girlfriend Hedy was very upset.

Shortly after he had started seeing Hedy, Ernie had separated from Norma, his wife of 15 years. Norma had been his first and only sexual partner until he met Hedy. With Norma, who was described as a "very nice woman," Ernie had no sexual problems. In the beginning, he had also come fast with Norma. But she was patient and supportive, and within several months Ernie had achieved excellent control. Thereafter, he had regularly lasted for "five to ten minutes" until they both climaxed.

But with the voluptuous Hedy, who was his sexual fantasy, Ernie was experiencing his old problem more severely than ever, and this showed no signs of abating. Worse still, Hedy was so upset about this that she was threatening to break off the relationship, which upset Ernie greatly.

## THE TREATMENT OF PREMATURE EJACULATION

As always, I felt happy when I heard that this patient had PE because I know the chances are good that within three months or so that man will have attained good ejaculatory control, and that he and his partner will be having a much better sex life together. That is because the causes of PE are so well understood, and the treatment methods are so effective that out of about 1,000 PE patients who my associates and I have treated over the past 20 years, there were only a handful (six) of treatment failures.[1]

The sex therapy treatment of PE consists of certain therapeutic sexual exercises which the patient or the couple conduct in the privacy of their homes. These "homework assignments" are integrated with weekly sessions in the doctor's office, where the patient's progress or lack thereof is reviewed, and deeper emotional, sexual, and relationship problems are taken up.

The behavioral exercises are designed to supply corrective sexual sensory feedback. This intervention is based on the theory that the patient has failed to learn adequate voluntary control over his ejaculatory reflex because he is not sufficiently aware of the erotic sensations emanating from his genitalia as he nears climax.[2–5] More specifically, the exercises center around interrupted penile stimulation, which is usually supplied by the partner. These exercises force the man to pay close attention to his rising excitement so that he knows when to tell his partner to *stop*. She stops stimulating his penis briefly, until the acute sensations abate, and resumes on his signal. He is allowed to ejaculate after the third interruption.

In our experience, in most cases, 5 to 15 successful manual stop-start experiences serve to program the brain's "ejaculatory control center" sufficiently, so that the man is ready to proceed to the stop-start *intravaginal* exercises.[2–5]

Because Ernie only came rapidly in situations where he was insecure, I did not have to do an extensive medical workup to rule out physical causes, as I certainly would have done if his sexual symptom occurred all the time, whenever he ejaculated. So, with a great deal of confidence that Ernie would soon have good voluntary control (and also some regret because I was at that time taking mostly more difficult cases, while my associates were getting to see all the "easy" cases like this one) I worked out a treatment plan with my colleague Dr. Richard Kogan, who would conduct the actual treatment.

Therapy did not go quite as smoothly as we had anticipated. Ernie was guilty about leaving Norma, obsessively overconcerned with pleasing Hedy, and frantically worried about losing the relationship. This made it difficult for him to concentrate on his stop-start exercises. Further, this patient had an unusually high sex drive which added to the problem of controlling himself. For this reason, Dr. Kogan asked him to do the exercises more than is usual, so that he ejaculated every day. This tactic reduces the sexual pressure and often helps severe PErs who are highly sexual to gain control.

The most difficult treatment issue, however, was Hedy's resistance to treatment. Very experienced sexually, she disparaged Ernie's sexuality by comparing him unfavorably with former lovers. This fueled his overconcern with pleasing her, and raised his performance anxiety, as well as his fears of rejection, to epic and obsessive proportions.

Initially, Hedy had refused to join Ernie in the therapy sessions, claiming that this was his problem and she was too distressed and "turned off" to help with the exercises. When this happens, we are often able to "bypass" the partner's reluctance to cooperate by having the patient conduct the stop-start exercises by himself. But this maneuver can backfire, and must be introduced very carefully, because some partners feel "left out" and rejected by the idea that their lover is masturbating instead of making love to them.

But Richard Kogan was extremely skillful in his work with this couple, and intuitive to Hedy's vulnerabilities, and he succeeded in enlisting her full cooperation and her support of Ernie's doing the masturbation exercises.

Soon there was notable improvement in Ernie's control and in the couple's relationship, and by the end of treatment they got married.

Richard and I experienced the "high" which is the therapist's reward for a job well done—when you know you have made a real difference in improving the quality of a couple's life.

But this was not the end of the story. Five years later, Ernie again consulted me because his PE had recurred and the couple were now having sex very infrequently. Moreover, the marriage was in deep trouble, presumably because of the sexual difficulty. Still totally in love with Hedy, Ernie was the picture of misery. He told me that things had gone well for awhile, but that he never gained the consistency of voluntary ejaculatory control he desired. He was still overcome by the fear that he would ejaculate before Hedy could climax, with the result that he almost always lost control when his wife started to thrust. Understandably, this would frustrate and enrage her.

In contrast to other types of sexual disorders, the recurrence of PE in patients who have been cured is very uncommon. However, there had been some unusual stresses in this couple's marriage. More specifically, Ernie and Hedy had made a big, emotionally draining effort to have a baby, but they had not been successful. Recently they had adopted Billy, "a wonderful baby boy." According to Ernie, except for his sexual problem, which created a threatening cloud over the marriage, their life would now be perfect.

Since Dr. Kogan was on vacation, it was decided that this time around I would conduct the therapy.

First I started Ernie doing the sexual exercises again while prohibiting intercourse. I did this in order to interrupt the cycle of negativity and frustration in the couple's lovemaking. However, I modified the stop-start exercise and suggested the slow-fast version of interrupted penile stimulation. In this exercise, the patient is asked to assess his erotic excitement on a subjective scale from "0" to "10" (0 being no excitement at all and 10 being ejaculation) and to stimulate his penis rapidly and forcefully until he reaches "8." Then, instead of stopping, he slows down sufficiently for his excitement to abate, to where he feels only a "5" sensation, although his erection remains firm. The patient is asked to continue to stimulate himself, slowing down at "8" and accelerating again when he reaches "5," with the aim of keeping the range of penile sensations between "5" and "8" for a period of five to ten minutes before he ejaculates.

But this time Ernie resisted. He complained that he found the exercises "boring" and that he had "been there before." In addition, when I suggested that he temporarily take an orgasm-delaying drug, which is very helpful in some cases, he strongly objected to this idea. When Dr. Kogan had originally seen Ernie, he had also offered him a drug which slows ejaculation as an aid to treatment. Ernie had refused, but since treatment had gone so well without medication, the matter was dropped. However, under the present circumstances—that is, Hedy's disappointment in her husband's sexual inadequacy, and Ernie's fear of losing her—I felt that the use of a drug to help Ernie get a "jump start" on control would have been very worthwhile. But once again, Ernie refused to consider medication.

## RESISTANCE TO SEX THERAPY

I was a little frustrated, but not surprised. In virtually every case, patients with sexual disorders or their partners show some temporary resistance to sex therapy.

Resistant patients miss their appointments, "misunderstand" the therapist's instructions, fail to comply with their therapeutic sexual homework assignments, start fights with their lovers, get "too busy," get pregnant, become ill, get into accidents, don't pay their bills, have affairs, attack the therapist, tell lies, hold back important information, rationalize, fill the sessions with irrelevant material, etc.

Sometimes resistances come from the sexually symptomatic patient only, whereas the partner is cooperative. In other cases, it is the partner without the sexual problem whose anxieties are raised by the other's improvement and who resist treatment on that account. In many cases such as this one, both partners take turns sabotaging treatment.

Some patients resist primarily because the *process of sex therapy* involves assignments that are emotionally threatening or objectionable to them for reasons apart from improving their sexual functioning. For example, very religious Christians and Jews may feel too guilty to comply with assignments that involve masturbation, erotica, or fantasy on moral grounds.

*Process resistances* seldom pose insurmountable obstacles to treatment. As long as patients are basically conflict-free about improving their sexual functioning, and if the therapist is flexible and uses a little creativity, it is usually possible to find alternatives to the particular intervention that is mobilizing the resistance. In this case, I felt Hedy's objection to joining her husband in sex therapy arose mainly because, like many wives, she found the "stop-start" exercises mechanical and tedious. It was for this reason that I asked Ernie to practice "by himself", and also why I tried to accelerate treatment with medication.

More commonly, the source of patients' resistance is ambivalence, on an unconscious level, about *a successful treatment result*. In other words, the goals of treatment—the attainment of better ejaculatory control and of a more passionate and intimate relationship with the wife—poses a threat or mobilizes guilt. Resistances that grow out of such inner conflicts are usually beyond the patient's conscious awareness and are more difficult to resolve than those that involve only the process of treatment. Although this had not been apparent at first, Ernie was unconsciously deeply conflicted about a successful treatment result, although on a conscious level, he would have given anything for success.

The resolution of resistances to treatment is an exceedingly important aspect of sexual therapy. The therapist's astuteness in analyzing the hidden and unconscious sources of the couple's resistances, and his or her technical skills in managing these effectively, is the key to the successful outcome of the majority of cases, and this constitutes the true art of psychosexual therapy.

### "Bypassing" the Unconscious Sources of Resistance

According to our psychodynamic sex therapy model, if the patient or the partner resists, the assumption is made that these obstacles are manifestations of deeper unconscious intrapsychic conflicts about sex or ambivalence toward the partner. These are the same issues which presumably gave rise to their sexual symptoms in the first place. However, although we precede on this theory, we do *not* switch to insight-promoting therapeutic interventions as soon as the first resistances emerge.

Our first-line strategy for dealing with a patient's resistances to the stop-start exercises is to attempt to "bypass" these with an orderly and systematic sequence of gradually intensifying behavioral and cognitive interventions. These progress from simple *repetition* of the assignment, to *reduction* of its intensity, to the *cognitive reframing* of the problem, to *confrontation,* and if these more "superficial" measures fail, we then try to help the patient gain insight into his or her underlying sexual conflicts.[3–6]

When resistances first begin to surface our first move is to simply ask the patient to "*repeat* the therapeutic homework assignment, several times if necessary." Repetitions that are bolstered by the therapists' unfailing support, encouragement, and "permission" to enjoy sexual pleasure often suffice to resolve the therapeutic impasse. And this worked with Ernie the first time, although he relapsed.

If encouragement and the repetition of the assignment do not diminish the patient's anxieties sufficiently to resolve his/her/their resistances, we then *reduce* the assignments so that this entail smaller and less threatening steps. For example, stop-start intravaginal thrusting is usually the next step after a patient has learned control on manual stimulation. But this was too exciting for Ernie, so initially I asked him to insert his penis and stay quietly inside his wife's vagina, without thrusting, to become accustomed to the sensations.

If repeated and reduced assignments continue to mobilize resistance, we may *reframe* a particular point of resistance and reconceptualize this in terms that are less "toxic" to the patient emotionally. Thus, for example, I often attempt to neutralize a patient's guilt about masturbating (which is very common in our culture) and to defuse the resistances this mobilizes to the masturbation exercises, by encouraging the patient to change his old perception that masturbation is a "dirty and impure" act, and to embrace the more rational notion that this is a normal phenomenon and a healthy rehearsal for eventual partner-related sex.

If the patient continues to resist after repetitions and reductions of the assignment, and if my reconceptualization of the anxiety-producing issues has failed to move treatment forward, I then *confront* the patient with his resistances in the attempt to make him aware of his/her sexual self sabotage.

For example, I said to Ernie when his claim that he was "bored" by the slow-fast masturbation exercises made it clear that he was resisting treatment, "I know that one part of you wants very much to gain better ejaculatory control. You are clearly crazy about Hedy and you would give anything to please her, and I understand your terror that she will leave you unless you learn to function better. But it looks like another part of you, a part that you don't seem to be aware of, is sabotaging this effort. How else can you explain why you suddenly can't find time to do your masturbation "homework"? Or why you won't even give the drugs a try when you know very well that this might be helpful?"

I had to be careful that I did not to come off like a "critical momma" when I confronted Ernie, for he was a typical "good boy." Negative judgments from me could easily have made him defensive, and that would be countertherapeutic. I needed to phrase my confrontations in a manner that would be "heard" by him constructively, as coming from me as an ally, a coach, who was trying to help him develop winning strategies to make him more potent and to rescue his marriage.

### Insight into the Deeper Causes of Resistance

Often, especially when treating patients who have orgasm phase dysfunctions that are usually easier to cure than those who have erection or sexual desire problems—these "superficial" tactics succeed in "bypassing" or "bridging over" the deeper sources of the patient's resistances. There are many cases in our files in which patients' sexual functioning and control improved to normal levels, even though they had gained virtually no insight into the unconscious roots of their sexual symptoms or into their resistances to treatment.

However, we have also seen numerous other cases where the patient or the couple were impervious to the therapeutic sexual exercises, sensory awareness training, sensate focus assignments, communication skills training, cognitive restructuring, the therapist's support and "permission" to have sexual pleasure, as well as medication, which constitute the treatment armamentarium of psychodynamically oriented sex therapy.[2–6]

When sexually dysfunctional patients show no improvement in response to such behavioral and cognitive interventions, and *in sharp contrast with therapists who don't believe in unconscious motivation nor in insight therapy, we do not give up on the case. Rather, we shift to our second-line psychodynamic mode.*

Many patients who were initially unresponsive to behavioral and cognitive approaches have been salvaged from becoming treatment failures by the addition to our treatment regimen of psychologically "invasive," insight-promoting, psychodynamically oriented interventions.

As is typical of our approach, in this case the psychodynamically oriented methods were deferred until it became quite clear that the patient was truly resistant to the cognitive/behavioral approaches.

One reason that I don't like to introduce psychodynamic methods early on is that these are not particularly effective in the initial stages of the treatment of premature ejaculation. At that stage, the patient needs sexual strategies to help him or her function more effectively rather than insight. In fact, the outcome with long-term, individual psychotherapy or marital counseling is very poor for sexual dysfunctions,[7] and patients with PE are not likely to be helped by these treatments. Further, psychodynamic interventions are not always necessary for successful outcome. While there is little doubt in anyone's mind that the vicissitudes of early life play a significant role in shaping adult sexual destiny and psychopathology, it does not necessarily follow that each patient's childhood history needs to be explored extensively, nor that patients must always obtain insight into the deeper causes and the early origins of their sexual inhibitions or their resistances to treatment in order for their sexual functioning to improve.

## THE PSYCHODYNAMIC ASPECTS OF THERAPY

It is very difficult to describe the psychodynamic aspects of sex therapy in a meaningful way because the process varies with each individual case. The method is unique in that a dynamic interplay regularly take place between the therapeutically structured sexual homework assignments and the therapist's active relentless psychodynamically informed interpretations and clarifications of the couple's resistances to their becoming sexually adequate, and to improving their relationship.

When patients remain resistant after a reasonable trial of the behavioral/cognitive maneuvers of sex therapy, the therapeutic objective shifts from *bypassing* the deeper causes and resistances with behavioral and cognitive tactics as described above, to attempting to foster *insight and resolution.*

At this psychodynamic phase of treatment, the therapeutic sexual exercises are *not* suspended. In fact, these assume additional importance because they now *become vehicles for analyzing the patient's resistances and for fostering insight* into his or her deeper problems.

I don't agree with clinicians who believe that there is an essential conflict between behavioral and psychodynamic methods. To the contrary, I believe that astutely devised therapeutic assignments that are shaped by the therapist's understanding of the patients' or the couples' deeper dynamics can be powerful transducers of insight and effective triggers for significant memories and free associations. I have come to this conclusion on the basis of my experience with my own patients, and also because a number of psychoanalysts whose patients I was seeing for the treatment of sexual symptoms while they were continuing their analytical work have remarked on great flood of significant dreams, associations, and memories that were precipitated by the patients' experiences in sex therapy.

Thus, after the shift to the psychodynamic mode, the therapeutic homework assignments are used in a dual manner: behavioral and psychodynamic. In other words, the stop-start exercises whose purpose it is to raise the patient's sensory awareness of his erotic genital sensations, and to "reprogram" his ejaculatory control mechanism by providing sensory feedback, continue, but his reactions, associations, and resistances to these experiences are now also used to illuminate his unconscious sexual conflicts. Further, this material is now actively interpreted on a deeper level, with the aim of fostering insight and resolution. To illustrate, I will briefly describe how dreams were used in treatment of this patient.

After I gave Ernie the "slow-fast" assignment, which he found "boring," he brought in several dreams which seemed to reflect his guilt about divorcing his first wife and his unconscious impulse to punish himself. Another major dream theme was Ernie's immature dependence on and rage at women, and his fears of being rejected. Ernie was not consciously aware of these hidden problems, but these were keeping him from becoming sexually adequate.

### Dreams in Psychosexual Therapy

Although I have successfully treated numerous patients without working with their dreams, in many cases dream work has proved extremely useful. The use of dreams in psychosexual therapy is based on two assumptions: (1) dreams often deal with current emotional issues in the dreamers' life and therapy; and (2) dreams have symbolical meaning above and beyond their manifest content.

The aims and methods of dream interpretation in brief dynamic sex therapy are consistent with the strategic nature of this modality and differs in some respects from dream work in psychoanalytic therapy. In contrast to the aims of the psychoanalysis and psychodynamic couples therapy, in this brief treatment we are not interested in trying to reconstruct the patient's neurotic personality or in changing the basic dynamics of the couples' problematic relationship (unless this is clearly necessary to implement the major aim of sex therapy—namely, to improve sexual functioning). Therefore, whereas in psychoanalysis dreams are interpreted at the deepest and earliest sources of psychic damage, at the Oedipal and preoedipal levels, in sex therapy dream interpretation is used mainly to illuminate and resolve the unconscious sources of the patient's resistances to becoming sexually adequate and also to further the therapeutic transference, which is very important in this form of treatment.

For example, in one dream Ernie was driving an attractive red convertible (his associations led to a vehicle that belonged to his former company) with Hedy. They left the car to go out for a walk and a large truck promptly smashed into the little red car and pushed it over a cliff where Ernie could not retrieve it. He felt very bad.

On the theory that his former employer's red car might symbolize Ernie's former marriage, I told Ernie that I thought the dream meant that he felt the divorce was destructive to his first wife and that he still harbored guilt about this. I further said that the dream might be a warning from his unconscious, about his own self-destructive impulses. In other words, I let Ernie know that I believed that he was in danger of punishing himself for the "hit and run crime" of leaving his wife.

On a deeper psychic level, this dream might have been interpreted as a castration dream—the red car being symbolic of the patient's penis and the large truck as the punitive father, or his own cruel superego. But Ernie would have thought I was crazy if I made such an interpretation, and I would have lost my credibility. Nevertheless, my more "ego-syntonic" interpretation led to an important insight. Ernie admitted that he did feel guilty about the divorce and that he was paying far too much alimony to Norma on a voluntary basis. Not surprisingly, this was a sore point between him and Hedy. I pointed out that Ernie's guilt was irrational. He had actually been a good and responsible husband. The marriage simply had not worked for either party. His excessive alimony reflected his neurotic need to punish himself and was also a sign of his resistance to committing himself fully to his new marriage.

I must have been on the mark because the patient was very receptive, and in fact a few weeks thereafter he negotiated a more reasonable alimony arrangement. This had a salutory effect on his relationship with Hedy.

A week after Hedy had refused to cooperate with the "silent vagina" homework assignment, Ernie had another dream which symbolized his fear of losing control of his anger. He dreamt he saw some cute small birds in a cage. As he watched to his horror, the birds got bigger and more threatening and he felt frightened when he woke up.

In a related dream which dealt with his unacknowledged anger at Hedy, Ernie dreamt that he was with his wife's family. Everyone was playing a game which involved a typewriter. Ernie was troubled because the keys were "different." He felt frustrated and did not want to play, but he felt there was no way out.

On the assumption that both dreams dealt with Ernie's unconscious ambivalence toward Hedy, I told him, with compassion and sympathy, that his dreams seemed to show that he was feeling a great deal of anger. I said that this was very understandable in view of Hedy's unrelenting demands and criticisms, despite his best efforts to please her. I also reassured him that he had never lost control of his angry impulses, that he didn't have to "put himself into a cage." I suggested that there were more constructive strategies to deal with the situation.

Ernie seemed relieved that I did not reject him because of his anger, and he told me about another anger dream which he had been reluctant to disclose. In this dream, he had taken his shirt to a laundry. The "laundry man" tells him that he can't promise how the shirt will come out. Ernie is seized with fury and gets into a violent, screaming fight with the laundry man. Hedy left with a fellow named Monty.

I thought that this was a clear resistance dream, and that I was the "laundry man," at whom he is so angry. In other words, Ernie was giving me a message which he would not express in real life, that he was furious with me because the therapy was "not coming out" as he wished and because I did not promise to "clean up" his shirt—that is, his "dirty" sex life and his marriage. This patient was mad at me because I was not curing him and because his wife was still dissatisfied. However, he was afraid to express anger at me or for that matter at Hedy directly, because he was afraid of rejection. The latter was symbolized by Hedy's leaving with "Monty," the "other man," when he became overtly angry. My response to this dream was to give the patient "permission" to vent his anger. I told him that his feelings of frustration and hostility seemed perfectly reasonable and justified under the circumstances, and that this would not harm our relationship. I assured him that I do not terminate treatment with patients who express their angry feelings. I also pointed out the reality that, although she might be angry and frustrated, Hedy was not about to leave him because he was an exceptionally good husband, and had given her a beautiful life—a baby, respect, love, a secure home, all the things she had always wanted. This led to a discussion of this patient's neurotic fear that women would abandon him unless he was "perfect" and performed "perfectly."

The most important interpretation generated by this dream involved Ernie's passivity and his infantile reliance on "mother figures." This was a major source of his resistance to using sex therapy to help himself. More specifically, I told Ernie that I was no "laundry man." That he would have to "clean up" his own dirty linens, but that I would be glad to show him how.

Shortly thereafter, Ernie brought in what I believe was a "break-through" dream that ushered in the successful resolution of his resistance to treatment.

Ernie was riding in the back seat of an automobile. His father was at the wheel. The father looks "old and doddering," "in a fog." The father *sneezes*— Something comes out of his nose. Ernie feels disgusted and asks his father "Why don't you use a kleenex?" His father replies, "Your mother won't let me."

I made the assumption that on a symbolic level Ernie's nose was his penis, the snot was semen, and the sneeze an uncontrolled ejaculation. I took the father to be a symbolic representation of himself, while the mother might have been a combination of his real mother, Hedy, and me. I strongly empathized with the feelings of shame and self-disgust that plagued Ernie on account of his premature ejaculations. Then, once again, I took up the issue of his blaming his "mother" for the mess, instead of assuming responsibility. To get the point across, I used a technique that can sometimes get patients in touch with the more constructive and active aspects of their personalities. I asked Ernie to "change the dream" as though this were a movie or TV show that he were directing. At first Ernie had difficulty assuming an active and "winning" role, even in fantasy, and he tried to circumvent dealing with the problem by changing the dream so that his father did not sneeze. But I did not let him off the hook, and asked him to start with the father's snot. After a few false starts, Ernie became more sympathetic toward his father (i.e., himself), and more effective. He realized that his father could not help sneezing, and that better solutions were possible. In the final version of the dream, Ernie gave his father a beautiful linen handkerchief to use.

My compassionate understanding of how this patient's sexual difficulty was lowering his self-esteem, and my confidence in his ability to solve his problems, served to deepen our therapeutic alliance even further. Moreover, Ernie was fascinated by my interpretation of the nose equaling the penis and that his father's disgusting snot equaled his ejaculate, and he became more responsive to the idea of helping himself. In this context, I again brought up the matter of medication.

In the past we had been using Dibenziline, an antihypertensive agent which has the fortuitous side effect of slowing ejaculations as an adjunct to sex therapy for the treatment of premature ejaculation. Since that time, we have found that low doses of SSRIs, such as Prozac, Zoloft, and Paxil, are much superior for this purpose. Very low doses of these drugs often suffice to slow ejaculation, and with such small amounts patients rarely experience unpleasant side effects.

This time Ernie did not resist the idea of medication, and he had an excellent response to daily doses of 10 mg of Prozac.

I gave Ernie the following assignment: After sufficient foreplay for him to become erect and for Hedy to lubricate, he was to enter and thrust in his partner's vagina very slowly, without coming, for about a minute. Then he was to withdraw and ejaculate by manual stimulation. Thereafter, he was to ask Hedy what he could do to please her.

The following week after the successful completion of the intravaginal thrusting assignment, Hedy urged Ernie "not to listen to Dr. Kaplan," and she seduced him into having regular intercourse. This succeeded beautifully. Ernie lasted for ten minutes and both partners had "terrific" orgasms.

## Enlisting the Partner's Cooperation

This time, I thought we were really home free. But I was wrong again. After about a week or so, Hedy resumed her complaints about their sex life. Once more she became critical of Ernie, and she showed her anger by sulking and by refusing to have oral sex with him.

I asked Hedy to come in for a solo session so I could gain a greater understanding of why she was sabotaging treatment and her marriage.

The other reason I wanted to see Hedy alone is that I needed to confront her sharply with her destructive behavior. This is difficult to do when the couple is attending the session together, for one must be careful not to place one partner in a poor light vis-a-vis the other. This risks undermining their relationship which is, after all, contrary to the whole point of the therapeutic effort. If the resistant partner must be confronted in a conjoint session, the negatives should always be simultaneously balanced by complimentary remarks about the other person or support of the relationship.

I stand by my often-repeated statement[2-5] that enlisting the partner's unqualified cooperation is an absolute prerequisite for a successful outcome in the treatment of couples with sexual difficulties. Many unnecessary treatment failures can be attributed to the therapist's inability to fully understand the partner's vulnerabilities and needs, and to overcome his or her resistance to treatment. This case was no exception.

Hedy was very pleasant to me, and she tried to draw me into colluding with her in devaluating her husband.

---

You know how it is, Dr. Kaplan. I am a very experienced woman. I have had wonderful lovers and great sex in the past. Ernie is a good guy and wonderful father for Billy. But he is simply a lousy lover. He is uptight in bed, he doesn't know how to touch, how to kiss, he is tense, he is a big baby. Do you know that he actually tries to kiss me face on, so our noses bump into each other! Dr. Kaplan you are a woman, you understand, don't you? that one simply can't get turned on with a klutz like Ernie.

---

When working with a couple together, the therapist must always remain aware of the impact that the confrontations with and interpretations to one partner are having on the other. Thus, while one constantly turns toward one and then the other partner, like a slalom skier, one must always swing back to the center fall line—that is, the improvement of the couple's relationship, which is the major focus of treatment.

Although I am usually pretty nimble in working with both partners, in this case I had concentrated too much on Ernie and had not paid sufficient attention to Hedy's problems. But now I learned that this young woman had a repetitive pattern choosing destructive men. Ernie was actually the first decent, loving man she had ever been involved with.

Hedy's history clued me in to her unconscious fear of successful romantic relationships,[8] which explained why she was about to destroy her marriage to Ernie. On the basis of this insight, I agreed with her that her husband's sexual skills were nothing to write home about. But at the same time I also pointed out that Hedy was literally "turning herself off" to a potentially good relationship by selectively and obsessively focusing on his shortcomings while ignoring his attractive qualities and all the positive things about her marriage.

## Improving the Couple's Fit

All of us have a notion of what a good relationship should include: sensitivity, intimacy, love, trust, mutuality, equal sharing of power, and so on. In reality, however, there is no way of knowing if there is such a thing as an ideal human love relationship, and what this would be like.

On a strictly empirical level, I consider a relationship "good" if it makes both partners happy, and "bad" if it is destructive to one or both.

Arrangements that work for different couples are infinite in their variety and frequently quite unconventional. From the viewpoint of the clinician, social conventions and politics are irrelevant as long as the relationship works for both partners.

As my colleague Dr. Stella Chess, put so aptly, nothing else matters "as long as the bumps on his head fit into the holes in hers."

In training hundreds of professionals over the years, I have found one of the most important qualities of a good sex or marital therapist is the ability to visualize what it would take to make a couple's relationship work better for them or to improve the fit between them. The therapist's own prejudices and biases can get in the way of helping couples accomplish this by blinding him or her to potentially constructive but unconventional strategies and solutions.

For the purpose of sex or marital therapy, neither the husband nor the wife is the patient. It is their *relationship* that is ailing and needs to be healed. If we wish to help couples, we must put aside all personal biases, whether feminism or chauvinism, and focus exclusively on making their interactions more harmonious.

In the best of all possible worlds, I would have wanted Ernie to become more mature and assertive, sexually and otherwise. I certainly prefer my own husband to be an effective "alpha male." But I really don't think that would have been doable in brief treatment, nor do I think that it would have made this particular marriage work. I sensed that despite her complaints about Ernie's passivity, on a deeper level of consciousness Hedy was more comfortable being in charge. On that assumption, I tried to improve the fit between these two people by getting Hedy to see that while an experienced, smooth rascal of a lover might provide more erotic excitement, she was basically a strong independent woman who was much better off with a compliant and gentle man like Ernie. I told her I thought that she had made an excellent choice in Ernie, and I also got her to see that her obsession with vaginal orgasms was, under these circumstances, self-destructive. Hedy came to realize that Ernie would do anything for her, and that she would likely get more pleasure out of their lovemaking if she firmly but lovingly took the lead. At the same time, I did not neglect helping raise Ernie's awareness to his wife's sexual and emotional needs, and also to developing greater sexual confidence.

## THE END OF TREATMENT

Within just a few weeks there was a remarkable improvement. Ernie was now less obsessed with lasting until Hedy had her orgasm, with the result that he did. He could now thrust vigorously, even when Hedy was in the throes of passion, without losing control. On her part, Hedy stopped being so intolerant and hypercritical, and the couple seemed really happy together. More important, they understood what had gone wrong and what it would take to deal with the minor sexual and emotional problems that are bound to come up in any marriage.

During the last session, when I terminated treatment, all three of us were happy, and we knew we would have no need to see each other again.

### Notes

1. These patients were seen by myself and by my colleagues at the Human Sexuality program of the New York Hospital-Cornell Medical Center, and in our private practice group in Manhattan.

2. Kaplan, H.S. (1982). *The new sex therapy.* New York: Brunner/Mazel.

3. Kaplan, H.S. (1975). *The illustrated manual of sex therapy.* New York: Quadrangle.

4. Kaplan, H.S. (1979). *Disorders of sexual desire.* New York: Brunner/Mazel.

5. Kaplan, H.S. (1989). *PE: How to overcome premature ejaculation.* New York: Brunner/Mazel.

6. Kaplan, H.S. (1995). *The sexual desire disorders: dysfunctional regulation of sexual motivation.* New York: Brunner/Mazel.

7. O'Connor, J., Stern, L. (1972). Results of treatment in functional sexual disorders. *New York State J. Of Medicine, 42,* 1972, 1927–1972.

8. Friedman, M. (1982). *How to overcome the fear of success.* New York: Warner Books.

# PART V

# MOOD DISORDERS

Some people are so incapacitated by changes in their emotional state that they cannot function on a day-to-day basis. Intense depression may lead an individual to such depth of despair that suicide seems like the only alternative. Mood disorders have as their central feature a disturbance in emotional state. There are two types of mood disorder: depressive and bipolar. In depressive disorders, individuals feel episodes of overwhelming sadness. People with bipolar disorders experience periods of mania, in which they feel elated and grandiose. The term "bipolar" is used because many, although not all, individuals with bipolar disorders experience fluctuations between the "two poles" of sadness and elation. The cases in this part illustrate two of the major types of mood disorders. A third case focuses on the tragic response to debilitating depression, suicide.

# 10

## About the Authors

*Donald F. Klein* received his M.D. degree from the State University of New York, College of Medicine in 1952, and in 1976, joined the faculty of the Department of Psychiatry at the College of Physicians and Surgeons of Columbia University. He is currently Professor of Psychiatry, Attending Psychiatrist at the Presbyterian Hospital and Director of Psychiatric Research and of the Department of Therapeutics at New York State Psychiatric Institute.

Dr. Klein has also been a Visiting Professor of Psychiatry at the University of Hawaii, Albert Einstein College of Medicine, and the University of Auckland in New Zealand. He is Past President of the American College of Neuropsychopharmacology, Psychiatric Research Society and the American Psychopathological Association. He is a Life Fellow of the American Psychiatric Association and the American College of Neuropsychopharmacology. Currently, he is President of the American Society of Clinical Psychopharmacology and President of the National Foundation for Depressive Illness.

Dr. Klein is the author of fifteen books, 400 original articles in refereed journals, 113 book chapters, and approximately 130 other publications.

*Gerald I. Hurowitz* received his M.D. degree from Jefferson Medical College in 1984, and at graduation was awarded the Baldwyn L. Keyes Prize in Psychiatry.

In 1988, Dr. Hurowitz joined the psychiatry faculty at Columbia University College of Physicians & Surgeons. In 1994, he became the Director of Psychopharmacology on the McKeen Behavioral Service of Columbia-Presbyterian Medical Center.

# Irene: A Case of Bipolar Disorder

**About**

**the**

**Disorder**

Bipolar disorder is a mood disorder in which a person experiences intense and disruptive periods of mania, lasting at least a week and involving euphoric or irritable mood. Most, but not all, people with bipolar disorder suffer from depressive episodes as well. During a manic episode, a person has abnormally intensified levels of thinking, behavior, and emotionality and may become incapable of functioning. In some instances, the individual experiences psychotic symptoms such as delusions and hallucinations.

Someone in the midst of a manic episode may be perceived by others as outgoing, alert, talkative, creative, witty, and self-confident. To a large extent this is true. However, the experience of people in a manic episode is far more complicated. Their thinking can be so grandiose and their self-esteem so grossly inflated that they take on a psychotic quality. Thoughts race through their mind as they jump from idea to idea and activity to activity. They may be more talkative and louder than usual, and speak with such rapidity that others find it difficult to keep up with them or to interrupt. For the most part, these individuals "feel on top of the world." However, the euphoria may suddenly turn into extreme irritability, even aggressiveness and hostility, especially if other people thwart their unrealistic and grandiose plans.

The case that Dr. Klein and Dr. Hurowitz describe illustrates a variation in the expression of bipolar disorder, known as Bipolar II disorder, the diagnosis used to describe a clinical course in which the individual experiences one or more manic episodes with the possibility of having experienced one or more major depressive episodes. This case illustrates the fascinating twists and turns that the disorder might take over the life course of the individual.—*Eds.*

## IRENE'S HYPOMANIA AND DEPRESSION

### Initial Presentation

As a consultant, I first met Irene just prior to her discharge from New York State Psychiatric Institute in 1964. She had been admitted for a severe depression. A married 38-year-old mother of two young sons, Irene had been in and out of three hospitals over the past year. When we met, I learned the following information. Irene's last depression had occurred in 1957 when, at age 31, she had moved with her husband and two year old son from New York City to Long Island. She had stopped all of her activities, which were quite numerous, and began to spend much of her time either in bed or driving around aimlessly in her car. Irene briefly entered treatment with a psychiatrist who prescribed medication and provided supportive psychotherapy. But when no improvement came, she found another psychiatrist. He began a three-day-a-week psychotherapy that lasted until 1960, when her second son was born. During this period, the patient first developed unmistakable symptoms of hypomania. She became the board chairperson of her son's nursery school and managed it extremely well. At the same time, she began to get by with very little sleep, on occasion going entirely sleepless for three consecutive days. Political issues became an intense area of interest. She would spend hours in bookstores, avidly reading up on various topics more or less relevant to her interest. At home, Irene began to socialize much more than usual, throwing several lavish dinner parties.

This hypomania persisted with some minor fluctuations until March of 1963, when slowly she began a fall back into a depression. During the first three years of her second son's life, Irene had become very involved in physical fitness, exercising frequently and intensely. She became very invested in "being a good mother" which involved, among other things, "keeping up with" her young toddler. However, by the spring of 1963 Irene began to feel her energies wane. She felt she could no longer keep up, and began to feel "like a robot." With her enthusiasm and zest for life depleted, she ultimately became incapable of child care and took to her bed much of each day. She returned to psychotherapy with yet another psychiatrist, who began twice-a-week treatment. The depression cleared almost immediately, but recurred within just 10 days. Now severely depressed, she was referred for her first psychiatric hospitalization, at Mt. Sinai Hospital in New York, in June 1963.

Shortly after admission Irene began to manifest a swing back into hypomania. She became an "organizer" on the unit, leading several patient groups, but despite her activity she was somewhat superficially involved in the psychotherapy. Instead, she felt she was able to push her problems out of her mind. Her discharge came after only three weeks of inpatient treatment. However, within days of her return home she relapsed into depression. She reported feeling disorganized and began to fret over a planned addition to her home. After 4 weeks elapsed without respite, she was rehospitalized at Mt. Sinai, where she remained for 6 weeks. Again, she recovered shortly after admission and, yet again, relapsed into a state of anxiety and self-reproach upon returning home, saying "I feel like I'm falling apart." She began treatment at a day hospital program three days a week, but continued to deteriorate, complaining of depression, loss of appetite, crying spells, and insomnia. Increasing the frequency of her attendance seemed to be of little further benefit, and Irene began to have thoughts of slashing her wrists. She was transferred to the Psychiatric Institute in an acute agitated depression, with plans for evaluation for possible electroconvulsive therapy (ECT).

At Psychiatric Institute the decision to utilize ECT was deferred and a trial of an experimental antidepressant was initiated. When this agent failed to bring remission, Irene was begun on the antidepressant Tofranil and the major tranquilizer Thorazine. Ultimately, she began to respond to the Tofranil at 300 mg a day. Having noted her tendency to relapse rapidly upon being discharged home, the Psychiatric Institute staff identified Irene's marriage as a primary source of stress. Her husband would withdraw emotionally when they were at odds, and she responded by becoming angry and more confrontative, but also more involved in her various projects. During her time outside the hospital, the staff found that the husband would often not be at home, and some of them suspected he was involved in an extramarital affair. This situation clearly stressed the patient and destabilized her moods. Apparently in response to these circumstances, Irene developed a strong attachment to a male patient on the unit who had also been suffering from depression. The hospital record reports the conjecture that this relationship provided the patient with emotional support not available from her husband.

After discharge, Irene began treatment in my private office. Unfortunately, within several months of her discharge, her marriage was beginning to come apart. Husband and wife began to lead nearly separate lives. Claiming that he no longer was in love with her, Irene's husband asked for a divorce. She agreed to the divorce, but soon fell back into a severe depression. Outpatient ECT was recommended, but Irene objected vociferously, claiming that her depression had been entirely the result of a (psychological) conflict over her "rejecting, worthless husband," whom she felt unable to give up. For some time she continued agitated, unable to sleep, without appetite, suicidally preoccupied, and incessantly active and complaining. Despite her negative feelings about the treatment modality, she ultimately consented to the ECT and her response was dramatic.

### Case History

The first of two daughters, Irene was born in 1926 to a well-to-do Jewish couple in Shaker Heights, Ohio. Her sister arrived two years later. Her recollections of her earliest childhood involve memories of a family maid rather than of her mother. The patient always found her mother emotionally somewhat distant and difficult to please, but said she was nonetheless very involved in her daughters' upbringing. She always endeavored to foster an appreciation of culture, often taking the two girls to museums, concerts, plays, and dancing lessons. Irene describes fond memories of her father, whom she described as warm and overindulgent with her. She considered him to be "a gentle leader and a soul saver." However, at times he was also perceived as being "henpecked," under the control of his wife, who could be subtly manipulative and demanding.

Irene felt that her sister was "sloppy, demanding, and irresponsible," in stark contrast to her own neatness and compulsiveness. But despite her own sense of superiority, Irene never believed this was reflected in her mother's opinion of her. The sisters competed throughout childhood, and especially during their adolescence in the area of athletics. Both were tomboys who took pleasure in competing with boys as well with each other. With consistently good grades through high school, Irene matriculated to a small, highly regarded liberal arts college, where she moved for her freshman year.

In 1944, 18 years old and in her sophomore year at college, Irene first became depressed. She would spend much of each day in bed, and was cared for by a classmate. At the time, she could not identify any precipitant. After several weeks of severe anhedonia (a lack of response to normally pleasant experiences), with much of each day spent in bed, she returned to her normal state.

She remained well until 1947 when, in the context of some uncertainty over her career choice, Irene suffered from a brief depressive episode. While she considered herself an actress, she was actively working as a modern dancer in a local troupe, aspiring to move up into the Martha Graham Troupe. At the same time, Irene taught dance to children in a local school program. She felt torn between these various occupations, but was unable to find a compromise or make a choice: during dance auditions she felt guilty for not spending the time with the children, and vice versa. She later described herself as having "too many irons in the fire" prior to the depression, a pattern observed many times subsequently in her adult life.

Another period of euthymia (normal mood) followed this depression, and lasted until the spring of 1950. But in anticipation of her marriage, Irene, now 24 years old, became anxious and depressed, and began to suffer from panic attacks. She had passive suicidal thoughts of turning on the gas to asphyxiate herself. In addition to her engagement, at that time she was also upset by her father's involvement in a substantial delinquent tax debt. She sought out psychotherapy, and entered into her first marriage in a chronically anxious state. Before the first year of marriage had passed, she went on to become more acutely depressed, losing 30 pounds from lack of appetite.

She entered four-day-a-week psychoanalysis, beginning in 1950 and lasting until 1955. Irene reported that she began to feel better almost from the very start of her analysis. She felt supported when the analyst interpreted her intense drive to self-accomplishment as typical of "a dethroned elder child," who sought through accomplishment to master the rivalry of her younger sister. The treatment was terminated after "a successful analysis," during Irene's first pregnancy in 1955. By this time, she had given up her career in performance, and focused on teaching dance at a community center. She earned an M.A. in teaching at a local teaching college between 1953 and 1954. She continued to feel well, with generally stable moods, until 1957, when she and her family moved to Long Island at the behest of her husband.

## Diagnosis

At the time of our first meeting, Irene had recovered from a major depressive episode with the help of Tofranil. Her clinical course over the previous seven years led me to diagnose Bipolar Disorder, type II (major depressions alternating with hypomanias). In 1964, this nomenclature had not yet been established, and so patients such as Irene were lumped in the category "manic-depression," a term that is now referred to as Bipolar Disorder, type I.

There was no compelling evidence at the time of our initial contact (nor since) of any character pathology (in modern terms, there was no Axis II diagnosis), as the patient's coping skills and psychological functioning had been too much affected by her acute illness. Likewise, there was then no significant general medical condition (Axis III) affecting the patient's functioning at that time. Life stressors were severe (Axis IV), owing to the divorce that was initiated within months of our initiating treatment. Finally (for Axis V), the patient's global level of functioning would now be represented by a Global Assessment of Function (GAF) rating of 25, as Irene had become nearly totally disabled by an agitated depression shortly after our treatment commenced.

| | |
|---|---|
| Axis I: | • Bipolar disorder, type II |
| Axis II: | • None |
| Axis III: | • None |
| Axis IV: | • 4 |
| Axis V: | • GAF = 25 |

## Course of Treatment

Within one month of her ECT, Irene, now separated from her husband, was situated in an apartment in Manhattan with her two young sons. During this period of transition, she had maintained contact with her male friend from the recent hospitalization, Robert, an attorney who had continued well since his own discharge. The two courted over the following six years, and Irene found this relationship very satisfying. Despite evidence of a drinking problem, Robert continued to function well at work and provide emotional support to Irene. Eventually, she became interested in marriage. However, apparently ambivalent about this commitment, his proposal was not forthcoming. Irene started dating other men and began to develop a relationship with another lawyer, a recovering alcoholic. Apparently, this development motivated Robert to finally propose marriage.

Lithium had just been introduced as a treatment for manic-depression with reports of dramatic success. I decided to offer Irene a trial of lithium shortly after the completion of her ECT course, and she accepted. Her response was clearly positive from the very start. Over the following several years, her mood swings were very attenuated. In 1965, at age 38, she obtained a clerical job at a local hospital. After a little more than one year, she moved on to become a field representative for the Girl Scouts of America, a job that suited her interest in public service and exposure to "the people." She enjoyed this work and performed well.

In 1971, now 43 years old, Irene married Robert. She soon quit her position with Girl Scouts, after a total of about five years of service, and began to work for Cancer Care, a community program of volunteers who helped terminally ill cancer patients. Irene was very active and successful in this position, starting many new volunteer chapters around the city over a period of seven years. In 1979, she quit working and entered a local post-graduate program in counseling, where after three years she obtained a Master's degree.

During her early fifties Irene had experienced relatively minor mood swings that were addressed through supportive psychotherapy and manipulations of her lithium and adjunctive thyroid medication. The major stressors at this time were the difficulties her two sons were experiencing, and her second husband's heavy alcohol use. Her younger son, Noah, had persistent behavioral problems at home and at school. He was impulsive, frequently involved in fights, and often brought before school officials for misconduct. After several suspensions, Noah was sent to live with a family upstate and enrolled in a boarding school. Meanwhile, her older son, David, who was suffering from emotional problems himself, failed out of college and moved in with his father. For support with her husband, Irene began to attend Al-Anon meetings in 1976. She began to threaten to leave if Robert's drinking did not cease. By February of the next year, her husband had begun attending Alcoholics Anonymous and began a period of sobriety. For the most part, Irene felt productive and most "even-keeled" when she was very active, which seemed to protect her somewhat from these considerable life stresses.

However, by late 1977, the patient had become depressed once again. A trial of an antidepressant, an monoamine oxidase inhibitor (MAO-inhibitor), was initiated, and by early 1978 there was a clear response, even a question of hypomania. Irene had "divorced" herself from her two help-rejecting sons, began to run avidly for exercise, and lost 23 pounds attending the Weight Watchers program. She ran in a marathon that year. The antidepressant was withdrawn and through the end of that year the patient continued stable, but mildly hypomanic. She continued to be embroiled in her sons' difficulties despite her "divorce," was somewhat overextended and scattered, and continued to run 20 to 30 miles a week.

I had observed a slowing down of Irene's thyroid function, probably precipitated by her lithium use, and therefore recommended the addition of the thyroid agent, Cytomel. On a combination of lithium and the Cytomel, Irene remained stable through 1979. She performed field work as an alcohol counselor as part of her training in graduate school. During this period, she began to cut herself off from her sons and ex-husband. Meanwhile, Robert had returned to drinking and dropped out of AA. Irene began to express feelings of jealousy toward her stepchildren, who were "too successful" in comparison to her own sons. This issue would trouble her repeatedly over the following years.

In September of 1980, Robert suffered a heart attack. By this time, both sons were on Medicaid for psychiatric disabilities, and were now once again more involved in Irene's life. In December, the patient accidentally overdosed on lithium, confirmed by blood test. She had apparently increased the lithium on her own, attempting to treat a hypomanic episode. With the dosage temporarily reduced, Irene's underlying hypomania re-emerged, but when the medication was returned to its original dose, her blood level was somewhat higher than usual and she became subdued and slightly downcast. She was advised to reduce the dosage slightly, but a repeat blood test produced the surprising result once again of a toxic level. Irene was advised to hold the medication for two days, reduce the dosage further, and was sent to her internist for an evaluation of her kidney functioning. Although he uncovered no evidence of an abnormality, over the following year Irene's lithium continued to rise on lower daily doses. At the same time, her blood pressure, previously well controlled, was elevated to 150/100. Her internist switched to a new antihypertensive, and her blood pressure returned to normal.

Over the following year, Irene continued to experience mild fluctuations in her mood states. The jealous feelings toward her stepchildren once again came to the forefront, to the point where her husband commented that the issue "makes her manic." Irene herself admitted to feeling angry over her sons' conditions. She and I discussed in several of our meetings the idea of her returning to psychotherapy. Although she expressed an interest, she delayed making contact with a psychotherapist. She continued to busy herself, among other things working in alcohol counseling at a local clinic.

I observed another development around this time. Irene began to pray and attend church, expressing to others a "faith in God." Her mood over the second half of 1983 was more down intermittently, but at the same time, some of her life stresses had begun to settle down. Robert had maintained sobriety and quit smoking, largely out of a fear of death. Noah was now 23 years old, and while his antisocial behaviors continued, it was easier for Irene to maintain her distance emotionally as he was no longer a dependent. The patient's ex-husband remarried during this period.

Over the following year, things continued to stabilize. David, now diagnosed with Schizoaffective Disorder, was more committed to treatment himself and had begun to work productively as a security guard at an art gallery. Robert reached four years of sobriety. But despite these changes, Irene would often erupt angrily at home, inciting arguments, once again consumed by her jealous feelings toward her step-children. She continued to attend church regularly, deriving some solace and a feeling of participation. She continued to work in alcohol counseling, but as she moved up into administrative duties, she enjoyed herself less, and soon she began to look around for other positions. During this period, Irene felt less able to shrug off bad feelings; she increased her eating and exercised less. She took long walks, claiming that she enjoyed solitude.

In 1985, at age 59, Irene found a new position at an outreach program that served the homeless mentally ill. She remained intermittently irritable at home. I found it difficult during this period to distinguish between the patient's anger related specifically to her sons and generalized irritability due to hypomania. She continued during this period to attend her community church and was "trying to be Christian." By early 1986, Irene appeared to be somewhat less angry and less preoccupied with her children and stepchildren. She expressed the idea, born of her religious involvement, that all children are spiritually equal. Her interest in solitude continued, but now seemed to have a less depressive cast to it. She said that she was less interested in material things. She was much more physically active once again: up early each morning to pray, meditate, exercise, "raring to go." She attended several support groups for families of the mentally ill, as well as school and church meetings.

The patient began to report bladder incontinence and underwent a urologic evaluation, which found "spastic bladder." She was treated for her symptoms over the following several years. In the summer of 1986, David had a psychotic depression from which he recovered by August. As Irene suffered an increase in depressive symptoms herself, her Cytomel was increased. However, on this higher dose, she experienced chest pain. A cardiac angiogram was negative, but the dose of Cytomel was returned in any case to its original level. Her internist added atenolol to her treatment regimen for high blood pressure. The patient stabilized once again.

In mid-1987, the patient's husband suffered a seizure that was blamed on medication. However, in retrospect, this was more likely secondary to a small stroke, as he later died of a larger stroke in October. Irene went through a period of mourning, including early morning awakening, but she denied depression. She felt that her son, David, was supportive, as were her sister and stepsons. She began to volunteer in a Gay Men's Health Crisis clinic and at a soup kitchen. Around this same time, Noah was arrested for drug possession.

Late in 1988, the patient had another unexplained episode of lithium toxicity after a period of increased hypomania. She was again told to discontinue the lithium, which was later restarted with the dosage adjusted downward, eventually to a quarter of her original dose. Her blood creatinine level, a measure of kidney function, was noted to be elevated, and since that time has continued slightly elevated. Through the first half of 1989, Irene was stable though mildly hypomanic. By May, I decided to begin a trial of an alternative mood stabilizer, with the hope that it might ultimately replace the lithium. Tegretol was therefore begun, first as an adjunct to the lithium. Over the following two months, however, the Tegretol failed to control the patient's hypomania, which in fact seemed to be worsening. In August, it was discontinued and replaced with Depakote. Finally, by early 1990, Irene's hypomania began to dissipate, and ultimately she was tapered off the lithium. Depakote was now her mood stabilizer.

Through the latter half of 1989, Irene continued mildly hypomanic. However, in October, after receiving word from the IRS that she would be audited, the patient sank slowly into a depression. She was begun on Tofranil, in addition to the Depakote, but she nonetheless continued to deteriorate through the end of the year. Irene also developed a resting tremor and difficulty with her gait, and sought the opinion of a neurologist. It was discovered that the patient was slightly parkinsonian, and the possibility of initiating treatment with the antiparkinsonian medication Sinemet was raised. By mid-January, 1991, because of her worsening mental state and the question of an additional neurological problem, hospitalization was recommended.

Inpatient evaluation by a neurologist found evidence of normal pressure hydrocephalus (NPH). This finding was believed to account for the patient's parkinsonian signs, but also her gait disturbance, and possibly her (long-standing) urinary problems. The department of neurosurgery was consulted and ultimately decided in February 1991 to place a ventriculo-peritoneal shunt, a small tube placed into an open space within the brain (a ventricle) that drains into the abdomen (the peritoneum), thereby siphoning off excess cerebrospinal fluid. Irene recovered well from this procedure and was discharged from the hospital in early March.

Over the following year, Irene began a pattern of rapid cycling of her moods, from highly energetic hypomanias to lethargic depressions. These swings of mood and energy lasted from two to eight weeks, and were complicated initially by a changing thyroid status, requiring thyroid medication adjustments (at one point she fell into a slightly hypothyroid state), and by her neurological condition. She continued on Depakote and Tofranil, and later, during a depressive episode, the stimulant Ritalin was added. The Depakote was increased slowly, but her mood swings continued. At this point, in early April 1991, I turned over the direct treatment of Irene to Dr. Hurowitz, but continued to provide supervision of the case.

For the first time, periods of mild confusion were evident, leading in May 1991 to a recommendation by her neurosurgeon that the shunt be revised. Once the shunt was operating well again, the episodes of confusion vanished. However, the NPH had also interfered with the patient's gait, and while there was some improvement after the shunt revision, to date, her walking is quite clumsy and labored. This gait disturbance was particularly troublesome in the period immediately after the procedure, when intermittently her walking was still rather disturbed. During her periods of hypomania, Irene would be prone to rise and walk impulsively, taking insufficient care to avoid losing her balance. She fell while in such a state in July, requiring an emergency room evaluation, where a CT scan of the head revealed a small subdural hematoma. Fortunately, since it was small, no treatment was required.

During a period of depression, in February 1992, a second fall occurred and led to an admission to the neurology service. It was advised that the patient's Depakote be reduced, despite a nominally nontoxic blood level, as it was conjectured that Irene was less tolerant of the medication because of her neurological problems. The Depakote was therefore gradually reduced. Upon discharge, the patient was encouraged to obtain the temporary support of a visiting home nurse. But even before she arrived home, Irene's depression had lifted entirely, and as she was soon back to her busy personal schedule, the home attendant soon became superfluous. She returned to volunteer at the soup kitchen where she had worked before, socialized, took long walks with her dog, and again expressed an interest in church. Unfortunately, after two weeks she slipped back into a depression, and for the following five months continued depressed with only occasional, brief hypomanias while on her standard Tofranil dose. By now it had become evident that Irene's neurological status deteriorated somewhat during each downturn into a depression. Just days after her visiting home nurse was dismissed, Irene once again was in need of the extra support.

Wellbutrin, a new antidepressant, had recently been cited in the literature as less likely to precipitate hypomania and rapid cycling among susceptible bipolar patients. As with most new treatments, Irene consented to a trial, starting in May 1992, that replaced her Tofranil. Yet, despite substantial doses of Wellbutrin, a trial of adjunctive Cytomel, and the addition of Ritalin, Irene's mood continued mostly down through the summer. Brief bursts of energy, lasting several days each, began by August, but failed to bring lasting relief. In late September, the Wellbutrin was discontinued and the antidepressant Pamelor was initiated. By early October, Irene entered into another period of hypomania that lasted four months. Once again, she threw herself into numerous activities, including her volunteer work, socializing, and going out more often for walks and for local shopping. She rekindled her interest in cooking and began to read cookbooks, looking for new dishes to prepare. Yet, there continued to be signs that this period would once again come to an end. In particular, Irene would keep herself awake until 2 or 3 A.M., busy with reading, listening to radio talk programs, or organizing her memorabilia, but would be awake again no later than 6 or 7 A.M. By mid-afternoon, Irene would find herself very drowsy, even prone to doze off while at a restaurant, but by the time she returned home, a "second wind" would come and sustain her until the middle of that night. The patient passively resisted suggestions to get more sleep, admitting that she relied on sleep deprivation to sustain her feelings of well-being.

By February, 1993, Irene, now 67 years old, slowly sank back into a depression, starting at first with a tendency to want more sleep and to report increased tiredness in general. By the end of that months, she was depressed to the point where she could not reliably administer her medications. She was readmitted to the hospital, where she stayed for a period of two months. Ritalin was added to the Pamelor, and for her anxiety, made worse by the stimulant, the tranquilizer Xanax was briefly added as well. This final addition seemed to catalyze her response to the antidepressant regimen. Prior to discharge, the stimulant and tranquilizer were successfully weaned, and she left taking Depakote, Pamelor, and the thyroid medication, Synthroid. The Synthroid was raised to relatively high levels in an attempt to gain better control over Irene's mood swings. After discharge in May, Irene was once again mildly hypomanic.

Our inability to sustain Irene's remissions continued to be a major source of concern. It was clear that the lithium was a superior maintenance medication for Irene, especially in that it protected her from the more severe depressions she was now experiencing. Yet, because of her compromised kidney function, I have not felt it prudent to reintroduce this medication. As there has been growing evidence that antidepressants in the maintenance phase of treatment may actually destabilize moods in some bipolar patients, the decision was made in early June to taper and discontinue the Pamelor. Over the following nine months, Irene was consistently mildly hypomanic. Again Irene tended to "burn the candle at both ends," but in many ways, and especially in terms of her sleep, she was less hypomanic than she had been during her last "high" period. In all, this period of mild hypomania lasted 11 months.

The patient's son Noah returned to the scene in March 1994. He had been living upstate and for some time had been relatively out of contact with his mother. Irene was aware that Noah had been abusing drugs, and when he arrived at her apartment building unexpectedly, seeking money and shelter, she refused him. Unable to gain entrance to her building, he made a loud scene in the lobby and Irene responded by contacting the police. His apprehension resulted ultimately in a court order remanding him to inpatient psychiatric and drug treatment, an outcome that pleased Irene.

However, this incident apparently precipitated her fall back into depression, ending her longest well period in several years. Wellbutrin was initiated, and low doses of the stimulant Dexedrine were added shortly after in an effort to augment the antidepressant. One week later, Irene required emergency hospitalization after her visiting home nurse discovered a rapid, irregular heartbeat, diagnosed as atrial fibrillation in the emergency room. On the medical service, Irene's Synthroid dose was returned to a moderate level and the Dexedrine was discontinued, as these agents were implicated in the precipitation of the arrhythmia. Unfortunately, Irene continued quite depressed, and in view of her weakened physical state, she consented to transfer to psychiatry. There she spent another two months, the depression remitting once again quite slowly, perhaps independent of her medication regimen. On discharge, early in July, 1994, Irene was prescribed combined antidepressants, Pamelor and Zoloft (she had failed to respond earlier to Pamelor and Zoloft given alone). Her mood state had returned to her baseline hypomania.

An effort was made to slowly taper her antidepressants, which was completed by mid-August. Her mood remained very good during this period, and she continued well through early October. Irene again developed symptoms of atrial fibrillation and was rushed to the emergency room. In this case, the patient's arrhythmia was complicated by respiratory problems, ultimately diagnosed as a pulmonary bloodclot. Unfortunately, a series of complications ensued: after her Synthroid was overlooked for a week, it was later restarted mistakenly at just one-sixth of her required dose. By the time the error had been discovered, Irene had become severely hypothyroid. To make matters worse, during this same period, she suffered from a severe pneumonia and an outbreak of shingles. The hypothyroid state apparently precipitated a recurrence of her depression.

The new antidepressant Effexor was begun and slowly increased over the subsequent weeks but in February, 1995, Irene manifested a discrete mental status change. She became confused and exhibited a marked inability to find words. Neurological and neurosurgical consultations found equivocal evidence of shunt malfunction and eventually it was decided to attempt a revision. But in addition to her cognitive problems, the neurologist found increased parkinsonian signs that were especially prominent on the right. At that time, notwithstanding these neurological considerations, I was concerned as well that the Effexor was perhaps playing some role in Irene's confusion. However, without specific treatment, Irene's cognitive problems were slowly resolving, and her depression was beginning to remit as well. Therefore, pending her response to a scheduled shunt revision, the antidepressant was continued.

The neurosurgical procedure, however, found that the shunt had been functioning adequately. An MRI scan of the head revealed several pointlike lesions within the internal capsule of the left cerebral hemisphere. This finding was believed to account for the recent mental status change, but also for the increased parkinsonian signs on the right side. It was now felt that her parkinsonian symptoms were a result of these "microstrokes" rather than primary Parkinson's disease. Despite the suddenness of her mental status deterioration, Irene was now being considered for transfer to a nursing home. Fortunately, with the input of Dr. Hurowitz, she was transferred instead to the rehabilitation medicine service. Just prior to her transfer, Irene's depression finally lifted, and before two days had passed, she was once again hypomanic.

Lingering concerns that the Effexor was adversely affecting her cognition led to the decision to slowly taper and discontinue it. By this time, Irene had been feeling markedly improved for two weeks. She went on to make tremendous gains in her overall strength and her ability to walk (now with a cane for support) during this inpatient stay. Nearly all of the acute mental status and neurological changes had been reversed. A follow-up neurological examination found that her parkinsonian signs were nearly back to her recent baseline. Irene was once again enthusiastic and actively took part in planning her return home. She was discharged home after nearly one month on the rehabilitation medicine service, once again taking only Depakote and Synthroid. Upon her return home, Irene again obtained the help of a visiting home nurse.

Unfortunately, at age 68, Irene's mood ups and downs continue to the present time. After just two weeks at home, she fell back into a moderately severe depression. Because it was never clear that the Effexor had caused any of the mental status changes noted in the hospital, and because it seemed effective in treating her depression, it was decided to restart this medication. After several shortlived periods of brightened mood, Irene's depression has continued through the present. In partial remission, Irene denies feeling depressed, but is unable to motivate herself and is somewhat excessively self-critical. She recently experienced some isolated days during which her mood was mildly elated, and almost immediately she began to plan her "return to life."

## Outcome of Case

Irene's history illustrates how very complicated the treatment of a bipolar condition can be. Numerous interactions of social, psychological, and biological factors influence Irene's functioning and her sense of well-being. The difficulties encountered in treating such patients require that attention be focused on all three of these realms.

Prior to my involvement with her, Irene's treatment had centered on her psychological response to childhood experience. Of course, this was in part a function of the Zeitgeist, as these were the days of the psychoanalytic hegemony within psychiatry. Even today, Irene's original presentation for treatment might lead, erroneously, to a recommendation for psychotherapy alone. Despite the patient's interest and motivation, a "successful psychoanalysis" failed to provide adequate "glue" to withstand the vicissitudes to come. By this time in her life, Irene had only begun to manifest the mood swings that have characterized much of her adult life.

A limitation of psychoanalysis, recognized by Freud himself, is that the intensity of the instinctual drives cannot be reliably quantified. Freud[1] speculated that drive intensity was a constitutional factor, varying across the population. For patients with bipolar spectrum disorders, what appears as drive intensity may be a function of the individual's current mood state. In Irene's case, the demands she placed upon herself became less problematic as energy levels increased into a hypomanic range. However, when her hypomania became more intense, aggressiveness, irritability, and single-mindedness led to interpersonal conflicts, which in turn receded into the background once the hypomania had passed its peak. In such patients, when interpretive interventions are called for, these must be indexed to the current mood state. This is not to demean the value of self-understanding for patients with bipolar conditions, but merely to point out that biological factors have the potential to wipe away apparent ego-strengths gained over long periods of time in psychotherapy. When this fact is overlooked by the clinician, the patient may suffer by experiencing his or her difficulties as a personal failure in the psychotherapy.

During her hypomanias, Irene develops coping skills less available to her at other times: she becomes tireless, active, creative, and altruistic. Her ability at these times to act within the bounds of social propriety has enabled her to achieve a great deal in her career and in her work in the community. Unfortunately, at home her irritability is often less effectively suppressed, and so it was here where angry outbursts often took place. For some time, the conflicts she felt over her second husband's drinking, his sobriety, and his children's successes in comparison to her own sons' difficulties would unsettle and threaten to destabilize her. At other times, during her depressions, Irene feels unable to handle the numerous affairs that sustain her during her hypomanic periods. As her competence begins to wane, feelings of *incompetence* become the focus of all of her thoughts. She becomes obsessively self-critical, and this demoralizing preoccupation further bars her return to activity, until a gust of enthusiasm for life returns.

Distinguishing the mood swings of Bipolar Disorder from "everyday" sadness or irritability is difficult to accomplish with an "either-or" biology-versus-psychology mentality. In considering a pharmacological intervention, one must look for patterns in the patient's affect and behavior that indicate some relative autonomy of the mood. Recognizing such *endogenomorphic* mood shifts requires that the clinician be familiar with his or her patient's desires, motivation, and characteristic coping patterns. With new patients, changes indicative of a mood swing may not be evident to the clinician, who has yet to learn to perceive such changes. In such instances, there is a risk of withholding medication beyond the time when the patient has developed impaired control over his or her moods. The ability to handle stresses may appear intact one day, yet slowly erode as the momentum of a mood swing overcomes the patient. The clinician must be flexible enough to provide psychological "anti-demoralization" support that changes as the patient does, but there is no reason to consider such support an *alternative* to medication.

Over the years, Irene's illness has changed in very interesting ways; some of these changes are relevant to other patients with Bipolar Disorder. It is clear, for example, that her mood swings have become more frequent, though not more severe, and perhaps somewhat more refractory to treatment. This sort of progression is consistent with our knowledge regarding the natural course of bipolar disorders, independent of treatment.[2] Post[3] has suggested, based on his kindling model of mood disorders, that mood episodes tend to promote further episodes—just as under the right circumstances a fire may smolder, burst into flame, return to smolder, and so on. For many individuals this tendency results in increasing cycle frequency, while prophylaxis with mood stabilizers may retard or halt this progression. Lithium treatment never fully protected Irene from minor mood swings, as she often required adjunctive antidepressant treatment, but without the lithium, her mood cycling has clearly become more frequent.

The natural course of bipolar disorders may also be affected by antidepressant treatment. In contradistinction to the mood stabilizers, antidepressants are now believed by some to potentially increase the frequency of mood cycles, with rapid cycling (greater than four mood episodes a year),[4] mixed states (simultaneous occurrence of symptoms of depression and hypomania or mania),[5] or a continuous circular course (depressions alternating with mania or hypomania with no interposed euthymic phase) all possible.[6] As these phenomena are believed to be more refractory to treatment, many now endeavor to limit the use of antidepressants in patients with bipolar disorder. Of course, in many cases this is easier said than done. Over the past several years, since Irene has suffered from more frequent depressions, efforts to shorten her exposure to antidepressants have provided mixed results: in one case, she entered her longest lasting period of remission in several years, and in the other (most recently) early withdrawal of her antidepressant may have led to an acute relapse.

Several researchers[7,8] believe that hypothyroidism plays a role in the development of increased cycling among bipolar patients, even when this condition is only evident with sensitive blood tests. Irene first became clinically hypothyroid while taking lithium, but after its withdrawal she continued to require thyroid supplementation, suggesting that she suffers from a primary dysfunction of the thyroid gland. This observation leaves open the possibility that a primary thyroid disorder has played some role in the progression of her bipolar illness. Following Bauer and Whybrow,[9] who report success using supranormal thyroid levels for the treatment of rapid cycling bipolar disorders, Irene was briefly maintained on doses of Synthroid that made her slightly hyperthyroid. Unfortunately, an episode of atrial fibrillation may have been precipitated, and so this approach had to be modified. At present, Irene is maintained in the high-normal thyroid range, which she seems to tolerate very well. Of course, clinical hypothyroidism is often associated with depression. This is exactly the state Irene found herself in when, during her recent hospitalization, she was accidentally underdosed with Synthroid for some time. The depression that resulted required, in addition to the correction of her thyroid state, that antidepressant treatment be initiated.

Akiskal[10] and Koukopoulos et al.[11] have reported that patients whose temperament is on the bipolar *spectrum,* which includes cyclothymia or hyperthymia, may be a risk factor for the development of rapid cycling or a continuous circular course. Hyperthymic individuals are described as extroverted and energetic, often requiring less sleep, with moods that are predominantly cheerful or irritable. It is unclear whether Irene's temperament could be described as hyperthymic prior to her first depression, although there is some indication that it was. We do know that she was an energetic, extroverted, and socially active individual, often risking involvement in too many activities at once. Frank hypomanic behavior first became manifest after her second episode of depression. What is clear now is that Irene's periods of euthymia have diminished over the years. Of late, her recovery from a depression leads quite rapidly into mild, hypomania, which in turn leads into her next depression. This pattern is the continuous circular course of bipolar disorder.

Biological factors account primarily for this change in cycling pattern, but it is noteworthy that the patient has adapted her behavior in a way that may also play a role. Irene has expressed a belief that excessive activity and sleep deprivation are "techniques" for avoiding a fall back into depression. It is well known that sleep deprivation can precipitate mania or hypomania in susceptible individuals. Is it possible that through lack of sleep Irene's hypomania may be "augmented" or prolonged? While "keeping busy" is for many of us a way to stave off the doldrums, among bipolar patients the antidepressant effects of "burning the candle at both ends" are often much more profound. Of course, overactivity and a reduced need for sleep are themselves components of hypomania, and so in practice it is difficult to know whether such behavior is a cause or an effect. In any case, once such behavior has begun, patients should be encouraged to get adequate sleep, and should be sedated to facilitate sleep if necessary. As in Irene's case, this goal is often difficult to achieve. During her hypomanias Irene often fails to discipline herself to get the requisite amount of sleep, and so her frenetic pace usually gives way only when she is no longer able to push herself to extremes, typically at the onset of her next depression. Might this pattern of behavior forestall the onset of her next depressive episode or sustain the patient in a hypomanic state until the last possible moment, thereby creating the circular course of bipolar disorder? Perhaps more important: does this behavior, by increasing or lengthening the hypomania, *increase* the likelihood of an ensuing depression or affect its severity? Unfortunately for Irene, efforts to treat her hypomania, and to perhaps slow this process, have been less effective since the discontinuation of her lithium.

Irene's medical history has complicated her treatment over much of the past decade and a half. The patient's hypertension, long requiring medication treatment, may have placed Irene at greater risk for depression, as many antihypertensives, especially the older ones, are now known to precipitate depression. As already mentioned, when her thyroid function first showed signs of slowing down, presumably hastened by her lithium use, this development may have begun a period of relatively less stable moods. And, of course, kidney toxicity resulting from Irene's accidental lithium overdoses ultimately forced us to stop this medication entirely. Nothing has adequately replaced the lithium as a prophylaxis against future mood swings.

The effects of aging have had a definite impact on the course of Irene's illness. In particular, her parkinsonian syndrome, resulting from multiple "microstrokes," may have caused her depressions to become more refractory to antidepressant treatment. The normal pressure hydrocephalus and its after-effects have complicated treatment as well. Now somewhat compromised neurologically, Irene's tolerance for many medications is reduced, thereby placing greater constraints on treatment options. Moreover, to some extent her physical limitations prevent Ms. A. from engaging in many of the activities that formerly galvanized her out of her depressions.

Fortunately, a number of possibilities for future treatment remain. We are most eager to find a maintenance mood-stabilizing regimen that will replace and perhaps even improve the lithium treatment that served her so well for two decades. Tegretol seemed ineffective in aborting an acute hypomanic episode, yet could this provide superior prophylaxis against future depressions? Verapamil, a calcium-channel blocker normally used to treat cardiac conditions and hypertension, has also shown some promise as a replacement for lithium among patients intolerant to lithium's side effects. Finally, would future depressions respond more rapidly to treatment that utilized antiparkinsonian agents to augment the effects of an antidepressant?

With all of these numerous issues, this case emphasizes the need for the treating psychiatrist to be expert in the fields of internal medicine, neurology, and pharmacology.

## EMPIRICAL CONTRIBUTIONS TO
## UNDERSTANDING BIPOLAR DISORDER

In the mid-1960s, when I first encountered Irene, the conceptualization and categorization of mood disorders was reaching a critical juncture. Although the unipolar-bipolar distinction had long been recognized, the existing theories of psychopathology tended to obscure this highly significant dichotomy. Psychiatry's prevailing paradigm, which influenced even the fledgling discipline of psychopharmacology, was based on psychoanalysis. One indication of this influence was the division of depressive disorders into the *neurotic* and *endogenous* subtypes. Neurotic depression was held to be less severe, a reaction to stress, typically a loss, that brought about the redirection of aggressive impulses onto the ego. In contrast, the endogenous subtype was defined as a depression without environmental precipitant, and included characteristic changes in sleep, appetite, and energy indicative of a biological substrate. Ostensibly, patients suffering from endogenous depression were more severely ill. While outpatient psychotherapy was indicated for reactive depressions, the endogenously depressed patient was prescribed the newly discovered antidepressants and often would require hospitalization.

The course of Irene's illness belied this distinction between depressive subtypes. Her depressions were complicated by changes in sleep, appetite, and activity level, and could be quite severe. Yet in almost every instance, there were stresses that seemed to precipitate her fall into depression. My experience with Irene and similar patients began to undermine my confidence in the existing categories. While I was convinced of the existence of precipitating stress in these cases, here were patients suffering from depressions of a severity and type consistent with the endogenous subtype as defined. By 1974, my thoughts on this matter had coalesced, and I wrote an article that first sought to define the term *"endogenomorphic."*[12] My purpose was to initiate a reexamination of our nomenclature based on a new, biologically based theory of depression.

The division into neurotic and endogenous subtypes placed emphasis on the existence of a precipitating stress and on severity of illness, but overlooked other relevant variables. I believe this indifference to readily observable clinical variables resulted from psychiatry's preoccupation at the time with what was "below the surface"—that is, with ego and superego functioning. Such thinking tended to lump together subtypes readily distinguishable by observation of symptom patterns. In *Endogenomorphic Depression,*[12] I introduced a new way of conceptualizing the observable differences among patients. This reorientation of theory gave birth to a new paradigm in our approach to understanding the mood disorders.

I suggested that the characteristic symptom pattern found in the endogenous depression subtype was more important than the existence of a precipitant and the severity of illness. The prevailing viewpoint suggested that the changes in sleep, energy, and appetite characteristic of endogenous depression were secondary features, variables that were a function of illness severity. The same was held true of anhedonia, an insensitivity to pleasure found in many depressed patients. I argued that these symptoms are not secondary features of the illness, related solely to severity, but are indeed essential to a subtype of depression I termed *"endogenemorphic."* The existence of a precipitant was no longer held to be relevant. While some patients might develop an endogenomorphic depression without apparent precipitant, this factor was no longer held to be a *sine qua non.* The emphasis was now placed on the relative *autonomy* of the symptoms once established. Because anhedonia is the feature that most typifies a patient's lack of response to his or her environment, I placed great emphasis on this symptom, believing that a dysfunction of the brain's reward system must be at the core of this type of depression.

In 1975, together with several colleagues, I[13] reported three cases, patients with histories of unipolar or bipolar depressions, who denied depressed mood but reported feelings of listlessness and of a dulled response to normally pleasant experiences or pastimes. As with Irene prior to her ECT, these patients felt "certain" that the changes in their mental state were a natural reaction to recent, adverse circumstances in their lives. It was for this reason that two of the patients at first refused medication. But ultimately their anhedonia developed further into a full depressive episode, and the patients then accepted the recommended treatment with positive results.

The concept of endogenomorphic depression served as a scaffolding in the development of our modern-day diagnosis of a *typical* major depression. Together with other observable changes in a patient's activity and sleep, prominent anhedonia now defines the *melancholic* subtype of major depression. Of course, these changes left untouched the concept of reactive depression, which for many years continued to be largely defined by psychodynamic formulations. But as with the inadequately characterized endogenous subtype, I was convinced that neurotic or reactive depression could be reconceptualized in terms of observable symptom clusters. Furthermore, I had observed, among a number of patients with reactive depression, a superior response to the MAO-inhibitor phenelzine, as compared to the tricyclic antidepressants. I became convinced that the depressions these patients suffered formed a biologically distinct group. And indeed, careful, statistical analyses of symptoms among a large group of patients with nonendogenomorphic depression has borne this out.

The collaboration of several psychiatric investigators at Columbia University has led to the refinement of the concept of *atypical* depression. This condition is characterized by low mood in the setting of intact mood reactivity, increased sleep and appetite, extreme lethargy (referred to as "leaden paralysis"), and a marked sensitivity to rejection. The superior response of this group of patients to the MAO-inhibitors has also been confirmed. As with typical depression, we have now come a long way toward a biological model of atypical depression.

## EMPIRICAL CONTRIBUTIONS TO TREATMENT
## OF BIPOLAR DISORDER

As noted above, the unipolar-bipolar dimension had also been overlooked despite observations several centuries old of this natural division among patients with depression. Again, indifference to this finding was the result of the mentalistic (nonbiological) bias within the field of psychiatry that persisted into the early 1970s. As with the advent of antidepressant medication, with its far-reaching effects on our understanding of depression, the introduction of lithium played a large role in the expansion of our understanding of bipolar illnesses. When lithium was introduced for patients with manic-depression, of whom Irene was one of the first, the effects were quite astonishing. Much of what had been attributed to personality or character pathology, behaviors alternately pathetic and incorrigible, could now be placed within the realm of biological disturbance.

Yet, whereas the efficacy of lithium in the acute mania was readily demonstrated (mania has a very low placebo-response rate), larger studies were needed to determine whether long-term use was warranted to help prevent recurrence. In addition, guidelines for antidepressant use in bipolar patients was not yet available. In 1975, Quitkin, Rifkin, and I[14] reviewed the existing literature describing controlled studies of lithium and antidepressant use for prophylaxis in mood disorders. We found there was good evidence that lithium protects bipolar patients from recurrences of mania, and evidence suggestive of a similar effect for bipolar, as well as unipolar, depressions. The limited research to date also suggested that antidepressants could help reduce recurrence among unipolar depressed patients.

In the late 1970s, I was one of a group of investigators[15] who undertook to investigate the benefits of lithium and antidepressants among unipolar and bipolar patients. We split the bipolar group into bipolar type I (depressions alternating with mania) and bipolar type II (depressions alternating with hypomania) subgroups, as there was growing evidence that these two groups may have distinct pathophysiologies. The unipolar and bipolar II patients were randomly assigned under double-blind conditions to one of four treatment groups: lithium plus imipramine, lithium plus placebo, imipramine plus placebo, and double placebo. Bipolar I patients were assigned to treatment with either combined lithium-imipramine or lithium-placebo. We found that lithium was of benefit in all groups, reducing the frequency of recurrence of hypomania or mania and depression. In fact, even among the unipolar depressed patients, lithium was superior to imipramine in preventing recurrences of depression. For the bipolar type I patients, imipramine combined with lithium provided superior protection against recurrences of depression, but among the female patients imipramine was also associated with an increased risk of breakthrough mania.

In 1974, Rifkin, Quitkin, Blumberg, and I[16] undertook a study of thyroid function among two groups of patients randomly assigned to lithium and then placebo, or vice versa. We found clear evidence that lithium interferes with the release of thyroid hormone. This was the first study to test a single diagnostic group under controlled conditions, lending greater strength to the conclusion that it is lithium and not the illness itself that caused the reduction in thyroid function in Irene and other patients. Routine evaluation of thyroid function among patients receiving lithium is now the standard of care. Because of the negative effects of low thyroid function for patients with waning thyroid hormone levels, replacement therapy is often critical for the maintenance of mood stability.

Although the main findings in these studies have now been replicated, much additional work has been done since—work that has helped to refine rational treatment strategies for our patients with bipolar illness. One interesting development has been the finding of increased mood cycling in some patients exposed to long-term antidepressant treatment. A similar risk of *rapid cycling* has been reported among patients with borderline thyroid functioning. Both of these phenomena may have figured in Irene's course, although the removal of lithium from her treatment regimen has confounded the evidence.

### Notes

1. Freud, S. (1955). The disposition to obsessional neurosis: A contribution to the problem of choice of neurosis. In *Standard edition of the complete psychological works of Sigmund Freud,* Vol. XXII. Translated and edited by J. Strachey. London: Hogarth, p.317.

2. For summary and review see Goodwin, F.K., & Jamison, K.R. (1990). *Manic depressive illness* (pp. 134–138). New York: Oxford University Press.

3. Post, R.M., Rubinow, D.R., & Ballenger, J.C. (1986). Conditioning and sensitization in the longitudinal course of affective illness. *British Journal of Psychiatry, 149,* 191–201.

4. Wehr, T.A., Sack, D.A., Rosenthal, N.E., & Cowdry, R.W. (1988). Rapid cycling affective disorder: Contributing factors and treatment responses in 51 patients. *American Journal of Psychiatry, 145,* 179–184.

5. Himmelhoch, J.M. (1992). The sources of characterological presentations of mixed bipolar states. *Clinical Neuropharmacology, 15,* Suppl. 1, A:630A–631A.

6. Koukopoulos, A., Reginaldi, D., Laddomada, P., Floris, G., Serra, G., & Tondo, L. (1980). Course of the manic-depressive cycle and changes caused by treatments. *Pharmakopsychiatr Neuropsychopharmakol, 13,* 156–167.

7. Cho, J.T., Bone, S., Dunner, D.L., Colt, E., & Fieve, R.R. (1979). The effect of lithium treatment on thyroid dysfunction in patients with primary affective disorder. *American Journal of Psychiatry, 136,* 115–116.

8. Cowdry, R.W., Wehr, T.A., Zis, A.P., & Goodwin, F.K. (1983). Thyroid abnormalities associated with rapid-cycling bipolar illness. *Archives of General Psychiatry, 40,* 414–420.

9. Bauer, M.S., & Whybrow, P.C. (1990). Rapid cycling bipolar affective disorder II: Treatment of refractory rapid cycling with high-dose levothyroxine: a preliminary study. *Archives of General Psychiatry, 47,* 435–440.

10. Akiskal, H.S. (1980). External validating criteria for psychiatric diagnoses: Their application in affective disorders. *Journal of Clinical Psychiatry, 41,* 6–15.

11. Koukopoulos, A., Caliari, B., Tundo, A., Minnai, G., Floris, G., Reginaldi, D., & Tondo, L. (1983). Rapid cyclers, temperament, and antidepressants. *Comparative Psychiatry, 24,* 249–258.

12. Klein, D.F. (1974). Endogenomorphic depression: A conceptual and terminological revision. *Archives of General Psychiatry, 31,* 447–454.

13. Quitkin, F.M., Gittelman-Klein, R., Rifkin, A., & Klein, D.F. (1975). Atypical signs of relapse in affective disorders. *Diseases of the Nervous System, 36,* 145–146.

14. Quitkin, F.M., Rifkin, A., & Klein, D.F. (1976). Prophylaxis of affective disorders: Current status of knowledge. *Arch of Gen Psychiatry, 33,* 337–341.

15. Quitkin, F.M., Kane, J.M., Rifkin, A., Ramos-Lorenzi, J.R., Saraf, K., Howard, A., & Klein, D.F. (1981). Lithium and imipramine in the prophylaxis of unipolar and bipolar II depression: A prospective, placebo-controlled comparison. *Psychopharm Bulletin, 17,* 142–144.

16. Rifkin, A., Quitkin, F.M., Blumberg, A.G., & Klein, D.F. (1974). The effect of lithium on thyroid functioning: A controlled study. *Journal of Psychiatric Research, 10,* 115–120.

## Recommended Readings

Goodwin, F.K., & Jamison, K.R. (1990). *Manic depressive illness.* New York: Oxford University Press.

Jamison, K.R. (1993). *Touched by fire: Manic-depressive illness and the artistic temperament.* New York: Free Press.

Klein, D.F., & Wender, P.H. (1993). *Understanding depression: A complete guide to its diagnosis and treatment.* New York: Oxford University Press.

Klein, D.F. (1974). Endogenomorphic depression: A conceptual and terminological revision. *Archives of General Psychiatry, 31,* 447–454.

# 11

## About The Author

*Albert Ellis* *has a Ph.D. in clinical psychology from Colum-*
*bia University, is the president of the Albert Ellis Institute for*
*Rational Emotive Behavior Therapy in New York, and is the*
*founder of Rational Emotive Behavior Therapy (REBT) and*
*the grandfather of Cognitive Behavior Therapy (CBT). He*
*was an innovator of sex and relationship therapy starting in*
*1943, a practicing psychoanalyst from 1947 to 1953, and*
*the pioneer practitioner of REBT and CBT starting in Janu-*
*ary 1955.*

*At first, he was greatly reviled because of his forthright*
*studies of sexuality, his forceful espousal of active-directive*
*psychotherapy, and his outstanding use of cognition and con-*
*structivism in REBT theory and practice. But he refused to*
*give into widespread condemnation of his views and contin-*
*ued to vigorously promulgate REBT and CBT methods and*
*they have become some of the most popular and empirically*
*substantiated modes of psychological treatment. In the pro-*
*cess, he has won many of the highest academic and profes-*
*sional awards, including those of the American Psychological*
*Association, the American Counseling Association, the Associ-*
*ation for the Advancement of Behavior Therapy, and the*
*American Humanist Association.*

# Flora: A Case of Severe Depression and Treatment with Rational Emotive Behavior Therapy

**About**

**The**

**Disorder**

A person with major depressive disorder experiences acute, but time-limited, episodes of severe depressive symptoms. First and foremost, such episodes involve a dysphoric mood whose intensity far outweighs the ordinary ups and downs of everyday life. The dysphoric mood may appear as extreme dejection or a dramatic loss of interest in most aspects of life. Depressive episodes last continually for at least two weeks, during which time the individual suffers a variety of symptoms. Not only does the individual feel emotionally deflated, but there are a number of physical symptoms that accompany the dysphoria. These can include a slowing down of bodily movement or, paradoxically, an agitated physical state in which behavior has a frenetic quality. Eating disturbances are common and people experiencing a depressive episode also show a significant change in their sleeping patterns.

Low self-esteem and feelings that they deserve punishment are cognitive symptoms that also characterize depression. The tendency to dwell on one's past mistakes may lead people with depression to become tyrannized by guilt and unable to believe that they are ever really doing well enough. Unable to think clearly or to concentrate, people in a depressive episode may be unable to make the most insignificant of decisions.

Dr. Ellis has a unique perspective on the causes and treatment of depression. He brings together very different techniques in which the therapist plays a central role in collaborating with the client.—*Eds.*

# CONFRONTING PHILOSOPHIC ABSOLUTISM

Flora came to see me after she had attended two of my Friday Night Workshops at the Institute for Rational Emotive Therapy in New York and had been struck with the fact that I was extremely active and directive in the course of interviewing volunteers with live problems and quickly got to the main philosophic sources of their disturbances. She had been in psychoanalytic therapy with three different analysts for the past 10 years and was amazed at my ability to zero in on people's neurotic difficulties in a half-hour public session, showing them what they seemed to be telling themselves created most of their problems, and then demonstrating how they could change their absolutistic musts and demands by making them only into strong preferences, and thereby quickly stop upsetting themselves. Flora's analysts had mainly listened to her complaints during the past 10 years, had formed intense relationships with her, and had endlessly explored her early childhood and her other family relationships, but they had not done much to reveal her self-defeating philosophies and to help her dispute and act against them.

## Initial Presentation

"I was particularly impressed," Flora said in the first few minutes of her first session with me, "that you always seemed to know exactly what the volunteers at your workshops were thinking to upset themselves, and that you quickly helped them to see these thoughts for themselves. What was also startling in the case of each of the four people I saw you work with, was that you always suspected that they were not only disturbed, but also disturbed about their disturbances. In all my years of psychoanalytic therapy, this was never quite pointed out to me; and now that I've seen you point it out to several others, all of whom agreed that you were right, I'm beginning to see that this is also one of my main problems. I have not only been anxious for practically my whole life, but I have also been seriously depressed. After watching you in action with several people, I'm beginning to suspect that my depression and my feelings of great inadequacy that go with it mainly stem from my horror of being anxious— from continually putting myself down for my anxiety. I may be wrong, but this is the way it now seems to me, and I want to check this out with you and use your system of Rational Emotive Behavior Therapy—which I see is in many ways the opposite of psychoanalysis—to finally overcome my depression. Also, of course, to get rid of my lifelong feelings of anxiety."

I was very happy that Flora had been benefitting from merely observing my public therapy sessions with several of my Friday Night Workshop volunteers. I thought, from the start, that she was probably already getting on the right track—after years of being sidetracked from it by her classical psychoanalytic therapy—and that, with her cooperation, we might quickly get to the root of her neurotic problems and discover what she could do to work at overcoming them.

Like most of my regular clients, as well as the many people I see for public therapy sessions each year, Flora had two major forms of disturbances: First, her original disturbance, which led to severe and almost steady anxiety; and second, her disturbance about her disturbance, which led to serious feelings of depression, including frequent suicidal ideation, about her original problems.

According to the theory of Rational Emotive Behavior Therapy (REBT), most people are like Flora in this important respect. They consciously and unconsciously choose to upset themselves by taking some of their important desires and goals—such as to perform well and to be loved and accepted by others—and they irrationally (that is, self-defeatingly) make them into grandiose demands: "Because it is good for me to succeed and to win others' approval, I *absolutely must* do so, and it is *horrible* when I don't!" Then, when their unrealistic necessitizing—or what I call musturbation—makes them feel quite disturbed, and often to act in destructive ways, they note how self-sabotaging they are, take their *preference* for not behaving that way and make it into another dogmatic *demand*: "I *absolutely must* not feel disturbed and I *ought not* behave foolishly!" They then get—or rather make themselves—upset about their upsetness, and create an emotional problem that is much worse than their original one.[1]

Not all people and all clients, of course, do this. But probably the majority of them do—as I often quickly show them. I found it refreshing, therefore, that Flora, in her first interview with me, was beginning to see this important facet of human disturbance for herself, and that her attendance at my Friday Night Workshop was already beginning to pay off.

## Case History

Flora was a 48-year-old manager of a dress shop who had been anxious since about day one of her life. Her father, an accountant, and her mother, a school teacher, had been very happy to have her as their only child, had given her emotional support all her life, and were still happily married themselves. But they were both highly anxious people: The mother was quite hypochondriacal and the father worried incessantly about having enough money for his approaching retirement, even though the family's financial condition was unusually secure. On both sides of her family, her aunts and uncles and grandparents tended to be well-functioning people, but often very anxious. Several of them were also depressed.

Flora, like her parents, married in her early twenties, constantly worried about her husband being unfaithful, and felt devastated when, after 18 years of marriage, he actually ran off with his secretary, saying that he no longer could stand Flora's pandemic anxiety and her constant checking on his activities. Her 22-year-old son also tended to keep a distance from her, though he said he loved her, because she kept nagging him to lead a highly respectable life and to avoid getting into any trouble.

After her husband divorced her, Flora was so hurt and depressed that she stayed out of the dating scene for a few years, although several men were attracted to her and wanted to form a close relationship. She finally started dating Joe, a 50-year-old widower who also was wary of deep involvements. He saw her every Saturday night, enjoyed being with her sexually and companionably, but refused to get any closer. She convinced herself that this was all right, but she really yearned for a closer relationship and was afraid to talk to Joe about this, for fear that he would stop seeing her completely.

Recently, another suitor, Ed, showed great interest in Flora, and even talked about living with her and marrying her when his divorce became final. But Flora was very anxious about seeing Ed, because she would ultimately have to tell Joe about it and might end up losing both of them. Ed, though a better candidate for a close relationship than Joe, had monetary difficulties, and Flora was afraid that if she decided to live with him, she might not be able to continue enjoying her middle-class life-style and that she would have great anxiety about their monetary difficulties. So she saw Ed, who lived 50 miles away, occasionally, but still saw Joe every Saturday and felt guilty about having sex with both of them.

## Diagnosis

Flora was a college graduate, had done well in school, and I judged her to have high average intelligence. On the Millon Multiaxial Inventory II, her main high scores were for Anxiety, Depression, and Avoidant Personality. Her *DSM-IV* diagnosis is as follows.

| | |
|---|---|
| Axis I: | • Generalized anxiety disorder |
| | • Recurrent depressive disorder |
| Axis II: | • Avoidant personality disorder |
| Axis III: | • Irritable bowel syndrome |
| Axis IV: | • Relationship difficulties |
| Axis V: | • GAF = 55 |

## Case Formulation

Flora's case was pretty much as she herself presented it during our first session and was similar to hundreds of cases of anxiety, depression, and avoidance that I have seen over the years. For both biological and environmental reasons, she first had severe performance anxiety. Like most other people in the white middle-class culture in which she was raised, she wanted to do well in school, in her social relations, in her marriage, and in her subsequent life. But she almost always raised her strong preference for doing so into an absolutistic demand: "I *absolutely must* succeed at the important things that I do, I *have to* be seen as competent and as being a nice person by significant others, and I *must* have a guarantee that these others will continue to like and love me and never reject me. If I don't succeed in these respects, I am really an incompetent and unlovable person. So I must always make sure that I am doing well and am respected and loved." Flora's demands for guarantees in these respects made her continually anxious and produced constant feelings that, even when she was doing well, she was not doing well enough, and therefore she was never really an adequate and acceptable individual.

In addition to her steady performance and relationship anxiety, Flora also had some degree of discomfort anxiety or low frustration tolerance. She irrationally believed that she had to be comfortable and must not be frustrated or deprived of life comforts. Thus, she strongly believed "I must get my important wants fulfilled and must not be deprived. It's *awful* when I am balked or thwarted, and *I can't stand it!*" She consequently was angry and upset when the conditions of her life were not going well and when people (such as her ex-husband) deprived her of what she wanted—and presumably *should* have![2]

Flora clearly was damning herself on two levels: First, for not doing well enough in her own life and wanting guaranteed approval from others; and second, for making herself so anxious about these "horrible inadequacies." She was also damning life, and especially her love life, for often being *"too* difficult." We explored her rage against others, including her ex-husband, which people like her often create. But although she seemed to be at times angry at them, she was much more angry at herself for *her* "awful failings."[3]

## Course of Treatment

REBT is unusually philosophic, because its ABCs of emotional disturbance assume that practically all people, when they suffer from or think about adversities (A's) and feel as a consequence (Cs) severely upset, have conscious and/or unconscious beliefs (Bs) which largely "cause" their upsetness. Their Bs include, first, rational preferences—such as, "I don't *like* failing, and getting rejected and *wish* that I succeeded." Second, they include irrational musts and demands—"Therefore I *must* not fail or I'm no good!" "My living conditions *must* be better than they are, or else my life is horrible."

REBT does not question clients' goals and preferences, but helps them clearly see their rigid musts and demands and change them back to preferences—for example, "No matter how much I'd *like* to succeed, I don't *have* to do so, and I'm okay *as a person* even when I fail."

To help people make this kind of profound philosophical change, and to give up their grandiose *demandingness*, REBT uses a number of cognitive, emotive, and behavioral methods and is therefore always multimodal. Scores of studies have shown that REBT, along with Beck's Cognitive Therapy and Meichenbaum's Cognitive-Behavior Therapy, has been effective with many individuals with severe anxiety, depression, rage, and other disturbances.[4]

I therefore used several cognitive methods of therapy with Flora and taught her how to use them between sessions and after therapy ended. I especially showed her how to Dispute (at point D) her irrational Bs and how to change them. For example, "Why *must* I not foolishly make myself anxious about not succeeding and not being approved?" Answer: "There's no reason why I *must not* be anxious, though I would highly *prefer* to stop creating such feelings." "Why is it *terrible* for me to fail at important things and get rejected?" Answer: "It isn't. It's distinctly *unfortunate* and *inconvenient*, but I can still accept myself and lead an enjoyable life."

When Flora kept Disputing her irrational Bs, she began to feel sorry and disappointed about her feelings of anxiety—but not depressed and self-deprecating about having them. Once she accepted herself *with* her anxiety, she found it relatively easy to also accept herself when she failed or got rejected, and to reduce most of her original anxiety and feelings of inadequacy.

Flora was also taught to use several use other cognitive methods of REBT.

### Rational Coping Statements

She worked out, wrote down, and steadily told herself several coping statements, such as: "I *want* other people to like me, but I do not *need* their approval." "I'm a fallible human who often does foolish *things,* but I'm never, never *a rotten fool* for doing them!"

### Recordings

Flora recorded our sessions together and listened to each of them several times to get their full *impact.*

### Psychoeducational Study

She read a number of REBT books and pamphlets and listened to cassettes of lectures and workshops. She kept attending my Friday Night Workshops and other Institute Public Workshops.

### Modeling

She modeled herself after friends and relatives who were more rational than she was, after effective people she read about, and to some extent after my own remaining unupset when she resisted my disputing her irrational beliefs.

### Philosophy

Flora worked on acquiring the philosophy of tolerance, of accepting human fallibility, and of long-range instead of short-range, hedonism.

Flora kept vigorously using several REBT emotive-experiential methods, such as the following.

### Rational Emotive Imagery

She imagined some of the worst things that might happen to her—such as failing at an important project—let herself feel very anxious or depressed about this, and then worked at changing her disturbed feelings to healthy negative ones, such as sorrow and disappointment.

### Shame-attacking Exercises

She deliberately did some foolish and "shameful" things in public and made herself feel *un*ashamed and only sorry and regretful about doing them and being criticized by others for doing so.

### Forceful Coping Statements

She said to herself, very forcefully, many rational statements like: "I really *want* to have things go my way, but they never, never *have to!* I can *still* definitely lead a fine life when I am frustrated!"

### Forceful Disputing of Irrational Beliefs

She stated, on a tape recorder, self-defeating beliefs, such as "I *must* be liked by all significant people at all times!" and she then very strongly disputed them until she truly disbelieved them.

### Reverse Role Playing

I took the role of Flora, held on vigorously to some of her dysfunctional Beliefs, and gave her practice in vigorously talking *me* out of them.

### Unconditional Self-Acceptance

I unconditionally accepted Flora, even when she did badly and didn't do the REBT homework that she had agreed to do. But I also showed her how to unconditionally accept herself *whether or not* she performed well and *whether or not* other people (including myself) respected and approved of her.

### Interpersonal Relating

Because Flora had an avoidant personality disorder, and was particularly distrustful of men, I at first refrained from attempting to get her attached to me and perhaps resistant to such an attachment. I showed her that I liked her for her intelligence and honest efforts to change herself, but was neither going to be fatherly (I was 30 years older than she was) nor husbandly. I was very honest with her about how disturbed I thought she was, but showed confidence that she could overcome her disturbance. I indicated that seeing her was a good learning experience for me, because her depression about her anxiety tested my theory of the importance of secondary disturbances and gave me a chance to partially validate this theory. So I made her into a collaborator, a kind of co-therapist who would look into herself for the data that might confirm or deny my theory, report these data back to me, and help me check on and expand my theory. She seemed to appreciate this collaborator role and became much more trustful of me than she had been of any of her previous therapists. Her trusting me seemed to help her be more trustful of the two main men in her life. In turn, I liked and trusted her for helping me to check on one of my own favorite theories.

Flora and I also used a number of REBT behavioral homework assignments which she agreed to do in between sessions, especially these:

### In vivo Desensitization

She tried "risky" situations, like telling both Joe and Ed that she was dating the other man and would continue to do so until she made up her mind which of them, if either one, she chose to be monogamous with.

### Staying in Difficult Situations while Working on her Upsetness

She deliberately kept having sex with both partners until she stopped putting herself down for doing so, and then decided which one of them was better for her.

### Reinforcement

She reinforced herself when she did her cognitive and emotional homework by allowing herself to spend money on herself only *after* she did it. When she ate too many sweets and gained more weight than she wanted to, she punished herself by restricting her social life until she cut down on her food indulgences.

### Skill Training

I talked with Flora about her methods of relating to and managing her relationships with men and showed her how she could be more assertive without being aggressive.

## Outcome of the Case

Flora had 12 sessions of REBT, over a period of four and a half months. We first worked on her self-deprecation for her symptoms and helped her unconditionally accept herself *with* her severe anxiety. Once she was able to do this, she was also able to stop making herself anxious and self-deprecating when she didn't perform "well enough" and when other people didn't accept her as well as she presumably *should* have induced them to do.

Flora actually took only a couple of months to start accepting herself unconditionally, in spite of her long-standing anxiety and not doing well enough and experiencing rejections by significant others. So she did remarkably well in achieving unconditional self-acceptance, which is almost always a prime goal of REBT.

Paradoxically, she had more difficulty in achieving the second important goal that is usually worked for in effective therapy: achieving higher frustration tolerance or long-range hedonism. When she reduced her ego-demandingness, she kept insisting that life—and sometimes other people—absolutely must give her what she wanted when she wanted it. But by continuing to dispute these irrational beliefs on her own and by continuing to use REBT materials and workshops, she ultimately decreased her whining about life's "horrors" and made herself less self-indulgent and more disciplined. Three years after ending therapy, she still comes regularly to my Friday Night Workshops. In the discussion period after I conduct a public session with a volunteer, Flora often helpfully presents some of her own experiences and sensible suggestions to the person with whom I am counseling.

## EMPIRICAL CONTRIBUTIONS TO UNDERSTANDING DEPRESSION

My theory of REBT, which I derived mainly from philosophers, says that people largely depress themselves by taking their strong desires for success and relationships and irrationally raising them to absolutistic *musts* and demands. I tested this with many clients in the 1950s and found it to be basically sound. I also tested my theory that if depressed people give up their insistent "musts" and make them into preferences, they become significantly less depressed. I conducted a study in 1957 that showed that when severely depressed clients were treated by me in classical psychoanalytic, or analytic-oriented, or REBT, they functioned better in REBT, second best in psychoanalytically oriented therapy, and worst in classical psychoanalysis.

I collaborated on a number of other studies which showed that REBT was more successful with depressed individuals than other therapies or nontherapy groups. In the 1960s, Aaron Beck, using cognitive-behavior therapy (which is closely related to REBT), started to conduct many studies, as did other cognitive-behavior therapists, that found that REBT and related therapies are effective with severely depressed people.[5]

During the early 1960s, I saw, from studying my clients and from other research, that severe depression often included an endogenous element and was often accompanied by personality disorders which also had biological as well as environmental roots. Endogenous depression, as well as reactive depression, encourages many sufferers to denigrate themselves for being depressed and to develop low frustration tolerance. They define their disturbance as hopeless and thereby interfere with their working forcefully to cope with and alleviate it. I therefore developed several REBT techniques for helping depressed individuals (with and without personality disorders) to unconditionally accept themselves with their disturbances and to increase their tolerance for frustration.

Irene Elkin and her associates at the National Institute for Mental Health conducted a large collaborative study comparing cognitive therapy, interpersonal therapy, and the antidepressant imipramine. They also used a placebo control group and found few remarkable differences for the therapy effectiveness among all the groups studied. Individuals in all groups, including the placebo group, were given a good deal of support and encouragement.[6]

My interpretation of this and most other studies of depressed (and otherwise disturbed) people is that they really explore whether people *feel* better rather than *get* better through therapy. *Getting better,* as I define it, means not only reporting that they feel better at the end of therapy, but that they become less "disturbable" in the future, that is, less prone to disturb themselves about unfortunate events again. REBT specializes in trying to help people become less prone to depression and anxiety for the rest of their lives, and in this sense is different from Beck's cognitive therapy and Klerman's interpersonal therapy.[7] I predict that future studies of depression will provide empirical evidence to support REBT's *getting better* hypothesis. I hope that such research will soon be conducted.

## EMPIRICAL CONTRIBUTIONS TO TREATMENT OF DEPRESSION

Let me summarize how I usually treat individuals with severe symptoms of depression. I first try to determine, from their initial presentation and from their (and their family's) history, whether they are mainly reacting to serious losses, disabilities, or traumas, and therefore have reactive depression. Or, I ask myself, do they suddenly feel depressed, lethargic, and lose interest in many activities out of the blue—for no special reason? If so, do they have endogenous—or biochemically related—depression? I also ask them about present and past medication for emotional or other problems.

If I suspect that they have endogenous depression, I elicit more details about their personal and family history, and discuss with them the advisability of getting a psychopharmacological evaluation by a reputable psychiatrist and of considering antidepressant (and other) medication. If they resist medication— as many of them do—I tell them that we will try REBT by itself, which may work quite well *if* they strongly and persistently use it. But I also say to myself, "We'll both try to do our best with REBT. If this patient seems to be too disturbed, however, I'll see if I can later make it clear that it is also probably advisable to try medication." Occasionally, when my client is nonfunctional or suicidal, I refuse to continue appointments without psychiatric consultation, and sometimes insist on hospitalization.

By far most of the time, whether or not the client is on medication, I actively reveal the chosen and self-created irrational Beliefs that probably instigate the reactive depression—absolutistic shoulds, musts, and other grandiose demands on the patient, on others, and on external conditions. I briefly explain the ABCs of emotional disturbance—as I did in Flora's case. I show how the patient can independently discover irrational Bs, actively dispute self-depressing insistences, and considerably reduce them and change them, instead, to healthy preferences.

I particularly show my depressed clients that they frequently have two very debilitating musts: One, "I must perform important tasks well and be approved by people I find important, or else *I* am an *inadequate, worthless person!*" This kind of self-downing is most common in depressed people.

Two, "People and conditions I live with *absolutely must* treat me considerately and fairly, give me what I *really* want, and rarely seriously frustrate me! Or else, I *can't* stand it, my life is *awful,* and I can't enjoy it at all!"

I check my depressed clients to see whether they have either of these two main dysfunctional beliefs—or any of then innumerable variations—and rarely find that they don't have them. Even if they are endogenously depressed, their biochemistry encourages them to think crookedly, so that their thoughts, feelings, and behaviors are *all* involved in their moodiness. So I usually find some of their irrational beliefs in the first session to two, show them how these cause or contribute to their depression, and also start teaching them—as time permits—how to discover and dispute their self-sabotaging beliefs.

In other words, I quickly start teaching these clients some of the main principles of REBT, tell them to *un*devoutly consider them, and preferably to *experiment* with applying them to their own emotional problems. I explain, as I did in Flora's case, how undesirable activating events or adversities (As) often importantly *contribute* to clients' negative feelings and behaviors, but that their own beliefs (Bs) and interpretations about these As also lead to their disturbed consequences (Cs)—and particularly to their depressed feelings. Often, moreover, the As of their lives are presently unchangeable and uncorrectable. But not so their Bs. These are almost always in their control and therefore changeable. Thus, they can change their self-defeating *demands* that they *must* do better and *have to* experience better conditions to strong healthy *preferences*. If so, pop goes much of their depression!

I suspect, on the basis of my REBT theory and practice, that most of my depressed clients also use their grandiose musts to create important secondary disturbances. Thus, they often devoutly believe, "I *must not* feel depressed! It's *awful* to be depressed! I *can't stand* my depressed feelings and actions!" They thereby make themselves—yes, *make* themselves—depressed about their depression. Or anxious, guilty, or enraged about it. If so, they then have a double whammy—two symptoms for the price of one! Moreover, their depression *about* their depression usually interferes with their finding and unraveling their original irrational beliefs and blocks their making themselves better.

So I explore this important possibility, show my clients how to ferret it out for themselves, and if they find it to think, feel, and act against it. Thus, I show them how to first reduce their depression about their depression, and then to reduce or eliminate their original depression. Quite a trick! But I find that, interestingly enough, many of my clients are at first more likely to conquer their secondary symptom without too much trouble. However, they often feel fine about this and yet find it difficult to convince themselves that their original failures or losses are not awful, but only highly inconvenient. So it may take them a much longer time to overcome their primary depression.

As I note in Flora's case, I almost always employ a number of cognitive, emotive, and behavioral methods to help my depressed clients minimize their disturbances and their disturbance about these disturbances. This is because people think, feel, and act dysfunctionally; and their thoughts, feelings, and actions importantly interact with and exacerbate each other. Moreover, although practically all depressed people have significant similarities, they also are unique individuals in their own right. What works with one easily may not work with another. But REBT methods are so many and so varied that they provide much leeway to use different strokes for different folks. And I often do vary REBT techniques with each client.

"How long will it take," many of my clients ask me, "to overcome my depression?" I reply that it "depends on several important factors: first, on how depressed you are and for how long you have been disturbed; second, on whether your biochemistry is seriously out of whack; and third, on the kind, degree, and persistence of the adversities in your life. Over these kinds of factors, you have relatively little control. But you do have a great deal of choice of how you choose to think, feel, and behave about the adversities that afflict you. Like practically all humans, you are born and reared with two opposing tendencies. On the one hand, you are easily disturbable, and can upset yourself over both little and big things. On the other hand, you are born and raised with real tendencies to change and to correct your self-defeating behaviors. You are potentially proactive and self-actualizing, if you *use* your healthy potentialities."

"How do I do that?" many of my clients ask.

My response is, "By seeing and using three of REBT's main insights. Number 1: See what we have been talking about in these sessions. You largely, though never completely, help create your own depression and other disturbances. Especially when you are reactively depressed after suffering losses and failures. Number 2: No matter how and why you originally depressed yourself, you still, *today,* are thinking crookedly, feeling inappropriately, and acting dysfunctionally. So you are *continuing* to make yourself depressed and, often, depressed about your depression."

"I see. And the third insight for me to achieve?"

"Oh, yes, the important third insight. There is usually no way but work and practice—yes, much work and practice—for you to change your depressed thoughts, feelings, and actions. No magic. No miracles. Only much work and practice."

"So I have to push myself to change myself?"

"Yes, almost always. If you do, within a few weeks or months you will probably make yourself feel much better—much less depressed. No guarantees—but a high degree of probability. However, if you want to achieve what I call the *elegant solution* to your emotional problems and make yourself both less disturbed and less disturb*able,* that usually takes longer."

"And that is?"

"That is, use REBT so strongly and persistently that you first significantly reduce your depression. Then go on to make a profound philosophical-emotional change where you endorse your healthy goals, desires, and preferences and minimize your absolutistic musts, insistences, and demands."

"Can I really do this?"

"Not easily! But with continued work and practice, you can. If you do, you then will rarely depress yourself in the future—no, not never, but rarely. If and when you do, you will give yourself unconditional self-acceptance, refrain from putting yourself down, and return to using the kinds of REBT methods that you used to undepress yourself before."

"Sounds good."

"And fascinating. You control most of your emotional destiny. If you *think* you do and if you *work* at doing so."

Naturally, I don't convince all my depressed clients to make themselves significantly less depressed. Even when I do, I hardly help all of them to make themselves elegantly less disturb*able.* But I always try, and I often succeed. So do they.

### Notes

1. Dryden, W. (1995). *Brief rational emotive behavior therapy.* London: Wiley; Ellis, A. (1988). *How to stubbornly refuse to make yourself miserable about anything—yes, anything!* New York: Lyle Stuart; Ellis, A. (1994). *Reason and emotion in psychotherapy, Revised and Updated.* New York: Carol Publishing; Ellis, A. (1996). *Better, deeper, and more enduring brief therapy.* New York, Brunner/Mazel; Ellis, A. & Harper, R.A. (1997). *A Guide to Rational Living.* North Hollywood, CA: Wilshire; Walen, S., DiGiuseppe, R., & Dryden, W. (1992). *A Practitioner's guide to rational-emotive therapy.* New York: Oxford University Press.

2. Ellis, A. (1987). A sadly neglected cognitive element in depression. *Cognitive Therapy and Research, 11,* 121–146; Hauck, P.A. (1973). *Overcoming Depression.* Louisville, KY: Westminster.

3. Ellis, A. A sadly neglected cognitive element in depression. *op. cit.;* Ellis, A. *How to stubbornly refuse to make yourself miserable about anything—yes, anything!* op. cit.; Ellis, A. *Reason and Emotion in Psychotherapy, Revised and Updated.* op cit.; Hauck, P.A., *Overcoming Depression.* op. cit.

4. Hollon, S.D., & Beck, A.T. (1994). Cognitive and cognitive-behavioral therapies.

In A.E. Bergin & S.L. Garfield, (Eds.), *Handbook of psychotherapy and behavior change* (pp. 428–466). New York: Wiley; Lyons, L.C. & Woods, P.J., (1991). The efficacy of rational-emotive therapy: A quantitative review of outcome research. *Clinical Psychology Review, 11,* 357–369; McGovern, T.E., & Silverman, M.S., (1984). A review of outcome studies of rational-emotive therapy from 1977 to 1982. *Journal of Rational-Emotive Therapy, 2*(1), 7–18; Silverman, M.S., McCarthy, M., & McGovern, T.E. (1992). A review of studies of rational-emotive therapy from 1982–1989. *Journal of Rational-Emotive and Cognitive-Behavioral Therapy, 10*(3), 111–186.

    5. Beck, A.T., Rush, A.J., Shaw, B.F., & Emery, G. (1979). *Cognitive therapy of depression.* New York: Guilford Press, 1979.

    6. Beck, A.T., Rush, A.J., Shaw, B.F., & Emery, G. (1979) *op. cit.*; Elkin, I (1994). The NIMH treatment of depression collaborative research program: Where we began and where we are. In A.E. Bergin & S.L. Garfield (Eds.), *Handbook of psychotherapy and behavior change* (4th ed., pp. 114–139). New York: Wiley; Klerman, G.L., Weissman, M.M., Rounseville, B.J., & Chevron, E.S. (1984). *Interpersonal psychotherapy of depression.* New York: Basic Books.

    7. Ellis, A., *Reason and emotion in psychotherapy, Revised and updated,* op. cit.; Ellis, A., *Better, deeper, and more enduring brief therapy,* op. cit; Ellis, A., & Dryden, W. (1997). *The Practice of Rational Emotive Behavior Therapy* 2nd ed. New York: Springer; Ellis, A., Gordon, J., Neehan, M., & Palmer, S. (1997). *Stress Counseling: A Rational Emotive Behaviour Approach.* London: Cassell.

### Recommended Readings

The books included in the notes for this chapter by A.T. Beck, et al., M.E. Bernard, W. Dryden, A. Ellis, P.A. Hauck, G.L. Klerman, et al.; and S. Walen, et al. are recommended.

In addition:

Bloomfield, H.H., & McWilliams, P. (1994). *How to heal depression.* Los Angeles: Prelude Press.

Burns, D.D. (1980). *Feeling good.* New York: Morrow.

Ellis, A., & Tafrate, R.C. (1997). *How to control your anger before it controls you.* New York: Birch Lane Press.

Seligman, M.E.P. (1991). *Learned optimism.* New York: Knopf.

Simon J.L. (1993). *Good mood.* LaSalle, IL: Open Court.

# 12

## About the Author

*Bruce Bongar is Professor of Psychology at Pacific Gradu-
ate School and Consulting Professor of Psychiatry and the Behavioral Sciences at Stanford University School of Medicine.
He is the co-editor of the* Comprehensive Textbook of Psychotherapy *(Oxford, 1995) and author of* Suicide *(Oxford,
1993) and* The Suicidal Patient, *(American Psychological Association, 1991) and is Series Editor for the* Oxford Text-
books in Clinical Psychology. *Dr. Bongar is a diplomate of
the American Board of Professional Psychology, a chartered
psychologist of the British Psychological Society, and a fellow
of the American Psychological Association and the Academy
of Psychosomatic Medicine.*

# Mary at 16: A Case of Attempted Suicide

**About**

**the**

**Disorder**

Treatment of a suicidal person is one of the most challenging and troubling aspects of clinical work. A person who is suicidal has reached a crisis point so that taking his or her own life seems like the only available course of action. The clinician's initial task is to evaluate the suicidal person's risk and come up with a short-term plan that will defuse the crisis. Once the crises passes, the clinician and client can work together to address the underlying problem. Crucial to the success of this approach is the quality of the therapeutic relationship.

No formal diagnostic category in the *DSM-IV* exists that specifically applies to people who attempt suicide. Most, though, are seriously depressed, suffering from a mood disorder such as major depressive disorder. Suicidal behavior may also be associated with other disorders, such as schizophrenia, somatoform disorders, or anxiety disorders. Suicidality is also a prominent feature in some personality disorders, particularly borderline personality disorders, in which suicidal gestures and attempts are common.

The case of Mary illustrates the many complex features of treating people who are suicidal, particularly those whose life histories are marked by experiences of trauma. Dr. Bongar's treatment of Mary emphasizes the importance of being empathic and committed to the ultimate well-being of the client.—*Eds.*

## CONSULTING ON MARY'S SUICIDAL IDEATION

### Initial Presentation

Patient suicide is a terrifying specter for patients, their families, and the mental health professionals who care for them.

Several years ago, I was called by a local psychiatrist and asked to see "Mary," the 16-year-old patient in this case. Her psychiatrist at the local inpatient emergency psychiatry unit was terribly concerned about Mary's continued wish to die and her impulsive and angry behaviors. What he needed was a consultation to help his inpatient team sort out this complex case. More specifically, the young psychiatrist wanted me to perform a family consultation and evaluate Mary's suicidality in order to determine whether she could safely go home. The doctors and nurses on the inpatient unit were especially concerned about Mary's suicidal ideation, self-mutilation, previous suicide attempts, lack of self-worth, feelings of hopelessness and helplessness, use of alcohol to reduce her stress, and the intense levels of conflict in her family.

### Case History

Like many young suicidal patients, Mary had been admitted to the emergency unit because of suicidal ideation while intoxicated. Tragically, even at this young age, Mary already could be seen as an alcoholic with episodic bingeing, blackouts, and DTs (delirium tremens). She told the staff that she had been drinking for the last four years. She was dating an older high-school dropout who was also a drug abuser, and she had constant fights with her parents about this boyfriend. She was sexually active, and reported a half-dozen boyfriends since age 13. As often happens, Mary had a previous history of suicidal ideation and behavior. At age 13, she attempted to hang herself with a silver-plated studded belt buckle. Complicating the danger, a friend of Mary's actually completed suicide by hanging himself a few weeks before I saw her. Mary was in the 10th grade, on probation for the fourth time for trespassing and alcohol violations. At the age of 11, Mary had been raped and sodomized by her uncle. After her parents found out and reported this to the police, Mary had to testify against her uncle in a lengthy court proceeding. The uncle was later convicted and imprisoned. The patient's paternal grandfather had a history of substance abuse. Mary's father had his own drinking problems in the past.

Before I saw her, I checked the chart and her history. Mary had no previous history of psychotherapy except a session or two at the time of the rape with a sexual abuse counselor.

## Diagnosis

> Axis I: • Alcohol dependence
>
> • Adjustment disorder with mixed distur-
> bance of emotions and conduct
>
> Axis II: • Possibility of personality disorder not oth-
> erwise specified
>
> Axis III: • While there was no long-term medical
> disorder, the patient did have a history of
> delirium tremens
>
> Axis IV: • Primary support group (family conflict
> and lack of trust between patient and
> parents)
>
> • Social environment (conflict with boy-
> friend, running with "fast" crowd)
>
> • Education (poor performance in school)
>
> • Other (suicide attempts, close friend re-
> cently committed suicide
>
> Axis V: • GAF – 49

Mary met many of the criteria on Axis I of the DSM-IV (at that time, DSM-III-R) for alcohol dependence, and an adjustment disorder with mixed conduct problem. The staff were also concerned that Mary might suffer from a mild to moderate level of depression. There was also the possibility of a personality disorder not otherwise specified. There were no Axis III medical conditions.

## Case Formulation

In working with suicidal individuals like Mary, and with the families of suicidal patients over the years, I have always believed that it is essential to involve the family and patient as collaborative risk management partners.

In Mary's case, I believed it would be essential to provide pertinent information to both Mary and her family over the course of the assessment and during any subsequent treatment. This would allow not only active collaboration, but also would foster close monitoring of the patient's and family's concerns. Indeed, under the rules of informed consent, Mary and her family had a right to be told about the risks and benefits of the suggested course of action and of any reasonable alternative treatments. It has also been my experience, and that of other clinicians who work extensively with suicidal patients, that in the highly charged area of determination of elevated risk of suicide and subsequent precautionary action, both competent patients and their families should be provided with as much information as possible to allow them—except when it is clinically contraindicated by a toxic interpersonal matrix—to collaborate and participate as active partners in each facet of the treatment plan. What this meant was that I needed to involve Mary and her family in a detailed exploration of all available options, including a discussion of the nature and purpose of the proposed treatment, its risks and benefits, and the availability of alternative treatments and their risks and benefits.

## Course of Treatment and Outcome of the Case

I see therapy for patients such as Mary as the opportunity to translate our knowledge (albeit incomplete) of risk factors for suicide into a plan of action.[1] Treatment of patients who are at high risk for suicide should address those risk factors that are most likely to result in suicide.

To illustrate this approach, I have included a few selected segments from the transcript of the consultation with Mary and her family to provide an example of the information that might well be collected to determine elevated risk, and how a clinician involves the patient and family as active collaborators in the creation of a management/treatment plan.

> *Interviewer:*  Well, what do your folks know about what brought you here? I don't want to put words in anybody's mouth, but what do you think about all of this? It's pretty scary! It's pretty scary and pretty serious, too.
>
> *Father:*  It goes beyond pretty scary.
>
> *Interviewer:*  Yeah, I was trying to sort of not use very inflammatory words. It is incredibly scary to have your child come to a hospital and talk about damaging herself— that's one of the scariest things a parent can handle.
>
> *Mother:*  When she told us she tried choking herself with the belt, I guess she was also running razor blades across her wrist. I mean we didn't even suspect anything like that. We knew she was depressed, but I guess we both thought she had some type of handle on it and kept trying to reassure her that things are going to be better as soon as we move out and get our own house and stuff. But we didn't know it had reached that point where she would contemplate something like . . . we just didn't know, we had no idea and when she told us the other night we were both totally shocked, you know.
>
> *Interviewer:*  Um uh . . . Were you surprised that your parents were surprised?
>
> *Girl:*  I don't know what I thought. I don't know what I thought when they found out.

*Interviewer:* Did your brother know about this stuff?

*Girl:* He knew I was depressed before. But I don't think he knew about what I tried doing.

*Interviewer:* Have you ever tried to do more than just superficial cuts or hitting yourself?

*Girl:* No, the only thing was the belt, that was about it.

After extensive history-taking, and rapport-building with Mary and her family, the interviewer then proceeds to talk about the purpose of the interview—namely, discharge planning from the unit.

*Interviewer:* Cause and effect is something we always want to know the answer to. We all want to know why. We want to know why we're feeling a certain way, why we do certain things, and just based on the little time that we've spent together, one of the suspicions that I have is maybe underlying some of the feeling of harming yourself that you have, are some pretty deep feelings of being depressed. And I wonder if that's true, if sometimes you get real down in the dumps and you get real depressed.

*Girl:* Yeah. It all depends if too many things happen at one time.

*Interviewer:* A lot of stressful things happen. Then the feeling is to get real depressed. What about Mom? When she would get overloaded, would she feel depressed? Maybe that was one of the reasons that you (*Mother:* Oh, yes) that you turned to the pills and stuff like that.

*Mother:* Definitely. I was overwhelmed; I was trying to be the perfect person, trying to—my husband was gone a lot —trying to handle everything. And be perfect about it. Be perfect at work and be perfect at home—it was an overload—I had to realize that—and I didn't want to dump any of my problems on anybody, so I kept them to myself and it was. . . .

*Interviewer:* I guess what I'm trying to say, is that the most important thing that I would like to see everybody in this room do, is not look for any reasons why anybody has to blame themselves as to what is going on here. That usually when people do things that are bad for themselves, it is because they are in a lot of pain at the time. And my guess is that when you were opening that car door or when you were putting the dog collar on your neck or slashing yourself or burning yourself, it is because you were in a lot—you were just incredibly upset and in a lot of pain at that time. And the problem is that we sort of cope and grope to find ways to deal with these intense feelings of upset and we find solutions that maybe ain't the best possible solutions, but it seemed like a good idea at the time. I think that the critical thing is to say what are we going to do as a family. Not to have perfect solutions, but to follow through here, so that when you get in a lot of pain, I'm not going to pretend to you when you been here for—how many days you been here now . . . (*Girl:* 2, 3) are your problems cured, you're going to walk out of here and you'll fight with your boyfriend or something pisses you off or you're upset that evening, you're never going do anything to harm yourself or be depressed again.

**Girl:** I know I'm going to get upset again. I feel fine—I'm not going to do anything now.

**Interviewer:** Sure, sure—no, no, they wouldn't be discharging you if they thought you were. My concern is, there are ways to cope with pain that I think you haven't learned. I'm not saying that your life is going to be free from pain and that Mom and Dad know that life is full of failure and pain and people upsetting you, people disappointing you and things not going the way you want and one of the things that is tough to learn is how to roll with the punches. It doesn't mean that you won't want to take a drink or do something to calm yourself down. But my concern is that right now the main way that you have for dealing with this is to turn it on yourself. And maybe that's not such a great idea. I'm not suggesting that we're going to be able to replace it with anything right away—but that there are some things you can do in talking as a family and talking as an individual where you really can learn that when you feel in a lot of pain, and when you feel a lot of stress, there are ways to deal with this. And I am not saying they are going to be perfect ways, but the ways to just muddle through and hope until you feel a little bit better. That scares me when you tell me that when you get real angry that's when you feel hopeless. Is that how it feels?

**Girl:** It just feels like you want to fix it—somehow, sometimes you can't or it won't get fixed.

**Interviewer:** What's it, is it the pain?

**Girl:** Yeah, once—it's weird, like sometimes it will bother me where I can't sleep or if I can sleep I am wide awake in the morning and all I want to do is fix whatever is wrong. And when I can't fix it, it just drives me crazy or it hurts inside so.

**Interviewer:** It hurts inside. What is that feeling like?

**Girl:** Lonely—it's hard to explain.

**Interviewer:** You think your Mom or Dad or brother ever felt like that?

*Girl:* You know, sometimes I don't think so, because you don't have to fix everything. To me, in order to make myself better, I have to fix it; it has to be OK.

*Interviewer:* Do you ever think of asking if they ever felt that way?

*Girl:* No because they would say, you know, don't worry about it. I have to, I don't feel better till I fix it, till I know it's better, till it's fixed myself. You know something goes wrong, you know, I just feel I have to fix it, if I don't, I don't feel better. Sometimes I don't think they understand that.

*Interviewer:* That's a wide responsibility that you have taken on yourself.

*Father:* That's one of her problems. She becomes so obsessed with

*Mother:* It has to be fixed right now, we can't wait two hours, it can't wait till the next morning, it has to be right now.

*Father:* So the sun is going to come up tomorrow, you'll wake up and it may not bother you so much tomorrow as it does now.

*Mother:* But she says she can't sleep,

The family and the interviewer then spend some time talking about perfectionism, and Mary's being so hard on herself whenever she feels she has failed, or when a relationship is threatened.

The interviewer then turns to the practicalities of the discharge question.

*Interviewer:* Let's say hypothetically, that you get out of here and in a week or two, you get in a terrible fight with Sandy. Sandy is the guy you're going out with.

*Girl:* I don't think so anymore, but . . .

*Interviewer:* Let's say for the sake of argument, you guys make up, everything is OK—Mom rolls her eyes like "please, don't make up"—

*Mother:* You can use it, but that is not going to happen.

*Interviewer:* Well you never know, you know the story of Romeo and Juliet

*Mother:* Yeah, but he's no Romeo, let me tell you

*Interviewer:* He's your Romeo right now.

*Girl:* He can be really nice when he wants to.

*Interviewer:*   That's the sort of thing I am concerned about. You know what happened to Romeo and Juliet, don't you?

*Girl:*   I mean I can talk to people a lot, but even if I do, I mean they can't solve it for me. I mean they can help me, but it's . . .

*Interviewer:*   I want to talk with you when it hurts real bad.

*Girl:*   and what my feelings are to fix things. They can't, nobody can help me.

*Interviewer:*   Then you go in

*Girl:*   Nobody can help me—you can say whatever you want to say, you know tomorrow morning you'll feel better, or it can wait until tomorrow morning, but to me it can't.

*Interviewer:*   That takes on all the responsibility and you get a burden.

*Mother:*   That is right, she blames herself for everything that goes wrong.

*Father:*   Everything. Absolutely everything. A guy could have been a real jerk and done something wrong, but she'll say well it was my fault, so I have to fix it. When the guy obviously don't care and I went through all the stuff where she was to the point she was going to steal a truck and go down there and the guy couldn't even be bothered with her when she got there.

*Mother:*   She still felt it was her fault

*Father:*   She felt it was her fault.

*Interviewer:*   You're a real intense person, you know that, too intense. Do people tell you that you're real intense?

*Girl:*   No

*Interviewer:*   You think you're real intense?

*Girl:*   Maybe.

*Interviewer:*   You feel things intensely—you say that's true.

*Girl:*   Yes.

*Interviewer:*   That's not bad, it's just powerful—it's sort of like riding. Did you ride—have you ever ridden horses? In California, when you lived there, did people surf there at all? When I was a kid, we used to body surf in the water.

*Girl:*   I used to boogie board, surf all the time.

*Interviewer:*   Did you ever catch a wave, one that is real powerful?

*Girl:*   Like a really big wave?

*Interviewer:*   Yeah, and the more powerful it is, the harder it is to ride, to keep your balance. And that's what I'm talking about. I think with these feelings that you have—they are real intense—and there is nothing wrong with intense feelings, but I think that the way—whoever taught you to ride that boogie board as far as your feelings go didn't do a very good job. My guess is maybe that you taught yourself.

*Girl:*   Yeah, the boogie board.

*Interviewer:*   Ride the boogie board of your feelings. And I guess one of the things that—we have to stop in a few minutes—that I would like to talk with you about is—that there really are some good people who work as counselors and therapists, and my biggest concern is whether I can convince you that is true in the few minutes we have left. Whether you might be willing to take a chance at talking to somebody again after the bad experience you had with the rape counselor. Maybe even have Mom and Dad and your brother from time to time—all of you get together and talk about these things. How would you feel about that?

*Girl:*   All right, as long as I like the person.

*Interviewer:*   How about if we make that a condition that you get to say thumbs ups or thumbs down. 'Cause one of the things that we've learned as psychologists and psychiatrists is that there are all sorts of specific things that we can do, specific things that I can tell you, this is good, this is not good. But one of the most important things is that you got to feel OK talking with the person you're talking with. And if it doesn't feel right, it doesn't feel right. And you guys are the ones who decide whether it feels right. Not me. Not Dr. King, none of the other people on staff here. If you don't like talking to somebody and you don't feel right talking with them, you feel like they don't understand you, if you feel like this is not going well, and this is making you feel worse, guess who's in charge. Not us. You—and the problem is that psychologists and psychiatrists understand that—they realize that—that they got to check in all the time, make sure that we're actually tuned in and know what is going on. Doesn't mean that they are always going to say things that make you happy, or that we won't piss you off, because you partly have to say things that people don't necessarily want to hear. But I think the critical thing that the ball got dropped the last time you ever had to see a counselor or therapist, and my biggest concern is that we get you linked up with somebody real good who you, in particular, feel this person is OK—I can talk to them, they are not a jerk, they're not pissing me off every time I go in there—I think if that connection can be made that is a critical step, for what goes on afterwards. Again, I don't think it's going to solve all your problems, I don't think it's going to solve what's going on with Sandy or with the drinking or anything right away, but I think at least it is the initial step.

*Father:*   I have a problem with that. We're just concerned when Mary leaves here today she has no tools to . . . I mean the reason she's here because she thought of taking her life, it was—she was so intense and so angry when she came out with this, she just scared us and the first thing I said, "You're going to the hospital."

*Mother:*   She admitted that she didn't know

*Father:*   And didn't know that she needed the help—it's something she knows she got a problem and she needs the help and she's been here for two or two and a half days, somebody spoke to her yesterday for 15 minutes—our concern is, if she's not here, I mean this place is fine for the purpose it serves, which is to make sure that they don't hurt themselves. Our question is, where does she go from here? Do you send her back home and say we'll see you in a week? We'll start some kind of therapy. The problem is like my wife said, she has no tools at all. I think that is the heart of the problem she has.

*Interviewer:*   I think there are two critical steps. The first is to get Mary linked up with somebody she feels is OK. Second is to get the whole family linked up with somebody you all think is OK and that you can talk to. And by that I mean someone that you can call any time day or night.

*Father:*   You mean me, too?

*Interviewer:*   Yes, and I mean you, too. So that if you were seeing somebody and felt like it got too much, then instead of thinking about harming yourself, then you go and you pick up the phone and you call them up and you know it might take 15, 20 minutes or a hour to get them, but they're going to call you back. And that they're going to talk with you about what is going on. And then if you, Mom and Dad, are concerned about things, you have somebody to call, too. Not just once a week, but you have that as a resource, so you have some backstopping is what I am saying. I think the critical thing is for us to make sure that the ball doesn't get dropped, that you get linked up with somebody good and the family gets linked up with somebody good. You have Central Health Clinic Care through your insurance?

*Mother:*   That's right.

*Interviewer:*   OK, that is fortunate because they have some very good people over there.

*Mother:*   I don't know. I saw someone over there a couple years ago and I didn't think he was so hot.

*Interviewer:*   Let me suggest something. I know the Chief at Central well. I've known him for many years. And the Director of the Clinical Services, I know. Would it be OK if I talk with them and see who is available and see if we can get you somebody who is at the top of their hit parade rather than at the bottom of the hit parade and see if I can coordinate that a little bit? Because everything we talked about here is confidential, so I need your permission to do that. The other thing that I'm going to ask is what did it feel like talking with me today?

*Girl:*   It feels good.

*Interviewer:*   How did that feel? (Interviewer looks at other family members) It felt OK?

*Mother:*   Oh yeah.

*Girl:*   There's a real nice lady here I liked. I forgot what she looks like. She came in and talked to me earlier and she had this blue thing on or something, curly hair, red-brown hair, she's a real nice lady.

*Interviewer:*   (in a joking manner): So it has to do with curly red hair, you like my red curly hair? That is just a coincidence—you liked talking with curly haired therapists? I'm just kidding. Let me see what I can do to make sure the ball doesn't get dropped this time. Sometimes you have to go through a couple of psychiatrists or psychologists before you click. Hopefully, you don't marry the first person you date and yet, I think, if you are seeking services, people sometimes feel like wall plaster, I'm stuck with whomever they assign me. And that is not the truth. If you went to a dentist, this happened to me, where every time I went to this dentist, I would feel so awful afterwards that I would be in pain for days. And finally I realized that it was the dentist's problem not mine, and I switched dentists and I found a decent dentist who—I still don't like going to the dentist—but at least I wasn't taking all those aspirin and other stuff for two or three days after I went to the dentist—the incompetent dentist just didn't have the touch. Should have been baking bread. And with your permission, let me see what I can do to try to get you both individually and as a family linked up.

Mary and her family kept their appointment at the Central clinic and participated in both individual and family sessions. The clinic also involved Mary in a special group for teenagers who had problems with alcohol and substance abuse.

## EMPIRICAL CONTRIBUTIONS TO UNDERSTANDING YOUTH SUICIDE

For all ages, the combined suicide rate in the United States during this century has remained at approximately 12 per 100,000 individuals.[2] However, suicide rates have increased alarmingly for youth (those aged 15 to 24). Although the suicide rates among the young are lower than those older age groups (especially men over the age of 35), the rates for older persons have decreased during this same time period.[3] Here it is important to note that, although, in the United States, suicide accounts for roughly 2% of all deaths, it accounts for more than 15% of the deaths among adolescents.[5]

Smith and Crawford[6] found, in a study of "normal" high school students, that 62.6% of their subjects reported some degree of suicidal ideation or action, and 8.4% had made an actual attempt. Holinger and Offer[7] have documented a significant positive correlation between adolescent suicide rates, changes in the adolescent population, and changes in the proportion of adolescents in the population.

Traditionally, suicide has been considered a mental health problem among older white males. However, since 1980, more than half of all completed suicides occurred among persons under the age of 40, according to the Alcohol, Drug Abuse, and Mental Health Administration.[3] The National Conference on Risk Factors for Youth Suicide found that for youths (ages 15 to 24), there were a number of risk factors for suicide, among them the following:[3]

1. Substance abuse, both chronic and acute, within the context of the suicidal act (as well as substance abuse as an exacerbating factor in concurrent psychiatric illness), dramatically increased the risk of completed suicide.

2. Other specific psychiatric diagnostic categories that placed youth at risk were affective disorders, schizophrenia, and borderline personality.

3. Familial characteristics, including genetic traits such as a predisposition to affective disorders, increased the risk.

4. Low concentrations of the serotonin metabolite 5-hydroxyindoleacetic acid (5-HIAA), and the dopamine metabolite homovanillic acid (HVA) in the cerebrospinal fluid.

5. Parental loss and family disruption, along with being a friend or family member of a suicide victim, a history of previous suicidal behavior, impulsiveness and aggressiveness, media emphasis on suicide, homosexuality, rapid sociocultural change, and ready access to lethal methods were also clearly linked to youth suicide. (pp. 1–59)

## EMPIRICAL CONTRIBUTIONS TO THE TREATMENT OF THE SUICIDAL PATIENT

For a number of years, I have believed in an integrative approach to the understanding and care of suicidal patients and their families.[8] I do so in the belief that the integration of this voluminous material can best occur in practice, not merely by virtue of integrating theoretical constructs from different schools of thought, but also by providing a more comprehensive framework that would encompass the clinical observables.[9]

In the case of Mary and other troubled young people, it is important to understand that when clinicians select assessment criteria and then implement an appropriate intervention strategy with such suicidal patients, they may find that traditional theories of psychotherapy, and traditional psychiatric diagnostic categories, are of limited practical value in precisely assessing suicidal risk. In particular, I have found that with patients like Mary, it is crucial that one remembers one's own humanness. Simply put, I show Mary and her family that I care deeply about her and her safety. It is not uncommon for clinicians who see many suicidal patients to truly extend themselves in their management efforts to demonstrate their commitment to doing whatever needs to be done to keep the patient alive—that every effort will be made to help the patient to decrease the amount of pain, perturbation, and lethality.

Furthermore, in working with Mary, one of the key factors in assessing her risk of suicide and determining her safety was the quality of the therapeutic alliance that I had established with her and her family.[7,10] The presence or absence of a good working therapeutic alliance can be utilized as an ongoing and robust measure of the treatment's effect on the patient's vulnerability to suicide.[7]

Unlike a number of more straightforward clinical problems, working with suicidal patients and their families is a high-risk, highly individualized endeavor. As clinicians, we would do well to heed Professor Edwin Shneidman's basic maxim for working with suicidal patients,[11] a rule that borrows heavily from the "philosophy of crisis intervention—namely, to see our involvement with the suicidal patient not as an attempt to ameliorate the patient's entire personality or to cure all emotional illness, but rather as an attempt to meet the immediate need to keep the person alive."[7]

## Notes

1. Brent, D.A., & Kolko, D.J. (1990). The assessment and treatment of children and adolescents at risk for suicide. In S.J. Blumenthal & D.J. Kupfer (Eds.), *Suicide over the life cycle: Risk factors, assessment, and treatment of suicidal patients* (pp. 253–302). Washington, DC: American Psychiatric Press.

2. Hirschfeld, R., & Davidson, L. (1988). Risk factors for suicide. In A.J. Frances & R.E. Hales (Eds.), *American Psychiatric Press Review of Psychiatry* (Vol. 7, pp. 307–333). Washington, DC: American Psychiatric Press.

3. Alcohol, Drug Abuse, and Mental Health Administration. (1989). *Report of the secretary's task force on youth suicide Vols. I–IV.* DHSS Pub. No. (ADM) 89-1621-1624. Washington, DC: U.S. Government Printing Office.

4. National Center for Health Statistics. (1986). *Annual summary of births, marriages, divorces, and deaths: United States, 1985.* Washington, DC: Author.

Dorwart, R.A., & Chartock, L. (1989). Suicide: A public health perspective. In D.G. Jacobs & H.N. Brown (Eds.), *Suicide: Understanding and responding: Harvard Medical School perspectives on suicide* (pp. 31–55). Madison, CT: International Universities Press.

6. Smith, K., & Crawford, S. (1986). Suicidal behavior among high school students. *Suicide and life-threatening behavior, 16,* 313–325.

7. Holinger, P., & Offer, D. (1982). Prediction of adolescent suicide: A population model. *American Journal of Psychiatry, 139,* 307–309.

8. Bongar, B., Peterson, L.G., Harris, E.A., & Aissis, J. (1989). Clinical and legal considerations in the management of suicidal patients: An integrative overview. *Journal of Integrative and Eclectic Psychotherapy,* 8(1), 53–67.

9. Goldfried, M. R., & Wachtel, P. L. (1987). Clinical and conceptual issues in psychotherapy integration: A dialogue. *International Journal of Eclectic Psychotherapy,* 6(2), 131–144.

10. Bongar, B. (1991). *The suicidal patient: Clinical and legal standards of care.* Washington, DC: American Psychological Association.

11. Shneidman, E.S. (1985). *Definition of suicide.* New York: Wiley.

## Recommended Readings

Bongar, B., Berman, A.L. Litman, R.E., & Maris, R. (1992). Outpatient standards of care in the assessment, management and treatment of suicidal persons. *Suicide & Life-Threatening Behavior, 22,* 453–478.

Clark, D.C., & Fawcett, J. (1992). Review of empirical risk factors for evaluation of the suicidal patient. In B. Bongar (Ed.), *Suicide: Guidelines for assessment, management, and treatment* (pp. 16–48). New York: Oxford University Press.

Peterson, L.G., & Bongar, B. (1989). The suicidal patient. In A. Lazare (Ed.), *Outpatient psychiatry: Diagnosis and treatment* (2nd ed, pp. 569–584). Baltimore: Williams and Wilkins.

Yufit, R.I., & Bongar, B. (1992). Suicide, stress, and coping with life cycle events. In R.W. Maris, A.L. Berman, J.T. Maltsberger, & R.I. Yufit (Eds.), *Assessment and prediction of suicide* (pp. 553–573). New York: Guilford Press.

# PART VI

# SCHIZOPHRENIA

➤ Chapter 13: Schizophrenia

Schizophrenia and related disorders fall into the category of psychotic disorders, disturbances that share the
central feature of a severe dysfunction in the individual's
experience of reality regarding the world and the self.
People with psychotic disorders such as schizophrenia
have difficulty formulating coherent thoughts and
speech. They may be distracted to the point of torment
by vivid visual images or sounds such as voices speaking
harshly to them. Because of the severe nature of these
symptoms, psychotic disorders are among the most
frightening and tormenting of human experiences.
Schizophrenia is a psychotic disorder with a range of
symptoms involving disturbances in the content and
form of thought, perception, affect, identity, motivation,
behavior, and ability to relate to other people. These disturbances are seen most clearly during the active phase
of the disorder, but also may affect the individual during
the early, prodromal phase and the late, or residual
phase. There are several variants of schizophrenic disorders based on the particular types of symptoms that the
individual is experiencing, ranging from those involving
primarily odd bodily movements to those that appear
more diffusely throughout the individual's behavior.

# 13

## About the Author

*Nancy C. Andreasen,* M.D., Ph.D., is Andrew H. Woods Professor of Psychiatry at The University of Iowa College of Medicine. She is actively involved in neuroimaging research, which involves the use of MR imaging, echoplanar MR, and positron emission tomography. In addition, she leads a team working on three-dimensional image analysis techniques to integrate multi-modality imaging and to develop innovative methods for analyzing structural and functional imaging techniques in an automated manner. She has been given a Research Scientist Award from NIMH for her work in this area, directs a Mental Health Clinical Research Center and a training program that emphasizes neuroimaging, and conducts several investigator-initiated projects in the area.

Dr. Andreasen is past president of the American Psychopathological Association and the Psychiatric Research Society, as well as a member of the Institute of Medicine. She has received the American Psychiatric Association Prize for Research and the Dean Award from the American College of Psychiatrists, as well as the Distinguished Service Award from the latter organization. She is Editor-in-Chief of The American Journal of Psychiatry and has written a book on neuroimaging (Brain Imaging: Applications in Psychiatry, American Psychiatric Press Inc., Washington D.C., 1989), as well as several hundred articles and seven books on other related topics.

# Jeff: A Difficult Case of Schizophrenia

A complex and multifaceted disorder, schizophrenia can take one of many forms in different individuals. However, before this disorder can be diagnosed, some general characteristics must be present. Symptoms of marked disturbance must be experienced for at least six months. Within this six-month period, there must be an active phase of symptoms that lasts for at least one month. During this active phase, at least two of the following symptoms must be evident: delusions, hallucinations, disorganized speech, disturbed behavior, and so-called "negative symptoms," such as speechlessness or lack of initiative or interest in life.

The most striking symptoms of schizophrenia are the "positive" symptoms—delusions, hallucinations, disturbed speech, and disturbed behavior—which are exaggerations or distortions of normal thoughts, emotions, and behavior. Many people with schizophrenia also have negative symptoms, those that involve a level of functioning that is below that regarded as normal. The most common negative symptoms are emotional unresponsiveness, deficient communication, and loss of motivation. It can be difficult to diagnose negative symptoms, because most people at one time or another may act in these ways, especially when they are fatigued or depressed. Although less commonly noted, some people with schizophrenia also experience anhedonia—the loss of interest or ability to experience pleasure from activities that most people find appealing.

For the person with schizophrenia, every facet of human functioning becomes affected by these disturbances in thoughts, feelings, and behavior. Interactions with relatives, acquaintances, even strangers are characterized by turmoil, particularly during episodes of active symptomatology. Dr. Andreasen's case of Jeff provides a glimpse into the devastation caused by this disorder, particularly when the symptoms have a slow onset and are primarily of the negative type.—*Eds*.

## THE CHALLENGE OF JEFF'S CASE

From the outset, I had the sense that Jeff was going to be a difficult case—
difficult to diagnose and difficult to treat. When he was admitted to our inpatient unit at age 19, he had already had a long psychiatric history. He had been
seen in our outpatient clinic for the past two years with a diagnosis of depression, and he had been given every kind of treatment that could be provided: all
classes of antidepressant medications, many types of antianxiety medications,
and most forms of psychotherapy (including behavioral, cognitive, and dynamic
approaches). Nothing had worked. One does not need to be an astute clinician
to wonder whether the diagnosis might not be wrong under such circumstances.
On the other hand, of course, some patients are treatment-refractory. Yet the
majority of depressions eventually do remit spontaneously. The case notes in
Jeff's chart indicated that he had gone steadily downhill for the past two years.
He managed to finish high school, but his efforts to attend college had been a
complete flop: six hours of credit over three semesters with a GPA of 2.1. This
academic performance did not match expectations. His father was a distinguished professor in the history department, and his mother also had a Ph.D.

### Initial Presentation

I walked down the hall to Jeff's room and knocked on the door. A voice responded softly and slowly with "Come in." Jeff was lying on his bed with his
eyes closed. I pulled up a chair, sat down next to the bed, and introduced
myself. He lay there like a lump for the first 5 or 10 minutes of the interview,
answering questions briefly and often monosyllabically. By joking around and
making small talk, I finally managed to get him to sit up and pay attention, but
getting him to talk about what was going on just wasn't easy. That initial interview went on for about an hour and a half, and extracting a history was like
trying to get blood from a turnip. He couldn't seem to think or say anything. He
also showed no animation and had minimal facial expression. Although he had
been diagnosed as having depression, he denied feeling sad. His own word to
describe his inner state was "empty." He said that he didn't feel anything. He
had no interests, no drive, no energy. His mind, he said, just didn't work any
more. It was blank. This smelled like negative symptoms,[1-7] not like depression.
That would mean his diagnosis was within the schizophrenia spectrum.

Efforts to elicit a history of psychotic symptoms led nowhere, however. I
tried both the usual questions ("Have you ever had the experience of hearing
voices when no one is around?") and the more oblique ones ("Do you feel like
people are down on you sometimes?" "Do you ever feel like you have lost control
of your body or your mind?"). These efforts led nowhere.

In the absence of a clear diagnosis, I decided to take Jeff off his current
medications, which were a modest cocktail of antidepressants and anxiolytics
(anti-anxiety medications). Simple observation might help clarify the diagnosis.
In addition, I scheduled an appointment with his parents. They were caring,

concerned, but bewildered. They indicated that Jeff had been a very normal, but somewhat shy kid until about two years ago. His troubles began when he went on a high school trip to France, had become acutely anxious, and had returned home early. They sought psychiatric treatment on an outpatient basis, and the initial diagnosis was mixed anxiety and depression. From that point forward, Jeff had begun to withdraw and to spend most of his time alone in his room. He no longer wanted to be around his friends. Although he had been on the football team during his junior year, he dropped out in his senior year. His grades plummeted, but he was able to graduate. His parents commented that a gradual but dramatic personality change had taken place over the past two years. They concurred with his perception that he just seemed "empty." All their efforts to encourage him, to help him find new directions, or to reassess his goals seem to have led nowhere.

Jeff began coursework at the local university after finishing high school, but was unable to study. In fact, much of the time he was even unable to get out of bed in order to attend class. This was a striking change, since he had been an A or B+ student throughout most of his academic career. He had also tried several jobs that were considerably below his intellectual ability, such as delivering pizzas. He couldn't even seem to find his way around the town he had grown up in and to get the pizzas to the right address! His parents reported that he seemed suspicious much of the time and that he had no desire to be around friends or peers of either sex. His grooming and hygiene had deteriorated. During his freshman year of college, he spent one semester in an apartment on his own, but his parents eventually moved him back home when they discovered that it was filthy beyond the level that one would expect even from a single young man who was an inexperienced housekeeper or cook. The apartment steadily became full of decaying food and dirty laundry. Jeff just didn't seem to care about anything. There was no history of drug abuse of any type. The admission was precipitated by two years of frustration with failed treatment for a disorder diagnosed and treated as depression.

It still smelled more like the negative symptoms of schizophrenia than depression, but other options needed to explored before making a diagnosis with such a bad prognosis, particularly in the absence of florid psychotic symptoms. Did Jeff have a brain tumor, for example? Had some traumatic event occurred during the trip to France that he had never been able to discuss? Could that be brought out through a sodium amytal interview? Or did he have an atypical depression that was treatment-refractory and that might respond to ECT?

I was not particularly surprised to find that Jeff's EEG and MR scan were normal. Psychological testing showed diffusely poor performance with an IQ in the low normal range, considerably below what one would expect for a former A student, the son of two Ph.D.s, and the younger brother of a woman who was getting A's at Stanford Law School. The amytal interview yielded nothing as well. Jeff really couldn't explain why he had become anxious in France and had to come home. He said he just got lonely and scared. The most striking thing about the amytal interview was how little he actually was able to say.

More probing of the family history shed a bit of additional light. Jeff's maternal grandmother had become extremely suspicious (in fact, clearly delusional) in her late twenties and had never returned to normal. The family tolerated her, but they knew that she was chronically ill. A maternal second cousin had also developed a psychotic illness in his early twenties and had shown prominent negative symptoms as well. He has been in and out of hospitals, is unable to function, and is maintained with Social Security disability.

I discussed the difficulty of differential diagnosis with Jeff's family, explaining that he could have an atypical chronic depression, or he could have a somewhat atypical form of schizophrenia that had not manifested prominent psychotic symptoms. The treatment choice was between ECT for the former or low-dose neuroleptics for the latter. I also discussed the quandary with Jeff, explaining that if he responded to ECT, it might confirm the diagnosis of depression and help him feel considerably better. He did not wish to have ECT, however, and so I finally decided to place him on a low dose of haloperidol (2 mgs, bid). He was discharged in late May with the self-stated goal of taking a course in summer school. It would be a freshman English course, that being one of his favorite subjects.

## Case History

Jeff had a normal birth and milestones. Most of his early history was unremarkable, apart from the fact that he was always somewhat quieter than his older sister, Sarah. He was also a slightly less successful student, although he had always gotten A's and B's. He had one or two close friends, but he was always a little socially awkward, while his sister had clearly been a natural leader: she was class president, involved in a singing group and debate, and class valedictorian. Nonetheless, Jeff had gone out for football all through junior high and high school and had made the first team. He seemed to enjoy his friends, his school work, and participation in sports. He was fond of Sarah and seemed to enjoy her success. His relationship with his parents was also relaxed and pleasant. Jeff denied any history of substance abuse, and discussions with both his family and with one close friend confirmed that this history was probably correct. The only real clinical tip-off in the past history was the family history of probable schizophrenia and the absence of a family history of mood disorder.

## Diagnosis

| | |
|---|---|
| Axis I: | • None, using DSM criteria. The most likely diagnosis for this patient (schizophrenia) could not be made, since he lacked the delusions and hallucinations required for this diagnosis. Yet this was the diagnosis in my judgment. |

Axis II: • The only possible diagnosis on this axis is schizoid personality disorder. This diagnosis would be made with a low level of enthusiasm, however, since personality disorders typically manifest themselves relatively early, represent a stable or enduring pattern of functioning, do not have the sort of acute onset that Jeff displayed, and do not lead to the type of deterioration that Jeff has shown.

Axis III: • None

Axis IV: • Jeff has not experienced any obvious stressors, but he has some psychosocial problems. These are largely educational and occupational and appear to be secondary to his illness.

Axis V: • His GAF is around 30. Jeff is unable to function in almost all areas. He stays in bed all day, has no job, and no longer has any friends.

## Case Formulation

This case illustrates the extreme difficulty that arises when a particular patient "has not read *DSM-IV*." In his initial presentation, Jeff did not fit neatly into any of the categories in *DSM-IV*. Although he had been diagnosed as having a mood disorder, he lacked genuine dysphoric mood. Although he might be forced into this category through counting criteria, he clearly was not depressed. His chronic nonresponsiveness to aggressive treatment of all kinds for mood disorder makes this diagnosis extremely unlikely. Further contributing to the unlikelihood of mood disorder is the inexorable downward course of his illness. The course and pattern of symptoms are most consistent with schizophrenia characterized by prominent negative symptoms. In the absence of psychotic symptoms, he would be considered to have classic Bleulerian simple schizophrenia,[8] which appears in the appendix of *DSM-IV* as "simple deteriorative disorder." He seemed to fit the criteria for this diagnosis almost perfectly. This disorder is defined by progressive development over a period of at least a year of all of the following: (1) Marked decline in occupational or academic functioning; (2) gradual appearance and deepening of negative symptoms such as affective flattening (blunting of emotional responsiveness), alogia (poverty of speech and thought) and avolition (diminution of drive and will). (3) poor interpersonal rapport, social isolation, or social withdrawal. His family history also supported the likelihood that he had a disorder within the schizophrenia spectrum.

## Course of Treatment

Jeff returned home to live with his parents. He remained isolated, apathetic, and avolitional. He was not able to get out of bed to go register for his summer school course. He spent most of every day either lying in bed or sitting around smoking cigarettes. Sometimes he sat in front of the television, but he was usually unable even to describe what he was watching. After a week or two, he refused to take the prescribed neuroleptics.

Two months after discharge, Jeff's condition showed a change. He began complaining that his father was tormenting him. Specifically, he began to experience severe electrical sensations in his head that he believed were being transmitted through his father's mind. He also began to have "horrible thoughts" that were put there by his father. His apathy began to be intermixed with agitation, and he began pacing, often through much of the night. One night, he became so agitated by the tormenting experiences to which his father was subjecting him that he grabbed a knife, went to his parents' bedroom, and threatened to slash his father's throat if he would not stop tormenting him. Fortunately, his father was able to talk him into dropping the knife and going to the emergency room.

## Outcome of the Case

Jeff was readmitted to the hospital and given a diagnosis of schizophrenia. He was placed on a higher dose of neuroleptic medication. Within about three weeks the psychotic symptoms diminished, and he returned to his baseline negative symptoms. He continued to have serious difficulty in functioning due to the negative symptoms, however, and he has been on medication and in residential treatment for the past two years. He has been living in a halfway house, receiving psychosocial rehabilitative therapy in conjunction with his neuroleptic medications. He has not been able to return to school or hold any type of regular job.

# EMPIRICAL CONTRIBUTIONS TO UNDERSTANDING SCHIZOPHRENIA

Although Jeff did not originally fit easily into the *DSM-IV* classification, he is not an unusual case. Many patients with schizophrenia present initially with negative symptoms and are diagnosed as suffering from depression, because the latter diagnosis carries a better prognosis. Since the *DSM* definition of schizophrenia has become steadily narrower, giving patients this diagnosis tends to imply a bad outcome, and clinicians are reluctant to use it until they are convinced of the diagnosis. In Jeff's case, my own intuitive reaction was that he had schizophrenia, since I have seen many patients with this pattern over the years. I felt reasonably comfortable discussing this possibility with his parents.

Much of my own descriptive work has been devoted to the study of negative symptoms.[1-7] These symptoms are really the classic core symptoms of schizophrenia. The early founding fathers of schizophrenia research, Emil Kraepelin and Eugen Bleuler, emphasized the importance of negative symptoms, although they did not use that specific terminology.[8,9] Kraepelin talked about the importance of affective blunting and loss of volition, while Bleuler emphasized "six A's": affective blunting, avolition, associative loosening, autism (social withdrawal), ambivalence (inability to make a decision), and attentional impairment. Bleuler pointed out that delusions and hallucinations occur in many conditions, including the mood disorders, but that the "fundamental symptoms" encompassed in the "six A's" tended to occur only in schizophrenia. Both Kraepelin and Bleuler stressed the severe cognitive impairment and loss of inner psychological unity that one senses in patients with schizophrenia.

When I first began to work with patients suffering from schizophrenia in the late 1960s and early 1970s, we were taught that we could prevent deterioration if we treated the psychotic symptoms aggressively with neuroleptics. We did so, but it gradually became evident that most patients were unable to return to normal lives, even though they were no longer psychotic. For some reason, they continued to have no interest or drive and were unable to return to school or to hold a job. Observing this pattern triggered my interest in what eventually came to be known as negative symptoms.

I have been consistently drawn to studying symptoms of schizophrenia that are considered difficult to evaluate, and much of my original work focused on defining forms of thought disorder.[10,12] As I did this work, I noticed that thought disorder tended to fall into two general categories: positive and negative. Positive thought disorder was characterized by derailment and incoherence, while negative thought disorder consisted of poverty of speech and poverty of content of speech. These two kinds of thought disorder emerged from factor analysis. I also became interested in developing methods for rating affective blunting precisely.[13,14] This work occurred in the context of the development of diagnostic criteria such as the Washington University (or Feighner) criteria.[15] The authors of those criteria, as well as the Research Diagnostic Criteria (RDC), were very reluctant to emphasize "soft" signs and symptoms, such as affective blunting or thought disorder.[16] Consequently, the various Bleulerian symptoms were considered as important, and the diagnostic criteria instead stressed the importance of delusions or hallucinations. These symptoms were much easier to rate reliably, since they tend to be "all or none" phenomena.

I participated actively in the development of *DSM-III*.[17] The *DSM-III* approach to schizophrenia followed the Washington University criteria and the RDC in emphasizing the use of delusions and hallucinations to define schizophrenia. I always felt uncomfortable about it, however, since I knew that a number of patients like Jeff would not easily fit the criteria and could not be given an appropriate diagnosis if the criteria were followed rigidly.

When I was asked to chair the Schizophrenia Workgroup for *DSM-IV*, I decided it was time to stress the importance of including negative symptoms in the criteria, and the entire workgroup concurred with this decision. It is now clear that negative symptoms are a core part of the illness, much as Kraepelin and Bleuler suggested. A substantial body of evidence indicates that they have a variety of important correlates: poor premorbid adjustment, poor educational achievement, structural brain abnormalities, poor prognosis, and more severe cognitive impairment.[2–7] It is very important that clinicians learn to recognize their presence and to use them as an aid in diagnosing schizophrenia. Although they overlap superficially with symptoms of depression (e.g., loss of interest, diminished emotional expression), an astute clinician can sense that negative symptoms are qualitatively different from depressive symptoms. In general, patients suffering from negative symptoms experience less obvious psychological pain and instead seem "empty," as Jeff did.

I personally would have preferred to broaden the criteria so that we could also include simple schizophrenia as a subtype of schizophrenia, but the majority of the committee members did not concur with this approach.

## EMPIRICAL CONTRIBUTIONS TO TREATMENT OF SCHIZOPHRENIA

Because negative symptoms have received less attention prior to their inclusion in *DSM-IV*, little research has been done on the treatment of negative symptoms. But this situation is now changing, in part because *DSM-IV* has included negative symptoms in the criteria and in part because the new atypical neuroleptics (e.g., clozapine, risperidone) are thought to have possible efficacy for negative symptoms.[18]

Historically, negative symptoms were seen as equivalent to the "residual state." A great deal of the treatment research on neuroleptic medication has defined "remission" in terms of remission of positive psychotic symptoms.[19] Patients are said to have "improved" or "recovered" when they no longer have delusions and hallucinations. As a clinician who still sees schizophrenic patients on a regular basis, I feel this approach is inaccurate and even unfair. Only the clinician feels better when he or she says that the patient has "recovered," when in fact the patient is unable to return to school, to hold a job, or to have close friends. Therefore, I was especially pleased when negative symptoms were included in *DSM-IV* as part of the characteristic symptoms of schizophrenia. One can no longer say that the patient is "recovered" when he has "active symptoms" as defined by the A Criterion for schizophrenia.

Now that negative symptoms have moved again to the forefront as core symptoms of the illness, initiatives are being developed to improve their treatment. These initiatives will proceed on two fronts: the development of better medications, and the development of psychosocial and cognitive rehabilitation strategies.

Traditional or "typical" neuroleptics were the mainstay of the treatment of schizophrenia for nearly three decades. Beginning with the development of chlorpromazine in the 1950s, a variety of neuroleptics were developed that had essentially the same goal: to block dopamine type 2 receptors, which were thought to be the major neurochemical abnormality in schizophrenia. This situation began to change when the work of Kane and Meltzer showed that some treatment-refractory patients were able to respond to clozapine, a medication that is not a potent D2 blocker, but instead acts on serotonin receptors and D1 receptors.[19] The observation of the therapeutic efficacy of clozapine led to a paradigm shift in thinking about the pharmacologic profile of an ideal neuroleptic.

Pharmacologic treatment of schizophrenia increasingly is emphasizing the use of "atypical neuroleptics." Atypical neuroleptics are defined in a variety of ways. Like clozapine, they have a mixed pharmacologic profile, acting on serotonergic, adrenergic, and even histaminic receptors, in addition to dopamine receptors. In general, they are less potent D2 blockers. A second characteristic of atypical neuroleptics is their low rate of extrapyramidal side effects. This is particularly advantageous, since patients are more comfortable and therefore more willing to take medication. A third characteristic of atypical neuroleptics is that they may be more efficacious for negative symptoms.

Very little work has been done so far on psychosocial and cognitive rehabilitative strategies for the treatment of negative symptoms. I see this as an area that should receive increasing emphasis during the coming decade. One wonders what might have happened to a patient like Jeff if he had been diagnosed early and treated aggressively with an atypical neuroleptic in conjunction with active cognitive and psychosocial rehabilitation. Perhaps he would have been spared the deteriorating course that he has experienced.

### Notes

1. Andreasen, N.C. (1983), *The Scale for the Assessment of Negative Symptoms* (*SANS*). Iowa City: The University of Iowa.

2. Andreasen, N.C., & Olson, S. (1982). Negative versus positive schizophrenia: Definition and validation. *Archives of General Psychiatry, 39,* 789–794.

3. Andreasen, N.C. (1982). "Negative symptoms in schizophrenia: Definition and reliability." *Archives of General Psychiatry, 39,* 784–788.

4. Andreasen, N.C., Flaum, M., Swayze, V.W., Tyrrell, G., & Arndt. S. (1990). "Positive and negative symptoms in schizophrenia: A critical reappraisal." *Archives of General Psychiatry, 47,* 615–621.

5. Andreasen, N.C., Arndt, S., Alliger, R., Miller, D., and Flaum, M. (1995). "Symptoms of schizophrenia: Methods, meanings, and mechanisms." *Archives of General Psychiatry,* 52, 52:341–351.

6. Arndt, S., Andreasen, N.C., Flaum, M., Miller, D., & Nopoulos, P. (1995). "A longitudinal study of symptom dimensions in schizophrenia: Prediction and patterns of change." *Archives of General Psychiatry* 52, 332–360.

7. Andreasen, N.C., Nopoulos, P., Schultz, S., Miller, D., Gupta, S., Swayze, V., & Flaum, M. (1994). "Positive and negative symptoms of schizophrenia: Past, present, and future." *Acta Psychiatrica Scandinavica, 90,* 51–59.

8. Bleuler, E., translated by Zinkin, J. (1950). *Dementia praecox of the group of schizophrenias (1911).* New York: International Universities Press.

9. Kraepelin, E., Barclay, R.M., & Robertson, G.M. (1919). *Dementia praecox and paraphrenia.* Edinburgh: E&S Livingstone.

10. Andreasen, N.C. (1979). "The clinical assessment of thought, language, and communication disorders: I. The definition of terms and evaluation of their reliability." *Archives of General Psychiatry, 36,* 1315–1321.

11. Andreasen, N.C. & Grove, W.M. (1979). "The clinical assessment of thought, language, and communication disorders: II. Diagnostic significance." *Archives of General Psychiatry, 36,* 1325–1330.

12. Andreasen, N.C., & Grove, W.M. (1986). "Thought, language, and communication in schizophrenia: Diagnostic and prognostic significance." *Schizophrenia Bulletin, 12,* 348–359.

13. Andreasen, N.C. (1979). "Affective flattening and the criteria for schizophrenia." *American Journal Psychiatry, 136,* 944–947.

14. Andreasen, N.C., Alpert, M., & Martz, M.J. (1981). "Acoustic analysis: An objective measure of affective flattening. flattering." *Archives of General Psychiatry, 38,* 281–285.

15. Feighner, J.P., Robins, E., Guze, S.B., Woodruff Jr., R.A., Winokur, G., & Munoz, R. "Diagnostic criteria for use in psychiatric research." *Archives of General Psychiatry, 26,* 57–63.

16. Spitzer, R.L., Endicott, J., & Robins, E. *Research diagnostic criteria* (3rd ed.). New York: Biometrics Research, New York State Department of Mental Hygiene.

17. American Psychiatric Association. (1980). *Diagnostic and statistical manual of mental disorders (DSM-III).* Washington, DC: Author.

18. Miller, D.D., Perry, P.J., Cadoret, R.J., & Andreasen. N.C. (1994). "Clozapine's effect on negative symptoms in treatment-refractory schizophrenics." *Comprehensive Psychiatry, 35*(1), 8–15.

19. Kane, J., Honigfeld, G., Singer, J., & Meltzer. H. (1988). "Clozapine for the treatment-resistant schizophrenic. A double-blind comparison with chlorpromazine." *Archives of General Psychiatry, 45,* 789–796.

## Recommended Readings

Andreasen, N.C., (1982) "Negative symptoms in schizophrenia: Definition and reliability." *Archives of General Psychiatry 39,* 784–788.

Andreasen, N.C. (1985). "Positive vs. negative schizophrenia: A critical evaluation." *Schizophrenia Bulletin 11,* 380–389.

Andreasen, N.C. (1986). *Can schizophrenia be localized in the brain?* Washington, DC: American Psychiatric Press.

Andreasen, N.C. (Ed.) (1990). *Positive and negative symptoms and syndromes.* Basel: Karger.

Andreasen, N.C., & Carpenter, W.T. (1993)."Diagnosis and classification of schizophrenia." *Schizophrenia Bulletin 19,* 199–214.

Andreasen, N.C., Flaum, M. (1991). "Schizophrenia: The characteristic symptoms." *Schizophrenia Bulletin 17*, 27–49.

Andreasen, N.C., Flaum, M., Swayze, V.M., Tyrrell, G., & S. Arndt. (1990). "Positive and negative symptoms in schizrenia: A critical reappraisal." *Archives of General Psychiatry, 47*, 615–621.

Marneros, A., Andreasen, N.C., & Tsuang, M. (Ed.). (1991). *Positive versus negative schizophrenia*. Heidelberg: Springer-Verlag.

Andreasen, N.C., Nopoulos, P., Schultz, S., et al. (1994). Positive and negative symptoms of schizophrenia: Past, present, and future. *Acta Psychiatrica Scandinvica* 90(suppl 384), 51–59.

# AGE-RELATED DISORDERS

In this part, two cases reflect the ways in which psychological disorders can be experienced at different points in life. In the first case, we see one of the many forms of disorders that originate in childhood; the second case reflects a disorder that strikes in later adulthood. Both can be considered age-related disorders, based on when they most commonly occur in the lifespan. An important difference between these two particular disorders is that attention-deficit/hyperactivity disorder is treatable, whereas Alzheimer's disease is irreversible. These disorders share the feature that others in the family are typically involved in caring for and helping the individual cope with the disturbing symptoms of the disorder.

# 14

## About

## the

## Authors

*Russell A. Barkley,* Ph.D., *is Director of Psychology and Professor of Psychiatry and Neurology at the University of Massachusetts Medical Center. He received his Master's Degree in 1975 and Ph.D. in 1977 in Clinical Psychology from Bowling Green State University of Ohio. Subsequently, he received internship training at Oregon Health Sciences Center University in Portland. Dr. Barkley is the author of six books, co-editor of two others, and creator of six professional videotapes. He has published over 140 book chapters and scientific papers on Attention-Deficit Hyperactivity Disorder and related subjects. His most recent books are* Taking Charge of ADHD: The Complete Authoritative Guide for Parents *(Guilford Press, 1995), and* Child Psychopathology *(Guilford Press, 1996). He is also the founder and editor of the bimonthly clinical newsletter,* The ADHD Report *(Guilford Press).*

*Gwenyth Edwards, Ph.D., is currently Chief of the ADHD Clinic at the University of Massachusettes Medical Center. She is an Assistant Professor of Psychiatry and Pediatrics and a licensed psychologist in clinical practice for over 20 years. Dr. Edwards completed her doctoral studies at the University of Rhode Island. Her particular interests include behavior management training and family therapy for parents of children with both ADHD and Oppositional Defiant Disorder; the role of fathers in the lives of children with behavior problems; and the assessment of complex combinations of ADHD, learning disabilities and emotional dysfunction.*

# Paul: An Instructive Case of Attention-Deficit Hyperactivity Disorder

**About**

**the**

**Disorder**

Children with attentional problems and heightened activity levels commonly act in ways that are disruptive and provocative. When a child's everyday life is characterized by these behavioral patterns, the diagnosis of attention-deficit/hyperactivity (ADHD) disorder probably fits.

There are two components to the diagnosis of ADHD: the inattention component and the hyperactive-impulsive component. Inattention involves a set of behaviors such as carelessness, forgetfulness, and other attentional problems. The hyperactive-impulsive component is further subdivided into hyperactivity and impulsivity. Hyperactivity is characterized by fidgeting, restlessness, running about inappropriately, experiencing difficulty playing quietly, and talking excessively. Impulsivity is evident in children who blurt out answers, cannot wait their turn, and interrupt or intrude on others.

One of the most common treatment methods for ADHD involves stimulant medication such as Ritalin, which has a paradoxical calming effect. The behavioral approach is also widely used in understanding and treating ADHD and, in some cases, may replace medications for children with ADHD. Implicit in the behavioral approach is the belief that both the family and the school must be directly involved in reducing the child's disruptive behaviors.

The model of treatment outlined by Drs. Barkley and Edwards illustrates the importance of careful assessment, early intervention, and willingness to integrate a variety of modalities.—*Eds.*

## PAUL'S CASE

### Initial Presentation (Edwards)

Paul arrived with his parents to be evaluated for learning disabilities at the clinic where I consult once per week. He had recently been through a battery of psychoeducational tests given by his public school system, and his parents were dissatisfied with the conclusions. They felt that the school either misunderstood or disregarded Paul's needs. He was repeating seventh grade, despite the fact that he appeared to be very bright.

The parents admitted, however, that even though 13-year-old Paul seemed capable, he was unable to finish assignments in class and had frustrating organizational problems, such as a tendency to lose his papers and forget his homework. They also acknowledged his oppositional behaviors and difficulty handling his feelings when frustrated or agitated. They wondered if he had an attention-deficit/hyperactivity disorder (ADHD). So did I.

### Case History

I asked Paul's parents when they started to notice history and age of onset of these behavioral difficulties. They informed me that Paul had been trouble from the word go. Colicky as a baby, by nine months of age he was climbing out of his crib and his parents could never trust him to be left unattended unless he was literally on a leash. I then asked whether Paul had been evaluated previously by any other professionals. The parents responded that even though five day-care providers had expelled him from their programs because of his disruptive behavior, his pediatrician assured them, after just a 15-minute exam, that Paul was a normal but active four-year-old boy. Yet multiple complaints and criticisms of Paul continued from other family members, who seemed to conclude that Paul must be "crazy" when he did impulsive things, such as when he threw a whole pizza at his mother at a family gathering. Despite such atypical behaviors, Paul was seen by a general psychiatrist who said Paul appeared to be a normal, healthy child.

Next, I investigated Paul's school history with the parents. They described school as a nightmare for Paul. His kindergarten teacher frequently sent notes home such as the following:

---

Paul is very kind, sweet, and sincere. He is liked by all his classmates. What concerns me most about Paul is his difficulty focusing. He wanders around the room, takes frequent walks, trips to the bathroom, and has many, many excuses as to why he cannot participate in an activity that involves academics. More effort goes into avoiding activities than participating.

---

The parents further noted that Paul's kindergarten teacher viewed him as "socially immature." And so they felt that Paul entered first grade with a well-established reputation as a child who needed firm limits. His mother informed me that she had told the school guidance counselor during the fall of first grade, "we are seeing an eager-to-learn child who has looked forward to going to and learning at his school turn into a child who is starting to lose his attention span, is making excuses, and is feeling inadequate." I sought to learn from the parents just how the school staff were reacting to Paul's difficult behavior. They stated that routine discipline at school for Paul apparently took the form of being made to stand against the wall during recess if he spoke out of turn in the line of children filing outside to the playground. Day, after day, after day, the parents said, Paul was stood against the wall as a consequence for his misconduct. By November, the parents said that Paul was throwing up before school, refusing to get on the school bus, and had to be dragged by his mother from her car into the building.

Like many parents of children with ADHD, Paul's parents had a need to ventilate more about Paul's school experiences and their frustrations with them. So I asked that they continue describing his later school years. His parents readily verbalized that Paul continued to have difficulties in second and third grades, especially when he was required to do any independent work. He became more argumentative with his teachers. His parents recalled requesting that the school provide Paul with some sort of special education. This, they said, led to Paul's meeting with a school counselor from time to time toward the end of the third grade. Although this seemed to be helpful, Paul's parents decided to place him in a different school within their city, hoping that Paul might make a fresh start and develop a more positive attitude toward school. I was interested to know how well he adjusted to this new school setting, realizing that it might indicate to what extent Paul's behavioral problems stemmed from his incompatibility with the former school staff. His parents told me that Paul adjusted well to his new school, but unfortunately the family needed to move within the city, which necessitated another change of schools in fourth grade. "And what of this new school situation?" I asked. The parents commented that the new teacher attempted to work with Paul around improving organizational skills and work habits, and his grades briefly improved. But despite the new school setting, I was told, Paul became increasingly inattentive and disruptive. "What then?" I inquired. His parents told me that they then made the surprising decision to pull him out of school and tutor him at home for the remainder of the fourth grade. He actually remained at home and received home schooling for the next two years. An unusual reaction, I thought to myself, given the increased rights children with ADHD have recently won within the school system for access to special educational evaluations and related resources. Most parents I have evaluated would have sought another teacher within the school, another school, or more likely requested a formal evaluation for special education under the public laws governing the rights of disabled children in schools (the Individuals with

Disabilities in Education Act, or IDEA, and Section 504 of the Civil Rights Act).

I encouraged the parents to complete the story of Paul's rocky educational course. They said that Paul returned to public school for the second half of sixth grade because his mother had a new baby and also had to take in her own mother, who had been diagnosed with Alzheimer's disease. I mentally noted this as a potential stressor event on the family that could place Paul at risk for increased oppositional-defiant behavior (research literature has found family stressors to have such an impact on boys). Paul was able to return to public school at grade level and underwent his first formal psychoeducational testing at that time. Results of that testing, I was told, indicated that Paul had an average IQ, a not-atypical finding for ADHD children, I thought to myself. His reading skills were found to be above grade level, while math skills were somewhat below grade level. The parents stated that Paul successfully progressed to seventh grade, which was in a middle school with all of its attendant increases in work load, number of teachers, and added responsibility for self-organization and self-control. I was not surprised, then, when the parents told me that Paul stopped completing his homework, left his tests unfinished, and appeared to be totally disorganized. Surely, I thought, the school would now move to provide support services for Paul. Instead, he was recommended to repeat seventh grade, but because of his defiance and argumentativeness with teachers, he was placed in a special program for at-risk students with small classes and assistance with organizational skills. I considered this response of the school staff to be not unusual; disruptive behavior from ADHD students often led to treatment for the disruption, but often overlooked the cognitive deficits in concentration, organization, and self-control that accompany ADHD. Later, I was informed, because of the school's perception that Paul was poorly motivated, along with his chronic absenteeism, Paul was suspended and then put in regular classes, with resource room support once per week.

It is often necessary at such junctures in the clinical interview to discover how the parents felt the school staff viewed the parents' role in all of Paul's difficulties. They gladly obliged by telling me that the personnel at Paul's school were outspokenly critical of them in their job as parents. In part, I could see the school's perspective because, at first glance, the family was certainly unusual. Paul's mother told me that she was at home with the three children from her second marriage, having four adult children from a first marriage, all of whom had either learning or behavioral difficulties or both. Paul's father, she said, worked as a security guard, despite the fact that he was extraordinarily articulate and well read. Both parents described themselves as learning disabled and the father believed that he experienced attentional difficulties similar to Paul as a child. I had learned over the years from both clinical work and the research literature that this familialness of ADHD symptoms is quite common in families of ADHD children and so it only corroborated my suspicions that Paul may well have ADHD. Paul's mother also reported that she had thyroid problems which contributed to her obesity and depression. There was also a positive family history for manic-depression, alcohol abuse, antisocial behavior, and narcolepsy. I could see, then, how school staff unfamiliar with the substantial hereditary nature of ADHD and the increased risk it conveys for other mental health problems among the relatives of such children might easily and erroneously conclude that Paul's problems stemmed from his parents' problems.

I carefully reviewed with the parents the diagnostic criteria for the more common childhood psychological disorders. They indicated that Paul displayed eight out of nine inattentive behaviors and eight out of nine behaviors associated with hyperactivity and impulsivity from the list commonly used to diagnose ADHD. These included his difficulty sustaining attention to tasks requiring some mental effort, his tendency to lose things and be disorganized, and his constant fidgeting. Many of these behaviors had been typical of Paul since he began public school, and the hyperactive and impulsive behaviors perhaps even as a toddler. And so in my mind, it all began to come together in formulating a diagnostic impression. The early onset of his behavioral problems, their cross-situational nature, the fact that Paul had more than sufficient symptoms to reach the threshold for diagnosis, and the apparent family history of difficulties consistent with ADHD were all contributing by now to my clinical sense that ADHD may well be present in this child, though additional corroborative evidence was needed from other components of my evaluation procedure.

In addition to having some of the classic symptoms of ADHD, Paul was described to me by his parents as having five out of nine behaviors associated with oppositional defiant disorder when I reviewed these with them. For example, he was described by his parents as argumentative with adults, tended to blame others for his mistakes, and had frequent temper outbursts. These sorts of problems had been evident since Paul was in first grade. Apart from occasional fighting with other boys at school, however, Paul displayed no evidence of a conduct disorder, characterized by delinquent and antisocial acts and a disregard for the rights of others.

I routinely question families about a child's peer relationships. When I did so in this case, the family described Paul as a happy boy who had been relatively successful in establishing and maintaining peer relationships. I immediately realized that this provided a positive or resiliance factor for Paul, as many ADHD children have serious peer relationship difficulties and it bodes poorly for their long term social adjustment. I found that Paul also had no history of depression or anxiety, nor of any trauma. This, too, I thought was good news, as emotional problems have also been found to be associated with poorer long-term outcome in ADHD children. Paul had apparently experimented with cigarettes and alcohol, but his parents did not suspect any ongoing substance abuse. He had never had psychiatric treatment of any kind, although his parents acknowledged that their parenting was quite inconsistent and they had wondered if they themselves could use some help. Here then, I reflected, was an added positive factor for Paul's prognosis—motivated parents who had already recognized that their own behavior might be contributing to some of Paul's behavioral difficulties, even though I recognized they were not directly causal of the ADHD.

To buttress the information I received from the parents, I sought opportunities to observe Paul's work-related behavior directly. I had two opportunities to do so, once at school and once in the clinic. I went to his history class one day and unobtrusively observed his conduct. In class, Paul spent much of the time with his head on his desk. He did not interact with other students. When the teacher called on him, he did have a response. However, his involvement in the lesson was minimal. At various moments, I wondered whether he was sleeping. Clearly, I thought, this boy's investment in school was waning and placed him at high risk for dropping out of school when the first opportunity might arise, as may happen with up to 36% of children with ADHD. I interviewed the teachers during my observation visit, and they communicated their concern for Paul's disruptive behavior in the classroom. He challenged authority regularly, they said, and took little responsibility for his work and assignments. They did feel that he could academically handle the curriculum, and they did not believe he had either learning disabilities or ADHD. This caused me to mentally note that educating the school staff about the true nature of ADHD would be a priority on my list of recommendations to make to the family and school.

As for my observations in the clinic setting, I found Paul to be impressively personable, interactive, and attentive. I knew this to be common; only a minority of ADHD children, I had learned, misbehaved seriously in the clinic. I reflected upon earlier research in our clinic that had demonstrated that normal behavior in the clinic was not predictive of such behavior at home or school, but that abnormal behavior, when it did occur in that minority of ADHD children, was highly predictive of school behavioral difficulties. I noted that Paul completed all tasks presented to him in the clinic playroom and seemed to work hard, displaying a fair amount of motivation. In a one-to-one context, Paul was very socially skilled and interested in relating. This, too, I thought, fit well with my knowledge that many children with ADHD show far fewer symptoms in such one-to-one encounters. His conversational skills, I found, were excellent. Both in his oral and his written language, Paul demonstrated to me a mastery of complex and sophisticated sentence structures. Paul was quite talkative throughout our session. He was also very curious and extremely fidgety.

Following these observations, I took time to conduct achievement testing with Paul so as to have more current test scores addressing the matter of his skills development to date. Based on a standardized achievement test, Paul seemed to have acquired grade level skills in all academic areas. However, his weakest skills were in his broad knowledge in areas such as social studies, science, and humanities, reflecting, I believed, Paul's poor attention in school, as well as somewhat impoverished life experience. Paul's reading skills were extremely strong, especially when compared to his more average math skills. His IQ was again tested to be in the average range. In fact, his teachers were correct in this regard: he did not have a specific learning disability if by that one follows the traditional definition that a learning disability is a significant discrepancy between Paul's broad cognitive ability (i.e., IQ) and his specific academic achievement skills.

It is routine in my clinical evaluations to use well-standardized rating scales of child behavior so as to gauge the degree of deviance of a child's behavioral problems relative to same-age, same-sex normal children. Paul's mother completed the Child Behavior Checklist, a frequently used questionnaire containing over 113 different behavior and emotional problems. Her responses resulted in a profile highly significant for both ADHD and oppositional-defiant disorder. Symptoms of hyperactivity were reported to occur to a greater extent than 93% of other youngsters his age, while symptoms of defiant and aggressive behaviors fell at the 98th percentile. In addition, social withdrawal and a tendency to daydream were also reported. I knew that a benefit of such scales was their capacity to cover a variety of behavioral and emotional problems in a short period of time and often revealed behaviors not directly reported during the clinical interview, which the scale had in this case.

It is also my custom to get these same rating scales completed by the child's teacher, and so I had seen to it that a set was forwarded to Paul's teacher prior to my initial evaluation. Paul's seventh grade basic skills teacher also completed this questionnaire. The results indicated that he showed symptoms of ADHD to a greater degree than 98% of other boys his age. In addition, aggressive and defiant behaviors and social immaturity were reported to a similar severity level. Also reported was Paul's tendency to daydream in the classroom. Another rating scale concentrating specifically on ADHD symptoms (the Children's Attention Profile) was also sent to this teacher. This short questionnaire specifically inquires about inattention, impulsiveness, and hyperactivity; here Paul also placed above the 98th percentile.

Although I have found, as have some studies, that ADHD children may underreport the presence and degree of ADHD symptoms in themselves, I nonetheless make a habit of having my child patients complete a scale about their own ADHD symptoms. Their perspective on their own behavioral adjustment can be enlightening even if not diagnostically useful. I had Paul complete the ADHD Self-Report Rating Scale. The questionnaire asks the child to evaluate his or her own behavior, using the same behaviors that are part of the diagnosis of ADHD (see Table 1). The responses revealed an awareness of 9 out of 18 behaviors related to ADHD occurring on a frequent basis. These included difficulty staying seated and a tendency to be fidgety, difficulty with concentration and paying attention to schoolwork, a tendency to lose things and be disorganized, and a tendency to not think ahead. I was pleased to note that Paul's answers to a questionnaire on depression, as well as one on self-esteem, fell within the average range.

As with the self-report rating scales, the clinical interview of the children with ADHD should not be used to determine the presence of the disorder, but can still prove informative. During our interview, Paul acknowledged that he had behavior problems in school. He said that he liked school at times and very much did not want to be retained another year. Paul admitted that he tended to "joke around" too much in class, but explained that he got bored easily and had trouble listening to the teacher. Such insight, I realized, is relatively rare in

## TABLE 1. Diagnostic Criteria for Attention Deficit Hyperactivity Disorder

A. Either (1) or (2):

(1) *Six* (or more) of the following symptoms of **inattention** have persisted for at least six months to a degree that is maladaptive and inconsistent with developmental level:

*Inattention*
(a) Often fails to give close attention to details or makes careless mistakes in schoolwork, work, or other activities
(b) Often has difficulty sustaining attention in tasks or play activities
(c) Often does not seem to listen when spoken to directly
(d) Often does not follow through on instructions and fails to finish schoolwork, chores, or duties in the workplace (not as a result of oppositional behavior or failure to understand instructions)
(e) Often has difficulty organizing tasks and activities
(f) Often avoids, dislikes, or is reluctant to engage in tasks that require sustained mental effort (such as schoolwork or homework)
(g) Often loses things necessary for tasks or activities (e.g., toys, school assignments, pencils, books, or tools)
(h) Is often easily distracted by extraneous stimuli
(i) Is often forgetful in daily activities

(2) *Six* or more of the following symptoms of **hyperactivity-impulsivity** have persisted for at least six months to a degree that is maladaptive and inconsistent with developmental level:

*Hyperactivity:*
(a) Often fidgets with hands or feet or squirms in seat
(b) Often leaves seat in classroom or in other situations in which remaining seated is expected
(c) Often runs about or climbs excessively in situations where it is inappropriate (in adolescents or adults, may be limited to subjective feelings of restlessness)
(d) Often has difficulty playing or engaging in leisure activities quietly
(e) Is often "on the go" or often acts as if "driven by a motor"
(f) Often talks excessively
*Impulsivity:*
(g) Often blurts out answers before questions have been completed
(h) Often has difficulty awaiting turn
(i) Often interrupts or intrudes on others (e.g., butts into conversations or games)

B. Some hyperactive-impulsive symptoms or inattentive symptoms that caused impairment were present before age seven years.

C. Some impairment from the symptoms is present in two or more settings (e.g., at school [or work] and at home)

D. There must be clear evidence of clinically significant impairment in social, academic, or occupational functioning.

E. The symptoms do not occur exclusively during the course of a Pervasive Developmental Disorder, Schizophrenia or other Psychotic Disorder, and are not better accounted for by another mental disorder (e.g., Mood Disorder, Anxiety Disorder, Dissociative Disorder, or a Personality Disorder).

Code based on type:

314.00 *Attention-deficit Hyperactivity Disorder, Predominantly Inattentive Type:* If criterion A(1) is met, but criterion A(2) is not met for the past six months

314.01 *Attention-deficit Hyperactivity Disorder, Predominantly Hyperactive-Impulsive Type:* If criterion A(2) is met, but criterion A(1) is not met for the past six months

314.01 *Attention-deficit Hyperactivity Disorder, Combined Type:* If both criteria A(1) and A(2) are met for the past six months

Coding note: for individuals (especially adolescents and adults) who currently have symptoms that no longer meet full criteria, "In Partial Remission" should be specified.

---

ADHD children, but was commensurate with his parents' reports that Paul was not without some perspective on his own difficulties and appreciated that he was having problems at school that were, to some extent, his own doing. Subsequently in the interview, he said he did a lot of daydreaming. He also said that he had trouble finishing his work and tended to forget his homework and his notebooks. When asked what might help him improve his behavior at school, Paul thought that assistance with organizational skills was most helpful. He also thought that his performance improved when his teachers were able to be friendly toward him rather than angry. This led me to recall that many ADHD children, like Paul, see the negative and often punitive reactions of others to their inattentive, impulsive, active, and disorganized behavior at school as inherently unfair; given that they perceive themselves as unable to control these difficulties to a large degree, cannot the teachers see this as well? Small wonder many come to see themselves as dumb, stupid, and less capable than their peers.

## Diagnosis

I judged from the school and clinic testing of Paul that learning disabilities or specific cognitive deficits could be ruled out as an explanation for his academic performance problems. He had, however, been displaying a chronic and pervasive pattern of inattention, impulsivity, and hyperactivity, dating back to early elementary school and possibly to his toddler years. Such problems also were evident in his current behavior, both from his responses to interview questioning as well as from observations of his behavior. Likewise, his parents' responses to the interview questioning, his mother's rating scale responses, and the rating scale responses and information obtained from his seventh grade teachers were extremely consistent in identifying the behavioral concerns related to ADHD as being deviant for his developmental stage. Since the frequency and severity of Paul's inattention, impulsivity, and physical restlessness would not be found in

### TABLE 2. Diagnostic Criteria for Oppositional Defiant Disorder

A. A pattern of negativistic, hostile, and defiant behavior lasting at least six months, during which four (or more) of the following are present:

   (1) Often loses temper
   (2) Often argues with adults
   (3) Often actively defies or refuses to comply with adult requests or rules
   (4) Often deliberately annoys people
   (5) Often blames others for his or her own mistakes or misbehavior
   (6) Is often touchy or easily annoyed by others
   (7) Is often angry and resentful
   (8) Is often spiteful or vendictive

*Note:* Consider a criterion met only if the behavior occurs more frequently than is typically observed in individuals of comparable age and developmental level.

B. The disturbance in behavior causes clinically significant impairment in social, academic, or occupational functioning.

C. The behaviors do not occur exclusively during the course of a Psychotic or Mood Disorder.

D. Criteria are not met for Conduct Disorder, and, if the individual is age 18 years or older, criteria are not met for Antisocial Personality Disorder.

*Source:* Copyright by American Psychiatric Association. Adapted with permission from the American Psychiatric Association. (1994). *Diagnostic and statistical manual of mental disorders* (4th ed.). Washington, DC: Author.

any more than 5% of the general population of boys his age, I concluded that Paul met the criteria for a diagnosis of ADHD, as well as for oppositional-defiant disorder (see Table 2).

| | |
|---|---|
| Axis I: | • Attention-deficit Hyperactivity disorder |
| | • Oppositional defiant disorder |
| Axis II: | • No diagnosis |
| Axis III: | • None |
| Axis IV: | • Educational problems |
| | • Problems with primary support group |
| Axis V: | • GAF = 35 (current) |

### Case Formulation

Paul's ADHD clearly had roots going back to age three when he started having trouble in day-care. Like many ADHD children I see, he was viewed as having an "attitude" problem and deliberately defying adults. As a consequence, he received far more punishment than encouragement, so that oppositional and defiant behavior problems then developed. I am especially chagrined when ADHD children are punished for symptoms of their disorder that are not under their control, such as being denied recess for talking. Although his parents were inconsistent in their parenting style, they encouraged Paul's native intelligence and supported his self-esteem. It was to their credit, as well as Paul's, that he had not developed more serious conduct problems or difficulties with depression. Moreover, since his parents recognized the role that the semi-chaotic nature of the household might be playing in some of Paul's difficulties, they were motivated to cooperate with advice on treatment recommendations, and were capable of buffering Paul when necessary from the social slings and arrows of criticism that often get directed at ADHD children for their undercontrolled behavior pattern. Paul was also an attractive and likable boy, well accepted by his peers. This, also, can be a quite favorable prognostic sign and good news for parents who may fear the worst for the future social adjustment of their ADHD children. The major factor working against a more favorable prognosis was his age. Parents of teenagers simply have less control over their child's activities, and opportunities for remediation in the school are fewer. Another factor that had to be considered was just how much the large family size, greater family stress, and diminished parental time for Paul was further contributing to his oppositional behavior.

I believe that engaging in diagnostic classification is a useful endeavor with children. It is often one reason parents are seeking professional advice (Does he have a problem or not? Should we as parents worry or not?), and it can provide a sense of relief to parents seeking some answers. It is rarely the sole reason for referral, however, and I considered this fact as I formulated my opinion of Paul's circumstances. I do not, as some clinicians do, eschew labelling or consider it a harmful exercise. To the contrary, many treatment decisions are categorical (yes/no) in nature, and they require that categorical decisions be made about the presence of a disorder sufficiently severe to warrant such treatments. The decision to use medication with a child, to request and be eligible for special education, to seek private educational tutoring, to request a new teacher, change schools, engage in home schooling, and so on, are all categorical decisions that are, in part, driven by the diagnostic process. And, given the legal rights to special education, Social Security benefits for the disabled, insurance, etc., that those with ADHD have gained over the years, diagnoses must be considered and given, or access to these rights may be precluded.

Yet as I have counseled professional trainees in my clinic, so I counseled myself to go beyond a simple diagnostic exercise to contemplate the other issues inherent in this referral. It is often necessary in such evaluations to "read between the lines," articulating what goes unsaid but may be critical to a better understanding of *why* the referral to me has occurred and, more important, why it has occurred *now*. This is the art and wisdom of the evaluative process that comes from clinical experience. "What are the real issues here?" I ask myself. The responses that came to mind in Paul's case were as follows:

1. *Help us, we are losing our child:* Parents who eventually decide to seek a professional evaluation may have come to realize that something precious in their relationship with their child is being undermined, and they seek help to restore that relationship. Whether it is the tarnishing of that sacred bond between parent and child by the demands of schooling or its disruption by defiant and antisocial acts within the home and community, the fact is that parents may sense that something fundamental to their sense of family and bonding with their child is being lost by the problems that ADHD and its comorbid conditions can create. Perhaps, at some level, there is a grief reaction surfacing surrounding such a loss that drives the parents to seek professional answers. No matter its source, the skilled, sensitive clinician will recognize its importance and address it beyond just giving a diagnostic label to the child as part of the clinical feedback conference.

2. *Do something, we can't take this anymore:* Parents are typically not just seeking a more formal acknowledgment of their perceived loss in their relationship with their child, they are desperate for solutions. If unaddressed, such desperation can lead many parents to flirt with or even fully embrace sham remedies for ADHD, such as complex dietary regimens, megadoses of vitamins and minerals, brain-wave training, visual-motor exercises, and other countless yet groundless treatments available for ADHD. A sound, reasonable, empirically based treatment plan must be provided that addresses this issue or dissatisfaction with the clinician is likely to ensue.

3. *Reassurance against unnecessary fears:* I believe that parents like the Wagners may also be seeking some consolation for their fears that things are at their worst. And so I find that noting and elaborating upon the positive prognostic factors in the case, physical, cognitive, and social strengths of the child, and constructive factors associated with the parents and family unit can be just as critical as delineating the nature of Paul's difficulties and the developmental risks which they may be associated with. Put bluntly, I find that parents often want to know what is necessary to worry about and what is not, and clinicians are obligated to help parents negotiate this thicket of potential concerns.

4. *Affirmation of performance as parents:* I am fond of recalling the campaign slogan of Ed Koch when he ran for his multiple terms as Mayor of New York City. He used to say to people he would pass while walking about New York City, "How'm I doin?" Part of the motivation of some parents in referring a child is to learn how they as parents are performing in their parental role. Leaving this issue unaddressed can often leave parents only partially satisfied with the clinical evaluation, I believe. Something needs to be said during the feedback conference about how they, as parents, may be performing with this ADHD child, both good and bad. I find it helpful not to "pull my punches" but also not to pummel the parents with too many negative factors about their child's case. Instead, I will note the positives, even if few, so as to strike a balanced evaluation of parental performance where this issue seems to arise, as I thought it did with the Wagners.

Undoubtedly, I have found that other issues than these can arise in clinically evaluating children, but these are the ones that arose foremost in my mind as I formulated my impression of this case.

## Course of Treatment

My contacts with Paul's school system had initially shown me that they had considerable resistance to the diagnosis of ADHD. From the school system's point of view, Paul had an "attitude problem" that was a result of his parents' lack of discipline. Paul's parents, on the other hand, were relieved to hear that there was an explanation for Paul's behavior. They were confused, however, about the distinction between ADHD and oppositional-defiant behavior and were unclear about which behaviors were under Paul's control and which were not. This is a common question of parents of ADHD children and requires great tact to address. Poor organization, the failure to sustain effort throughout completion of tasks, impulsive verbal, behavioral, and emotional reactions are all easily attributable to ADHD. But refusal to perform a task at the outset, intentionally spiteful and vindictive conduct, extreme temper outbursts, and direct disobedience of a request are oppositional behavior and, as a result, can be viewed as learned, hence, malleable to some degree. Therefore, education about ADHD and ODD are critical before any other form of intervention can be started.

Following some consultation with Paul's school, I found that his teachers were agreeable to making several modifications. Paul would check in weekly with his guidance counselor, who talked to the teachers on a regular basis about Paul's classroom behavior. The guidance counselor served as a "coach" or "case manager" and would assist Paul with ensuring that he had his daily assignment notebook and that it was completed, that his materials for upcoming classes and homework after school were organized, and provide him with daily feedback about his performance at school. I requested that Paul also be allowed to have an extra set of books to keep at home so he would be less likely to lose them. I encouraged his teachers to grant him access to a computer at school in order to learn keyboarding and eventually word processing skills. Paul learned to sit regularly at the front of the classroom so he would be less prone to daydreaming, and his teachers agreed to give him weekly outlines of material being covered in class. Paul eventually ended up taking his tests in the resource room with extra time allowed because he needed more time to complete them, and his homework assignments were modified to accommodate how exhausted his attentional abilities were by the end of the day.

I requested that Paul's parents also attend seven sessions of a parent behavior-management training group, and they willingly did so. As they learned more about ADHD, it became apparent that Paul's father had many of the symptoms himself. As is the case with nearly 25% of parents of ADHD children seen in our clinic, Paul's father was referred to our Adult ADHD Clinic for further evaluation and management of his adult ADHD. His father had realized that his own ADHD made it more difficult for him to consistently follow through with the home-based incentive system for Paul. While Paul's parents were able to see improvement in his self-esteem as a result of their increased praise and the special, one-on-one time they began spending with him, they had more trouble following through with the rewards and penalties I teach parents to use with children for following household rules. They found that their control over Paul's behavior outside the home was a particular problem. While he would be more compliant with his chores in order to earn time at the video arcade, he was caught on more than one occasion buying cigarettes illegally for older boys at the arcade and even smoking himself.

## Outcome of the Case

Paul's parents eventually made the decision to place Paul on a stimulant medication, Ritalin (methylphenidate). This drug is commonly used in the treatment of children with ADHD. His pediatrician placed him on 20 milligrams of the sustained release form because it lasts longer during the day (six to seven hours) than the regular form (three to four hours). Because of financial constraints, the pharmacist recommended the generic version. Paul resisted taking the medication at first and said that he was used to being the class clown and did not like himself on medicine. At last contact, his parents were still struggling with Paul over medication, and they had started family counseling.

# EMPIRICAL CONTRIBUTIONS TO UNDERSTANDING ADHD (BARKLEY)

In many ways, I found Paul's case to be rather typical, characterized by many of the most common findings associated with children and adolescents having ADHD as reported in the empirical literature. His difficulties with his temperament, even as an infant, distinguished him as a difficult baby to care for, being more irritable and emotional than most normal children. These problems are often reported in the histories of children with ADHD.[1] His difficulties upon entry into formal schooling with his ability to organize his work and persist in completing assignments, likewise, are highly typical of children with ADHD.[2] Recently, I have encountered research that has found that the symptoms of hyperactivity and impulsiveness in these children often emerge in the preschool years while the problems with sustained attention and persistence of effort toward work assignments often emerge several years later, usually by entry into school.[3] This fact, along with other research findings, implied that the problems with inattention are somehow secondary to those arising from the hyperactivity and impulse control. The latter two problems have, for some time, been recognized as actually comprising a single deficit, that being a problem with inhibition.[1,4] In short, I believe that the problems with inhibition arise first in development, and are manifest as difficulties with excessive movement and behavior (hyperactivity), as well as with difficulties inhibiting urges to act (impulsiveness) during the preschool years. Later, they seem to lead to problems with sustained persistence to tasks. I have come to think of the problem with persistence (sustained attention) as resulting from a combination of problems: (1) the poor inhibition of immediate responses to potentially rewarding events happening around the child while working (distractibility); (2) the diminished ability to return to work once interrupted; and (3) a commensurate inability to self-regulate one's own drive or motivational states supporting goal-directed behavior in the absence of immediate consequences for doing so.[3]

In my clinical opinion, Paul's behavior was quite consistent with the Combined Type of ADHD, as shown in Table 1. During his preschool years, he would likely have fallen into the Predominantly Hyperactive-Impulsive Type, I felt, until such time as his poor inhibition began to create problems with persistent, goal-directed or task-oriented behavior (sustained attention), when he likely moved into the Combined Type classification. It has been my opinion that the available research indicates that the Predominantly Inattentive Type of ADHD actually is not a subtype of ADHD at all. Instead, I believe that the research increasingly supports the possibility that it is a distinct disorder apart from ADHD. I interpret the existing empirical literature as showing that this form of ADHD carries far fewer developmental risks, and comprises a different gender ratio, pattern of co-existing disorders, and constellation of potential causes that is different from those seen in the other two types of ADHD. Those types are simply separate developmental stages of the same disorder, in my opinion.[1] The Inattentive Type likelyrepresents a true disorder of attention (known focused or selective attention, most likely), whereas the other types of ADHD are actually a disorder of behavioral inhibition. The remainder of this chapter concentrates on the latter group.

My sense of the developmental literature on ADHD is that by age five to eight years, between 45 and 70% of children with ADHD have begun to show significant problems with defiance, resistance to parental authority, hostility toward others, and quick-temperedness, much like Paul.[1,2] This behavior pattern is often called oppositional defiant disorder and is rarely seen in the Inattentive Type of ADHD.[1] This hostile/defiant/aggressive behavior seems to be a harbinger of a much higher risk for later school disciplinary actions, peer rejection, and antisocial or delinquent behavior within the community.[1,4] When combined with greater-than-normal stress events within families, inconsistent parental management of a child's behavior, as well as a tendency to use harsh and unpredictable discipline by the parents, can provide fertile soil for early oppositional behavior. In such soil, the early proneness to becoming easily upset, emotional, and angry often seen in ADHD children like Paul seems to blossom or escalate into more severe forms of defiant and aggressive behavior and, possibly later, to delinquency.[5] One critical feature in determining which oppositional children progress to conduct disorder or delinquency, I have found, is the degree to which parents monitor their children's activities, especially while the children are out of the home.[5,6] This fact helped me to see how Paul's emerging antisocial behavior (stealing cigarettes and other goods from stores) may first have started at times when he is away from home and from his parents' supervision.

This combination of problems I witnessed in Paul with uninhibited behavior and poor persistence in work, as well as defiance to rules and authority, has been shown to lead readily to difficulties in school. And so I could see how Paul, like 35 to 50% of children with ADHD, carried a risk of eventually being retained in grade and even suspended from school at least once. Knowing that 10 to 20% of ADHD children will be expelled as a disciplinary measure, I realized that Paul was at risk for such consequences should his behavioral problems at school continue.[1,7] Such conduct, I realized, placed Paul at significant risk of not completing high school, which seems to occur in up to 35% of children with ADHD followed into young adulthood.[8] Unlike a large minority of children with ADHD (30% or more) who also have learning disabilities, Paul did not seem to show the classic discrepancy between his intelligence and some area of academic skill, such as reading, math, or spelling, necessary for that diagnosis. Instead, comparable to the vast majority of ADHD children, his discrepancy, I concluded, was between his intelligence and his productivity or actual work performance at school. This meant that Paul's ADHD was best thought of as a disorder of performance (doing what you know) rather than one of skill (knowing what to do)—of when he should be doing something and not how to do it.

A similar type of discrepancy between mental ability (i.e., IQ) and performance has also been noted in the larger sphere of fulfilling more general responsibilities appropriate to a child's developmental stage. These include things such as dressing, bathing, and otherwise caring for oneself, being trustworthy to follow rules when away from parents, cooperating with other children, and performing assigned chores at home reliably. These areas are often referred to as adaptive functioning. Children with ADHD are frequently found to be substantially behind their peers and siblings, as well as below that level predicted from their own intellectual potential in such adaptive functioning.[9,10]

Paul's case also shows just how stressful a child with ADHD can be to raise and the types of reactions his uncontrolled behavior is likely to elicit from others. I have found in my studies on the interactions of children with ADHD with their parents that such children are less compliant with parents' directions, more negative toward their parents, less able to follow through on instructions, less able to play quietly for sustained periods of time, and request more help from their parents when working.[11,12] Such behavior, I have found, can make parents more likely to respond with excessive commands, hostile reactions, and punishment, as well as to become less responsive to their children's interactions and requests for help. My own follow-up study and those of others have shown me that these interaction conflicts will continue into the adolescent years for many families of ADHD children.[1] Over time, I believe that parents may spend less of their available time in recreation with an ADHD child like Paul because such children are so stressful to supervise and interact with compared to normal children.[13] Such parenting stress seems to be especially acute during the preschool years, yet research by my colleagues at our medical center has shown that it continues to be higher than normal throughout childhood. They have also found that the level of stress is similar to levels experienced by parents of children with more severe developmental disabilities, such as autism.[14,15]

Is it any wonder, I thought, that Paul would bring out the same kinds of reactions from his teachers? I frequently find in my studies that other adults besides parents who must supervise, teach, and care for children like Paul often view the children's uncontrolled and negative behavior as willful, lazy, or part of a generally poor attitude toward work and responsibility. Paul experienced just such social judgments from his teachers, I felt. The problem, as seen by teachers, is one of motivation or poor self-discipline and, as in Paul's case, is often attributed to poor child-rearing by the child's parents. As a result, teachers, for instance, may respond to children with ADHD with more commands, punishment, and censure than they would show toward other children.[16] I have also found that the normal peers of these children, will likewise react with increased attempts to control and direct the ADHD child's undercontrolled behavior, but will eventually reject and ostracize such a child from the normal play groups.[17] I would not be surprised, then, to find in my practice that children like Paul are often friendless in adolescence or drift toward a peer group that is similarly deviant in their conduct. This increases the risk that the child or teen will engage in antisocial acts, such as lying, stealing, underage use of alcohol and tobacco, and using illegal drugs.[7,8] Unless tightly supervised by parents during adolescence, Paul carries a similarly higher risk for such outcomes. Yet I find it is the rare parent who will react to the problems at school as Paul's parents chose to do, by removing the child from school for home-schooling or transferring the child to a different school. Most stay with their neighborhood school and continue to advocate for whatever special accommodations or formal special educational services they can obtain for their children while personally striving to assist the child in meeting the demands of school. This often means sacrificing time with other family members or time needed for personal renewal.

My experience shows that Paul's own reactions to these responses from others is rather typical. I have noted that children with ADHD, especially those with oppositional disorder,[1] often come to view others as the cause of their problems, disappointments, and failures in succeeding in home, school, or social settings. They frequently do not see their behavior problems as being as severe as others, such as parents and teachers, see them[18] and, consequently, find it hard to understand what everyone is so upset about. I have found that many, though not all, children with ADHD believe that things would be better for them if others would simply "get off their case" and let them do as they wish to do.

The experience of Paul's parents in initially seeking help for his behavior problems is, regrettably, rather typical in my experience. The majority of children with ADHD have often been viewed as being relatively normal during brief visits to their pediatrician's office,[19] much as Paul was. This situation is improving greatly as more primary care physicians come to realize that symptoms of ADHD are less likely to be seen in one-to-one encounters with the child, in novel settings, for short periods of time, and with strangers. Yet my travels have taught me that the current situation, particularly outside of North America, is still woefully inadequate in this regard. The strong recommendation to incorporate well-standardized parent and teacher rating scales into the evaluation process, as was done with Paul, is but one means of collecting more reliable and valid information about the deviance of children's behavior problems in place of so heavy a reliance on office behavior.[1,4] Children's self-reports on such scales should not be given as heavy an emphasis in the diagnostic decision-making, given that, as with Paul, such reports are often underestimates of the actual level of deviance demonstrated by such children, particularly relative to parent and teacher ratings.[18]

## EMPIRICAL CONTRIBUTIONS TO THE TREATMENT OF ADHD

The theoretical model I have developed elsewhere[3] helps to provide a framework not only for the understanding and assessment of children such as Paul, but provides a deeper understanding of the need for particular treatments and what their likely success will be. For instance, my own early reviews on the subject,[20,21] as well as later work on the clinical use of medications,[22,23] has found the stimulant medications to be the most effective treatment for children, like Paul, with ADHD. Between 70 and 90% of such children over the age of five years and with IQs higher than 50[24] display a positive response to these medications—a response that continues to be favorable into adolescence and adulthood, contrary to clinical lore. Moreover, such medications produce dramatically higher rates of normalization (behavior brought to within the normal range) than occurs with any other medications or psychological or educational treatments. The side effects of these medications are commonly minor and benign, the risk for addiction or later substance abuse trivial to nonexistent, and the cost-effectiveness relative to psychoeducational treatments highly favorable. Thus, medication remains the treatment of choice for managing ADHD. This makes sense because, as the model shows, the treatment which helps to improve or resolve the underlying neurodevelopmental deficit in behavioral inhibition has the greatest likelihood of improving those psychological functions dependent on inhibition that are also impaired in those with ADHD.

I have found in my practice and discussions with numerous other professionals, however, that the greatest problem with using medication for children in Paul's age group is compliance. The recommendation of medication at this age often conflicts with the natural tendencies of adolescents for greater autonomy, a greater voice in decision making that involves them, and a greater sensitivity to the social judgments of their peers about taking a "psychiatric drug." Cooperation, not treatment efficacy, is more often the dilemma faced by clinicians treating adolescents with ADHD and their parents. This often results in the need for short-term family therapy around communication and conflict negotiation skills to assist parent and teen with resolving the numerous issues that arise in this developmental stage in those with ADHD.[25]

The use of medications, however, is often not a sufficient treatment plan for many children with ADHD, though it can be for a large minority in my experience. This need for additional treatment is often driven by several factors: (1) degree of initial response to medication; (2) comorbidity of other disorders, such as ODD, CD, learning disabilities, and affective disorders with the ADHD; and (3) the psychological integrity of the parents to manage such difficult children. For any or all of these reasons, additional treatments are going to be needed, such as: (1) training the parents and teachers of children with comorbid ADHD and ODD in more effective child management skills, as was necessary for Paul; (2) obtaining additional special education services and making curriculum adjustments to accommodate the deficits caused by several disabilities (ADHD, LD, etc.); (3) providing psychological counseling to the children in cases of comorbid Post-traumatic Stress Disorder, depression, or other emotional disorders; (4) referring parents to mental health services for their own psychological difficulties or psychiatric disorders; (5) encouraging parents to become involved in parent support groups for families raising children with ADHD, such as Children and Adults with ADD (CHADD) or the Attention Deficit Disorders Association (ADDA) in North America, LADDER in England, and a number of regional support groups increasingly available in Australia; and (6) in the 8 to 10% of cases in need of such intensive treatment, assisting with placing the child in residential treatment programs.[1] As I have discussed above, Paul and his parents were in need of several such recommendations.

The model of ADHD I have developed[3] also leads to understanding why behavior modification programs will prove indispensable for many children with ADHD, why they must be maintained for long periods of time (often years), and why there are likely to be no enduring treatment effects once such programs are ceased. This is because such programs provide artificial or prosthetic consequences for goal-directed behavior. They do so, in a sense, by bringing the future into the moment so as to motivate and maintain appropriate prosocial, goal-directed, and future-oriented conduct by the child with ADHD. Such programs, as the model implies, are not done so much to teach the child a new skill (ADHD is not a skill deficit); they are meant to assist the child with initiating and persisting in the use of prosocial and productive behaviors already within their repertoire whose consequences naturally lay in the future (ADHD as a performance deficit). The model also demonstrates why purely cognitive-behavioral[26] or other skill-oriented training programs are unlikely to affect the deficits associated with ADHD adequately or be of much long-term benefit. They place too much emphasis on self-directed and internalized speech, which is downstream from the real deficit in inhibition. Also, such speech is not only immature in those with ADHD, but is less likely to guide their own behavior even when it occurs. The problem with self-directed speech, then, is *secondary* to the inhibitory deficit that goes unaddressed by cognitive or skill-focused therapies.

I have found it critical to stress to parents, teachers, and others that the neurodevelopmental nature of the deficits, along with the strong genetic or otherwise biological predisposition to ADHD and its significant stability over time,[1] are not intended to be used as excuses for the child's misconduct. It should not serve to free the child utterly from any form of accountability. Quite to the contrary, I stressed with Paul's parents and teachers the need to provide those with ADHD with *increased accountability*—the consequences for both prosocial behavior and misconduct must be more immediate, frequent, salient, and consistent than is often done with otherwise normal children.[1] Time, delays in consequences (accountability), and the future more generally constitute a nemesis for those with ADHD that can be defeated only by the organized and systematic management of the immediate context which surrounds them.

In conclusion, I believe that labeling the problems of those with ADHD simply as an attention deficit both trivializes and tragically underestimates the actual nature of this disorder and its developmental implications for later social maladjustment and a life of underproductivity relative to one's abilities. ADHD, I believe, is actually a developmental disorder of self-regulation and future-directed behavior that adversely affects an individual's self-discipline, social effectiveness, and general adaptive functioning. I have found that its diagnosis and proper management remove it from the realm of moral judgment and place it squarely within the realm of the mental health sciences where it belongs. Paul's case, I believe, nicely illustrates this process of reinterpretation and the important role clinicians play in it, by helping families to better understand, cope with, and raise a child with ADHD.

### Notes

1. Barkley, R.A. (1990). *Attention deficit hyperactivity disorder: A handbook for diagnosis and treatment.* New York: Guilford Press.

2. Loeber, R., Green, S.M., Lahey, B.B., Christ, M.A.G., & Frick, P.J. (1992). Developmental sequences in the age of onset of disruptive child behaviors. *Journal of Child and Family Studies, 1,* 21–41.

3. Barkley, R.A. (1995). *Inhibition, sustained attention, and executive functions: Constructing a unifying theory of ADHD.* University of Massachusetts Medical Center, Worcester, MA. Submitted for publication.

4. Hinshaw, S.P. (1994). *Attention deficits and hyperactivity in children.* Thousand Oaks, CA: Sage.

5. Loeber, R. (1990). Development and risk factors of juvenile antisocial behavior and delinquency. *Clinical Psychology Review, 10,* 1–43.

6. Patterson, G.R., Reid, J.B., & Dishion, T.J. (1992). *Antisocial Boys.* Eugene, OR: Castalia.

7. Barkley, R.A., Fischer, M., Edelbrock, C.S., & Smallish, L. (1990). The adolescent outcome of hyperactive children diagnosed by research criteria: I. An 8-year prospective follow-up study. *Journal of the American Academy of Child and Adolescent Psychiatry, 29,* 546–557.

8. Weiss, G., & Hechtman, L. (1993). *Hyperactive children grown up.* New York: Guilford Press.

9. Stein, M.A., Szumowski, E., Blondis, T.A., & Roizen, N.J. (1995). Adaptive skills dysfunction in ADD and ADHD children. *Journal of Child Psychology and Psychiatry, 36,* 663–670.

10. Barkley, R.A., DuPaul, G.J., & McMurray, M.B. (1990). Comprehensive evaluation of attention deficit disorder with and without hyperactivity. *Journal of Consulting and Clinical Psychology, 58,* 775789.

11. Barkley, R.A. (1985). The social interactions of hyperactive children: Developmental changes, drug effects, and situational variation. In R. McMahon & R. Peters (Eds.), *Childhood disorders: Behavioral-developmental approaches* (pp. 218–243). New York: Brunner/Mazel.

12. Danforth, J.S., Barkley, R.A., & Stokes, T.F. (1991). Observations of parent-child interactions with hyperactive children: Research and clinical implications. *Clinical Psychology Review, 11,* 703–727.

13. Cunningham C.E., Benness, B.B., & Siegel, L.S. (1988). Family functioning, time allocation, and parental depression in the families of normal and ADDH children. *Journal of Clinical Child Psychology, 17,* 169–177.

14. Mash, E.J., & Johnston, C. (1983). Parental perceptions of child behavior problems, parenting self-esteem, and mothers reported stress in younger and older hyperactive and normal children. *Journal of Consulting and Clinical Psychology, 51,* 68–99.

15. Anastopoulos, A.D., Guevremont, D.C., Shelton, T.L., & DuPaul. G.J. (1992). Parenting stress among families of children with attention deficit hyperactivity disorder. *Journal of Abnormal Child Psychology, 20,* 503–520.

16. Whalen, C.K., Henker, B., & Dotemoto, S. (1980). Methylphenidate and hyperactivity: Effects on teacher behavior. *Science, 208,* 1280–1282.

17. Cunningham, C.E., & Siegel, L.S. (1987). Peer interactions of normal and attention deficit disordered boys during free-play, cooperative task, and simulated classroom situations. *Journal of Abnormal Child Psychology, 15,* 247–268.

18. Fischer, N., Barkley, R.A., Edelbrock, C.S., & Smallish, L. (1993). The stability of dimensions of behavior in ADHD and normal children over an 8-year follow-up. *Journal of Abnormal Child Psychology, 21,* 315–337.

19. Sleator, E.K., & Ullman, R.L. (1981). Can the physician diagnose hyperactivity in the office? *Pediatrics, 67,* 13–17.

20. Barkley, R.A. (1976). Predicting the response of hyperactive children to stimulant medication: A review. *Journal of Abnormal Child Psychology, 5,* 351–369.

21. Barkley, R.A. (1977). A review of stimulant drug research with hyperactive children. *Journal od Child Psychology and Psychiatry, 18,* 137–165.

22. Barkley, R.A., DuPaul, G.J., & Costello, A. (1993). Stimukants. In J.S. Werry & M. Aman (Eds.), *A practitioner's guide to psychoactive drugs with children and adolescents* (pp.206–238). New York: Plenum.

23. Dulcan, M.K. (1990). Using psychostimulants to treat behavioral disorders of children and adolescents. *Journal of Child and Adolescents Psychopharmacology, 1,* 7–20.

24. Greenhill, L.L., & Osman, B.B. (Eds.), *Ritalin: Theory and patient management.* New York: Mary Ann Liebert.

25. Robin, A.L. (1990). Training families with ADHD adolescents. In R.A. Barkley (Ed.), *Attention deficit hyperactivity disorder: A handbook for diagnosis and treatment* (pp. 462–497). New York: Guilford Press.

26. Abikoff, H. (1987). An evaluation of cognitive behavior therapy for hyperactive children: A critical review. *Clinical Psychology Review, 5*, 479–512.

## Recommended Readings

Barkley, R.A. (1990). *Attention deficit hyperactivity disorder: A handbook for diagnosis and treatment.* New York: Guilford Press.

Sleator, E.K., & Pelham W.E. (1986). *Attention deficit disorder.* Norwalk, CT: Appleton-Century-Crofts.

Taylor, E. (1986). *The Overactive Child.* Philadelphia: Lippincott.

Weiss, G., & Hechtman, L. (1993). *Hyperactive children grown up* (2nd Ed.). New York: Guilford Press.

Werry, J., & Aman, M. (1993). *Practitioners guide to psychoactive drugs for children and adolescents.* New York: Plenum.

## Books for Parents and Teachers

Forwler, M. (1992). *CHADD Educators' Manual.* CHADD, 449 N.W 70th Ave., Suite 308, Plantation, FL 33317.

Fowler, M.C. (1990). *Maybe you know my kid: A parents' guide to identifying, understanding, and helping your child with attention-deficit hyperactivity disorder.* Birch Lane, 600 Madison Ave., New York, NY 10022.

Goldstein, S., & Goldstein, M. (1992). *Hyperactivity: Why won't my child pay attention?* Neurology, Learning and Behavior Center, 670 East 3900 South, #100 Salt Lake City, Utah 84107.

Gordon, M. (1991). *ADHD/Hyperactivity: A consumer's guide.* DeWitt, NY: GSI Publications.

Ingersoll, B. (1988). *Your hyperactive child.* New York: Doubleday.

Ingersoll, B., & Goldstein, M. (1993). *Attention deficit disorder and learning disabilities: Realities, myths, and controversial treatments.* New York: Doubleday.

Kennedy, P., Terdal, L., & Fusetti, L. (1993). *The hyperactive child book.* New York: St. Martin's Press.

Parker, H. (1992). *ADAPT: Attention deficit accomodation plan for teaching.* Impact Publications, 300 NW 70th Ave., Plantation, FL 33317.

Wender, P. (1987). *The Hyperactive Child, Adolescent, and Adult.* New York: Oxford University Press.

Wodrich, D. (1994). *What every parent wants to know: Attention deficit hyperactivity disorder.* Baltimore: Paul H. Brookes.

# 15

*Steven H. Zarit conducts research on mental health problems of later life, with a focus on family caregiving. He is Professor of Human Development and Assistant Director of the Gerontology Center at Pennsylvania State University. He received his Ph.D. from the Committee on Human Development, University of Chicago, with specializations in adult development and aging and clinical psychology.*

*Judy M. Zarit is a clinician in private practice in State College. Pennsylvania, specializing in clinical geropsychology. About one-third of her practice involves older people and their families. She received her Ph.D. from the University of Southern California with a specialization in clinical psychology and aging. Both Drs. Zarit have written several articles together in and one book* (The Hidden Victims of Alzheimer's Disease: Families Under Stress. 1985. *New York: New York University Press), with N. K. Orr and are at work on a new book about mental health and aging. Their interest in aging grows out of the recognition of what well-planned clinical interventions can achieve and the opportunities to make important changes, even in difficult circumstances, such as described in this chapter.*

# Esther and Milton, 'Til Death Do Us Part: A Case of Dementia

**About the Disorder**

Dementia is a form of cognitive impairment involving generalized progressive deficits in a person's memory and learning of new information, ability to communicate, judgment, and motor coordination. In addition to experiencing cognitive changes, people with dementia undergo changes in their personality and emotional state. Such disturbances in how a person thinks and acts impair the person's ability to work and interact with others. The symptoms of dementia may begin as mild forgetfulness; however, if the underlying brain disorder that causes the dementia cannot be treated, the symptoms will become increasingly obvious and distressing. As the condition of people with dementia worsens, so does their capacity for caring for themselves, staying in touch with what is going on around them, and living a normal life.

Dementia of the Alzheimer's type clearly affects more than the afflicted individual; it touches everyone in that person's life. The stress or burden of caregiving can lead the family member to experience severe depression bordering on despair. Furthermore, medical problems can complicate the diagnosis and treatment of Alzheimer's disease.

Unlike the other disorders in this book, the prognosis for people with Alzheimer's disease is always dire. There is no cure. The best that clinicians can hope for is finding ways to alleviate pain and discomfort for the afflicted individual. Furthermore, as is evident in Dr. Judy Zarit's sensitive case description, the focus of treatment may shift from the individual with the diagnosis to the caregiver. Dr. Steven Zarit's approach to understanding the problems of caregivers provides a theoretically and empirically sound foundation for such interventions.—*Eds.*

Of all the problems and illnesses associated with old age, none is as feared or devastating as dementia. Alzheimer's disease and the other disorders which cause dementia result in progressive impairment of memory and intellectual functioning, deterioration of behavior, and ultimately a loss of one's personal identity as the afflicted person no longer is able to recall even basic information about one's self or one's past. Although nursing home placement of dementia patients is common in the later stages of illnesses, families provide a great deal of care at home, often under considerable stress.

## CAREGIVING FOR DEMENTIA

The following case examines the consequences of dementia for one couple, the wife who has the illness and her husband who cares for her. They were seen clinically by one of us (J.Z.) over a period of several years, so the whole of a caregiver's career can be illustrated, from the early stages when the role is first assumed, through periods of struggling with overwhelming stresses and losses, to institutional placement, and finally the patient's death. While I follow one couple, the case is a composite incorporating elements from other families. This was done both to protect confidentiality and to illustrate a broader array of issues in treatment. The case is unique because of how long the dementia patient was able to participate in and benefit from brief counseling sessions. It also illustrates that intervention goes beyond a traditional office model of treatment to include home visits, interfacing with physicians and social service providers, and the use of a variety of skills, some psychotherapeutic, some based on an understanding of dementia and how to manage its consequences, and some having to do with practical life skills.

### Initial Presentation

My first glimpse of Esther and Milton was in the waiting room of my office, where they were arriving for an appointment with one of my associates. My clinician's sixth sense told me at a glance that Esther had early dementia. I remember asking myself then why that thought had occurred in the single moment my gaze fell on her. Was it the slightly puzzled, maybe even frightened look in her eyes? Or something about the musculature of her face? Or did I notice Milton's hand gently guiding her to the receptionist's window? Whatever the signal was, I was in no way surprised when my associate referred them to me.

### Case History

Prior to my initial visit with Esther and Milton, I received a neurological and neuropsychological evaluation. The neurologist had diagnosed Alzheimer's disease, based on mental status testing, neurological evaluation, and an MRI scan done in 1988 that showed pronounced cortical atrophy with compensatory ventriculomegaly. He was struck by Esther's tearfulness and requested the neuropsychological evaluation to attempt to differentiate between dementia and depression. He referred her to my associate for neuropsychological evaluation, which was completed in April 1989.[1]

Esther was observed to be both anxious and depressed during the neuropsychological testing. She was acutely aware that she was not performing at levels which she considered acceptable. She would tearfully cry out, "You see, you see, I just can't do it! What am I going to do?" Although many of Esther's abilities were at or above normal levels, immediate and short-term memory were severely impaired, both in verbal and visual presentations. Her general intellectual skills, particularly abstracting abilities, showed impairment. While she could perform simple arithmetic, she was unable to approach more complex problems, stating, "I can't even begin to understand."

Esther was a 67-year-old woman in 1989. She had completed college and had worked in secretarial positions until she married Milton, who had been her college sweetheart. They had two children, and Esther stayed active in community organizations while raising them, often assuming secretarial functions or working with Milton to produce newsletters for the various organizations. She was particularly gifted at writing personal notes of thanks to contributors in her lovely, flowing script. By the time the children left home for college, Esther and Milton were devoting most of their free time to their community work, usually working together. They took particular pleasure in working in community theater, both on the stage and behind the scenes.

In about 1983, Esther began having memory lapses during performances. Her mind would suddenly go blank and other cast members would either cue her or improvise around her errors. Gradually, she withdrew from performing, but she was continuing to serve as treasurer of the community theater when I first met her in 1989.

Milton is a retired professor and a very observant historian. He had originally thought that Esther had gotten over-involved in activities, and he attributed her memory lapses to overload. However, the number and kind of problems had reached a critical point by 1988, and he could no longer find explanations, which led to the neurological consultation. She was now having difficulty finding her clothing, and was wearing only those items of clothing she could find easily. Milton described visual-perceptual problems, such as Esther looking directly at an object while saying she was unable to find it. When the object was pointed out to her, she would say, "It doesn't look right."

Esther had recently stopped driving and had withdrawn from her friends, because she was no longer comfortable leaving home. She was also having some mobility problems resulting from arthritis in her knees and shoulders and being overweight.

## Diagnosis

Given the available data, I felt that while the neurologist's diagnosis of Alzheimer's disease was certainly *possible,* it was equally possible that this was a case of vascular dementia, especially because of a documented history of hypertension, the irregular pattern of deficits found in neuropsychological testing, and Esther's acute insight into her shortcomings.[2] In any event, both of those disorders have a progressive and unrelenting course, leading to severe impairments in cognition and everyday functioning. One thing quite clear was that she was (perhaps appropriately) depressed and anxious in response to her deficits. This pattern of comorbidity of dementia, depression, and anxiety is very common. The *DSM-IV* diagnosis was vascular dementia with depressed mood.

> Axis I:  • Vascular dementia with depressed mood
> Axis II:  • Deferred
> Axis III:  • Hypertension, osteoarthritis
> Axis IV:  • Limited social support network, difficulty accessing medical care, secondary mobility problems, and dementia, dependency on the primary caregiver
> Axis V:  • GAF = 45

## Case Formulation

Although dementia is an irreversible degenerative process, it can be helpful to treat a patient in the earlier stages, particularly someone like Esther who is aware of her deficits and is depressed over them. Goals of treatment would be to help her come to terms with her growing disability, to plan for her own care and to lessen feelings of depression and anxiety. In most cases, however, the focus of treatment shifts to the family caregiver. Milton appeared to be as depressed as Esther by all of these changes, although he clearly wanted to believe that Esther was the "client." Accordingly, I decided to establish a pattern of seeing them together for half of the session to process her current reported problems, then to see her alone for the remaining time to work more directly with her depression and anxiety. This strategy would also give me an opportunity to monitor his depression without spotlighting him as a client.

## Course of Treatment

### First Crisis: A Solution to Their Problems

The initial stages of therapy with Esther and Milton became complicated early on when Milton stated that he knew of a "solution" to their problems, and that was to end her life and then his own when things got too bad. Cognizant that there have been several news reports of similar acts, I took this threat very seriously. I pointed out that while each individual may have the choice of suicide, no one is morally free to end another person's life, and Milton agreed. He evidently was frequently asking Esther to agree to his plan in moments of despair, and she had not responded to it directly. I spend the next several months working with Esther to answer this fundamental question: If your memory was completely gone and you needed total care, would you choose to go to a nursing home or would you choose to have your life ended? I was aware of the problems that would result should she agree to his plan (which I would have been legally obligated to prevent), but I felt that she had not agreed to his repeated requests and did not want to be part of a double suicide. As a result, I felt I could have a useful role by helping her clarify what she wanted.

Esther was terrified of the prospect of being separated from Milton and, in particular, of "being put away" in a nursing home. Gradually, through a long, patient series of possible scenarios (for example, asking her what she would do if something happened to Milton, or if she were unable to take care of herself), Esther was able to say to me first, and then later to Milton, that while she did not under any circumstances *want* to go to a nursing home, she even more strongly objected to having her life ended prematurely. She stated: "I can't imagine deciding to commit suicide." Once she had been able to make her preference clear, Milton felt honor-bound not to pursue this course. In retrospect, it was critical to have resolved this issue early, since later on in her disease, she would have been too impaired to verbalize her thoughts clearly.

### New Symptoms and New Strategies

Suicide was such a "hot" therapeutic issue that it was alluded to or touched on during weekly sessions for over six months. At the same time, memory and behavior problems Esther was experiencing were being discussed, and a variety of problem-solving strategies were used. For example, Esther was now feeling panicky when the phone rang, for fear that she would not know what to say or that she would forget what was said to her. During this period, the solution that worked for her was to begin writing down all phone messages. It should be noted that with a progressive degenerative brain disorder, all "solutions" are short term and can be undone by further deterioration. Periodically, I would remind Milton that these were temporary solutions and described the types of strategies that might be necessary later on. When caregivers can anticipate future problems, they are often better able to cope with them.

During the first six months of therapy, which I now think of as the "getting to know you" phase, I learned many important things about Esther and Milton. I learned that they truly were a mutually dependent couple, who had been each other's best friend. While they were very involved in the community, they were not people who socialized a lot or who entertained in their home. Later I would learn firsthand why not. Their children had both graduated from college, had married, had families, and lived in distant cities. The children visited infrequently and were focused on their own families and careers. These distant relationships with their children intensified their mutual dependency and isolation. I observed, and Milton confirmed, that if he got depressed enough, Esther would rally and take care of him for awhile.

During the first year of therapy, Milton was struggling hard to keep up a semblance of normality to their lives. They attended theater and symphony performances. Milton continued to work outside the home a few hours a week, and they worked together on the sales of season tickets for the community theater. People had noticed that something was wrong with Esther, but Milton was still telling them that it was her arthritis that was limiting her activities. At home, Milton was making heroic efforts to keep Esther functioning at as high a level as possible. She had so much apraxia that she could no longer cook. They would go grocery shopping together, but with no real plan for meals. Gradually, Milton was accepting that Esther could not meaningfully contribute in these tasks, and he began buying more frozen dinners and prepared food from the delicatessen.

During this period, Esther continued to be frustrated and angry with herself for not being able to do things the way she used to. When she would talk about her frustration, I usually concurred and supported these feelings, but pointed out that when she was upset or angry her verbal fluency generally got worse. She had a wonderful vocabulary and struggled valiantly to capture the precise shade of meaning when she spoke. So it was doubly frustrating for her when her mind suddenly would go blank in the middle of a sentence (anomia). I learned that if I asked her to talk around the word, she could convey the meaning. Often, I could offer words until she recognized the one she sought. (Recognition memory is retained far longer than spontaneous or recall memory in the dementing illnesses.) Milton learned to use this strategy, although eventually Esther's language impairment progressed to the point that her speech was too "empty" for anyone to be able to guess at what she intended to say. And at times, I am sure he got very frustrated as the frequency of her lapses escalated.

One of Milton's issues at this time was how long it took Esther to do things. Dementia caregivers have told me that it can take several hours to get the patient dressed and ready to go out, although it is sometimes hard for them to explain exactly what takes so long. Milton was attributing some of Esther's slowness to her arthritis. But on closer questioning, it was evident that he was still expecting her to dress herself independently, perhaps reminding her, but then assuming she would proceed by herself. In reality, she would forget what she was supposed to do, and also how to do it. When Milton became aware of how her memory impairment was slowing her down, he stayed with her more during dressing to prompt her through the necessary steps. In other areas, such as laundry, making the bed, or loading the dishwasher, he let her take as long as she wanted, which gave him a few moments of peace as well.

*The Second Year: A Household in Disarray*

As the second year of treatment began, Milton was becoming visibly more depressed. The pressure of trying to keep all of his commitments in the community, while Esther became ever more housebound and limited in what she could do, was overwhelming. He admitted to crying in frustration and hopelessness. His sleep was poor and erratic, as was Esther's now that she could no longer keep the days and nights separated. She would, for example, fall asleep briefly, and then awake, thinking she had slept the whole night.

At this point in caregiving, it is often helpful to bring in formal services to relieve the caregiver of some tasks, or to provide respite. It quickly became apparent, however, that there were serious obstacles to bringing help into the home. Milton began confiding in me that the house had not been cleaned for two, maybe three years, since Esther became unable to do that. He also admitted they were both pack rats who had filled their house with all sorts of things. He felt ashamed of the house being the way it was and, as a result, would not consider getting any type of help in the home for Esther.

A few months later, Milton revealed he had not been opening his mail or paying his bills for several months. I made some attempts to help problem-solve with the bills, but while he could acknowledge that it was a symptom of his depression, and that he was symbolically saying, "We're just not functioning in this house," we made no progress in getting the bills paid. Finally, I asked if I could make a home visit so that we could work on the bills together. Initially, Milton balked, saying he was too ashamed. With reassurances from me, Milton agreed to a home visit. Thus, we began alternating home and office visits.

The home was, indeed, cluttered and dusty, and there were some potential hazards for Esther, mainly because she was becoming increasingly unsteady on her feet. But the house was by no means unsafe or unhealthful.

During the home visits, Milton would let me find and organize his current bills. Then he would write the checks and I would mail them. I told him it gave me a feeling of satisfaction to get checks in the mail (which is true), and he would tell me it gratified him to give me that satisfaction. While we sorted mail and wrote checks, he would talk about his and Esther's life together. She generally sat by companionably and listened. We learned early that it was important to seat her between us when I visited at home, or she would get jealous that he was paying too much attention to me. And in the office she would often complain that he was much nicer to other people than he was to her.

At this point in the disease, Esther was becoming more tearful and depressed over not remembering. To help her, I wrote positive statements for her on index cards, such as "My memory is not reliable, but I will remember what is important to me." These cards were helpful for a while in controlling her tearfulness.

Some significant signposts of memory deterioration occurred during the second year of treatment. Esther began having memory lapses where she could not remember if she had any children. Her language was more often empty. She would talk about "the thing," but was unable to specify what she meant or anything about it. She would say, "I know what I want to say, but I can't get the words out. I can't understand why he [Milton] can't figure it out." The two of them would get into long, protracted arguments in the middle of the night. She would perseverate on something she was trying to say, and he could not think of a way to end the conversation. Eventually, he stopped trying to make sense out of what she was saying, particularly after he realized that she was often not using the word she intended. That realization was another very disturbing loss for him. His once very articulate wife, who was so precise and particular in her use of language, no longer could even speak in meaningful terms.

Because of these changes, Milton decided that his children should come and spend some time with their mother while she could still appreciate it. Milton also agreed that they could sort through their own belongings that were still in the house and begin removing them. That would be a start to reducing the clutter. I received calls from both children, and we scheduled a meeting with just Milton and the children. At this point, Esther could not have participated in a discussion without having difficulty understanding and would likely become upset. Milton, in turn, did not feel comfortable talking about her condition and the problems he was facing in front of her. The children were overwhelmed with the amount of clutter and dirt in the house, but did not have the time or energy to do anything about it. They were in favor of hiring help to sort and clean, which Milton rejected. As it turned out, when the children actually tried to remove anything, Esther would get upset and cry. The clutter was what she was familiar with, and she relied on it for visual cues. Seeing her distress, Milton refused to let anything be changed.

### Bringing in Formal Services: An Uneasy Alliance

By the fall of 1991, Milton was taking Esther with him most of the time. Her declining mobility, and the possibility she would not be able to call for help if she needed it were growing concerns. Twice a week, he was still leaving her at home for a few hours, and she seemed to be tolerating his absence. When he returned, however, she would be tearfully happy, saying she thought he had left her for good.

I was continuing to see them alternate weeks at home and at the office. When alone, Esther would confide that "he'll want to get rid of me. Why would he want to be with a dull normal?" I would remind her of his commitment to her and ask her what she would do if the situation were reversed. Sometimes, she could still rally to this kind of explanation, saying, of course, she would have taken care of him, no matter what. Her insight into her condition, though fragile and fluctuating, was remarkable, given the level of cognitive impairment at this point. The time I spent with her was an important source of support, as she struggled with her weakening condition and her fears of being abandoned.

In November 1991, I got an emergency call that Esther had been incontinent, had slumped to the ground, and that Milton could not get her up. While this event could mark a worsening of her dementia, a number of treatable problems including acute illness and, especially, medications, could exacerbate her condition. I asked whether there had been any change in her medication, and Milton acknowledged that her primary care physician had prescribed Darvocet for her pain, since the less potent medications were not providing any relief. I suggested he call the physician and describe her symptoms. I also let him know I had seen this kind of catastrophic reaction in dementia patients as a consequence of this particular medication. After the medication was discontinued, she returned to her prior level of functioning.

By the following spring, however, Esther was even less mobile and her memory impairment was more severe. Their children arranged to come into town together again, and we met to try to problem-solve so that Milton could get some respite. The two alternatives were to arrange for home health aides to come into the house, or to arrange for Esther to attend a new adult day-care center that was just opening. Milton chose to pursue the option of home health aides first.

A nurse from the home health agency came out to the home to do an evaluation and scheduled an aide to come in twice a week to bathe Esther and do whatever other household chores would be helpful to Milton. Like many caregivers, Milton had expected that Esther would resist help from a stranger, but she surprised him by adjusting easily to the aide. Milton started feeling comfortable leaving Esther and running a few errands while the aide was with her.

After several months of this arrangement, I received two phone calls, one from Milton and one from the Area Agency on Aging. Milton was furious because a caseworker from the Area Agency had been called in by the home health nurse. The local Area Agency had been requesting that home health consult with them on all cases to determine eligibility for subsidized services. Milton had not wanted the Area Agency involved, since his financial situation was such that he would not be eligible for any benefits. The home health nurse, however, said that she had to comply with the request. At the time, I wondered whether the home health agency felt an obligation to report the condition of the house to the Area Agency on Aging because of the potential risk for harm.

The caseworker from the Area Agency on Aging made a home visit and quickly determined that Milton was not eligible for benefits. She focused instead on the issue that Milton still occasionally left Esther alone for a few hours a couple of times a week. The caseworker believed that leaving Esther alone constituted abuse under the state's new elder abuse regulations. She threatened to have Esther placed in a nursing home if Milton did not make a change. Her interpretation of what constituted abuse under the state's elder abuse statute turned out to be inaccurate, but the threat was frightening and real to Milton. In retrospect, the caseworker was probably upset as much by the clutter in the house as by Esther staying alone. She did not, however, find any reportable safety or health violations.

I spoke with the caseworker, explaining that Milton was a conscientious caregiver who was adapting to Esther's declining abilities as quickly as he could, that the process of bringing help into the home had been very delicate, and that I was overseeing the process. The caseworker agreed to back off if Milton would arrange to have someone with Esther when he went to work twice a week. He agreed to do so, but continued to be angry with the intrusion by the caseworker. It should be noted that Area Agencies on Aging function in a variety of ways, and that in some areas they would have offered help rather than sanctions. In fact, the caseworker in this instance offered no suggestions to Milton about how to arrange for help, and seemed indifferent to whether he continued his work or not. His twice-a-week work was virtually the only time he had contact now with other people and involvement in something other than caregiving. Giving up his one outlet could have been catastrophic for him.

During a visit to their primary care doctor in November 1992, his physician took Milton aside and told him that he had to make plans to place Esther in a nursing home. Milton was angry and depressed by this statement. He still wanted to try to keep Esther with him as long as possible. The in-home help he had arranged was providing him with the opportunity to keep working, which was a vital link between him and the community. Despite the gravity of the situation, as viewed by outsiders such as the physician and caseworker from the Area Agency on Aging, Milton believed it important to do everything he could to keep Esther at home. In each case, the attempt to cajole him to place his wife was greeted with anger, and then depression. In my work with Milton, I encouraged him to explore all of his options, including nursing homes, but remained supportive of his decision to keep Esther at home.

In April 1993, two significant events occurred to alter the situation. First, Esther stopped going out of the house altogether. She had become much less mobile, perhaps partially because of her arthritis, but more important, she panicked at the idea of leaving the house. She fought against using a wheelchair when she went outside, so her world had now shrunk to their bedroom, bathroom, and dining room. Second, Milton had noticed numbness and tingling in his left arm, caused by pressure on the cervical spine. He went to a surgeon who raised the possibility of surgery to correct the condition. His family physician again urged him to place Esther in a nursing home and have the surgery immediately. He tried to impress Milton with his sense of urgency about the need for surgery. Milton was very upset, but consulted with the surgeon, who felt that since he was only mildly symptomatic, he could afford to wait. The crisis of possibly having to go suddenly into surgery forced Milton to reach out to both his children and his long-time neighbors, who offered their help and support.

### Placement and Its Aftermath

Over the next year, Esther continued to decline in her mobility, needing help to move from what had become her three stations in the house: her bed, her chair in the dining room, and the bathroom. She was unable to perform any self-care and unable to speak intelligibly, but she could still respond with a warm smile to the people she recognized. Milton had a home-care worker to help with Esther's personal care and laundry, and he continued to have someone stay with her while he worked, but he otherwise took care of all her needs.

In January 1994, Esther began having episodes where she would suddenly slump to the floor while walking. Milton was unable to raise her by himself, and would call a neighbor to help get her up and put her to bed. One neighbor volunteered to help at any time, and literally came at all hours of the night to help Milton with Esther. But Milton knew that this arrangement could not continue. With bitter irony, he placed her in a skilled nursing facility on Valentine's Day. In the period leading up to the placement, he expressed to me his ambivalence and guilt over reaching this decision. His depression was as high at this time as at any point during his caregiving career.

The nursing home he chose only takes private pay patients and, as a result, is able to provide an aesthetically pleasing setting with many amenities. Nonetheless, it was painful for Milton to see Esther there, looking small, frightened, and helpless. But, like many caregivers, he went to visit her each and every day. Most of the time she seemed angry with him and sometimes would ask, "Why? Why me?" Of course, he felt even more guilty. I continued to see him to help him with his guilt and depression. We went over his search for alternatives, and at one point when he resolved he would take her back home, I helped him explore the practical steps he would need to take in order to do that. Gradually, though reluctantly, he realized he could not care for her any longer, and that she needed to remain in the home.

Two other events were important during this period. First, the nurses and nurse's aides varied in their skill in caring for Esther. Although Milton generally was charming and engaging when dealing with the staff, he could also be intolerant of their shortcomings. I worked with him to develop strategies for how to approach the staff in ways that would help him get the kind of care he wanted for Esther. He was able to develop friendly, joking relationships with many of the staff, and in turn they came to view him with affection. Second, I visited Esther in the nursing home. Because I am a regular consultant in that home, I could also make suggestions to the staff about her care. This arrangement was reassuring to Milton, because he felt that he had another advocate for her.

It looked as if this situation might go on indefinitely, when she suddenly became unresponsive. The staff of the nursing home managed her during what was the terminal phase of the illness in a dignified and skillful way, and the home's attending physician made her as comfortable as possible. Their children came and rallied around Milton. Within a week, Esther died. The cause of death was an internal hemorrhage of unknown etiology.

## Outcome of the Case

It has only been four months since Esther died, and I still see Milton every week. He needs company while he pays his bills, and support to put his life back together and to ward off continuing feelings of depression and guilt. We spent about a month talking about her death, about how she finally was at peace and no longer was afraid. We are moving to the more difficult part of grieving, where the images of Esther with dementia are gradually forgotten and Esther, the warm and gracious life partner, is remembered. Now the real loss is experienced. Milton is fortunate because he kept his job throughout her illness, so he is not as isolated as many caregivers often find themselves after their relative's death. He has also noted that friends, who avoided him or did not ask how Esther was doing when she was in the nursing home, now came forward to offer condolences and to invite him to social events. (Social norms and conventions following a death are much better developed than for nursing home placement.) Milton also feels some satisfaction because he was able to take care of her at home as long as he did, despite the threats of the Area Agency on Aging caseworker or the urgings of doctors and friends. What would have been gained if he placed her on their timetable, rather than his own? I like to think that the resources I helped Milton find and the support I gave were instrumental in his being able to provide care for Esther at home until he was sure he could no longer take care of her needs.

## EMPIRICAL CONSIDERATIONS FOR UNDERSTANDING DEMENTIA

The disorder in this case was dementia, but as has been illustrated in the case study, this disorder affects both patient and family. Assessment and intervention must reflect both an understanding of the disorder *and* its consequences for the family.

Turning first to the disorder, the term "dementia" or "senile dementia" refers to a syndrome of progressive memory and intellectual impairment, which can be brought about by many different diseases. Senility and old age were once considered synonymous, but we now know that dementia affects only a small proportion of the elderly, approximately 5 to 7 percent of people over age 65.[3,4] The prevalence, however, rises with age, so that by their late eighties about 30% of people have some form of dementia.[5]

The main illnesses causing dementia are Alzheimer's disease and vascular disease, particularly when there are repeated small strokes or infarcts.[2] Alzheimer's disease is the most common dementing illness, accounting for between 50 and 60% of cases.[6] Symptoms and problems associated with the various dementing illnesses differ, particularly earlier in the course of the disease, but as these disorders progress, impairment is generally widespread and severe, affecting most intellectual functions and interfering with even the most basic activities of everyday life, such as dressing, bathing, and feeding oneself.

Diagnosis of dementia is made in a three-step process. First, it is important to confirm that the patient has significant and pronounced symptoms of memory impairment. Everyone forgets at least some of the time, but because of the expectation that people become more forgetful in later life, it is not uncommon for older people to attribute ordinary instances of forgetting to dementia or old age. Incorrect attributions of this type are particularly common among people who are depressed.[7] As a result, the first step in assessment is to identify whether a significant degree of memory and other intellectual impairment is present. This process is accomplished by administering neuropsychological tests that assess memory, as well as other intellectual functions that often are affected by dementia, such as language, spatial ability, and conceptual skills. Test performance can be affected by several factors, including education and mood, which are taken into account when evaluating the results. Another consideration is whether there is a disruption of usual activities of daily living, such as work or leisure activities. As might be expected, it is relatively easy to detect obvious cases of dementia, because impairments are so pronounced, but relatively difficult to identify early cases, because small fluctuations in memory and other abilities can be caused by many factors other than dementia, including mood, motivation, and past learning.

Once a significant problem is identified, the second step is to rule out treatable or reversible causes of the dementia symptoms. A variety of treatable problems can produce symptoms that are similar or identical to dementia. Medications are probably the most common cause of reversible dementia symptoms. Psychiatric disorders, including severe depression and personality disorders, can also occasionally be exhibited with memory loss and other features similar to dementia.[8] The term "pseudodementia" has sometimes been used to denote these disorders.

Determining the type of dementia is less exact. A definitive diagnosis depends on examination of brain tissue, which can be done only after the patient's death. Clinical criteria have been developed, however, which make it possible to identify with a high degree of accuracy if a dementia is due to Alzheimer's disease or vascular dementia.[9] Other rarer dementing diseases sometimes have unique presenting symptoms, which makes identification possible.[2]

As this case illustrates, dementia places considerable strain on the family. Most dementia patients are cared for at home by family, often for long periods of time. The duration of a dementing illness can be quite long, extending 10 years or more. As their illness progresses, patients require around-the-clock care and supervision. It is not surprising, then, that caring for a dementia patient can have adverse effects on family caregivers, including high rates of depression and increased problems with their own health.[10]

The caregiving process has been likened to a career which has entry and exit points and major transitions.[11] There is a period of socialization into the role, during which caregivers realize, sometimes reluctantly, that the changes they are observing in their relative are not transient and that regular care and assistance is needed. During the period of role enactment, caregivers often provide extensive help, giving up many of their other activities and social contacts. Some become totally absorbed or trapped in their role. They also gradually experience the loss of their relative, who is slipping away because of the relentless progression of the dementia. The transition to nursing home care can produce extreme feelings of guilt. Contrary to widely held beliefs, placement does not relieve stress on caregivers.[11] We saw in this case that placement changes the types of problems caregivers are coping with, as new stressors are encountered in the institutional setting. When death finally comes, many caregivers feel relief, but they also mourn, trying to come to terms with the loss of their loved one and the terrible ordeal that has occurred.

## EMPIRICAL CONSIDERATIONS FOR TREATMENT OF DEMENTIA

As with assessment, treatment must address both the patient and family. Kahn[12] argued that dementia must be viewed as a "psycho-social-biological" phenomenon. While we currently have limited means for modifying the biological component, interventions can frequently change psychological or social dimensions of the situations.

Currently, two medications, Tacrine and Donepezil, have been approved for use with Alzheimer's patients, but their effects are limited.[13] Some people in earlier stages of the illness can benefit from these medications, which may reduce the progression of the disease for up to a year. People with vascular dementia sometimes benefit from administration of aspirin and similar medications.[2] Despite considerable progress in understanding the causes of these diseases, much needs to be done to improve treatment. Dementia patients are also very sensitive to the effects of medications, as illustrated by Esther's response to Darvocet. It is not uncommon to have adverse reactions to medications, which are marked by exacerbations of memory and behavior problems.

Although the underlying disease is progressive, some of the causes of stress to family caregivers are potentially remediable. Clinical treatments which identify and intervene in these modifiable aspects of the stress process can assist caregivers and patients. These interventions can be helpful in different ways throughout the caregiving process. In the early stages, treatment of patients can reduce their depression and anxiety, and, to the extent possible, help them come to terms with their illness. Over the long haul, interventions will focus more on the primary family caregiver, sometimes including his or her immediate family as well. These interventions can explore options and alternatives for caring for the patient, build effective coping responses, marshall support from family and friends, and manage the emotional and practical problems that arise around critical transitions, such as worsening of the patient's condition, problems with the caregiver's own health, or nursing home placement. A combination of individual and family therapy has been found to be an effective way of relieving the burden and emotional distress among caregivers of dementia patients.[14,15]

The treatment in this case has many unique features, but also illustrates common themes and problems that arise with dementia. Milton's distress and depression remained pronounced throughout much of the period of care. Rather than relieving stress, treatment had the effect of preventing the situation from getting worse. This case is also unusual for the length of time that Esther was able to participate in treatment. Esther's superior verbal skills, which were relatively spared until fairly far along in the disease process, allowed her to use the half-hour counseling sessions well. To what extent did treatment result in benefits for her? By involving Esther initially, it was possible to bring Milton into the process during the critical period when he was most despondent and suicidal. The sessions with Esther also enabled her to state her preferences about what should happen to her. Treatment may have relieved some of her fears and depression, at least for short periods of time.

This case was typical in many other ways, however. It illustrates the unrelenting stress that falls on the primary caregiver and the need to make continuous adjustments as the patient's condition worsens. With the patient's decline, caregivers often must assume responsibilities for which they are not prepared. In Milton's case, that was cleaning the house. For another caregiver, it might be arranging automobile repairs or assisting the patient to use the toilet. As in many similar situations, the amount of support Milton received from family and friends was limited. Some help was available to Milton from formal agencies, but as this case clearly shows, agencies are sometimes not helpful. Another key issue is that many people advise caregivers to place their relatives in a nursing home, without realizing how difficult or complex a decision that is, or without considering the costs of nursing homes (at least $35,000 a year). Placement is an issue that needs to be examined over time and in light of other available options. Caregivers should make that decision in a manner consistent with their values and sense of obligation, rather than someone else's preferences. Finally, it is important to understand that caregiving does not end at the institution's door, nor even with the death of the patient. The caregiver's needs for support are often greatest around these critical transitions, and after their loved one has died.

## Notes

1. Testing primarily consisted of the Luria Nebraska Neuropsychological Battery. While this particular instrument is not always the most useful in evaluating older adults, it yielded valid and useful information in this case. See Golden, C.J., Purisch, A.D., & Hammeke, T.A. (1985). *Luria-Nebraska neuropsychological battery: Forms I and II Manual* Los Angeles: Western Psychological Services.

2. Cummings, J.L., & Benson, D.F., (1992). *Dementia: A clinical approach,* (2nd ed.) Stoneham, MA: Butterworth-Heinemann.

3. Kay, D.W.K. (1995). The epidemiology of age-related neurological disease and dementia. *Reviews in Clinical Gerontology, 5,* 39–56.

4. Regier, D.A., Boyd, J.H., Burke, J.D., Jr., Rae, D.S., Myers, J.K., Kraemer, M., Robins, L.N., George, L.K., Karno, M., & Locke, B.Z. (1988). One month prevalence of mental disorders in the United States. *Archives of General Psychiatry, 45,* 977–986. Some estimates of prevalence are higher, but 5 to 7% represents an average rate across most studies in the United States, Canada and Europe.

5. Johansson, B., & Zarit, S.H. (1995). Prevalence and incidence of dementia in the oldest old: A study of a population based sample of 84–90 year olds in Sweden. *International Journal of Geriatric Psychiatry, 10*, 359–366.

6. Anthony, J.C., & Aboraya, A. (1992). The epidemiology of selected mental disorders in later life. In J. E. Birren & G. D. Cohen (Eds.), *Handbook of mental health and aging* (2nd ed., pp. 27–72). San Diego: Academic Press.

7. Kahn, R.L., Zarit, S.H., Hilbert, N.M., & Niederehe, G. (1975). Memory complaint and impairment in the aged: The effect of depression and altered brain function. *Archives of General Psychiatry, 32*, 1569 –1573.

8. Caine, E.C. (1981). Pseudodemenita: Current concepts and future directions. *Archives of General Psychiatry, 38*, 1359–1364.

9. McKhann, G., Drachman, D., Folstein, M., Katzman, R., Price, D., & Stadlan, E. M. (1984). Clinical diagnosis of Alzheimer's disease. *Neurology, 34*, 939–944.

10. Zarit, S.H. (1994). Research perspectives on family caregiving. In M. Cantor (Ed.), *Family caregiving: Agenda for the future* (pp. 9–24). San Francisco: American Society on Aging.

11. Aneshensel, C., Pearlin, L.I., Mullan, J., Zarit, S.H., & Whitlatch, C.J. (1995). *Profiles in caregiving: The unexpected career.* New York: Academic Press.

12. Kahn, R.L. (1975). Mental health and the future aged. *Gerontologist, 15* (1, Suppl), 15–24.

13. Committee on Aging: Group for the Advancement of Psychiatry. (1994). Tacrine in the care of patients with Alzheimer's disease: What we know one year after FDA approval. *American Journal of Geriatric Psychiatry, 2*, 285–289.

14. Whitlatch, C.J., Zarit, S.H., & von Eye, A. (1991). Efficacy of interventions with caregivers: A reanalysis. *Gerontologist, 31*, 9–14.

15. Mittelman, M.S., Ferris, S.H., Steinberg, G., Shulman, E., Mackell, J.A., Ambinder, A., & Cohen, J. (1993). An intervention that delays institutionalization of Alzheimer's disease patients: Treatment of spouse-caregivers. *Gerontologist, 33*, 730–740.

## Recommended Readings

Aneshensel, C., Pearlin, L.I., Mullan, J., Zarit, S.H., & Whitlatch, C.J. (1995). *Profiles in caregiving: The unexpected career.* New York: Academic Press.

Cantor, M. (Ed.). (1994). *Family caregiving: Agenda for the future.* San Francisco: American Society on Aging.

Coughlan, P.B. (1993). *Facing Alzheimer's: Family caregivers speak.* New York: Ballantine Books.

Knight, B. (1986). *Psychotherapy with older adults.* Newberry Park, CA. Sage.

Mace, M. (Ed.). (1990). *Dementia care: Patient, family and community.* Baltimore: MD Johns Hopkins University Press.

Mace, N.L., & Rabins, P.V. (1991). *The thirty-six hour day* (rev. ed.) Baltimore: MD Johns Hopkins University Press.

McGowin, D.F. (1993). *Living in the labyrinth: A personal journey through the maze of Alzheimer's.* New York: Delacorte Press.

Rosenbaum, J. (1993). *Caregiver's companion: A practical guide to food, feeding and community resources.* Portland, OR: Good Samaritan Hospital and Medical Center.

Zarit, S.H., Orr, N.K., & Zarit, J.M. (1985). *The hidden victims of Alzheimer's disease: Families under stress.* New York: New York University Press.

# PART VIII

# DISORDERS OF SELF-CONTROL

➤ Chapter 16: Substance Abuse
➤ Chapter 17: Eating Disorders

In this part, we cover two disorders which on the surface may appear very different, but share a common feature—behavior that is difficult to control and has disastrous consequences for the body. In substance abuse disorders and eating disorders, people are driven to engage in these self-destructive behaviors even though they may realize at some level that they are harming themselves. Diagnostically, these disorders appear in different categories, but researchers are increasingly recognizing that they may lie along a similar spectrum or dimension.

# 16

**About**

**the**

**Author**

*Marc Alan Schuckit, M.D., is a Professor of Psychiatry at the University of California, San Diego School of Medicine, and Director of the Alcohol Research Center at the San Diego Veterans Affairs Medical Center. He has been involved in research in alcohol and drug dependence since his first year of medical school at Washington University, St. Louis, in 1964. His research interests focus mostly on genetics of alcoholism, the relationship between alcoholism or drug dependence on the one hand and psychiatric syndromes on the other, and diagnostic issues in the alcohol and drug use field.*

*Dr. Schuckit has more than 350 publications, including seven books, the most recent of which are the fourth edition of his text* Drug and Alcohol Abuse *(1995, New York: Plenum) and a first edition of a book written for the general population entitled* Educating Yourself about Alcohol and Drugs *(1995, New York: Plenum). In addition to his research, teaching, and administrative responsibilities, he directs two alcohol and drug treatment programs, one for the Veterans Affairs Medical Center in San Diego and the other for the Scripps McDonald Program at Scripps Memorial Hospital.*

# John's Alcohol Dependence: A Casebook Report

**About the Disorder**

The use of mind-altering substances has become a central part of contemporary culture. Both legal and illegal substances are so easily available that anyone with a propensity for addiction encounters temptation on a daily basis.

The lives of people who abuse substances are affected in a number of ways. They neglect work and family obligations. They may take risks that are personally dangerous and put others in jeopardy, such as driving or operating powerful machinery while intoxicated. Legal problems arise if they are arrested for disorderly conduct, driving while intoxicated, or assaultive behavior. Lastly, and most commonly, their lives are characterized by interpersonal problems. Even when the person is sober, interpersonal relationships are usually strained and unhappy.

The main feature of abuse is a pattern of behavior in which the individual continues to use substances even when it is clear that such behavior entails significant risks or creates problems in living. A diagnosis of substance abuse does not, however, convey the notion of addiction. Substance dependence is the term that describes a maladaptive pattern of substance use manifested by a cluster of cognitive, behavioral, and physiological symptoms caused by continued use.

The treatment of John by Dr. Schuckit involved a multifaceted approach that included traditional outpatient treatment as well as participation in Alcoholics Anonymous. The outcome of John's case is a happy one, but such a positive result requires constant vigilance and commitment to maintaining a sober lifestyle.—*Eds.*

## JOHN'S CASE

### Initial Presentations

John is a 38-year-old, twice-divorced professor of chemistry. My clinical involvement with him began when, through my role on the Faculty Well-Being Committee, I was telephoned by his chairman, who was concerned about the quality of John's teaching and his overall academic performance. The week prior to this contact there had been a report from a colleague that when John was telephoned at home regarding a college matter he had sounded confused and incoherent—a complaint John explained away as a consequence of a recent bout of the flu. The chair also related that at a recent social gathering, John had slurred speech and an unsteady gait, and that there had been a complaint that a student had smelled alcohol on John's breath the morning of a class. Finally, the chair was worried that John had appeared sad and distant and that he might be depressed.

Because John and I were not close colleagues, I agreed to talk to him. In setting up these interactions, I followed the guidelines that I offer families seeking advice on confronting a relative with the evidence of his or her possible problem drinking. I chose a time for this discussion that would minimize the chances he would be intoxicated, setting up a lunch during the middle of the week. John appeared in our meeting neatly dressed and in no acute distress, with no signs of intoxication nor any evidence of a tremor or any other possible sequelae of withdrawal. I began the conversation by letting him know I had received a telephone call from his chair and that the people around him were quite concerned about a possible problem. I then listed specific items and days on which potential impairment was observed, avoiding generic discussions of global impairment.

John voiced shock that others thought that he might have a problem, and had excuses for all of the behaviors related by his colleagues. He did admit to having some difficulties sleeping and to being worried about the progress of his career, but pointed out that in the past his ratings as a teacher had been quite high. He denied any problems in the present marriage.

At this point in the intervention or confrontation, my goal was to enhance any motivation he might have for getting help. If that failed, I wanted to open up opportunities for further dialogue while not retreating on my level of uneasiness. I discussed the types of impairments that were likely to develop if alcohol-related problems were involved, stressing the probability that although alcohol-related difficulties would be likely to fluctuate over time, they would almost certainly increase in intensity over the years with continued drinking. I presented all this information in a concerned but unemotional way, emphasizing that while no one could make John do what he did not want to do, only he would bear the brunt of the consequences if a problem did indeed exist.

As part of our talk, I asked John when he had his last physical examination. I was concerned that if he was taking higher doses of alcohol and demonstrating more alcohol-related interference than he was willing to admit, he was also at high risk for a number of medical problems including high blood pressure, cardiac arrhythmias, gastritis, and an increased risk for cancers. I also wanted to observe the results of blood tests likely to demonstrate high-normal or slightly above normal values in the presence of heavy drinking. These state markers of heavy drinking, while not diagnosing alcohol dependence per se, are likely to identify an individual who has been drinking four to six drinks a day over a period of a week or so. In this context, a drink is the amount of alcohol contained in approximately 12 oz of beer, 4 oz of wine, or a single shot (1.5 oz) of 80-proof beverages. The specific laboratory tests likely to be of value include gamma-glutamyltransferase (GGT) results of 30 units or more, an average size of the red blood cell (abbreviated as mean corpuscular volume or MCV) of 91 or more cubic microns, or high values of other liver function tests. Unfortunately, these considerations were to no avail because John refused to get a physical exam.

Because of the anxieties expressed by his chair, my clinical evaluation also centered on attempting to evaluate the level of depressive symptoms. John admitted to middle-of-the-night insomnia several nights a week the prior month, and discussed feeling unfocused at work. However, he denied persistent depressive symptoms, feeling hopeless, difficulties concentrating, or other problems that characterize a major depressive episode as described in the *Diagnostic and Statistical Manual of Mental Disorders* of the American Psychiatric Association, Fourth Edition (*DSM-IV*).[1] He also expressed hopefulness regarding the future, and vehemently denied that he ever felt discouraged enough that he thought he might harm himself.

The session ended by my reminding him that I was available should any future problems develop. I was honest in sharing with John my opinion that I felt problems were apparent. Over the ensuing 18 months, I saw John occasionally on campus and at meetings. In each instance, I went out of my way to say hello and to be pleasant, and did everything possible to indicate through my actions that I was available if he wanted to talk more. However, in the absence of any further complaints from his chair, and without having personally observed any specific problems, additional interventions were not felt to be appropriate.

Then, one Sunday night at approximately 8:00 P.M., John telephoned me at home. He was crying, his speech was slightly slurred, but he was coherent. John told me that he and his wife had been feuding all weekend regarding his drinking. He said that he remembered little of their interactions on Saturday night, but that his wife had accused him of becoming verbally aggressive while intoxicated. She had also informed him that unless he sought immediate help, she would leave him. I agreed to come directly to his house.

John greeted me at the door with alcohol on his breath, slightly slurred speech, but no evidence of an unsteady gait or nystagmus (involuntary eye movements) (both common signs of moderate or severe alcohol intoxication). His eyes were swollen from crying, but otherwise he appeared in good physical condition. He was oriented to time, place, and person, and while he was sad regarding his present situation, he expressed a willingness to do anything he could to take care of the problem and save his marriage.

## Case History

That evening, the alcohol history unfolded through discussions with John and his wife. While John's first contact with alcohol was in his early teens, and his first mild intoxication occurred at approximately age 16, there were no persistent difficulties until the year before his first divorce at age 25. Up to this point, John's academic career had gone well, he was funded by a small grant, and he was known as an excellent teacher. His first wife, however, complained that John would spend excessive amounts of time drinking on weekends, and that during those bouts of intoxication he would become irritable and verbally abusive. She felt they had grown apart as he was spending more and more of his time drinking, and asked for a divorce. She was unwilling to consider marital counseling.

In an effort to demonstrate to himself and his wife that he was not an alcoholic, John stopped drinking and, despite the separation, he maintained a period of abstinence of over three months. He then convinced himself that the ease with which he avoided alcohol and the fact that he didn't suffer from any withdrawal symptoms indicated that he couldn't possibly have a major problem. He returned to alcohol, establishing rules that he would only drink beer and only on the weekends beginning on Friday after 5:00 P.M. John was able to maintain this pattern for almost a year, during which time he met his second wife and they moved in together. While it is difficult for John to pinpoint exact times during the subsequent years, the quantity of alcohol consumed increased to a case of beer each day over most weekends. At age 28, John was stopped by the police, who suspected him of driving while intoxicated, but he was able to convince the officer that he was not impaired, and was let off with a speeding ticket. By age 30, John's parents voiced concerns about the amount of alcohol he would consume on his visits. His pattern of spending a great deal of time drinking on weekends was interfering with his second marriage. This resulted in marital counseling, periods of abstinence, and months at a time of controlled drinking. By the age of 32, John's alcohol use pattern contributed to his second divorce.

In response to this crisis, he stopped drinking, but subsequently established rules for controlling his intake. By age 35, problems were apparent at work, mostly absences after weekends of heavy drinking. His third marriage was also in trouble, but John had been able to avoid further drunk-driving difficulties by making and rigidly upholding a vow to never drive after consuming alcohol.

## Diagnosis

The diagnostic formulation was as follows:

| Axis I: | • Alcohol dependence, with physiological dependence (based on the documentation of tolerance). |
|---|---|
| Axis I: | • Alcohol-induced mood disorder, with depressive features, with onset during intoxication. |
| Axis II: | • none |
| Axis III: | • none |
| Axis-IV: | • Marital problems |
| | • Occupational problems |
| Axis V: | • GAF = 60 |

## Case Formulation

The history indicated that by approximately age 30, John had developed at least three of the *DSM-IV* items related to alcohol dependence.[1] These included tolerance, spending a great deal of time using the alcohol, and regularly consuming higher doses than intended (as evidenced by his becoming intoxicated at social gatherings or after he had promised his wife that he would limit his drinking on a particular evening). There had been at least two periods of abstinence since age 30, one at approximately age 32, and one at approximately age 34, each lasting three to four months.

However, the history did not support a diagnosis of a major depressive disorder, pointing instead to an alcoholic-induced mood disorder.[2] As is my usual approach when attempting to evaluate psychiatric symptoms in the context of heavy drinking, I used the information provided by John and corroborated by his wife to construct a time line of John's life history.[3] On this line, I first noted the approximate age of onset of dependence, and then added in any subsequent periods of abstinence. For me, the onset of dependence is approximately the age where the third of the seven *DSM-IV* dependence items occurred for that drug, especially if the three or more problem areas continued concomitantly at that age. The third step in the time line for an individual who might demonstrate both a major psychiatric disorder (here a major depressive disorder) and a substance use disorder (here alcohol dependence) is to determine whether the individual met criteria for the full psychiatric syndrome either prior to the onset of alcohol dependence or during a period of abstinence lasting several months or more. The emphasis in this case was not on short episodes of sadness but on periods of multiple weeks or longer when he was depressed almost every day, all day. Through this evaluation, I found that while John's depressions had been severe in the past, and he may have been suicidal at times, a major depressive episode had never been observed outside the context of heavy drinking.

## Course of Treatment

After having established the diagnosis, the next step was to initiate treatment for possible alcohol withdrawal.[4] Both John and his wife reported that he had not consumed any alcohol over the four hours prior to my Sunday evening evaluation. Despite the period of abstinence, John's pulse was 80 and regular, his respiratory rate was 20, and he demonstrated only a slight tremor. He reported that he had finally had his routine physical examination the prior month, and no major medical problems had been observed (although it is likely the physician did not look carefully at state markers of heavy drinking). Thus, all indications were that in this otherwise healthy young man, the withdrawal syndrome related to alcohol would likely be relatively mild.

I briefly considered the possibility of inpatient rehabilitation, but he lacked any of the usual indications for inpatient programs. Thus, John had not failed at outpatient treatment, he had a relatively stable social situation, his withdrawal syndrome was likely to be mild, he did not evidence severe psychiatric syndromes (while he had an alcohol-induced mood disorder, he was not suicidal), and according to his recent physical examination and my brief evaluation, he did not have any major medical problems.

John's outpatient alcohol rehabilitation began that evening as I gave him and his wife some readings regarding alcohol and drug problems and their treatment.[5] He agreed to go to an Alcoholics Anonymous (AA) meeting every night for the next thirty days while his wife attended Al-Anon (a group for the spouses of alcoholic individuals). I helped them pick a self-help meeting appropriate for them, one composed of nonsmoking, highly educated individuals, and that held its meetings at a location near his home.[5] I also identified an AA member who was willing to serve as his guide and potential future sponsor.

John's initial intensive outpatient treatment included visits to my office each day for the next five days to be certain that withdrawal symptoms did not escalate, and to offer the necessary education and reassurance regarding withdrawal.[5] Had a significant abstinence syndrome developed (e.g., a markedly increased blood pressure or pulse rate, anxiety, or severe insomnia), I would have prescribed a benzodiazepine. My preference is chlordiazepoxide (Librium), using 25 mg tablets up to four times a day the first day, with several additional pills if needed between doses, but warning John to skip even regular scheduled pills if he became very sleepy. The first day's prescription is then decreased by 20% of the initial day's dose each subsequent day, in order to stop the medications by day five. This process could be monitored on an outpatient basis.

Beginning that week and continuing over the next months, we also began 30-minute general discussion sessions three times per week. As described in detail elsewhere, my goal during those meetings was to increase John's level of motivation for abstinence to the highest level possible.[3,5] In this regard I emphasized John's responsibility for his own actions, and frankly discussed the usual clinical course of severe alcohol problems (with serious medical as well as psychological sequelae). I emphasized that if he continued to drink, he would probably face repeated substance-induced depressions with a likely tenfold increased risk for suicide, his third marriage and subsequent relationships were likely to fail, and he would probably cut 10 to 15 years off his life by carrying a health risk for heart disease and cancer. However, I also told him that there was reason to be optimistic about the future because for individuals who are committed to abstinence and have stable life functioning, there is a 60 to 70% one-year abstinence rate—with one-year abstinence predicting the high likelihood of future abstinence over subsequent years.[5]

Over the first month, I also used the triweekly sessions to help John rebuild his life now that alcohol was no longer an option. I emphasized the need to avoid all "recreational" or "street" drugs because intoxication with any substance is likely to hamper motivation regarding alcohol. We focused on how John would now spend all the time previously occupied by drinking, emphasizing the need to learn how to interact with his spouse and colleagues while sober and exploring interests and hobbies. We also talked about the importance of continued participation in AA, and how John does not necessarily have to accept all its teachings but should borrow from that group all attributes that he found to be personally helpful. This intense first month of treatment was an opportunity to use relapse prevention strategies to begin to help John recognize those situations in which relapse would be likely to occur, and to help him develop ways to avoid such situations.[5] The risk of returning to drinking was also discussed, along with ways to make these "slips" as short and inconsequential as possible by developing coping strategies and rehearsing beforehand how they could be handled.

Consistent with my usual approach, no medications were used for the rehabilitation phase.[3,5,6] There was no obvious need for an antidepressant to help John with his alcohol-induced mood disorder because abstinence resulted in a slight improvement in depression over the first week to 10 days, with a subsequent marked diminution of depressive symptoms.[2,7] By the third week of abstinence, John no longer evidenced a consistent depressed mood. Nor were medications indicated for John's alcohol dependence.[6] As I discuss in the last section of this chapter, while there are some interesting and potentially helpful pharmacological approaches, careful controlled trials do not yet support their routine use.

Following the first month, and in light of John's relatively normal mood pattern, his level of engagement in AA, and his wife's attendance in Al-Anon, visits with me were decreased to once a week for the next three months. This was then followed by "reminder visits" (once every other week to once a month for the following six months). After that, John and I "touched base" occasionally.

## Outcome of the Case

The damage done to John's career contributed to his decision to accept a position at another university approximately a year after his treatment with me had ended. Since then, I continued to see him occasionally at meetings, and have spoken with him on the phone several times a year. It is now three years and he is still sober and functioning well in both his career and his marriage.

## SOME EMPIRICAL CONTRIBUTIONS TO UNDERSTANDING ALCOHOL DEPENDENCE AND EVALUATING DUAL DIAGNOSES

This case demonstrates both my own philosophy and my understanding of the literature on the substance use disorders. The first anchor is the recognition that substance dependencies are long-term, life-threatening disorders that can be reliably diagnosed.[8] The criteria for dependence identify a group of individuals with a pattern of severe problems, a prognosis for continued difficulties, and a potential shortening of life if they are not adequately treated.[9] This is a common psychiatric diagnosis affecting 10 to 15% of men and 5 to 10% of women, and clinicians should consider it as a possibility for all patients and clients coming for care, no matter what their presenting complaint might be.[1,5]

Despite this high prevalence, there are several reasons why substance dependence is often undiagnosed. As I discussed in an editorial for family physicians,[10] many people have an inaccurate picture of alcohol- or drug-dependent people. What typically comes to mind is a skid-row derelict. In truth, many individuals with these disorders are highly productive people with intact families and jobs, and the diagnosis of substance dependence (especially alcohol dependence) has a high rate in all socioeconomic strata. A second fallacy that interferes with our ability to establish a diagnosis is the erroneous belief that substance-dependent people always present with symptoms of intoxication or withdrawal, when in reality most regularly control their alcohol or drug intake temporarily. As John's case shows, the problem here is not in stopping substance use, but rather, it is in avoiding the escalation of problems when any use of the substance re-occurs. Several of our studies focusing on 600 to 2,000 alcoholic men and women have demonstrated those issues regarding the usual course of alcohol dependence, and another documents how rare severe withdrawal conditions are, even among hospitalized alcoholics.[4,9]

Another key point is the need to recognize that not all alcohol- and drug-dependent people respond positively to the first confrontation.[5] Thus, it is important to raise the possibility of a substance use disorder with them in as unemotional a way as possible, leaving the door open for future confrontations to help the person when problems escalate.

Consistent with our own work in this area, John's case also serves to illustrate how at least one in three alcohol- or drug-dependent people present for care with temporary symptoms that resemble other Axis I major psychiatric disorders, such as major depressive disorder, any of the major anxiety disorders including panic disorder or social phobia, and schizophrenia.[2,7,11] Such psychiatric symptoms are especially likely to be observed if the substances in question are either brain depressant drugs (alcohol, benzodiazepines, and barbiturates) or stimulants (including all the forms of cocaine and amphetamine, as well as all prescription and most over-the-counter weight-reducing products). Severe repeated intoxication with any of the brain depressants can cause a temporary, but severe mood disorder that resembles major depressive disorder and can be associated with suicidal behavior. Withdrawal from brain depressants is likely to include severe symptoms of anxiety, with perhaps one-third of individuals withdrawing from these substances having repeated panic attacks, social phobic-like behavior, or other major anxiety complaints.

Contrary to the major psychiatric disorders, such as major depressive or panic disorder, substance-induced psychiatric syndromes last only a matter of weeks and usually resolve without pharmacological treatment.[7,11] The distinction between long-term, independent psychiatric disorders that might require medications and a substance-induced depressive, anxiety, or other type of disorder rests first with the history. John's case demonstrates how one can use a time line to determine whether there is evidence of an independent major psychiatric disorder, or whether the symptoms are likely to be substance-induced.[7,11] The steps involve first establishing the approximate age of onset of the substance dependence (not just the first use or isolated problems), then noting any abstinence periods of several months or more, and finally determining if the full psychiatric syndrome (not just symptoms) occurred before the onset of dependence or during the subsequent abstinent periods. This systematic approach to evaluation is used in all our research projects and in my clinical work. In the absence of relatively strong evidence that an independent disorder exists, it is highly likely that the symptoms of depression or other disorders will disappear with abstinence. To corroborate the diagnostic formulation, patients should be observed for several weeks to a month to see whether the anxiety, depression, or psychosis do improve as predicted.

Observing the clinical course in these instances is ideally carried out in a hospital, but this is usually not available because of the high cost. If an evaluation is done on an outpatient basis, it is important to explain the need for the patient to abstain from all substances in order to determine whether medications are required for the psychiatric syndrome to disappear. Monitoring the person's abstinence can be aided by asking an additional observer (usually a spouse) to be available to indicate to the clinician if any drinking or drug use has returned. Also, the progress of abstinence can be monitored with state markers of heavy drinking such as GGT.[12] As shown by our research group, any increase of 20% or more of the enzyme indicates that the person has probably returned to drinking. If other drugs are involved, urine or blood toxicology screens can be used.

Even if a major depression independent of heavy drinking exists, I am reluctant to prescribe antidepressant medications for individuals who are actively drinking. Thus, for substance-induced mood disorders, or those cases where I can't be certain of the diagnosis because alcohol intake is continuing, I rely solely on behavioral and cognitive therapies, not antidepressants.

## EMPIRICAL CONTRIBUTIONS TO THE
## TREATMENT OF ALCOHOL DEPENDENCE

Dealing with this patient required that consideration be given to a variety of treatment issues addressed in our research and in the literature. While John's history involved alcohol dependence, the same general guidelines could be applied to individuals with almost any other type of substance dependence including cocaine, cannabinols, or opiates.[3,4] The first question is the reliability of a diagnosis of alcohol dependence, and whether this carries enough information about prognosis to warrant treatment. A recent *DSM-IV* field trial demonstrated a high level of consistency with other diagnostic schemes.[8] Both prospective and retrospective investigations of alcohol-dependent individuals have documented the probability of a progression to ever more complex and serious problems, with a potential for a significant shortening of the life span.[9] Death rates among alcohol dependent individuals are elevated for heart disease, cancers, suicide (with a lifetime risk of 8 to 15%), and accidents. Thus, the implications of the treatment literature are that this is not a trivial disorder and that some form of intervention is warranted.

A second question concerns the treatment implications of John's depressive symptoms. Most studies suggest that alcohol-induced depressive symptoms will markedly improve after several days to perhaps a month of abstinence, without the use of medications.[7] Thus, for the average alcohol-dependent individual who lacks clearly documented independent depressive episodes, antidepressants are not beneficial in alleviating the depressive symptoms. John's course is consistent with a spontaneous clearing of the depressive symptoms that occurred more rapidly than could have been expected had the antidepressants been invoked. On the other hand, if I had chosen to use antidepressants, I would have been obligated to consider continuing the medications for six to nine months, as one would do for any major depressive episode. In other words, even if the depression does clear, once medications have been started the physician is almost locked into continuing the dose for the usual course.

The next major decision point regarding John's treatment came with the determination that this detoxification could be carried out on an outpatient basis. This decision was supported by the literature, including one of our own studies, that demonstrates that 95% or so of alcohol withdrawal syndromes are of mild to moderate severity, while an agitated confused state (e.g., delirium tremens) or grand mal convulsions are quite rare.[4] The absence of such severe withdrawals in John's past, along with his modest level of clinical symptomatology despite relatively low blood alcohol levels at the time of evaluation, argued that outpatient detoxification would be appropriate.

This case involved a decision on whether a formal inpatient alcohol treatment program would be beneficial. Of course, the more intensive inpatient treatment would be more costly, force John to be separated from his wife, and also cause him to miss work. The literature does not indicate that such intense treatments are required for the average alcohol-dependent individual to achieve and maintain abstinence,[13] and thus it was decided to treat John as an outpatient. However, the data indicate that during the first several weeks to three months of abstinence, alcohol-dependent individuals are at the highest risk for relapsing to heavy drinking.[14] Therefore, John was seen frequently during that first month, and only slightly less often during the subsequent three months.

While it is difficult to generate data from controlled trials that self-help groups such as AA significantly improve recovery rates, there is a strong clinical impression that this does occur.[5,15] The lack of cost of such programs, the ability of AA to reach out to family members through Alanon, and the treatment philosophy of AA all argued for incorporating this mode of help into John's treatment. At the same time, it was important to recognize that AA groups are quite different in character, and efforts had to be made to help him find an AA group where he was likely to be most comfortable.

A literature review I recently completed underscores the reasons why I choose not to use medications as part of the routine approach to rehabilitation.[6] Our own work with disulfiram (Antabuse), coupled with more extensive studies in the literature, does not support the general efficacy of this approach.[16] While another pilot study from our group was consistent with a possible effect of the nonbenzodiazepine antianxiety drug buspirone, a finding made more persuasively in a recent study, and while two modest-sized studies point toward the possible importance of the opiate antagonist, naltrexone (Trexan), for alcoholism, the data are as yet too preliminary to justify routine use.[17] Double-blind controlled trials do not support the routine use of antidepressants, lithium or any other medication in the routine rehabilitation of alcohol-dependent individuals.[6,18]

One final note regarding treatment seems appropriate. Many clinicians might be surprised to learn that for relatively functional blue- and white-collar, alcohol-dependent individuals (i.e., the average alcoholic), the expected outcome is actually quite good.[5,19] Of course, there are biases in the data since the most thorough information is available on those who complete the more intensive first several weeks of an inpatient or outpatient alcohol rehabilitation program. Nonetheless, among these moderately functional individuals who have invested in the first phase of treatment, the one-year abstinence rate is likely to be 60% or higher. This is most likely to occur for those individuals who maintain contact with aftercare treatment programs or self-help groups such as AA.

### Notes

1. American Psychiatric Association. (1994). *Diagnostic and Statistical Manual of Mental Disorders.* (4th ed.). Washington, DC: American Psychiatric Association.

2. Schuckit, M.A. (1994). Alcohol and depression: A clinical perspective. *Acta Psychiatrica Scandanavia* Suppl, *377*, 28–32.

3. Schuckit, M.A. (1994). Goals of treatment. In, *Textbook of substance abuse treat-*

*ment* (pp.3–10). M. Galanter, & H. Kleber, (Eds.), Washington, DC: American Psychiatric Press.

4. Schuckit, M.A., Tipp, J., Reich, T., Hesselbrock, V., & Bucholz, K. (1995). *The histories of withdrawal convulsions and delirium tremens in 1,648 alcohol dependent subjects. Addiction, 90,* 1335–1347.

5. Schuckit, M.A. (1995). *Drug and alcohol abuse. A clinical guide to diagnosis and Treatment* (4th ed.). New York: Plenum.; Schuckit, M.A. (1995). *Educate yourself about alcohol and drugs: A people's primer.* New York: Plenum.

6. Schuckit, M.A. (1996). The psychopharmacology of alcohol dependence. *Journal of Consulting and Clinical Psychology, 64,* 669–676.

7. Brown, S.A. & Schuckit, M.A. (1988). Changes in depression among abstinent alcoholics. *Journal Studies in Alcoholism, 49,* 412–417; Schuckit, M.A., Irwin, M. & Smith, T.L. (1994). One-year incidence rate of major depression and other psychiatric disorders in 239 alcoholic men. *Addiction 89,* 441–445.

8. Schuckit, M.A., Hesselbrock, V., Tipp, J., Anthenelli, R., Bucholz, K., & Radziminski, S. (1994). A comparison of DSM-III-R, DSM-IV, and ICD-10 substance use disorders diagnoses in 1922 men and women subjects in the COGA study. *Addiction, 89,* 1629–1638; Cottler, L.B., Schuckit, M.A., Helzer, J.E., Crowley, T., Woody, G., Nathan, P., Hughes, J. (1995) The DSM-IV field trial for substance use disorders: Major results. *Drug and Alcohol Dependency 38,* 59–69.

9. Schuckit, M.A., Smith, T.L., Anthenelli, R. & Irwin, M. (1993). Clinical course of alcoholism in 636 male inpatients. *Am J Psychiatry, 150,* 786–792; Schuckit, M.A., Anthenelli, R.M., Bucholz, K., Hesselbrock, V.M., & Tipp, J. (1995). The time course of development of alcohol-related problems in men and women. *Journal Stud in Alcholism, 56,* 218–225.

10. Schuckit, M.A. (1987). Why don't we diagnose alcoholism in our patients? *Journal Family Practice, 25,* 225–226.

11. Brown, S.A., Irwin, M. & Schuckit, M.A. (1991). Changes in anxiety among abstinent male alcoholics. *Journal of Studies in Alcoholism, 52,* 55–61; Schuckit, M.A., Irwin, M. & Brown, S.A. (1990). The history of anxiety symptoms among 171 primary alcoholics. *Journal of Studies in Alcoholism, 51,* 34–41; Schuckit, M.A. (1992). Anxiety disorders and substance abuse in Tasman, A. & Riba, M. (Eds.). *American Psychiatric Press Review of Psychiatry* Vol. 11, (pp. 402–417). Washington, DC, American Psychiatric Press, Schuckit, M.A. & Hesselbrock, V. (1994). Alcohol dependence and anxiety disorders: What is the relationship? *Am J Psychiatry, 151,* 1723–1734.

12. Irwin, M., Baird, S., Smith, T.L. & Schuckit, M. (1988). Use of laboratory tests to monitor heavy drinking by alcoholic men discharged from a treatment program. *American Journal of Psychiatry, 145,* 595–599.

13. Cross, G.M., Morgan, C.W., Mooney, A.J., Martin, C.A. & Rafter, J.A. (1990). Alcoholism treatment: A ten-year follow-up study. *Alcoholism, Clinical and Experimental Research, 14,* 169–173; Holder, H.D. & Blose, J.O. (1992). The reduction of health care costs associated with alcoholism treatment: A 14-year longitudinal study. *Journal of Studies in Alcoholism, 53,* 293–302; Yates, W.R., Reed, D.A., Booth, B.M., Masterson, B.J., & Brown, K. (1994). Prognostic validity of short-term abstinence in alcoholism. *Alcoholism Clinical and Experimental Research, 18,* 280–283.

14. Woody, G.E., & Cacciola, J. (1994). Review of remission criteria. In Widiger, T.A., Frances, A.J., Pincus, H.A., First, M.B., Ross, R., & Ross, R. (Eds.). *DSM-IV Sourcebook* Vol. 1, pp. 67–80) Washington, DC, American Psychiatric Press.

15. Snow, M.G., Prochaska, J.O. & Rossi, J.S. (1994). Processes of change in Alco-

holics Anonymous: Maintenance factors in long-term sobriety. *Journal of Studies in Alcoholism, 55,* 362–371.

16. Litten, R.Z., & Allen, J.P. (1991). Pharmacotherapies for alcoholism: Promising agents and clinical issues. *Alcoholism Clinical and Experimental Research, 15,* 620–633; Fuller, R.K., Branchey, L., Brightwell, D.R., Derman, R.M., Emrick, C.D., Iber, F.L., James, K.E., Lacoursiere, R.B., Lee, K.K., Lowenstam, I., Maany, I., Neiderhiser, D., Nocks, J.J., & Shaw, S. (1986). Disulfiram treatment of alcoholism. *Journal of the American Medical Association, 256,* 1449–1455; Schuckit, M.A. (1985). A one-year follow-up of alcoholics given disulfiram. *Journal Studies in Alcoholism, 46,* 191–195.

17. Volpicelli, J.R., Alterman, A.I., Hayashida, M., & O'Brien, C.P. (1992) Naltrexone in the treatment of alcohol dependence. *Archives of General Psychiatry, 49,* 876–880; Anton, R. (1991, June). *Buspirone in alcohol* rehabilitation. Presented at the Research Society on Alcoholism Annual Meeting, San Marco Island, Florida; Kranzler, H.R., Burleson, J.A., Del Boca, F.K., Babor, T.F., Korner, P., Brown, J., & Bohn, M.J. (1994). Buspirone treatment of anxious alcoholics: A placebo-controlled trial. *Archives of General Psychiatry, 51,* 720–731.

18. Dorus, W., Ostrow, D.G., Anton, R., Cushman, P., Collins, J.F., Schaefer, M., Charles, H.L., Desai, P., Hayashida, M., Malkerneker, U., Willenbring, M., Fiscella, R. and Sather, M.R. (1989). Lithium treatment of depressed and nondepressed alcoholics. *Journal of American Medical Association, 262,* 1646–1652.

19. Finney, J.W., & Moos, R.H. (1991). The long-term course of treated alcoholism: I. Mortality, relapse and remission rates and comparisons with community controls. *Journal of Studies in Alcoholism, 52,* 44–54.

## Recommended Readings

Goodwin, D.W., & Guze, S.B. (1996). *Psychiatric Diagnosis* (5th ed., pp. 170–205). New York, Oxford University Press.

Lowinson, J.H., Ruiz, P., Millgram, R.B., & Langrod, J.G. (Eds.). (1997). *Substance abuse: A comprehensive textbook* (3rd ed.) Baltimore: Williams & Wilkins.

Schuckit, M.A. (1995). Alcohol-related disorders. In Kaplan, H.I., & Sadock, B.J. (Eds.) *Comprehensive textbook of psychiatry* (6th ed., pp. 775–791) Baltimore: Williams & Wilkins.

Schuckit, M.A. (1995). *Drug and alcohol abuse: A clinical guide to diagnosis and treatment* (4th ed.). New York: Plenum.

Schuckit, M.A. (1995). *Educating yourself about alcohol and drugs: A people's primer.* New York: Plenum.

# 17

## About the Authors

*W. Stewart Agras was educated in Britain and obtained his M.D. degree from London University in 1955. Emigrating to Canada, he completed training in Psychiatry at McGill University in Montreal. After moving to Vermont, he became interested in behavior therapy and phobia as a model for psychotherapy research, eventually leading to the discovery that exposure to the feared situation was a principal ingredient of treatment for the phobias. In 1973, he moved to Stanford University as Professor of Psychiatry, establishing one of the first behavioral medicine programs in the country. When the upsurge in patients with bulimia nervosa occurred in the late seventies, he began the research described in this chapter. He has been President of the Association for the Advancement of Behavior Therapy, and of the Society for Behavioral Medicine, and Editor of the* Journal of Applied Behavior Analysis.

*Robin F. Apple completed her Ph.D. degree at the University of California, Los Angeles, and her postdoctoral fellowship at the Oregon Health Services University. She has been on the staff in the Behavioral Medicine Clinic, Department of Psychiatry, Stanford University Medical Center, since 1993. She recently participated in a multicenter study investigating the effectiveness of interpersonal and cognitive-behavioral therapies for the treatment of bulimia nervosa and has taken part in numerous other clinical experiences, as well as teaching and writing projects, which focus on the treatment of bulimia and binge eating disorder and the match between the patient and the therapy model used for treatment.*

# Sally and Her Eating Disorder: A Case of Bulimia Nervosa

**About the Disorder**

Food has psychological meaning that extends far beyond its nutritive powers. For some people, food takes on inordinate significance, and they become enslaved to bizarre and unhealthy rituals around the process of eating. People with eating disorders struggle to control the way they think about food and, to the distress of those who are close to them, their disturbed eating behaviors can put their lives at risk.

People with bulimia nervosa alternate between eating large amounts of food in a short time (binging), then compensating for the added calories by vomiting or other radical measures. Binges are characterized by a lack of control over what or how much is being eaten. People with bulimia nervosa also engage in inappropriate behaviors that are intended to prevent them from gaining weight. Those with the purging type try to force out of their bodies what they have just eaten; to do this, they induce vomiting, administer an enema, or take laxatives or diuretics. Those with the nonpurging type try to compensate by fasting or excessive exercise. Both types get caught up in a vicious cycle of binging, followed by desperate attempts to cleanse themselves of the foods that were so gratifying during the binge. Following the purging, hunger will return and the cycle continues.

It may be difficult to imagine what would motivate a person to engage in such unusual behaviors. The case of Sally as described by Drs. Agras and Apple, provides insight into the factors that can contribute to the development of bulimia nervosa. The treatment described illustrates the need for examining the various contributors to the development and maintenance of bulimia nervosa. By participating in a therapy that combined behavioral treatment and a focus on interpersonal relationships, Sally was able to make remarkable gains and achieve a healthy level of functioning.—*Eds*.

## Initial presentation

Sally, an unmarried, 40-year-old Caucasian female from Australia on a temporary professional assignment in the United States, contacted our clinic to request treatment for bulimia nervosa after viewing a televised segment about eating disorders in which the Stanford Clinic was featured. Her call coincided with the initial phase of a multicenter clinical trial, and having agreed to participate, she was assigned to one of the study conditions—interpersonal therapy. To accommodate her itinerary, I agreed to meet with her twice weekly for 10 weeks rather than adhering to the more usual 19 sessions over 20 weeks.

Sally was a tall, thin, but not emaciated woman dressed in a highly feminine and youthful manner. She noted that her mother had selected the "frock" and jewelry that she wore to the session. While her affect was bright and upbeat, it had brittle, forced quality. She noted that her mood had improved during the few weeks she had been in the States. Prior to departing Australia, following a brief psychiatric consultation, she reported that she had ceased a years-long habit of daily binge-eating and vomiting, instead adopting a regular, but restricted, meal plan. She acknowledged that the consultation had been helpful not only by addressing maladaptive eating behaviors, but also by touching upon social history and relationship patterns. As a result, Sally had confided to a few colleagues and friends about her eating disorder. At the same time, she persisted in viewing bulimia nervosa as a "medical condition that would clear up" when she decided to eat.

Sally's most striking feature was her eagerness to please. She arrived several minutes before our first early morning session was scheduled to begin, with a well-organized, detailed, computer-printed chart chronicling her life history, the emergence of specific aspects of her eating disorder, and her treatment experience. I speculated that her meticulously prepared, "therapy-wise," overly solicitous presentation provided a significant clue as to the nature of her interpersonal issues. In my opinion, Sally's behavior inadvertently revealed an attempt to disguise her very strong need to rely upon and open up to someone who was willing and able to support and assist her. I guessed that she demanded of herself near-perfect performance and expected criticism and rejection from others should she fail to meet these high standards. At the same time, I experienced Sally, as somewhat controlling and off-putting; she had consolidated, on her own, the information I had hoped to help her navigate during our first four sessions together.

### Case History

Sally reported a 25-year history of disordered eating which began in her early teens in the form of intensified shape and weight concerns. She was sheltered and overprotected by her well-to-do parents, growing up as the only girl in the immediate and extended families and one of few girls in a small farming community. She was an outstanding student and athlete, who felt "better than" her peers, although she remembers competing with an older brother for attention and praise.

Her focus on weight and shape began during a period of transition in her life, as she prepared to go to a prestigious all-girls boarding school several hours away from home. She first became upset about her body shape and size after viewing a photograph of herself, her mother, and her maternal grandmother, in which she felt that she looked "chubby," "large-boned," and "overweight," like her female relatives. When she began a stint as a model shortly thereafter, these concerns were intensified. Some months later, when she was sent away to school, additional signs of an eating disorder emerged as she grappled with the many changes in her life. For the first time, Sally had to compete with girls who were equally talented. She restricted her food intake, began to binge-eat and purge, and developed a running program of up to one hour per day. During the first month at school, her weight dropped by ten pounds, and she found that this enabled her to feel somewhat unique and special. At the same time, she began to complain of weakness and malaise, behaviors which were reinforced in the form of more attention and passes to visit her family. She was depressed and lonely, but unwilling to ask for support from her classmates, whom she viewed as competitive and superficial. Instead, she immersed herself in a quest for personal achievement in academics, athletics, and modeling. She was so skilled at masking her emotional distress beneath a facade of success that she impressed peers and school administrators as a leader and role model and by the end of her first year had been elected as a "counselor" for other students.

Nevertheless, she remained unhappy and after two years transferred to a day school closer to home. She took an apartment with a roommate in a neighboring town and began to study for college entrance exams, but was "homesick" and wound up spending every weekend with her family, whom she described as her "best friends." She neglected opportunities to develop hobbies or relationships independent of them. Her time away from family was spent studying, training for competitive athletics (up to 30 hours per week), and binge-eating and vomiting, behaviors that had escalated over the years to a frequency of up to several times per day. When her weight dropped to its adult low of 66 pounds, she was admitted to the hospital for refeeding, weight restoration, and behavior stabilization, but she terminated this and a second hospitalization prematurely, when she began to perceive the environment as "too controlling." Both times, she was welcomed home by her parents, who reorganized their work and vacation schedules to care for her.

Sally's twenties and thirties passed similarly, with periods of high functioning alternating with episodes of intractable binge-eating, purging, and depression. She completed hotel management courses, college, and an advanced degree, became established and well respected in a business-related profession, and achieved international renown in competitive sports. However, she continued to be quite isolated in her social life, developing casual, superficial relationships, but no close friendships. For example, during her first year of college, she described herself as "well known on campus, always in the press" and participated in, and won, a "looks and popularity" contest, but had no real confidantes. She was also involved in a months-long romance with a man 20 years her senior, whom she described as controlling. She ended the relationship after receiving a failing grade in a course, turned her full attention to studying, moved off campus, and was socially reclusive for the remainder of college.

Sally eventually developed a large network of casual acquaintances through work and sports, but was careful to hide her personal problems from them, buying into her parents admonition that "you are put on this earth to be the best and to serve others." Thus, she spent most of her time alone, perfecting her performance in everything she attempted. She was equally committed to maintaining a "one up" stance in relationships by "knowing what it is that the other person needs and giving it to them, rather than having them give to me." She felt comfortable "being real" only with her family, and her behavior was quite childish, at times "throwing tantrums like a two-year-old." Her parents persisted in treating her in kind, referring to her as their "little girl" and repeatedly asking her to move home, despite her ability to support herself. Long after owning her own place in another city, Sally continued to refer to the family farm as "home," and felt "homesick" and guilty if she missed a family vacation or stayed at her own place for a weekend. It was with considerable difficulty that she left for the States alone. Her mother volunteered to accompany her because of her concern that Sally would not be able to manage eating on her own. Sally assuaged her parents by agreeing to write and call on a weekly basis, later describing her letters as "the highlight of my parents' week."

## Diagnosis

Sally exhibited a long-standing eating disorder which included the following symptoms in her history: maintenance of less than 85% normal body weight, disrupted menses, intense fear of gaining weight, persistent overconcern with body shape and size, out-of-control binge-eating episodes, compensatory purging through vomiting, laxative use, and excessive exercise. These symptoms warranted a diagnosis of bulimia nervosa with a past history of anorexia nervosa. She also complained of depression and her symptoms of low mood, poor self-esteem, insomnia, and feelings of hopelessness met criteria for dysthymia with a past history of recurrent major depression. Long-standing personality characteristics also contributed to the picture, suggesting obsessive-compulsive and avoidant tendencies. These included perfectionism, overconscientiousness, preoccupation with details, restricted range of affect, hypersensitivity to others' evaluation, shyness in social situations, and limited confidants. Finally, Sally experienced a number of physical sequelae secondary to the years of abusing her body through binge-eating, purging, and compulsive exercise. These conditions were listed on Axis III.

*DSM-IV* Diagnosis:

| Axis I: | • Bulimia nervosa (history anorexia nervosa) |
|---|---|
| | • Dysthymia (history major depression, recurrent) |
| Axis II: | • Obsessive-compulsive and avoidant traits |
| Axis III: | • Dental, musculoskeletal, and gastrointestinal problems and surgery to correct anal prolapse |
| Axis IV: | • Job changes: transfer to new position in different country; inadequate social support system |
| Axis V: | • GAF = 55 (current) |

## Case formulation

During the first four sessions (Phase I), a detailed assessment (linking together history of weight and eating disorder symptoms, mood, interpersonal relationships, and significant life events) led to the creation of an "interpersonal inventory" aimed at identifying one or more salient problem areas among the following four general categories: interpersonal role disputes, role transition, grief, and interpersonal deficits.

From the outset of my treatment with Sally, I felt convinced that her primary interpersonal problems involved role transition difficulties and interpersonal deficits. For Sally, the onset and worsening of eating disorder symptoms corresponded with times when she had difficulty negotiating transitions in her life. Her limited social skills were an added liability in these situations, preventing her from obtaining real support, while increasing the likelihood that she would fall back on perfectionism and drive in performance as a means to cope with unfamiliar situations.

Sally's history and presentation suggested that early on she bought into her parents' overvaluation of achievement and success at the expense of close personal relationships. She modeled her life according to their directives to "be the best" and to "serve others" without questioning the relevance of their rules for her life. While success in athletics, academics, and her profession came relatively easily to her, she pushed herself to the limit in order to uphold the perfectionistic standards that she had made her own. She learned to approach social relationships with the same competitive edge. Rather than allowing herself to enjoy a mutually satisfying connection to people, she prided herself on knowing exactly what was needed by another person, giving more than they could give to her, and masking her own needs behind a pretense of sound adjustment. Although this posture helped her to feel sought out by and indispensible to others, she began to regard herself as a "fake" who hid her "real self" from others at all costs. She lost sight of the possibility of developing a deeper and genuine connection with another person, since she had no conception or mastery of the necessary interpersonal skills.

## Course of Treatment

While Sally began the therapy with an interest in understanding the interpersonal and emotional contributions to her eating problems, she actually had very little understanding about these areas. In reviewing her history, it was clear that she was quite adept at discussing details involving the concrete aspects of her eating disorder—for example, aberrant eating behaviors, weight changes, physical sensations (such as hunger and fatigue), hours of exercise—but she had considerable difficulty giving all but sketchy details when asked to describe her mood state, important events, and significant relationships.

Not surprisingly, Sally was ill-at-ease when, following the first four structured and directive history-taking sessions, we moved to the second phase of treatment, in which she became responsible for initiating discussion of problem areas. While she had agreed with the formulation, she seemed overwhelmed by the expectation that she should broach these topics on her own. Thus, she fell back on the strategy of trying to say "the right things." Her presentation in session five seemed "canned" in that she relied on jargon and vague generalities pertaining to her desire to please others, lack of assertiveness, and difficulty identifying her own feelings. She discussed these topics in a mechanical and distant manner, referring to herself in the second person (as "you"), exhibiting minimal, and at times inappropriately cheerful affect, and presenting in a manner that suggested to me a fear of saying the wrong thing or showing her real self. Any attempt on my part to push her to explore the relationship patterns in more depth was met with resistance, and I realized that Sally did not have command of a language to describe her emotions or relationships in more detail. She was limited to describing her experiences in terms involving eating behaviors and varying levels of hunger, exhaustion, and illness.

Her awareness of this problem surfaced during session six, when in response to my querying about her feelings, she stated in an irritated tone, "I don't know what my feelings are." This revelation represented a pivotal point in the therapy because it was her first expression of genuine affect. I responded in an empathic, but nonintrusive manner, commenting on how difficult it must be for her to have me prodding her to talk about an aspect of her experience that she was not able to access. I wanted to reinforce disclosure of feelings without being overly critical or controlling. I was hoping that gentle encouragement would facilitate her emerging trust in our relationship and make it more likely for her to experiment with new ways of relating in the therapy room. I decided to bring the discussion of our relationship into the open, as it was relevant to the interpersonal problem areas we were working on. I hypothesized out loud that Sally's difficulty labeling her emotions might stem from her focusing her attention on what she thought I wanted to hear from her, rather than on what she was actually feeling. I shared with her my observation that up to that point, she had been acting in a manner that might characterize a "perfect patient"—arriving early for sessions, addressing the appropriate topics, thanking and complimenting me after each meeting—but hiding her "real self" from me in the process. I speculated that this way of relating was probably familiar and comfortable to her, and might be based on a history of having been the recipient of negative feedback at times when she did share her real feelings. But I cautioned her that our work would certainly be limited if she maintained a stance of saying and doing "what was right." I reminded her that our therapy goals involved changing interpersonal patterns and that the therapy hour itself provided an opportunity to take risks and experiment with new behaviors.

Sally disagreed with my perception of her as "playing a role" and assured me of her commitment to "be real" during our sessions. Her denial did not surprise me, and I was actually encouraged by her willingness to express a dissenting opinion. In any case, the process and tone of therapy changed after this session. She began to initiate discussions of the "difficult times" she had endured since our last meeting, typically involving the experience of loneliness and depression and urges to re-engage in problematic eating behaviors. She observed that she was most upset when she was alone with "nothing to do" during evenings and weekends. She described weekends as "time to fill before going back to work" and acknowledged less satisfaction from solitary pursuits. She began to talk movingly about a desire to make friends, admitting that she had never had a friendship with a female. She slowly began to accept social invitations from professional colleagues, joined a church group, and participated in a hiking club where she would not let herself "go all out and compete with the fast group," but instead allowed herself to enjoy a slower pace that would enable socializing along the way.

In session nine, Sally began to reflect on her history, noting considerable grief and regret about her relationship patterns. She characterized herself as a "sucker" who "wasted 40 years serving others." She described her previous interpersonal role as one of making herself indispensable, to avoid criticism, rejection, or dependence. She expressed anger toward herself for "being used" and toward those who had exploited her. She admitted feeling like a "social misfit" whose tangible achievements only served as a "cover-up" for being alone.

She also began to talk about her parents, admitting that, while they were adept at disguising their behaviors as parental nurturance and caretaking, their overprotectiveness and her devotion to them had taken from her many opportunities for personal and social maturation. Slowly, she began to address the here-and-now aspects of their relationship, expressing exasperation at the intrusiveness and triviality of their questions about what she was wearing, eating, or doing. She altered the tone of their relationship by attempting to deflect these questions and to limit self-disclosure about personal matters such as her progress in therapy. She expressed disappointment that her parents seemed unable to understand the process she was going through and upset when they interpreted her broadened perspective for understanding her problems as "blaming others." She considered that they may not have the capacity to really understand or connect with her, and started the process of grieving the loss of the ideal relationship she hoped to have with them. At the same time, she began an active search for trusted confidantes and became friendly with the wife of a colleague and members of a church social group.

Toward the end of the second phase of treatment, Sally's behavior in the sessions also began to change, with a greater willingness to discuss her feelings toward me. In session 15, after enthusiastically presenting me with a chart correlating her negative thoughts, feelings, and behaviors, she expressed disappointment that I reacted less positively than she expected, stating that I seemed to misunderstand her effort to "get in touch with feelings." A productive discussion about her frustration at our working at "cross purposes" ensued and she identified this interaction—a direct communication about negative emotions with the person involved—as a new form of relating. She added that our discussion had helped her feel more rather than less connected with me, although she was upset that we had not addressed these *real* issues earlier.

We began in the final sessions to consolidate gains, anticipate future problems, and plan for termination. Sally revealed a personal goal of "surrounding myself with people with whom I can relate genuinely," based on her experience in therapy and her view of me as the "first woman who could accept me for who I am." She continued to participate in social activities and limited her work hours to facilitate her new interests. Befriending others seemed to help her to treat herself with more kindness; she began to allow herself to eat and sleep to satisfaction on a regular basis, breaking long-standing, rigid behavioral patterns. She expressed concern that upon return to Australia she would resume "the empty shell of my former life." Thus, considerable time was spent in devising strategies for maintaining the gains made in therapy. Hence, she planned for the first time, to spend only half of an upcoming holiday vacation with her parents; she started to refer to her own house as home; and she re-engaged with former associates whom she hoped would be part of her new social circle. In discussing termination, she was open, expressive, and tearful. She was sad that the therapy could not continue, but was also ready to "test her wings" by putting the changes she made in the States into practice in her country. She felt that the therapy relationship had provided a model for future relationships in which the sharing of feelings would be primary. As a token of thanks and a means for saying good-bye, she presented me with a card elaborating on the value of friendship.

## Outcome of the case

When treatment ended, Sally reported weight maintenance (in the low normal range), no binge-eating episodes, and a few episodes of purging. Her exercise averaged out to be moderate (no more than one hour per day). She had radically altered her understanding of bulimia, viewing it as an attempt to manage certain feelings states, particularly those involving relationships with other people, rather than a medical condition.

Interpersonally, her gains were remarkable. With respect to the role transition issues, she came to terms with the fact that her habitual way of living her life, which had been based on living by others' rules and expectations rather than her own, was no longer effective and that there was a need for change. She mourned what was lost and prepared herself for a life style in which social relationships would be primary. She practiced social skills—assertiveness, limit-setting, self-disclosure—initially during the therapy hours, and later outside of the sessions, with family, colleagues, and friends. She adopted a new, more flexible and accepting way of relating to herself, based on these interpersonal changes.

Sally has remained in touch with me since completing treatment here 18 months ago. In her most recent FAX, she informed me that she had relocated to the States semi-permanently, following a requested corporate transfer. While she admits to "bad spells" involving poor physical health (secondary to the years of overexercise and bulimia), and intermittent, brief episodes of binge-eating, purging, food restriction, or overexercise, she continues to work hard to understand these behaviors in a psychosocial context and thereby attempts to address the underlying causes. Her relationship with her family remains changed to a degree (as evidenced by her move to the States), although she maintains very close ties to them, and finds it difficult at times to accept their limits in understanding her. At the same time, she has developed a few confidantes in church and sports activities and seems to be able to nurture these relationships without much difficulty. While she does reflect with sadness and regret upon the years consumed by the eating disorder and depression, she is able to uplift herself by shifting her focus to the richness and texture she has added to her life—through attention to emotions and personal relationships.

## EMPIRICAL CONTRIBUTIONS TO UNDERSTANDING BULIMIA NERVOSA

In the late 1970s there was a sudden and unexpected surge in the number of patients with bulimia nervosa seeking treatment in my clinic, a phenomenon later reported throughout the industrialized world. It was this that first sparked my interest in better understanding bulimia nervosa. From a clinical viewpoint it seemed that dieting to improve body shape and weight led to binge eating. Although it was, and still is, not clear whether the surge in the number of cases represented an increase in the prevalence of the disorder, it seemed reasonable to suppose that societal pressures for a thin body shape and low weight might be one factor contributing to the increase. So the first question I asked was whether societal views on the ideal female body shape had changed over the years, and whether there was a greater emphasis on thinness in the decade preceding the surge in new cases. Luckily, there is a documentary record of women's shape in the advertisements in magazines directed primarily toward women. Hence, an index of body shape from slim to curvaceous was devised

and scored for randomly selected depiction's of women in three women's magazines that had been continuously published over an 80-year span. In the first
two decades of the twentieth century, a plump body shape was preferred in
such pictures. However, in the 1920s—the era of the "flapper"—the ideal body
shape became one of thinness. Such a silhouette was achieved by means of a
dress style that gave women an elongated slim look. By the 1940s, the ideal
body shape had become curvaceous once more, remaining so until the mid-
1960s when thinness again became the rule. When the proportion of articles on
diet was determined in the same periodicals, the percentage was very low until
the mid-1940s, dramatically increasing in the 1970s. These two findings confirmed that there was a change in ideal body shape for women from curvaceous-
ness to thinness in the decade before the surge in cases of bulimia nervosa
occurred, and that diet, rather than dress style, had become the major method
of achieving such a body shape.

Since the majority of young women diet, and only 1 or 2% develop bulimia
nervosa, dieting cannot be the only risk factor for this disorder. This observation
led me to consider other factors that might precipitate binge eating. One of the
best ways to find out about such factors is to ask the patient in the context of a
semi-structured interview. Based on patient reports, it turned out that negative
emotional states such as anxiety, anger, and a sad mood were three times more
likely to lead to a binge than was dieting. These findings were paralleled in a
nonclinical sample of women binge eaters identified in an epidemiological study
carried out in the San Francisco Bay Area. Both these studies suggested that
the influence of negative emotions on binge eating had been underestimated.

This led me to investigate the effects of dietary restriction and negative
mood on binge eating experimentally. Binge eating can be reproduced in the
laboratory by serving individuals large amounts of attractive food, and in some
cases, giving instructions to binge. In the first of the experiments which I designed, participants with binge eating disorder and weight-matched non-binge
eaters, as well as a group of patients with bulimia nervosa, came to the laboratory in the morning for a standard breakfast, having eaten nothing since mid-
night. Half of each group were then randomly assigned to eat or skip lunch and
in mid-afternoon were served a large and appetizing buffet, about 25,000 calories worth, and told to eat as much or as little as they wished. I was interested
in whether participants who had skipped lunch, would eat more throughout the
day than those who had been served lunch. I speculated that binge eaters who
did not have lunch (analogous to dietary restriction) would lose control of their
eating and eat more than those who had lunch. It turned out that this was not
the case. Even though some of them binged at the buffet, the eating disorder
patients were able to accurately regulate their daily caloric intake. Binge eating
may simply represent compensation for previous dietary restriction, with large
binges making up for dietary restraint and purging.

In the second experiment, the effect of negative mood on caloric intake was
examined. Participants with binge eating disorder again came to the laboratory
for a standard breakfast and lunch, and were served a buffet in mid-afternoon.

The laboratory setting was private, and participants were not observed. Just before the buffet a negative mood was induced in half the participants and a neutral mood in the other half. Basically the negative mood was engendered by having the participant recall a recent upsetting event and reliving it as intensely as possible. The amount of food consumed was measured. Intriguingly, the participants' mood did not affect caloric intake either at the buffet or over the whole laboratory day. Nonetheless, there were some interesting findings. The more negative the participants' mood, the more likely they were to characterize their eating as "out of control" and describe the episode as a binge. Once again, there was evidence that negative mood, not dietary restraint, influenced aspects of binge eating.

What has all this to do with our case study in which interpersonal therapy was used to treat bulimia nervosa? One of the things that puzzled me most about findings that interpersonal therapy may be as effective as cognitive-behavioral therapy was the question of the mechanism of action of interpersonal therapy.[1] This was on my mind as we examined the factors contributing to binge eating. Could it be that interpersonal therapy reduces the emotional triggers associated with binge eating? Emotions are often generated through faulty interpersonal interactions. In Sally's case, for example, binge episodes were precipitated by loneliness and a depressed mood. The changes that she made in her interpersonal relationships, particularly forming genuine friendships, would reduce such negative affect, and hence reduce binge eating.

## EMPIRICAL CONTRIBUTIONS TO TREATMENT OF BULIMIA NERVOSA

Sally was a pilot subject for a two-center study designed to compare cognitive-behavioral and interpersonal psychotherapies. This comparison is interesting because the two therapies are conceptually and procedurally distinct. Cognitive-behavioral therapy (CBT) for bulimia nervosa directly addresses the disturbed eating patterns and distorted thinking regarding body weight and shape. In contrast, interpersonal therapy focuses on current interpersonal difficulties and, apart from the assessment phase, does not address the disturbed eating patterns.

In a study at Oxford University, interpersonal therapy was used as a control condition in a comparison with CBT in patients with bulimia nervosa.[2,3] Given the fact that CBT had proven more effective than many forms of psychotherapy, including nondirective therapy, manualized psychodynamic therapy, and stress management, it was surprising that the interpersonal therapy was as effective as cognitive-behavioral therapy in reducing binge eating and purging. At the time these results were published, my research focus had shifted to binge eating disorder, then known as nonpurging bulimia nervosa or compulsive overeating. I had found cognitive-behavioral therapy to be effective in treating binge eating disorder, with recovery occurring in about half of all patients, a proportion similar to that found in the treatment of bulimia nervosa. As a next step, I decided to find out whether interpersonal therapy was as effective as cognitive-behavioral therapy in binge eating disorder. There were two differences between our study and the Oxford study. First, as described, the patients suffered from nonpurging bulimia nervosa (binge eating disorder). Second, because patients with this condition are often overweight and wanted to lose weight, our treatment used a group format similar to that used in weight control programs.

Patients with binge eating disorder were allocated at random to one of three groups: CBT, interpersonal therapy, and a waiting list control group. Luckily, half the patients in each of the two active treatments regarded that treatment as their first choice, removing the bias of choice from the study. The results were quite straightforward. The two treatments were both more effective than the waiting list control group in reducing binge eating, and were no different from each other. At follow-up one year after treatment ended, although some relapse occurred in both groups, the two treatments continued to be equally effective. This study confirmed the findings of the Oxford group, suggesting that interpersonal therapy, a treatment that does not address the eating disorder directly, is as effective as cognitive-behavioral therapy. These findings provoked three questions. Are the treatments really equally effective, or do they appear similar because the studies were not large enough to detect true differences? How does interpersonal therapy work? Do individuals respond differently to the treatments? These questions led to the design of the multicenter study.

Interpersonal therapy is a newcomer in the treatment of bulimia nervosa. CBT, on the other hand, has a much longer history of development. In 1981, Fairburn at Oxford University wrote a paper describing the effectiveness of a new treatment, cognitive-behavioral therapy.[4] I decided to replicate his work, making one change—namely, modifying the treatment for use in a group setting, hopefully a more cost-effective mode of treatment. For the 13 female participants, self-induced vomiting, which averaged 24 times each week before treatment, fell to 2.2 times each week, a 91% improvement. Moreover, seven patients stopped purging following treatment, and only one relapsed in the next six months. These findings led me to conclude that CBT was a treatment worth investigating in more time-consuming, expensive, and controlled studies—the next step in the development of a new therapy.

In designing controlled studies of psychological treatments, it is necessary to devise a suitable control group against which to test the new therapy. When a standard treatment for the condition exists, the best design is to compare the new therapy with standard treatment. However, when no standard therapy exists, as was the case for bulimia nervosa at that time, it is necessary to choose a comparison treatment that controls for elements common to all therapies. These elements include a therapeutic relationship, a believable therapeutic rationale, and positive expectations for recovery. The therapy that I chose as a control for CBT was a form of nondirective psychotherapy, a believable treatment that, unlike cognitive-behavioral therapy, does not focus on disordered eating. Hence, in the next study, patients with bulimia nervosa were assigned at random to either group CBT or to group nondirective therapy. Participants rated the two therapies as equally credible for the treatment of bulimia nervosa. However, by the end of treatment, binge eating and purging had reduced to a significantly greater extent in the group receiving cognitive-behavioral therapy than in the group receiving nondirective therapy, confirming the utility of cognitive-behavioral therapy in the treatment of bulimia nervosa.

During the initial testing of the effectiveness of CBT, researchers at the University of Vermont,[5] had developed a therapy focused on purging rather than on dietary restraint. This treatment, known as response prevention, consisted of having bulimics consume binge food and then preventing purging by remaining with the patient until the urge to induce vomiting had passed. The reasoning here is that patients will see that the anxiety associated with binge eating dissipates if the anxiety is not avoided by purging. Hence, in the next study I decided to compare no treatment; self-monitoring of eating behavior and supportive therapy; CBT plus response prevention; and CBT alone, in a randomized controlled study. Two questions were addressed in this study, namely: Are there specific elements in CBT over and above self-monitoring that add to the effectiveness of treatment? Does response prevention add anything to CBT? In this study, individual therapy was used, since it is more difficult to keep treatments well separated in group therapy than in individual therapy.

The results surprised me. Response prevention decreased the effectiveness of cognitive-behavioral therapy. This may have been because patients receiving response prevention received less cognitive-behavioral therapy, as we had a fixed number of treatment sessions. A later study from Rutgers University[6] confirmed this notion. In addition, CBT was superior to self-monitoring of eating behavior, demonstrating that there are effective elements over and above self-monitoring and a therapeutic relationship in cognitive-behavioral therapy. Nearly 60% of the patients receiving CBT had stopped binge eating and purging by the end of treatment, and at six-month follow-up maintained these improvements. It should be noted that maintenance of therapeutic gains following CBT is for the most part excellent, a situation different from the psychological treatment of other conditions.

In parallel with the development of CBT, Pope and his colleagues at Harvard had made the surprising finding that antidepressant medication was effective in the treatment of bulimia nervosa.[7] Although the use of antidepressant treatment began with the notion that bulimia nervosa was a form of depression, this hypothesis has been shown to be erroneous, since both depressed and nondepressed bulimics respond equally well to antidepressants. In an early study, I confirmed the effectiveness of an antidepressant, imipramine, by comparing it with a placebo. As the number of studies of the effectiveness of antidepressant treatment grew, it appeared as though this treatment might be as effective as CBT. This led me to the next question: Would the combination of cognitive-behavioral and antidepressant treatments be more effective than either treatment alone? This is an important question since, on average, only slightly more than half of patients treated with CBT recover.

To address this question, I conducted a study in which patients with bulimia nervosa were allocated at random to one of three groups: CBT, antidepressant treatment, which is withdrawn after four or six months, and the combined treatments. Since there were now a large number of studies demonstrating that antidepressants were superior to placebo, it did not appear necessary (or ethical) to include a placebo condition in this study. There were several interesting findings. First, when the antidepressant was given for only four months, nearly all the patients showed a relapse in binge eating following withdrawal of the medication, a relapse that was prevented by the addition of CBT. Second, CBT therapy was more effective than medication. Third, the most effective treatment was the combination of desipramine (given for six months) and CBT, with 65% of patients stopping binge eating and purging.

One year after treatment had ended, 78% of those receiving the combined treatment, with the antidepressant withdrawn at six months, had stopped binge eating and purging, compared with 18% of those receiving four months of antidepressant without CBT. The other groups fell between these extremes. Interestingly, half the patients not recovering in the most successful combined treatment group had recovered at one year follow-up. Since medication had been withdrawn at that time, it would appear that CBT has delayed positive effects.

As can be seen, the development of new and effective psychotherapeutic treatments takes time. Programmatic research in which studies build upon each other is essential in such a development, and is facilitated if several centers follow somewhat similar paths. When sufficient evidence has accrued from single site studies, one or more trials, larger in scope than can be accomplished at a single center, are needed to firmly settle a particular question. As is the case in our ongoing study, this will often consist of a comparison of two active treatments, a comparison that of necessity involves a large sample size. The programmatic work involving several centers described in this chapter, leading to the multicenter study in which our patient made an important contribution as a pilot subject, will hopefully provide guidance as to the most effective form of psychotherapy for bulimia nervosa.

### Acknowledgment

The preparation of this chapter was supported in part by a grant (MH 49887) from the National Institute of Mental Health.

### Notes

1. Klerman, G. L., Weissman, M. M., Rounsaville, B.J., & Chevron, E.S. (1984). *Interpersonal Psychotherapy of Depression.* New York: Basic Books.

2. Fairburn, C. G., Jones, R., Peveler, R.C., Carr, S. J., Solomon, R. A., O'Connor, M. E., Burton, J., & Hope, R. A. (1991). Three psychological treatments for bulimia nervosa. *Archives of General Psychiatry, 48,* 463–469.

3. Fairburn D. G., Jones, R., Peveler, R. C., Hope, R. A., & O'Connor, M. (1993). Psychotherapy and bulimia nervosa: Longer-term effects of interpersonal psychotherapy, behavior therapy, and cognitive-behavior therapy. *Archives of General Psychiatry, 50,* 419–428.

4. Fairburn, C. G. (1981). A cognitive-behavioral approach to the treatment of bulimia. *Psychological Medicine, 11,* 707–711.

5. Leitenberg, H., Gross, J., Peterson, J., & Rosen, J. C. (1984). Analysis of an anxiety model and the process of change during exposure plus response prevention treatment of bulimia nervosa. *Behavior Therapy, 15,* 3–20.

6. Wilson, G. T., Eldredge, K. L., Smith, D., & Niles, B. (1991). Cognitive-behavioral treatment with and without response prevention for bulimia. *Behavior Research and Therapy, 29,* 575–583.

7. Pope, H. G., Hudson, J. I., Jonas, J. M., & Yurgelun-Todd, D. (1983). Bulimia treated with imipramine: A placebo-controlled double-blind study. *American Journal of Psychiatry, 140,* 554–558.

## Recommended Readings

Agras, W.S., Rossiter, E.M., Arnow, B., Scheider, J.A., Telch, C.F., Raeburn, S.D., Bruce, B., Perl, M., & Koran, L.M. (1992). Pharmacologic and cognitive-behavioral treatment for bulimia nervosa: A controlled comparison. *American Journal of Psychiatry, 149,* 82–87.

Agras, W.S., Rossiter, E.M., Arnow, B., Telch, C.F., Raeburn, S.D., Bruce, B., & Koran, L.M. (1994). One-year follow-up of psychosocial and pharmacologic treatments for bulimia. *Journal of Clinical Psychiatry, 55,* 179–183.

Agras, W. S., Telch, C. F., Arnow, B., Eldredge, K., Henderson, J., & Marnell, M. (In press). Does interpersonal therapy help patients with binge eating disorder who fail to respond to cognitive-behavioral therapy? *Journal of Consulting & Clinical Psychology.*

Fairburn, C. G. (1993) Interpersonal psychotherapy for bulimia nervosa. In Klerman, G.L., & Weissman M.M., (Eds.) *New Applications of interpersonal therapy.* Washington DC: American Psychiatric Press.

Fairburn, C.G., Marcus, M.D., & Wilson, G.T. (1993). Cognitive behavior therapy for binge eating and bulimia nervosa: A treatment manual. In Fairburn, C.G. & Wilson G.T. (Eds.), *Binge eating: Nature, assessment, and treatment* (pp. 361–404) New York: Guildford Press.

Wilfley, D.E., Agras, W.S., Telch, C.F., Rossiter, E.M., Schneider, J.A., Cole, A.B., Sifford, L., & Raeburn, S.D. (1993). Group cognitive-behavioral therapy and group interpersonal psychotherapy for the non-purging bulimic: A controlled comparison. *Journal of Consulting and Clinical Psychology 61,* 296–305.

Weissman, M.M., & Marcovitz, J. C. (1994). Interpersonal therapy: Current status. *Archives of General Psychiatry, 51,* 599–604.

# Index

*Frances and Roland Bee*

**Frances Bee** and **Roland Bee** are directors of Time for People Ltd, a personnel and training consultancy. Frances's career has spanned strategic planning, personnel and training in local government and senior management in the financial services and retail areas. Roland flew in the RAF for 12 years before entering the field of management services and HR. He has worked as a chief officer in local government and the electricity supply industry, and as personnel manager with a national finance organisation. Both have had wide experience of facilitating groups in learning situations and as managers. They are specialists in training and consultancy in the training/learning area – training needs analysis, design and development of training interventions, facilitation skills and training evaluation. Frances and Roland met on the MBA programme at the Management College, Henley-on-Thames, and have just celebrated their twentieth wedding anniversary. They now live in rural Suffolk in a converted barn and late medieval farmhouse surrounded by ten acres of new woodland and wildflower meadow. They are co-authors of the following CIPD books: *Managing Information Systems and Statistics, Training Needs Analysis and Evaluation, Project Management – The people challenge, Constructive Feedback* and *Customer Care.* They have also written a training package, *The Complete Learning Evaluation Toolkit,* also published by the CIPD.

In the TRAINING ESSENTIALS series leading experts focus on the key issues in contemporary training. The books are thoroughly comprehensive, setting out the theoretical background while also providing practical guidance to meet the 'hands-on' needs of training practitioners. They are essential reading for trainers and for students working towards training qualifications – N/SVQs, and Diploma and Certificate courses in training and development.

## Other titles in the series include:

The Chartered Institute of Personnel and Development is the leading publisher of books and reports for personnel and training professionals,  students, and for all those concerned with the effective management and development of people at work. For details of all our titles, please contact the Publishing Department:

*tel.* 020-8263 3387

*fax* 020-8263 3850

*e-mail* publish@cipd.co.uk   ·

The catalogue of all CIPD titles can be viewed on the CIPD website:

www.cipd.co.uk/bookstore

# FACILITATION
# SKILLS

*Frances and Roland Bee*

Chartered Institute of Personnel and Development

First published in 1998

Reprinted 1999, 2001, 2002, 2003

Typesetting by Fakenham Photosetting,
Fakenham, Norfolk
Printed in Great Britain by
The Cromwell Press, Wiltshire


*British Library Cataloguing in Publication Data*

A catalogue record for this book is available from the
British Library

ISBN 0-85292-733-9

Chartered Institute of Personnel and Development, CIPD House,
Camp Road, London SW19 4UX
Tel: 020-8971 9000   Fax: 020-8263 3333
E-mail: cipd@cipd.co.uk  Website: www.cipd.co.uk
Incorporated by Royal Charter.  Registered Charity No. 1079797.

# Contents

# Acknowledgements

We should like to thank David Nida and Commercial Union plc for giving us the opportunity to share in the development and introduction of a facilitation skills programme for their staff based on the principles in this book. Also our thanks go to Anne Cordwent, our editor, who was never other than unfailingly supportive and encouraging throughout the creation of this book.

# Introduction

This book is aimed at anyone who may be required to facilitate a group session of some sort – all those:

- internal or external trainers, managers and others who are involved in the learning process
- managers, internal and external consultants, in fact anybody who may need to help a group achieve its objectives through group sessions, eg project teams, departmental/functional teams, problem-solving/ quality groups, etc.

We set out to explain exactly what is meant by the word 'facilitation', what are and how to develop the knowledge and skills to become a successful facilitator, and why it is so important for today's organisations that there is a move towards facilitative approaches and away from the more traditional directive approaches.

Traditional management practice has had its roots in the Theory X (McGregor, 1961) style of management, which has led those who have sought to influence others – for example, managers and trainers – to take a more *directive* approach in working with their teams and training groups. This approach is based (in very simplistic terms) on the view that people:

- want to do as little work as possible
- are unreliable
- do not want to take responsibility

■ prefer to be directed rather than think for themselves
■ are motivated by money
■ need rules, structure, hierarchies and strong controls
■ lack creativity.

Translated into the training/learning situation, this has meant that training approaches have often been based on the view that:

■ people may not be motivated to learn
■ the trainer is primarily responsible for ensuring that the learning takes place
■ it is the trainer's role to tell the delegates 'how to do it' – the knowledge and skills reside with the trainer
■ training design should be highly structured with set training session plans.

Forward-thinking organisations have increasingly become aware that this traditional approach stifles innovation, the ability to respond quickly and effectively to changing situations and the ability to adopt a more flexible style of working. All of these requirements are becoming increasingly important as organisations seek to survive and grow in an environment of ever escalating change involving rising customer expectations, increasing competition, global markets and the challenge of technology.

Organisations are now seeing the benefits of adopting a *facilitative* approach which has its origins in the Theory Y (McGregor, 1961) view that people:

■ are generally interested in their work and want to do a good job
■ are motivated by a desire to learn and achieve their own potential
■ want responsibility and are comfortable with the philosophy that their own self-discipline will be stronger than any imposed controls

▊ have creativity and ingenuity that is greatly under-
used.

Translated into the learning/training situation, this
means that facilitative approaches are based on the view
that:

▊ people are generally highly motivated to learn and
develop their full potential

▊ responsibility for learning rests primarily with the
learner

▊ people have considerable existing experience – the
aim of the learning sessions is to use and build on this

▊ people want and can take more control over their learning

▊ the role of the modern trainer is to facilitate learning

▊ the learning plan needs to be flexible to meet the
needs of the learners.

Similarly, translated into general group sessions, the facilitative approach is based on the view that group members
are highly motivated and want to achieve the objectives of
the group; they want to share their knowledge and skills
and participate fully in solving the problem, or coming up
with new ideas; they can and want to share responsibility
for the outcomes of group sessions. The ability to solve
the problem/come up with new ideas resides with the
'participants'. The facilitator's role is to guide and support the group, not to direct it. A good example of this
was when we were asked to help a university which was
having problems with one of its major management
courses – it was receiving a lot of complaints from the
students about the quality and running of the course.
Our role was not to come up with the answers but to
facilitate the staff involved with the course, who had the
relevant knowledge and skills, in identifying the issues
and the way to deal with them.

Where trainers are moving into the role of internal consultants, with the brief to support managers and staff in

the learning process, the need to be able to facilitate general group sessions will grow. For example:

- working with stakeholders to identify training needs, agree learning objectives, etc
- facilitating participants of a training programme in providing feedback on that programme as part of an evaluation process
- helping members of a project team explore the learning from their project experience.

The facilitative approach is based on a vision of partnership, of shared objectives and of shared achievements. The goal is that everyone should be a facilitator, it becomes a 'way of life', part of the organisational culture. It is an essential prerequisite to the successful introduction of initiatives such as empowerment and the learning organisation. These differences in approach must encompass every part of the organisation's life – the way people learn, in the way group sessions are run and the way people are managed individually on a day-to-day basis. This book addresses the first two of these areas.

Whether you work for an organisation which is some way down the path of embracing a facilitative way of working or in one that is just setting out down that path, we hope that this book will provide both the motivation and the map to help you reach that goal. We look at:

- in Chapter 1, the difference in behaviours and outcomes between a facilitative approach and directive approach, and we examine some of the common concerns about adopting a facilitative approach – the element of risk, lack of control, issues of neutrality, time implications, confusion over roles and responsibilities.

- in Chapters 2 and 3, the core skills for facilitation:
  - building rapport

&#9633;  active listening and observing

&#9633;  masterly questioning

&#9633;  managing information

and how these skills can be developed and applied in facilitating learning groups and general group sessions.

■  in Chapter 4, behaving as a facilitator – using a well-known model of behaviour to throw light on the relationship between the facilitator and the group.

■  in Chapter 5, the implications for the design of learning sessions:

&#9633;  ownership of the learning objectives by the learners

&#9633;  flexible approaches to learning methods

&#9633;  emphasis on experiential learning

&#9633;  empowering the learner – the role of the trainer/facilitator.

■  in Chapter 6, useful processes that can help the facilitation of group sessions, covering:

&#9633;  preparing to facilitate

&#9633;  helping the group get started

&#9633;  use of tool and techniques to problem-solve, generate new ideas, take decisions, eg SWOT analysis, brainstorming

&#9633;  reviewing and learning from group sessions.

■  in Chapter 7, monitoring group processes and handling challenging people situations using a facilitative approach, eg dealing with lack of involvement, cynicism and anger.

■  in Chapter 8, continuing to improve your facilitation skills.

We make use of two important behavioural models, neuro-linguistic programming (NLP) and transactional analysis (TA), in the development of the core skills and behaviours of facilitation. We use many of these skills and behaviours intuitively; however, by understanding and structuring them we are able to deploy them more purposively and in more challenging situations.

For some people, moving towards a facilitative approach may seem a daunting prospect. We see the journey as a series of stepping-stones across a river – on one side is the traditional, directive approach and on the other side the facilitative approach. As you cross, you make sure that each stone is firm and secure, and that you feel quite comfortable resting on it, before you step on to the next one. Everyone will choose their own pace of crossing. However, what we guarantee is that you will enjoy reaching the facilitation side!

# 1

# What is Facilitation?

## Introduction

Facilitation is a word that is used a lot in the 'modern' organisation and crops up all over the place in the writings on current management practice. It has become fashionable to be called a 'facilitator'; however, what it means to be one is not always well understood.

Let's start with the area of training and development. It is salutary to recall the origins of the word 'trainer' – it comes through Norman French *trahiner* 'to drag' from Latin *trahere* 'to pull'. For us trainers, this can create a very vivid (and occasionally very realistic) image of dragging those unwilling delegates out of the darkness of ignorance and into the sunlit pastures of knowledge, skill and competence! Apparently the first usage of the verb 'to train' was in the context of training a plant or tree – for example, into a particular shape or up a wall. Again this conjures up the splendid image of taking a delegate and forcing his or her limbs into the required shape for effective organisational performance! In contrast, the origins of the word 'facilitator' has quite a different flavour and feel – it comes from the Latin *facilitas* meaning 'easiness', and the verb 'to facilitate' has the dictionary definition 'to make easy, promote, help forward (an action or result)'. This time we can visualise ourselves as holding out a helping hand, removing obstacles and generally creating a smooth pathway for the delegates to pursue *their* learning journey.

We now turn our attention to the second area that this book addresses – the use of group sessions for problem-solving, innovation, managing projects, etc. We traditionally talk about leading the discussion. The dictionary definition of 'leading' is 'to cause to go with one', 'to direct movements of', and group sessions are often run by the 'leader' or the 'manager' of the group. The implications are, and often the reality is, that this person does direct the session and feels a responsibility for the outcome. Facilitating a session has quite a different air about it – it is about making it easy for the group to discuss the issue or topic. There are no connotations of having a view about, or taking responsibility for, the outcome or result.

In both training/learning and general group sessions it is useful to consider the activity as having three main elements: content, process – technical, and process – personal and interpersonal (see Table 1).

We shall explore in more detail what we mean by training *v* facilitating learning groups and leading *v* facilitating general group sessions. We shall also examine some of the more common concerns that are expressed about taking a facilitative approach, namely those of:

▌ lack of control

▌ time implications

▌ issues of neutrality

▌ the element of risk

▌ confusion over roles and responsibilities.

## Training *v* facilitating learning groups

Bentley (1994) captured the spirit of the difference when he said:

> Facilitators concentrate on providing the resources and opportunities for learning to take place, rather than 'manage and control' learning.

We like to think in terms of a continuum of training styles – at one end we would put 'the instructor' and at

*Table 1*

## MAIN ELEMENTS OF GROUP SESSIONS

| Elements | Training/learning groups | General group sessions |
|---|---|---|
| Content | The subject area of the training/learning – the knowledge, skills, behaviours to be learned. | The subject matter of the session, eg the details of the problem or opportunity being addressed, the aspect of the project being discussed. |
| Process – technical | The training/learning methods being used to achieve the learning objectives, eg exercises, case-studies, role plays. | The methods or techniques that are being used to explore the problem or issue, eg brainstorming, SWOT analysis (see Chapter 6). |
| Process – personal and inter- personal | What is happening for the learners – are they interested, participating, worried, bored, etc? How the learners are interacting with each other – are they helping the process by sharing experiences or hindering the process by putting people down? How the group as individuals and as a whole relates to the trainer. | What is happening for the individuals within the group – are they participating, bored, angry, positive, etc? What the relationships are between the group members. How they are interacting – is anyone dominating, is there conflict, are sub-groups emerging? |

the other end 'the facilitator'. In reality, we all operate somewhere along this continuum and in a later section we shall discuss the factors that might influence where on the continuum we choose to be. It is important that we make the choice rather than falling into a rut of continually training in a particular way without considering the needs of each unique training situation.

We shall explore the continuum in terms of:

▮ the behaviours that are likely to be demonstrated

▮ the outcomes that are likely to result

▮ other issues that may arise.

Remember that the behaviours/outcomes, etc described are for the extremes of the continuum.

*Behaviours*

*Table 2*

## BEHAVIOURS OF TRAINERS/INSTRUCTORS V FACILITATORS OF LEARNING

| Directive trainers/instructors: | Facilitators of learning: |
| --- | --- |
| Set 'training' objectives – what they are going to achieve. | Set 'learning' objectives – what the learners are going to achieve. |
| Believe they are the experts, know best and their job is to instruct the delegates; they do a lot of 'telling'. | Believe that the learners already have great reservoirs of knowledge and skills and that their job is to surface that experience; they do a lot of 'listening' to the delegates. |
| Are centred on themselves and achieving their training objectives. | Are centred on the learners and supporting them to achieve their learning objectives. |
| Remain detached; see themselves as separate from the group. | Work hard to build and maintain empathy with the learners; see themselves as part of the learning group. |
| Concentrate very heavily on content – the knowledge, skills and behaviours – required to achieve the training objectives. | Concentrate on the processes – both technical and interpersonal – required to achieve the learning objectives. |
| Discourage participation except in specific areas and on specific issues. | Encourage learners to participate at all times, interested in learners' views on all aspects of the learning process. |
| Ask fewer questions and these are often closed or leading – seeking answers to specific questions. | Ask lots of questions, using open and probing questions to explore and structure learning experiences. |
| See themselves as in charge and in control of the learning to ensure that it happens – operating in Controlling Parent state a lot of the time (see Chapter 4). | See themselves operating in an equal partnership with the learners, with the learners in control of their own learning – in the Adult state (see Chapter 4). |
| Use detailed training session plans and stick to them to ensure consistency of training. | Use outline training session plans and like to be flexible to meet the needs of the learners. |
| Discourage feedback on the training process as it is owned by the trainer/organisation who are the experts. | Encourage feedback on all aspects of the learning process – see the learners as the owners of the learning process, the experts on their own learning. |

*Outcomes*

Consider the impact of these two different approaches on the following issues:

▌ *Delegates' motivation to learn.* Motivation generally is a complex issue and motivation to learn is perhaps even more difficult to understand and explain than other areas. However, there is considerable evidence to suggest that motivation is enhanced by individuals feeling that they:

☐ can participate fully in decisions that affect them – and what can be more important than decisions concerned with the development of their learning?

☐ have as much control as possible over their own lives – and what a key aspect of one's life is learning

☐ have challenging but achievable targets – their learning objectives – which they have been involved in setting

☐ are valued – their views actively sought and their experiences seen as valuable inputs to the learning process.

A quick look at the behaviour table above would suggest that the facilitative approach is more likely to motivate delegates.

▌ *Type and quality of learning.* Breen (1998), based on Bateson (1972), put forward a model of learning levels:

Level 0  Instinct
Level 1  Learning specific tasks by being shown how to do them
Level 2  Learning how to learn
Level 3  Learning how to learn how to learn
Level 4  Collective learning/evolution.

Directive/instructor-led training is very focused on the Level 1 type of learning – the emphasis is very much on breaking down the learning into manageable chunks and presenting it in as easy a way as possible for the delegates to learn. Facilitative learning is about moving into Level 2 and above. It is focusing on the learning process rather than just on the pure content of the training. It is providing the learners with the tools to learn themselves and be able to build on their existing skills and experiences and continue to learn in new areas of behaviour. It is perhaps one of the most valuable gifts you can give – the power to learn.

■ *Transfer of learning to the workplace.* This can be a major issue for many types of training, particularly in the so-called soft skills area of training, which focuses on behaviour rather than technical skills and knowledge. What seems easy and straightforward and makes sense in the training environment can quite often come a cropper in the real world of the workplace. Perhaps there are no opportunities to practise the new skills/behaviours, perhaps there are systems and procedures that get in the way, perhaps your manager or your colleagues are not interested or supportive of your new skills/behaviours. Suddenly you are faced with what appear to be these mountainous obstacles, there is no 'trainer' on hand to tell you what to do, how to handle the situation, and it is all too easy to let the learning go. Facilitative learning by focusing on the learners' needs, by putting the emphasis on the learning process and by giving the learners control and responsibility for their own learning, encourages the ability and confidence to tackle these obstacles and overcome them. The learners do not need the trainer to hold their hands: they have all the resources they need within themselves.

## Leading *v* facilitating group sessions

By group sessions we mean a group of people, who may or may not work together regularly, meeting to address an issue or issues. The sessions could take the form of project meetings, team briefings, departmental meetings, or one-off meetings set up to discuss a specific problem or opportunity. The spirit of the difference between leading and facilitating group sessions is very similar to that between directing and facilitating learning groups. Let's look at some of the behaviours:

*Behaviours*

*Table 3*

## BEHAVIOURS OF DIRECTIVE LEADERS *V* FACILITATORS OF GROUPS

| Directive leaders of groups: | Facilitators of groups: |
|---|---|
| Focus on their own needs and objectives and see the group as supporting them. | Focus on the needs and objectives of the group and see their role as supporting the group. |
| Concentrate on the content of the discussion. | Concentrate on the processes of the session to maximise the effectiveness of everyone's contribution. |
| Are centred on themselves and may have little interest in understanding others' views. | Are centred on others and build rapport – seek to understand others' perspectives, get alongside, get on the same 'wavelength' as their group. |
| Believe that they are the experts and know best; they do a lot of 'telling'. | Believe that the group members are the experts and do a lot of 'listening' to them. |
| Discourage participation in discussion except in specific areas and on specific issues; control the participation. | Encourage all members of the group to participate in the discussion – interested in a wide range of views. |
| Ask fewer questions and these are often closed and leading questions, seeking specific factual information or leading the group to a particular answer. | Are tenaciously effective questioners, using open and probing questions to explore issues. |
| Strive to put forward their own ideas and achieve their own solutions. | Coach and support the group to come up with ideas and solutions. |
| Make the decisions. | Seek consensus agreement, win-win solutions. |
| Operate in a Controlling Parent state a lot of the time – they know best and believe they should be in control (see Chapter 4). | Operate primarily in the Adult state, with occasional moves into Nurturing Parent and Free Child as required (see Chapter 4). |

## *Outcomes*

Let's look at the impact of these different styles of behaviour on the outcomes of group sessions:

*Quality of solutions/new ideas etc.* With the directive approach the solutions/new ideas are likely to be based primarily on the leader's knowledge and skills. Whereas with a facilitative approach the solutions/new ideas will be based on the corporate knowledge and skills of the group. Assuming that the group has been brought together because individual members have an important contribution to make, then it could well be argued that this latter approach would produce a higher-quality outcome. However, some people are concerned that there is a danger that the solution may be based on the lowest common denominator, ie the solution that everyone finds acceptable rather than the 'best' solution. We would argue that in a group using sound processes, where everyone is encouraged to participate, where there is an atmosphere of openness, trust and shared responsibility, the group will strive to reach the best solution.

*Commitment to the solution/new idea.* With a directive approach, the solution is more likely to be owned by the leader. With a facilitative approach the solution is more likely to be owned by the group. Now, it is perfectly possible that the group is happy with a solution that has been reached via the directive approach. However, we would argue that the facilitative approach, with its emphasis on ensuring that everyone participates and that a wide range of issues are aired, ensures that whatever solution is reached the individual group members will feel that they have played a part in arriving at that solution. The implications of individuals or the group feeling that they own the solution are very great. There will be a greater motivation and commitment to taking forward and implementing the new solution or idea. It is more likely that each individual member of the group will be willing to play his or her part in the implementation process. As a result, the process of implementation can be based on the principles of empowerment rather than those of delegation and close control.

*Learning and development.* The facilitative approach puts a great emphasis on the processes – both technical and interpersonal – that underpin the discussion. The manner by which the solutions/new ideas are generated is considered very important. With the best of facilitative approaches the process will include a built-in review loop – the group and facilitators will constantly be monitoring how the process is going and making any necessary adjustments. Also, the group may from time to time review the process formally – we talk in detail about this area in Chapter 6. Obviously, the purpose of these reviews is primarily to improve the quality of the outcome. However, in addition there are very important spin-off benefits in that both the individuals and the group as an entity will be learning about the processes themselves – what works well, what and how the interpersonal issues should be addressed, etc. With the more directive approach, the emphasis is primarily on the content of that particular session. Also, there is the learning that can take place about the content of the discussion. Perhaps at first glance it might be assumed that, given that the directive approach concentrates on content, the opportunities for learning in the content area are greater with this type of approach. However, with the directive approach the leader very much controls the scope and depth of the discussion. With the facilitative approach the emphasis is on exploring the issues as fully as possible. In which arena do you feel the greater-content learning is likely to take place?

## Issues arising from the facilitative approach

We hope that by now that most readers are totally convinced that the best approach is the facilitative one and are raring to go and find out how to do 'it'! However, there may be among you those who say 'Hang on a minute, this all seems to be too good to be true', and ask:

▌ Are there any concerns or issues around using the facilitative approach?

▌ Is the facilitative approach always the right one?

The most common concerns that are raised are to do with:

▌ control

▌ time

▌ neutrality

▌ risk

▌ confusion over roles and responsibilities.

## *Control*

In both learning groups and general group sessions, one of the major areas of concern for those in the 'lead' role, be it as trainers or as leaders of the session, is that of *control*. How do you ensure that the group learns or the group reaches a reasonable decision or generates a sensible solution or idea? You may say 'It is all very well handing over the control and responsibility of the group, but what happens if it doesn't work? When the chips are down I will be held responsible.' There are a number of responses to this concern:

▌ The degree of control that you pass over to the group is up to you. As we said earlier, there are not just two approaches – the directive and facilitative. In reality there is a continuum of approaches – you can generally choose where to place yourself (and the group). The sorts of factors that might influence your decision either consciously or subconsciously are:

   ☐ how well you know the group, how well they know you, how well they know each other

   ☐ what the standard of your facilitation skills is, how experienced the group is at working/learning together

☐ what the atmosphere/culture within the group/organisation is at present: is it one of suspicion and insecurity or openness and trust?

☐ how clear the overall aim and objectives are: can these be clarified if necessary?

☐ what the status of information in the group/ organisation is: is it unclear and concealed or transparent and accessible?

If the group is new or inexperienced at working together in a facilitative manner, or you lack confidence in your facilitation skills, or the culture is one of suspicion and insecurity, or the aims and objectives are confused and likely to remain so, or information is not clear and available – then you might choose to place yourself towards the directive end of the continuum, and vice versa.

▮ What are the penalties of passing over control to the group? (Note the phrasing of 'pass over', not 'lose' – we are talking about a positive act, not an outcome.) What is the worst that can happen? How likely is that to happen – what are the risks? How can we influence this outcome from a facilitative position? Often we worry unduly about the worst-case scenario and lose sight of the fact that we have considerable resources and skills that we can deploy to manage the situation other than from a position of control. The types of skills and techniques we discuss in the following chapters are all about how to support the group in controlling itself.

▮ Think about the benefits of sharing control – those of ownership, commitment and motivation. How important are these to you and what you are trying to achieve?

## Time

Another major issue often raised is that of time. The sceptical among you may comment 'It is all very well going for this facilitative approach, but surely it is going to take a long time? I only have a short period of time to achieve the learning objectives, reach a decision, generate a solution/idea.' Again there are several responses:

▌ Time is an important factor. If time is very short then it may influence what position you take on the directive–facilitative continuum. A directive approach may take less time, at least in the short term. However, what about the long term? A facilitative approach may take longer in the first instance, but the question you need to ask is how effective is the learning, or how robust is the solution/new idea.

▌ Can you influence at all the time you have? Is it a real constraint, eg do you have only two hours because the board meets that afternoon and the outcome from your meeting must be reported to them? You might ask yourself how you found yourself in that position and learn for next time, but if there is simply no choice then this will influence your approach. Or perhaps time is a constraint because of other pressures on you or other members of the group, eg the delegates can be spared for only a day for this training. The question then to consider is how important is the facilitative approach to achieving a successful outcome in the longer term. If you can convince yourself, then go and convince the relevant stakeholders involved in making the decision on timing!

## Neutrality

Neutrality is another important issue of principle for facilitators and one that causes a lot of *angst* in the aspiring facilitator. A 'true' facilitator in a group discussion will not be concerned with the content or outcome of that discussion. 'True' facilitators are only interested in process. In fact, many facilitators may have little or no knowledge of the subject area being discussed. The facilitator's role is purely to ensure that the group has the best chance to raise and explore the relevant issues and reach the 'best' decision it can in that situation. The 'true' facilitator must be neutral on content.

However, unless the facilitator is a consultant (internal or external) specifically brought in to facilitate a session then it is rare that he or she is truly neutral. Many facilitators will be either an ordinary member of the group chosen to take on the facilitator role or often the team leader or project manager, ie someone who is in some form of authority position. In both of these cases, and particularly the latter, those individuals will not be neutral in terms of outcome and may be very knowledgeable about the content. They may feel it is important to make a weighty contribution in terms of knowledge or express some strong views. So how can they operate as facilitators? The glib answer is – with difficulty! So, what are some options?

▌ The first issue is to decide whether you want to operate as a 'true' facilitator and are willing to forgo making your contribution as an ordinary member of the group. Perhaps you can ensure that another member of the group is available to make the content contribution. However, it will require tough self-discipline not covertly to influence the outcome that you want.

▌ You may feel that although you do wish to make some input and express some views your contribution will be relatively minor. If your contribution is likely to take place all at one time, one option is formally to hand over the role of facilitator to another member of the group at that stage and join the group as an ordinary participant. If your contribution is likely to be made in small interjections, then it may be possible simply to make the statement each time that you are joining the discussion as an ordinary group member. It may be helpful to establish with the group that you will stand or sit in a particular spot when you move out of your facilitator role, using the move to make the statement that 'Now I am taking off my facilitator's hat.'

▌ The last option concerns the person who has strong views and wishes to influence the outcome in a substantial way. Either you accept that you will be operating at the directive end of the continuum, but will try to make every effort to adopt facilitative behaviours as much as possible, or you find another facilitator! In some organisations they have a pairing arrangement whereby team leaders facilitate each other's teams, or a small group of people are trained as facilitators as part of their overall development and are available to facilitate on an occasional basis.

The important message is that neutrality is a key principle. It is very difficult to manage the process if you are trying to make a contribution to the content, and it is very hard to ensure a balanced and open discussion if you have already made up your mind on the issues!

We have talked so far about neutrality in terms of facilitating general group sessions. The issue is equally thorny in respect of facilitating learning groups. You could well argue that as a facilitator of learning you simply cannot be neutral about content; surely you will want to achieve the learning objectives and surely you need to be knowledgeable about the content? How on earth could you facilitate a learning session on health and safety, or on becoming a train driver, or on project management, or on managing people, if you knew nothing about the subject area? So the concept of neutrality has a rather different meaning in the learning situation. We would put forward the following criteria to distinguish the truly neutral facilitator of a learning group:

▌ a willingness to let the individuals or group decide what they want to learn – to set or amend the learning objectives – but within overall parameters about what is required in the workplace

▌ a flexible approach to the learning process – a willingness to share the decisions on how the learning will take place, on learning methods, etc

■ the commitment to make very clear distinctions between statements of fact and statements that involve a subjective viewpoint. This is analogous to the concepts used in giving constructive feedback. The person giving feedback is encouraged to describe exactly what they have seen or heard in terms of the behaviour, and similarly the outcome of that behaviour. They are discouraged from making generalised or evaluative statements. In the same way, the neutral facilitator of learning does not seek to impose overtly or covertly their opinions and judgements – their role is to help the learners to explore and understand the issues so as to form their own opinions and judgements.

■ the awareness, at times when content is paramount and there is a need to take on the 'expert' role, eg on health and safety issues, to make clear when they are shifting into that role and when they are moving back into the facilitator role.

## Risk

When one describes the facilitative approach – the avoidance of influencing outcomes, giving control to the group, being flexible on learning objectives and learning methods, the concentration on experiential learning, etc – it fills many potential facilitators with horror. 'Surely', they say, 'this is a very risky approach: who knows what might happen . . .?' We would reply, 'Yes, in part you are right – who knows what might be the outcome of the group discussion or how the learning will take place?' However, the skilful facilitator will ensure that the outcome is based on the optimum contributions from the group; that the learning meets the individual/organisational needs. It is rather like saying that you can ensure that you will reach Edinburgh although not which route you will take to get there. Yes, there are some risks that you might stray down the odd 'no-through-road', or take a precipitous route over the mountains. However, equally you will find yourself traversing unexpected peaceful roads surrounded by flower meadows and that precipitous route across the mountains will provide you with some breathtaking views. Hart (1992) describes facilitators as 'experimenters and risk takers'. In summary, there are risks but we would strongly make the case that with good facilitation skills and using appropriate facilitation techniques these risks can be minimised – and the rewards can be very great. The effective facilitation of groups can not only provide spectacular results but can also be enormous fun.

It is right to be aware of the risks and in later chapters we shall talk a lot about the importance of planning and preparation. Some people see facilitation skills as the ability to 'wing it' or 'live on your wits' – it is not. Yes, there is the need to be able to think on your feet; however, it is from a very solid foundation of planning and preparation. We would also argue that the risks of failure in taking what appears to be a safer path – a more directive approach in group discussions, a more trainer-centred and structured approach to learning – are in fact greater. So, have courage and read on!

## Roles and responsibilities

Traditionally, in the learning situation, the role of the trainer has been quite clear – to impart knowledge and skills to the delegates. The trainer has been seen as being responsible for ensuring that the delegates achieve the required standard – and if they do not, for furnishing reasons why not. Increasingly, there has been awareness that the trainer's role and responsibility is largely restricted to the training environment and that the very important stage of the transfer of learning from the training environment to the workplace is affected by many factors outside the trainer's control. Hence the shift of responsibility from the trainer to the learner has been fuelled from two sources:

▌ the recognition that responsibility for ensuring that

the transfer of learning to the workplace actually happens can rest only with the learner. Hence it makes a lot more sense to say that the responsibility for learning throughout the whole learning process should be with the learner.

▌ the greater understanding of the learning process, and therefore the desirability, and you might say almost inevitability, that responsibility can lie only with the learner. It is a bit like saying that the responsibility for eating lies with the eater rather than the cook/provider of the food. Clearly, it is crucial that the food is available, but with mature adults only the eater can choose to eat.

Traditionally, in the situation of groups discussing issues, solving problems, generating new ideas, the 'leader' of the group has been seen as having the role of taking the lead and responsibility for finding the solution or new idea. Often the leader has been in a position of authority over the group members – that is why he or she is the leader of the session. Taking responsibility for the outcome is a natural extension or part of his or her overall role as a manager. There has been a sea change in how the role of the manager is viewed, involving such concepts as the upside-down pyramid with managers supporting their staff rather than being in charge of them, and the concepts of empowerment, ie giving responsibility to those who can directly affect the outcome. The role of the leader of a group session has similarly changed – he or she is there to support and empower the group.

## The directive–facilitative continuum

We have talked at various points about the concept of a directive–facilitative continuum and the importance of making a conscious decision about where on the continuum you want to be, based on a range of factors. This continuum can be summarised as follows:

| Directive | Facilitative |
|---|---|
| *Use when:* | *Use when:* |
| working with immature groups that are inexperienced at working together | working with mature groups that are experienced at working together in a facilitative way |
| aims and objectives are unclear and will be difficult to clarify | aims and objectives are crystal clear or are capable of clarification |
| there are very tight time constraints | sufficient time is available or can be made available to meet the aims and objectives |
| the culture/atmosphere is one of suspicion and insecurity | the culture/atmosphere is one of openness and trust |
| the policy towards information is one of limited access and concealment | the policy towards information is one of accessibility and transparency |
| your facilitation skills are undeveloped | you are confident in your facilitation skills |

In practice, we are often faced with a mixture of factors, each showing characteristics of varying degrees of intensity. It will be a matter of judgement where on the continuum you decide to operate. We would encourage you to be determined and always push as far as possible towards the facilitative end. Look at ways of influencing the factors – what can you do to develop the maturity of the group, how can you relieve the time constraints, how can you develop your facilitation skills?

Where all the factors are positive, you will be working in the Utopian situation of hardly needing to take on the role of facilitator at all: every member of the group will be operating as facilitators themselves!

## Why a facilitative approach is important to you and your organisation

We have left this important issue to last. In part we hope we have already convinced you that there are many advantages to adopting a facilitative approach in learning and general group working situations. However, there are a number of factors in the work environment propelling this change in approach with an almost unstoppable force. These are:

▌ We are working in an environment of increasingly rapid change. Organisations, if they are to survive, have to be constantly scanning their environment both internally and externally. They need to be continually questioning the way they do things, continually investigating their customers' needs and continually ensuring that they are maximising all their resources – and particularly their human resources. They need people who relish change, who take every opportunity to be creative and innovative and are self-motivated to deliver the best customer service to both external and internal customers of the organisation. Such people do not want, and will not respond to, a directive approach; they need and will be energised by a facilitative approach.

▌ The structure of our organisations has changed almost out of all recognition. Our organisations are flatter with managerial span increased manyfold from the traditional span of six staff as suggested by Urwick (1947). Managers are having to adopt a different approach as it is simply not possible closely to manage and control very large teams in the old way. People need to be able to work relatively unsupervised, managing the operation and the quality of their work themselves. The team manager has to hand over responsibility to his or her team members and these team members need to be empowered to take responsibility. Managers are having to step back from the detail and nitty-gritty of the everyday work and take a more strategic role. Their role is to provide the resources and environment to enable their teams to deliver the results. They have become enablers not enforcers.

▌ There has been a tremendous shift to more flexible

working practices. This has taken the form of both multi-skilling, with staff being expected to handle a wide range of different jobs, and in terms of the mode of employment, ie the move towards Handy's shamrock organisation (Handy, 1989) of core workers, part-time workers and external contractors. This new structure of employment has inevitably required and resulted in new types of relationships between manager and managed. These are relationships based on mutual respect for each other's abilities and contributions.

▮ Much is said – and perhaps little is really understood – about what is meant by a learning organisation. It has become a bit of a 'hurrah' statement – everyone thinks it is the in-thing to be a learning organisation. In a way they are right, but from the wrong premiss. We believe that, because of all the factors we have described above, everyone has to be continually learning and continually hungry to learn. This must happen at the individual, team and organisational levels. It is not something that it would be nice to have, sounds good in the annual report or in your conference speech, ie is splendid on paper but a little short in reality. *It is an essential requirement for organisations to be able to survive and grow in this rapidly changing world.* A facilitative approach encourages and nourishes learning. It is about drawing out and developing everyone's potential. It is an approach that challenges but does not coerce, and is based on high expectations that everyone wants to achieve.

▮ Last but not least, an important change in the training/learning world is the move towards trainers taking on internal consultant roles. This requires developing the skills to get close to the business and in particular the type of facilitation skills described in this book.

We leave you with the lovely quotation, which for us sums up the spirit of facilitation:

No man can reveal anything which is not already in the dawning of your own knowledge. The teacher therefore gives of his faith for, if he is wise, he does not bid you enter the house of his knowledge but rather leads you to the threshold of your own mind.

(Long, 1992)

## In brief

■ The facilitative approach is based on 'making it easy' for groups to learn/solve problems/generate new ideas; it is about supporting and enabling individuals and groups to take responsibility and ownership for their decisions and for their learning.

■ There are significant differences in the behaviours and resulting outcomes between directive and facilitative approaches. In reality you operate along a continuum between these extremes and it is important to make a conscious decision where on the continuum you want to be. The decision will be based on a number of factors, such as the maturity of the group, time constraints, your own facilitation skills.

■ There are a number of issues that you need to think about – those of control, time, neutrality, risk, and roles and responsibilities.

■ Organisations of today face a large number of challenges: the facilitative approach is about providing an environment that encourages and nourishes learning and the development of the appropriate skills and behaviours in its people to meet those challenges.

# 2

# Getting Alongside the Group

## Introduction

The effective facilitator needs to have a very high level of communication skills. We would argue that the success of the facilitator depends critically on deploying four core skills:

- building and maintaining rapport between the facilitator and group members and between group members
- actively listening *and* observing group/individual behaviours
- masterly questioning to draw out and explore issues with the group
- effectively managing information derived from the facilitation process.

Surely, you might say, these are the same old skills we read about in every management book these days. In part they are – however, what we are setting out to do in this book is to provide some useful tips and techniques to help develop these skills specifically in the situations of facilitating learning and general group sessions. We would argue that it requires far higher levels of these skills to facilitate rather than direct a group. You never stop honing these skills and you continue to learn from every facilitation experience.

## Why these skills are important

*Building and maintaining rapport* helps you:

▌ to understand how individuals/the group are feeling, the way they see things, what 'bells' are ringing for them at a particular time

▌ to know what sort of process intervention to make, eg when to energise the group, take a break, move on to another subject area, take a different tack

▌ to move forward harmoniously with the group towards the objectives.

*Active listening and observing* helps you:

▌ to pick up quickly all the information on the *content* of the session that is being sent out by individuals

▌ to pick up all the signals, both verbal and non-verbal, being sent as to how participants feel about the *process*

▌ to demonstrate that you are involved, are interested in and value individuals'/the group's contributions

▌ to recognise the positive intent behind objections and potentially unhelpful interventions.

*Masterly questioning* helps you:

▌ to manage the session – most of your interventions will be in the form of questions – you are seeking to involve the group and build on their knowledge, skills and experiences

▌ to open up the discussion, broaden the issues, explore other angles, make connections and links

▌ to probe and follow up a line of thought, a specific proposal, to surface problems and constraints

▌ to get at key facts, clarify issues

▌ to use questions to 'oil' the process – bring people in, move the group forward, take different directions.

*Managing information effectively* helps you:

■ to gather and analyse the ideas/proposals/facts required to help the group meet its objectives

■ to focus the group and clarify issues by presenting the information in a structured format

■ visibly to demonstrate the value of contributions by recording them

■ to provide an accurate record of the outcomes of the session

■ to provide materials that will be useful to the participants for reference purposes, continuing their learning after the session.

## How we communicate

Research (Mehrabian and Ferris, 1967) has shown that we communicate our message using three channels, by:

■ what we say          7%
■ how we say it        38%
■ our body language    55%

We spend a lot of time thinking about what we say – the words we use – however, perhaps not enough about the type of language we use. Sometimes we think about how we say the words – the tone of our voice, its volume, pace, etc. We probably spend very little time thinking about our body language – the expression on our face, our gestures, our posture, etc – yet it is our body language that is conveying over 50 per cent of our message.

The skilled facilitator learns to use all the channels of communication in a very powerful way. For example, by sitting down, ie joining the group, and speaking in a quieter, slower-paced voice when you want the group to relax and discuss issues perhaps at length and in depth; by standing up and speaking at a faster pace when you want the group to move on or at a quicker pace. This book is all about helping you to become a master of communication – to learn to use the combination of all three channels positively and confidently to facilitate group sessions.

In this chapter we concentrate on the first of the core skills – building and maintaining rapport. Think of this as the central nervous system in the body, crucial to, and permeating, all the body's functioning parts. In Chapter 3 we concentrate on the other three skills – active listening and observing, masterly questioning, and managing information effectively. The concepts and techniques of neuro-linguistic programming (NLP) underpin much of the content of these two chapters. NLP's roots were in the study of excellent communicators and what NLP sets out to do is to identify and structure the behaviours that lead to excellent communication. Most of us will use some of the behaviours some of the time instinctively – NLP helps us to learn to maximise the use of these behaviours.

## Building and maintaining rapport

The term 'rapport' is hard to define, but being in rapport with the person with whom you wish to communicate is vital to the effectiveness of that communication. Here are some ways of describing what we mean by rapport:

■ achieving a harmonious and understanding relationship
■ feeling mutually at ease
■ getting alongside people
■ being on the same wavelength
■ seeing eye to eye with people
■ being in empathy with others.

### Maps of the world

Building rapport helps you understand a person's 'map of the world'. This is taken from the concept that we all have different 'maps of the world' based on our experiences. Our maps give meaning to our worlds and our filters, our assumptions, prejudices, etc, determine our view and the sense we make of the world we live in. Take a very simple example of three people walking in a wood; one is a botanist, one is an ornithologist and one is a forester. Each of these people will experience their walk in very different ways. The botanist will be focusing on the flora, probably spending a lot of time looking at the ground to identify the wild flowers. The ornithologist will have her eyes fixed on the birds swooping among the trees and probably will pay little attention to the flowers and trees. The forester will be looking at the trees to see which ones need attention or are ready for felling. We had a fascinating example of the power of these maps in talking to a craftsman who had come to repair the timber frame of our medieval cottage. He volunteered how when he walked through a woodland he saw the trees in terms of how they could be used in a timber frame – which would be best for curved braces, substantial corner posts, and so on.

Our filters can be used both to enhance and blank out different aspects of the world. At our home in Suffolk, we have just planted a natural woodland and hence have become very interested in trees – their size, shape, colour of leaves, etc. We are now very much more aware or sensitised to trees generally – this is a positive filter like those described above. Also, we are in the midst of a training course on timber-framed buildings, so now when we are travelling around we see them all around us, whereas previously we never noticed them.

Our filters can also lead us to be de-sensitised to information and experiences. For example, if in the past we have found reports with tables and statistics boring and unhelpful, our expectation will be the same of all similar sorts of report and we will tend to shut out information to the contrary. It works in respect of people too – if in the past we have found a colleague difficult to understand or have had difficulty in seeing the relevance of their work to our own, then it is unlikely that we shall be willing to listen to what they have to say. These are negative filters in action.

Understanding a person's map of the world will help us to see issues through their eyes, use words in the same way as they do, maximise the use of positive filters and take action to take account of the negative filters. Building rapport involves building trust and learning about their world. This can take time. We often have very good rapport with people we have known for a long time. However, in situations where we are facilitating a learning group, or facilitating a group in discussing a specific issue, we may be meeting some or all of the group members for the first time. We shall have a very short time to build rapport, so we need some ways to help us speed up the process. We all use these techniques instinctively in some situations. Being aware of the mechanisms behind our instinctive actions enables us to deploy them in a proactive way.

### *Matching body language and voice*

To build rapport with an individual, try the following:

▌ Actively observe their body language and then match it with your own body language, eg the way they tilt their head, the way they hold their shoulders, if they are sitting slumped or upright, if their legs are crossed or stretched in front of them. If someone is tapping their foot, you tap your foot in the same rhythm or alternatively tap with your finger in the same rhythm. The very expert learn to match breathing – is it shallow and fast or deep and relaxed?

▌ Actively listen to their voice and then match it with your own, eg if someone speaks quietly, you will speak quietly; if someone speaks rather fast, you will increase the pace of your speech.

This may seem rather strange and unnatural, but remember we do it instinctively. Look at couples or groups in social situations who are clearly getting on well – observe how similarly they are sitting, standing, the way they are using gestures, smiling, etc. Think about times when you were talking with someone who spoke rather quietly, did you not automatically adjust the volume of your voice? We try to match someone's mood – at the extreme, if someone is upset or distressed we usually try and empathise with them, not disregard how they are feeling and keep up a cheery banter!

The other commonly voiced concern is whether people notice this matching process. The easy and glib answer is that generally they do not. However, as a colleague facilitator once said to us, 'a little goes a long way'. Some tips are:

▮ You do not fully have to match the body language, tone of voice, etc. For example, if someone is using very strong body language, eg lying back in their chair with their legs outstretched in front of them, then it might look odd, and you might feel rather uncomfortable, fully trying to match this position. Our suggestion would be that you should lean back a little in your own chair and perhaps partly stretch your legs. If someone is speaking very loudly, then it will be enough just to raise your voice slightly above normal – you do not need to shout at each other!

▮ If someone changes their body posture, pace of speaking, etc, it is helpful to delay slightly (perhaps a few seconds or so) before moving to match their new position, or pace of speaking.

When you have achieved rapport you will notice that when you move your body posture, etc, the other person will follow your lead automatically, and vice versa. You can then start to use your own body language, voice, etc to lead the other person into perhaps a more positive state. So, for example if someone is feeling rather tense, you could use your own body posture and voice to lead them into a more relaxed state *once you have achieved rapport*. In the good old days, you may remember that the standard advice was that if someone was very tense the best way to relax them was to be very relaxed yourself. This advice was based on the same pre-miss, ie that we could influence others through the use of our body language and voice; however, it left out the vital step of joining them in their world first before lead-ing them out of it.

Another good example of the old style of communi-cation training was in customer care. The classic answer to how you deal with an angry or upset customer was to be very soothing yourself and in no way join them in their anger or upset. You may like to recall a time when you have been very angry or upset, perhaps about the non-delivery for the $n$th time of a new washing machine or other piece of vital home equipment, and how it feels when the sales person on the other end of the telephone speaks to you in a very soothing voice. They may be using the right words – apologising, promising to take action – but somehow they are just making you feel more cross. By not entering our world of being upset and angry, we feel that they do not really understand or accept the strength of our feelings or the urgency of the issue. These days we would suggest that you match the customer first – again, not to the full extent of shouting yourself or fully joining them in their distress – but by raising your voice slightly and injecting a feeling of ten-sion and urgency into your voice, *then* lead them into a calmer state.

Clearly, the appropriate level of matching is not always easy to gauge, and we suggest that you practise these skills in non-critical environments first, eg social situ-ations, non-contentious arenas at work, until you feel confident. However, remember that we find it easy to match those with whom we normally have a good relationship; the test and indeed the real power of these skills comes in using them with people whom you do not know or in some way you find challenging. For us, a real turning-point in the development of our skills came when we were dealing with a particularly difficult client. The client was the managing director of a medium-sized company. He was a very tall man who used his body language and voice in rather intimidating ways: by leaning forward, banging the table and speaking in a very loud and rather abrupt manner. We were discussing the introduction of a management performance scheme and were trying to suggest to the client that we consult with managers rather than just impose the new scheme on them. The client was from the school of 'just get on and tell them that's the way it's going to be'. We had begun to feel quite hopeless about the project – we had tried every line of argument and persuasion to no avail and were seriously contemplating withdrawing from the whole project. So we decided to use our matching skills for the whole period of an afternoon's meeting. All we can say is that the results were amazing. At that stage we were still slightly sceptical about whether matching really worked, and this experience was a milestone for us.

A useful exercise to use with a group experimenting with matching techniques is set out in Table 4 opposite.

The comments arising from this exercise are usually about how difficult it was to disagree about the topic, the differences seemed much less and there was less anger and conflict involved. The opposite occurred when the pairs were agreeing – they felt very uncomfortable and it was difficult to focus on the areas of agreement. Reversing the natural process – we tend to match when we are agreeing and mismatch when we are disagreeing – demonstrates very vividly the power of matching.

## Matching language

We have concentrated so far on matching body language and voice because these are by far the most powerful influences on quality of communication. However, there is also much to be gained by matching in terms of the

*Table 4*

## EXERCISE ON MATCHING

1 Ask the group to divide into pairs and each pair to decide:

▮ a topic on which they both agree
▮ a topic on which they both disagree

It is helpful if these are topics that they feel strongly about – this is the exercise when it is fine to bring in politics and religion! At this stage they merely decide on the topic, and do not start discussing it.

2 Label one member of the pair A and the other member B.

3 Ask the pairs to discuss the topic on which they *agree*:

▮ A to be themselves, B to mismatch A

then on the call 'change' from the facilitator

▮ B to be themselves and A to mismatch.

4 Ask the group to reflect on the experience quietly to themselves for a couple of minutes.

5 Ask the pairs to discuss the topic on which they *disagree*:

▮ A to be themselves, B to match A

then on the call 'change' from the facilitator

▮ B to be themselves and A to match.

6 Ask the group to reflect on the experience quietly to themselves for a couple of minutes.

7 Ask the group to comment on their experiences.

type of language we use. We are all aware that it is important to think about the technical terms, jargon and the complexity of the language we use. For example,

there is nothing that gets in the way of effective communication more than the misuse of acronyms. We recall
attending a conference on car crime (we were carrying
out some consultancy work for the police). The keynote
speaker constantly used the acronym 'IT'. To us IT
meant Information Technology but this made no sense
in the context of what he was saying. We spent the
whole of the speech trying to work it out – in fact, we
found out afterwards that it stood for Intermediate
Treatment, an alternative to a custodial sentence. The
rest of the content of that speech was completely lost on
us as a result! Excellent communicators automatically
adjust and match their type of language to their audience. For example, the architect who is helping us ren-
ovate our medieval cottage uses quite different language
to explain building concepts to us from that which he
uses with the builder. He is taking into account the limitations of our maps of the world as regards our understanding of building terms, such as tie beams, purlins,
collars, etc, and the whole science of building. He talks
to us as lay people and to the builder as an expert.

There is a less obvious pattern of language that we use.
It is concerned with the way we express ourselves in
everyday situations. We interact and gather information
from the world using our five senses and these form the
basis of five types of language patterns, although the following three are by far the most common:

■ *Visual language patterns* – when someone uses a lot
of words and phrases involved with visualising/
seeing things. So, for example, if they were describing a house they would talk in such terms as 'The
house was painted with a pale pink limewash, deco-
rated with a fancy pattern of geometric shapes drawn
out on the plaster; it looks bright and airy.' The language conjures up strong visual images. The pattern
will also be apparent from the use of phrases such as
'looking at it my way', 'this is my perspective on it',
'this report paints a picture of healthy growth'.

- *Kinaesthetic language patterns* – when someone uses words and phrases that are associated with how they feel about things or how they are physically experiencing things. So, for example, if they were describing the same house as above they might say, 'The house sits well within its gardens, it is has an air of permanence and solidity, it feels like a peaceful and happy home.' The language conjures up feelings and emotions. The sorts of phrases that might be used are 'getting to grips with something', 'rub you up the wrong way', 'let's walk you through this report'.

- *Auditory language patterns* – when someone uses words and phrases that are associated with hearing. So, for example, describing the same house, they might comment on 'the creaking timbers, the way the wind howls down the chimney, the whispering of the leaves in the trees'. The sorts of phrases they might use are 'being on the same wavelength', 'it does not ring true', 'sounding off about things'.

The other two are olfactory and gustatory, involving language patterns that conjure up smell and taste. If you listen to cookery experts or wine experts you will get superb examples: 'mouth-watering flavour of fresh coriander, the fragrance of a fine wine with a spicy bouquet, the aroma of fresh bread'. You will also hear it in the form of phrases such as: 'get a flavour of it', 'a whiff of trouble', 'smell a rat'.

We probably use all of these language patterns at some time; however, we usually have a preference for one of them. By listening very closely we can identify the preference and then choose to match it with our own language patterns. Identifying people's language patterns can be quite fascinating. You may find it hard at first, especially as people also use language that is non-specific in terms of the senses. However, if you listen consistently over a period of time you will begin to pick up a regular pattern. It is much easier to do if you are not trying to keep up a dialogue, so try listening first to people on the radio and TV, then perhaps when you are in a meeting where you are not involved for periods of time. A useful exercise to use with gatherings is to break them down into groups of three and ask each person in turn to describe a situation that they have really enjoyed or hated. The other two members of the group then try to identify the language patterns being used. Because we have a natural preference ourselves, we may find it quite hard to match someone with a different preference. Try the following exercise yourself or with a group:

*Table 5*

## EXERCISE ON LANGUAGE PATTERNS

> Try practising the different language patterns yourself when describing an object, like a house or garden, then move on to a situation such as a party, or an accident, or a meeting at work.
>
> This can be a fun exercise to do with a group – it works best with a maximum of about eight people. You all sit round in a circle – one person facilitates. A particular topic is chosen – perhaps one's home or a fictional story can be used, although it is usually easier to start with an object of some sort. The facilitator chooses who is to go first and which language pattern they should use, then indicates when the baton should be handed over to the next person in the circle and which language pattern to be used. The objective is to give everyone in the group the opportunity to try using each of the three main language patterns – visual, kinaesthetic and auditory. This can be a very useful energiser and not only does it enable individuals to identify which patterns they find easiest or hardest to use, but it also enables them to begin to build up the facility of moving between them.

The more you practise, the more adept you become at sliding in and out (notice our kinaesthetic preference here) of the different language patterns. Skilled facilitators will use a wonderful range of language patterns. Read these two very different examples of the use of a wide range of language pattern and notice, tune into, experience, the impact they have on you:

> Picture a beach on a bright sunny day. Notice how the light plays on the waves, shimmering and sparkling on the frothy white foam and how the colours are different in each wave, a heady mixture of blue and green translucent jewel-like colours . . . And as you watch the waves breaking, hear the sound as each wave breaks . . . one wave crashing on the top of another and listen to the swish of the shingle and then the gurgle as the waves pull back. And as you watch and listen, just walk to the ocean edge . . . and as the next wave breaks allow yourself to feel the warmth of the water on your feet, and the tingling sensation as it finds its way between your toes. Experience a deep sense of calm and wholeness, of being at one with the world.

> When you sit in the car the first thing you notice is how soft and supportive the seats are. You can adjust them to make them even more comfortable for you, and as you sink in, you will notice the smell of the real leather used in the upholstery. Take a deep breath and start driving, and what will be really striking is how quiet it is. Apart from a soft murmur and a gentle hum, you don't hear very much at all, because under the bonnet there is well-tuned and immaculate engine. It gleams, it looks compact and very tidy: it has been designed to make the best use of space. It's a lovely thing to look at, even if you don't know how it works.

> (Based on training material from *International Training Seminars* (McDermott, 1996), one of the main NLP training providers)

## Matching with groups

We have talked so far about how to build up rapport with an individual through the process of matching body language, voice and language patterns. How, you may well ask, does this work with a group that you are facilitating? This is not a problem, of course, if the whole group is in rapport and exhibiting the same body language and use of their voices. When a group is working really well together this will be the case. However, there will be many times when this is not the case and the question arises as to how you use your skills to best effect:

▌ If there are one or two individuals who seem to be particularly out of tune, ploughing their own furrow or out of line with the group (note – auditory, kinaesthetic, visual phrases), then it may be worthwhile spending some time in their world by matching them at an appropriate time. The appropriate time could be at a break or perhaps when the individuals are working on their own. This may throw some light on why they are out of sync with rest of the group and help you lead them back into the group.

▌ It is likely that people within the group will have a mix of preferred language patterns. The skilled facilitator will use a range of language patterns when talking to the group as a whole. This can be very important at key moments in the group – for example, at the start of the session or introducing a particular learning area or stage in the discussion process. It is well worth preparing these 'pieces' in advance while you build up your skills. For example, as a simple general introduction:

> It is a real pleasure to be working with you today and sharing the opportunity to learn about ... (kinaesthetic). I am very much looking forward to finding out about your perspectives on these issues ... (visual). There will be plenty of time to tune into each other's thinking and sound out ideas ... (auditory).

We had the fascinating experience of seeing the impact of such an approach. We were working with an engineering organisation which was training their supervisors in management skills. Part of our role was to coach and mentor a group of middle managers in presenting specific sessions on the business. One of these managers reported back that after his session one of the supervisors had come up to him and said that it was the first time that he had thought that the manager was speaking directly to him, Bill, and the session had really rung bells for him. This supervisor was highly auditory and the inclusion of even a few well chosen auditory words and phrases had suddenly meant that he was tuned into the session.

▌ Match the pace and energy levels of the group. This is a really key activity for both learning groups and discussion groups. It is unusual if a group that is working together over a period of time does not go through patches of low energy levels. If a group is in rapport it takes only two or three members of that group to lose their energy and motivation for that to affect the whole group. The key is to identify when it happens as soon as possible and take action. If you are in rapport with the group you will notice it almost automatically, as you will find yourself being led into a low energy state. Anyway, the signs are usually fairly obvious if you are actively listening to and observing the group. Some of you reading at this stage will be saying to yourselves 'You are telling granny how to suck eggs' (note the gustatory phraseology of this rather strange saying!). However, we have observed experienced trainers/leaders of groups ignore what seemed to us very overt signs. In one example, three-quarters of the group had ceased to say anything, were either sitting slumped in their seats or rather desultorily leafing through their notes – there was little or no eye contact between the trainer/leader and these delegates. In this situation the trainer/leader was very focused on himself and what he was doing and had lost touch with his group. He was operating in a world where he was centre stage, not the group – he was in what is known as *first position*.

A very important message here is that excellent facilitators spend very little time in first position. The concept of 'positions' is very important so we shall spend a little time introducing you to it in the context of facilitating groups:

- When you are in *first position* you are totally focused on yourself – what you are doing, thinking about, your own beliefs and values – regardless of other people. You are wrapped up in yourself, seeing the world solely from your own perspective, marching to your own tune. (We are sure now that you are picking up the range of language patterns we are using!)

- When you are in *second position* you are totally focused on another person(s). You are seeing the world through their eyes, experiencing life as though walking in their shoes, singing to their hymn sheet. Matching someone as described earlier takes you into second position. You are fully entering and understanding their map of the world.

- When you are in *third position* you are detached from yourself and others and are able to observe objectively the relationship between yourself and others. You are taking what is sometimes referred to as a helicopter view, standing back from the situation, eavesdropping on the world!

All three positions are important because they give different perspectives and insights into our experiences. There will be times when it is very important to be in first position – perhaps when we are thinking through a complex issue, clarifying our own views and values, resourcing ourselves to deal with a situation. However, spending too long in first position can cause problems as we described above: we lose touch with those around us.

Being in second position is vital to developing rapport and understanding other people's maps of the world. But spending too long in this position may cause us to be overly affected and influenced by others' issues. A good example is that if you are in second position for a long time with someone who is upset or despondent you may find you become too upset and despondent to be able to help in any way except empathise. Being in third position is often key to problem-solving in a relationship as you can take a dispassionate view of what is happening rather than being over-influenced by your own sets of views and feelings or others' views and feelings. Spending too long in third position can result in your becoming too detached from the whole situation and finding it difficult to re-enter and participate fully in it. The skilled facilitator is able to identify when it is helpful to be in particular positions and move easily between them. When facilitating a group you may decide to go into first position to plan the next process intervention you want to make, or go into third position to review how the group and yourself are functioning.

Apart from the usefulness of this model in helping the facilitator to function effectively, it is also very useful as a means of helping individuals and groups to think about the way they are behaving – more of this in Chapter 4.

## In brief

- There are *four core skills* of facilitation:
  - building and maintaining rapport between the facilitator and group members and between group members
  - active listening and observing of group/individual behaviours
  - masterly questioning to draw out and explore issues with the group
  - effectively managing information derived from the facilitation process.

▉ The skilled facilitator will make full and powerful use of *all three channels of communication* – our words and language, our voices and our body language.

▉ *Build and maintain rapport* by:

☐ matching voice and body language of individuals and groups

☐ matching and using a range of language patterns

☐ matching the pace and energy levels of groups.

▉ Be aware of, and consciously use, the *three positions*:

☐ first position – to plan and think through issues, resource yourself

☐ second position – to be in rapport with the group, to pick up and understand all the signals being sent out

☐ third position – to review and take stock of situations from a detached point of view.

# 3

# Picking up the Signals from the Group

In the previous chapter we described how to develop the core skill of building and maintaining rapport with individuals and groups. In this chapter we look at the core skills of:

▌ active listening and observing group/individual behaviours

▌ masterly questioning to draw out and explore issues with the group

▌ effectively managing information derived from the facilitation process.

## Active listening and observing

We all spend a lot of time listening to people face-to-face, on the telephone, radio, television, etc, but how effectively do we listen? How much of the message do we hear in the first place and then how much do we successfully decode so that we truly understand the message being sent by the sender? We are taught how to read and write and we learn both actively and passively how to talk. However, very little attention is paid to our abilities to listen actively to people and, we would say, none at all to observing them actively. In fact, we are instinctively picking up signals being sent out by others' body language and voices. For example, if our nearest and dearest comes home and responds to our question of 'How was your day?' with the words 'It was fine', but is

*Table 6*

## EXERCISE ON LISTENING SKILLS

1 Watch/listen to a short video tape of a single person talking about something that is important to them, eg someone giving a presentation, describing an event. First watch a one-minute clip – do not take notes – and then describe in your own words, either writing it down if you are on your own or having it scribed if you are working as a pair:

■ the content of what is being said, ie facts, views
■ the quality of the voice
■ the body language that is being used
■ the feelings about what is being said.

Compare your account with the real one. Note what you have missed and whether you have added things that were not there. At this point it is useful to have a second person to discuss the points that arise. Then go on and listen to a two-minute clip and then a five-minute clip, taking notes as required.

2 Repeat this procedure, but using a video tape of two people talking to each other, eg an interview. This time describe the list in 1 above for both parties in the discussion.

3 Repeat the procedure but using a video tape of a group of people talking with each other, eg a meeting. Concentrate on a maximum of five people in the group. This time we positively suggest you take notes in a structured manner. It is helpful to set out a sheet of paper, as below, for each member of the group and record the information for each episode of communication:

| NAME: | EPISODE | ESPISODE | EPISODE |
|---|---|---|---|
| CONTENT | | | |
| VOICE | | | |
| BODY LANGUAGE | | | |
| FEELINGS | | | |

standing there with his or her shoulders hunched over and using a dispirited tone of voice, which message do we believe? However, we often miss a lot of signals and particularly the more subtle ones. The emphasis here is on the word 'active' – this is something that we have to make a positive effort to do. Actively listening and observing is hard enough when we are not engaged in the communication – when we are purely observers/listeners of the situation – and it becomes a real challenge when we are trying to communicate as well. It requires intense concentration and practice. Try the exercise in Table 6. It will enable you gradually to increase your powers of active listening and observation.

The other two ingredients in the process of active listening/observing are:

▌ demonstrating to the other person that you are listening to them and giving them your full attention. The fairly obvious ways of doing this are the nods, the 'uh, uhs' and the crucial eye contact. The dead give-away that someone is not listening to you is when their eyes move away from yours. We give out these signals instinctively when we are listening and equally stop when we are not! However, the process also acts in reverse: if you maintain eye contact (not 100 per cent eye-balling, but the normal 70 per cent or so focusing in and around the eye area) and you positively nod your head, you will find that you have to give the person your full attention and listen. Anyone who has experienced the removal of someone's interest and attention as they start to look around the room or out of the window, etc, will know that it can cause powerful feelings of anger and rejection. It is a very valuable gift to give someone your *complete* attention, and a very easy way to lose rapport if you do not.

▌ reflecting back and summarising to the speaker what you have heard in your own words. This process has two purposes. The first is linked to the above process – it is part of demonstrating that you are actively listening to and observing them. However, in addition it allows you to check out your understanding of the message that has been sent. It is also a way of structuring the communication. If someone is speaking at length about a complex subject, then the reflecting process enables you to stop him or her and summarise and reflect back each chunk. So you might begin with phrases like:

– 'As I understand it, what you are saying is ...'
– 'Have I got this clear, what you mean is ...'
You can also use the process to check out not just the content but also the strength of feeling involved. Often these messages are based more on your observation of the signals from the body language and the tone of voice being used rather than the words. You might use phrases like:

– 'Am I right in picking up that you feel ...?'
– 'Can I check out that I have understood how you feel about this ...?'

There are many barriers to active listening and observing, things that get in the way of hearing and truly understanding the message at all levels. It is important to be aware of them and try to tackle them: see Table 7.

Active listening and observing becomes an even more complex activity when you are facilitating a group. Most of the time you are listening to only one person (although occasionally you may have to deal with several people speaking at once!), yet you will need to be *observing* all the group members all the time. You will be watching for those key signals that tell you that someone wants to enter the discussion, that someone has lost interest or that the group needs a break, etc. Thus at the same time as actively listening and observing the speaker to fully understand the communication, it is vital to scan the group continually. This has the added benefit of ensuring that the key eye contact which is normally engaged in one-to-one communication is not maintained for too long between you and the speaker. Sometimes, because as a facilitator you are 'holding the ring', drawing people into and out of the discussion, there will be a tendency for the speaker to address his or her comments to you. However, you want the speaker to communicate with the whole group and not just with you.

Active listening and observing is a skill that we can all develop to a very high level. But:

*Table 7*

## BARRIERS TO LISTENING

| BARRIER | TRY TO: |
| --- | --- |
| You think you know what they are going to say and make assumptions about what it is. | Positively keep an open mind. Tell yourself that the person has something new and interesting to say. |
| You are eager to get in and have your say. You may feel that the moment will pass unless you get in with your point now, or that your interjection is crucial. | Focus on what others are saying and doing. Jot down briefly the point that you wish to make so that you need not worry about forgetting it. Also, it is making a commitment to yourself that you will make the point at the appropriate time. |
| Your mind is elsewhere, you are thinking of something else, eg your next meeting, an important memo you have to write. | Consciously clear your mind of other thoughts. |
| You are anxious/nervous. | Relax, focusing closely on what others are saying; being centred on them rather than yourself will help. You might consider at the outset of the learning session or group meeting resourcing yourself to feel more relaxed/confident. |
| You are angry. | See the positive intent of what is being said or happening. This means searching for any positive reasons that the person might have for behaving in the way that is angering you, eg they are trying to improve your performance, rather than telling you off. |
| You are hot, cold, tired, thirsty, hungry, etc. | Make sure you and the group are as comfortable as possible. Take care about the physical environment – it does matter that the room is at an appropriate temperature, there is good ventilation. Monitor the energy levels of the group – do they need a break? |
| There are noises and interruptions. | Again, try to choose a venue that is quiet: put up signs about no interruptions, consider banning all telephones, particularly mobiles! |

▌ first of all, we have to be convinced that it is a key
  skill

▌ second, we need to accept that we are probably not
  very good at it at present – this is one of the best
  examples of a skill where most of us have a high
  degree of unconscious incompetence

▌ third, we must be prepared to practise it – luckily,
  every interaction we have gives us an opportunity to
  do so; but consider using exercises like the one in this
  section to speed up the learning process.

## Masterly questioning skills

Masterly questioning skills are a vital tool in the facilitator's
kit. Excellent facilitators ask lots of questions – questioning is how you move from a culture of 'telling' to
one of drawing out the learning or ideas from others.
Again, this is a skill we tend to take for granted – surely
we are asking questions all the time. However, effective
questioning involves asking the right types of question
at the right time. We shall concentrate first on what are
the most appropriate questions to use in different situations, and then offer some words of guidance on those
questions that you ought to try to avoid.

Use:

▌ *Open* questions (What, How, Why, Where and
  When) – when you want to open up areas for discussion or explore areas of learning, because they
  give you lots of information on the situation: eg
  'What happened when the last new product was
  launched?' 'How did you handle the angry customer?' Although traditionally we include the 'why'
  question in this list, it can be more powerful to turn
  'why' questions into 'what' and 'how' questions. For
  example, you could ask: 'Why was the product
  launch delayed?' If instead you ask: 'What were the
  causes of delay in the product launch?' you are focus-

ing the respondent's mind directly on causes, which is in fact the information you want.

The 'what' and 'how' questions are the most powerful of the open questions. The 'when' and 'where' questions are in fact asking for quite specific areas of information.

Although not actually questions, some other very useful phrases to use to obtain a wide range of information are:

- 'Tell me about ...'
- 'Describe ...'
- 'Paint the picture ...', 'Tell the story ...', 'Replay the experience ...' (using whichever matches the language pattern of your respondent).

∎ *Probing questions/greater response* questions narrow down and refine the information, eg 'What specifically do you not like about the new procedure?' and add depth to the discussion, eg 'How exactly did you explain to Jane what was wrong with her report?', 'Tell me in detail what happened when you spoke to your manager about the poor results.'

∎ *Challenging* questions. There is another set of probing-type questions which can be used to challenge certain types of statements. These are statements that are all-embracing, allow for no exceptions, and often include words such as 'never', 'always', 'everyone', 'all'. For example, 'I have *never* had any problems with customers' or '*Everyone* hates performance management interviews.' It is very important to challenge these types of statements, for discussions of topics and the process of learning can often be stopped by them. Your antennae should always be on the alert for these types of word and be ready to challenge them. However, sometimes they are more subtly expressed, for example as generalisations like 'External consultants are expensive' (an issue close to our hearts!) or 'Staff are not interested in first aid training.' The types of responses that you might make are:

| Statement | Questions |
|---|---|
| 'I have *never* had any problems with customers.' | 'Never?' (Direct challenge which can be softened by tone of voice.) Or: 'Have there *ever* been any occasions when you have had problems?' which invites people to hunt through their experiences for any examples of exceptions. |
| *'Everyone* hates performance management interviews.' | 'Does *everyone* hate performance management interviews?' |
| 'External consultants are expensive.' | 'Are *all* external consultants expensive?' |
| 'Staff are not interested in first aid training.' | 'Who says that?' 'What evidence do you have for that statement?' |

Another set of generalised statements are those that set rules or limitations on ourselves or others and often involve words like 'must', 'should', 'must not', 'can't'. For example: 'I must not give the information to the customer', 'I can't make presentations', 'I can't handle conflict'. There may or may not be good reasons behind these sorts of statements; it is helpful to find out:

| Statement | Questions |
|---|---|
| 'I must complete the filing by 10 am.' | 'What would happen if you did not?' This question invites people to explore the consequences of 'breaking' the rule. |
| 'You should call the supervisor to deal with machine breakdowns.' | 'What would happen if you did not call the supervisor?' We are sometimes so rooted in a particular way of doing things that we do not stop to question it. |
| 'I must not give this information to the customer.' | You now reverse the process and ask: 'What would happen |

| | if you did?' Again, you are inviting them to explore the outcomes or consequences of changing that belief. |
|---|---|
| 'I can't make presentations.'<br>'I can't handle conflict.' | Stronger rules and beliefs are often expressed by the use of the word 'can't'. These can be serious blocks on people moving forward. The way to try to unlock this is to ask: 'What is stopping you?' or 'What prevents you?' This puts the focus on eliminating whatever stands in someone's way – which may be real or in large part imaginary limiting factors. |

▌ *Detail-probing* questions. These are used when statements are made in a form of shorthand with bits missing – they might be made in this format deliberately or inadvertently. For example, statements like: 'That's not good enough' or 'Not enough is known about it'. In ordinary conversation we may let statements like this go by – we shall probably make assumptions about what exactly is meant by the 'that' or the 'it' or 'good enough'. However, in the workplace leaving such statements unchallenged is usually unhelpful. They can operate as serious blocks on the resolution of issues, so it is important to probe for the specific details:

| Statement | Questions |
|---|---|
| 'That's not good enough.' | 'What exactly do you mean by "that"?' 'What is it specifically that is "not good enough"?' Having established what the issue or behaviour is, then ask questions that probe the 'good enough' part of the statement: 'What are you seeing and hearing that tells you it is not good enough?' 'What would be an acceptable standard?' |

■ *Comparison-probing* questions. We will often hear, and indeed ourselves use, statements like 'I must manage my time better.' The probe is 'Better than what?' Do we mean better than we have done before (usually this is the assumption we make) or better than a colleague manager, or what? Terms such as 'better', 'worse', 'more', 'less' all beg the question 'than what?' If we are not clear about the comparator then it is hard to achieve our goal. For example, in the case of our time management we are up against some nebulous ideal standard. It is surprising how often we and others make these types of very unmotivating statements.

■ *Cause-and-effect-probing* questions. These are particularly useful and powerful questions for dealing with emotions and relationships. For example, if someone says 'You upset me', the implication is that you are doing something to upset them. So you might ask: 'What am I doing to upset you?' – but this is assuming and going down the path that it is something you have done. A more neutral question is 'How exactly do I upset you?' This invites the individual to review their experience and examine what is causing their upset. They may still blame you – feel that you were the cause. It is surprising that people are so willing to hand over responsibility for their emotions to someone else – such statements are in fact handing power to someone else. An even stronger question then is 'How do you make yourself feel upset in response to what I am doing?' Such a question has to be used with great care because you are inviting the person to take back responsibility for their emotional state. From their perspective it may seem that you are trying to shift the responsibility to them (which you are) *and* get out of it yourself (which you are not). In fact you are helping them to make what can be an enormously liberating shift in taking back control over their own emotional state. They can directly influence their response to the stimulus, even if they cannot impact on the stimulus itself.

▌ *Clarification* questions (a form of probing question). These are used when you need clarification of something that you have heard or observed. We have talked about these types of question within the 'active listening and observing' section and emphasised the crucial nature of them for ensuring complete understanding of the communication. In addition, they can also be used for closure on a particular issue, eg 'Chris, if I understand you correctly you are now in agreement with the rest of the group on ...?', 'Sarah, can you confirm that you are now clear on the outcomes required from this exercise?'

▌ *Redirection* questions. Sometimes a group member may ask a question which may lead the facilitator, in the case of a discussion group, into too much involvement in the content of the discussion. Or, in the case of the learning group, to providing answers when the facilitator believes that the learning lies within the group. In these situations the facilitator can redirect the question to the group as a whole or to a specific person in the group, eg 'Pat has just asked me what I feel about the cost of this piece of equipment. What do you feel as a group?' or 'Chris has asked what the process for handling disciplinary situations is – can anyone throw some light on this?'

▌ *Closed* questions. These are used to check facts and assumptions by soliciting a 'yes/no' answer, eg 'Were you involved in the pilot project?' or 'Did you attend the first module of this programme?' We are quite good at asking closed questions – in fact rather too good. We often ask a closed question when we really need to use an open or probing question. For example, 'Did you see how Janet reacted when you asked the question about her last employment?' The strict answer to this is yes or no. What you really wanted to ask was 'How did Janet react ...?' Many people will respond to the first question as an open question, but some will not. Also, the closed question invites the respondent to do a rather quick memory search – to note a reaction or not. In fact, you want them to replay that part of the interview in more depth and note the detail of Janet's response.

- **Pauses.** Although not questions, they can be a powerful way of generating responses. They give time for people (and yourself) to reflect and prevent the questioning process from becoming a grilling.

Avoid:

- *Leading* questions. These are questions where you suggest the answer in the question. For example, fairly obvious leading questions would be 'The computer system seems to be the best choice, don't you think?' or 'You are happy to move on to the next stage of the disciplinary process, aren't you?' You may be saying to yourself, 'They are indeed a bit obvious I am sure I don't ask questions like that!' However, we suggest you try the exercise in Table 8 before you dismiss this issue. Also, leading questions come in more insidious guises. For example, the question 'What have you liked about the programme?' is suggesting that the respondent has liked something about the programme. A truly open question would be 'What are your views on the programme?' However, we may have decided that we want to know about what they liked and disliked about the programme and asking both questions provides balance. So we need to take care and be very aware of where our questions are leading us.

- *Multiple* questions. These are ones that ask more than one question at once, which can lead to confusion, eg 'Are you clear on the specification and the process of getting it approved?' We often ask multiple questions when we are in a hurry; however, such questions are good examples of the 'more haste less speed' maxim. What does an answer of yes or no tell us – is the respondent clear on both the specification and the process or just the specification or the process alone? Such questions can also lead to real confusion in the minds of the respondents. For example, the question 'What were your experiences of coaching new starters and the existing team?' This is a very complex question: possibly you are asking the respondent to recall two completely different experiences, if not more. He or she will be tempted to range across them all and there is a risk of each experience becoming confused with the others and certainly the clarity of the individual experience may be lost.

*Table 8*

## EXERCISE ON QUESTIONING SKILLS

This is a very simple exercise, but a surprisingly powerful one. Work in groups of three – one person operates as the 'interviewer', one person as the 'interviewee' and one person as the 'observer'. The 'interviewee' chooses a subject that he or she would like to talk about, eg a holiday, hobby, the job. The 'interviewer' then asks questions to find out as much as possible about the chosen subject area in a three-minute period. The rules are to ask as many open and probing-type questions as possible and avoid leading and multiple questions. The 'observer' has a sheet which records the number of the types of questions asked and provides examples of particularly helpful open/probing questions and 'good' examples of leading/multiple questions. Each person has a turn at each of the roles. At the end of each questioning session there is a five-minute feedback session, which takes the form of:

- the 'interviewer' commenting on how he or she felt it went
- the 'interviewee' commenting on how it felt from his or her perspective
- the 'observer' providing objective feedback on the types of questions asked.

Even the most experienced communicators will usually comment on how difficult it is continuously to ask open and probing questions, and correspondingly how easy it is to fall into the trap of asking leading and multiple questions.

The exercise can also be extended to cover building rapport and listening/observing skills.

## *'Chaining' questions*

Skilled facilitators will often use questions in a sequence like a chain in order to enhance the group process. Using a chain of questions, the facilitator takes the initial idea, develops it by probing initially with the proposer, then invites the wider group to get involved, and finally closes down the issue while confirming the commitment of each member of the group. For example:

> Facilitator: 'John, why have you asked for this item to be put on the agenda?' John: 'Well, I think it is likely to be more important to us in the future.' Facilitator: 'Fine, why do you think it will increase in importance for us?' John: 'Well most people seem to think that trade with north-east France will develop due to the opening of the Channel Tunnel.' Facilitator: 'So trade in general will increase, but specifically how would that benefit us?' John: 'I think we can develop the franchising in France, don't you?' Facilitator: 'Possibly; what do the rest of the group think about the issue?' Mary: 'I think it's a great idea.' Facilitator: 'So Mary, you think we should discuss the idea of developing franchising in France as a result of the opening of the Channel Tunnel?' Mary: 'Yes, I do.' Facilitator: 'OK, is everyone happy that we include it as an item on the agenda? Everyone agree?' Assent all round.

This can be a particularly potent technique in the learning situation when you are seeking to draw out the learning from the delegates – for example, after an exercise:

> Facilitator asks Beth: 'What happened when you were the leader of the group?' Beth responds: 'I was dreadful. We got nowhere near completing the task.' Facilitator: 'What do you mean by dreadful?' Beth: 'I lost control, everybody did their own thing, there was no organisation!' Facilitator: 'At what point did you feel you lost control?' Beth: 'When our original plan clearly was not going to work and I think we all went into panic mode.' Facilitator:

'How would you like to have handled the situation differently at that stage?' Beth: 'I needed to get the group back into planning mode.' Facilitator: 'How specifically might you have achieved this?' Beth: 'I might have suggested that the group sit down and share ideas on what had gone wrong and how we might approach the task differently.' Facilitator then asks the rest of Beth's group: 'How do you think this would have worked?' And so on.

The facilitator is remaining completely neutral, not expressing any views on what happened or what might have been done differently, but seeking to explore with Beth and her group what lessons are to be learned. There is a lot of skill and judgement in choosing the appropriate question to draw out the sorts of learning points you want. Sometimes you will want to keep the questions as open as possible. At other times, you may want to steer the learning down a particular route. For example, David (one of Beth's team) might have said: 'Beth did really well.' The facilitator might decide, rather than probing what David meant by 'really well', to steer the discussion towards how well the team performed in terms of outcomes by asking: 'How well did the team achieve the task?' Or when Beth made her original statement that 'she was dreadful', instead of exploring what happened the facilitator might have wished to explore how she felt by asking: 'How were you feeling during the exercise?'

In both the learning situation and when the facilitator's role is to help a group resolve a problem or discuss an issue, the key to success is to be able to range through all the three 'positions' discussed in the previous chapter. Go into 'first position' to check out what you want to achieve from the feedback session or that part of the meeting; into 'third position' to get an overview on where the group is and how they are relating to yourself; then into second position – for example, with Beth, as you explore her experiences of being a team leader.

We now move on to our final core skill – the ability to manage information effectively.

## Managing information effectively

Here we are talking about the ability to capture thoughts and ideas in a *written* format. This is often a skill that is overlooked or that gets trivialised into whether or not you can write straight and clearly on a flipchart, or can spell. We are not denigrating either of these two skills – however, we feel that you do not need any help in learning to write clearly on a flipchart, and spelling is such a fundamental skill in written communication that we have to make an assumption that you have it. However, if you are not confident about your ability to spell words that are in general use (nobody expects people necessarily to be able to spell technical terms or jargon words), then it is helpful to tackle this. We say this for two reasons:

■ If you are having to spend time worrying about how to spell a word, you will cease to listen to what is being said and key information may be lost.

■ The group's acceptance of the facilitator's role depends on mutual respect – this can be undermined as much by poor written skills as poor interpersonal skills. This can be a particular issue with certain types of groups – taken at an extreme: if you are facilitating a group of academics or very senior managers, they will expect you to match them at their level of skills.

There are often two stages involved in the recording of information:

■ during the facilitation session – to capture ideas/ agreements, to help focus the group and structure the learning

■ after the facilitation session – to provide a permanent record of the session and its outcomes for group members and others who might need the information.

## *During the session*

First, it is helpful to review the tools of your trade, ie the physical means of recording information. Do not take these for granted – they can make a big difference to your ability to operate as an effective facilitator. During the session the emphasis is on media that provide:

▮ high visibility so that the whole group can easily see what has been recorded

▮ flexibility to amend and update the record as the discussion/learning progresses.

The media that are commonly used are:

▮ flipcharts
▮ whiteboards and electronic whiteboards
▮ overhead projector slides/strip
▮ computer-assisted presentation systems
▮ bespoke systems – designed for a specific purpose.

Appendix A (pages 165–8) sets out the advantages and disadvantages of using these different media and offers some helpful tips to on how to use them to best effect. It is well worth thinking about the basics of how you are going to record information. The act of recording information is in fact a highly skilled activity and the better prepared you are in terms of the tools for the job, the easier it will be. Also, be creative – design your own bespoke systems; they can add interest and fun to your sessions!

So, on now to the challenging art of recording information. The first question to ask is whether you as the facilitator or another member of the group should take on this role. The expectation is often that it should be the facilitator; however, there are both advantages and disadvantages in being the 'scribe'.

The main advantage is that it gives you more control over what is written and how it is structured. Very often you will have to summarise what is being said and make a decision on where – for example, in which column or group – the comment/idea should be placed.

There are two main disadvantages. It tempts you into being a 'gatekeeper' of the information, and into the danger that, consciously or unconsciously, you start to filter the information and interpret it according to your map of the world. Not only can this compromise your neutrality but there is the additional problem that the group may start to see you as in control and acting as the expert. This is fine if at any stage you want to take on this role, perhaps because you feel the group is stuck or going down a wrong route, but do not let it happen by default. The second major disadvantage is that it is quite difficult to do the physical recording and still actively listen to and observe the group. You may miss some of the content – and again, surprisingly often, the group will allow this to happen and not repeat a comment or draw your attention to the omission. Also, and equally important, you may miss some of the process signals, eg that some group members are not participating, that some people are being blocked and talked over, that some or all of the group are unhappy about what is going on.

The great benefit of not being the scribe is that you can devote all your attention and energy to managing the process. You can then monitor the neutrality of the scribe and help him or her to capture and structure the information in the most effective way. The ideal situation, which is luxury in these days of tight resources, is to have two facilitators – one to act as the scribe and the other to manage the process. However, it can also provide a valuable learning opportunity for someone to practise these skills.

In the case of there being only one facilitator, we would recommend that you make a conscious decision on whether to scribe yourself or pass the role to someone else on each occasion, based on the following factors:

■  the extent to which you want to control the way the information is recorded. Perhaps in a learning situation you want to structure the comments in a particular way, but not to share this at the outset with the group. For example, when considering the outcomes from an exercise to identify behaviours used in performance management interviews, you might wish to divide them up into behaviours that occur before, during and after the interview.

■  the complexity/difficulty of the recording role. It may be that the issue under discussion is particularly complex or difficult to understand, eg the merits of a new computer system or the results from an exercise to plan a project, and you feel that your skills are needed to deal with this.

■  the availability of a member of the group who may be, or wishes to be, less involved in this particular part of the session and who can therefore more comfortably take on the role. For example, in a team meeting of planners, the administrator might take on the scribe role at the stage in the meeting when the team is discussing a particular planning application. This is an important factor because asking a member of the group to take on the scribe role may affect their participation in the discussion in one of two ways. They may end up simply scribing and not contributing their ideas, or they may go in the other direction and use their position to influence the information recorded by including their ideas at the expense of others, or by filtering the ideas of others.

■  the 'recording' skills of the individual members of the group. Some group members may not feel confident to take on the scribe role, eg in a focus group session or learning session involving people in jobs where written skills may not be a large part of that job, such as cleaners, shop-floor workers in factories.

■  your own 'recording skills'. You may find it difficult to take on this role. For example, we were working with a manager who needed to facilitate her large team in discussing a major restructuring initiative. She found it very difficult to listen actively and record information and felt very pressured when she took on the 'scribe' role, so we suggested she rotate the role around the team. This worked very well – the manager felt she was able to facilitate the process better and the team members felt they owned more of the process.

If you choose to use a scribe, then it is helpful to give him or her as clear a brief as possible.

Tips on how to record information effectively:

- Be very clear on the purpose of the specific recording session. For example, are you trying to capture all ideas verbatim without any attempt to structure or evaluate them, perhaps in a brainstorming session to identify all possible ideas on how the organisation might celebrate the millennium? Or are you going to use a very clear structure for recording the information? For example, in a session to examine the role of a department, you might choose to use a process such as SWOT (strengths/weaknesses/opportunities/threats) analysis and ask participants to analyse the department under these headings.

- Be very clear about the process that you are using, eg SWOT analysis, brainstorming. It is crucial that you understand the model that you are using – not only to help the group to use it effectively but also to ensure that the information generated by using it is captured correctly. We talk about the need to prepare in Chapters 5 and 6; an important area is ensuring that you are very comfortable with the application of any processes/models used. You are there as the *expert* in the processes – make sure that you are. If you are not, the difficult job of recording the information will become even harder as you struggle to make sense of the input versus the structure of the model.

▮ If the information is to be recorded using a particular pre-set structure, then it is sensible to pre-prepare the flipchart or whatever medium you are using. This both saves time and looks very professional.

▮ Perhaps the most important tip of all – if you are not capturing the exact words used, it is best whenever possible to check back with the speaker that you have interpreted his or her comment or feeling or idea correctly. This is important for three reasons:

  ☐ It is easy to mishear/misunderstand what has been said; or sometimes, as discussed earlier, we find ourselves filtering the information to what we think was meant or should have been said. This is particularly tempting in the learning situation, where we are often looking for specific learning points to come out from an exercise or discussion. Surprisingly often people do not challenge any misinterpretation – perhaps because they pick up that the information has been filtered and do not want to challenge this filter, or because they are embarrassed to intervene again, or simply because they have moved on to their next point and do not notice.

  ☐ Often, through the filtering process described above, the really wacky ideas can be lost. But these might be the very ones that lead to the breakthrough in terms of the way a group looks at an issue or problem and generates innovative solutions. In learning terms, they can be the very ones that unlock a learning block or throw new light on a way of doing things.

  ☐ It is important that the ownership of the comments/ideas remains with the group and very firmly not with yourself.

▮ A very useful device to deal with ideas/comments/ learning points put forward by group members that are not appropriate to or helpful for that part of the session is to 'car park' them. Set up a separate recording area – often a flipchart sheet on a wall – to record such ideas so that they are not lost and can be revisited at a more appropriate time. This is a very useful approach as it can be a tactful way of dealing with the contribution of someone who has really gone off on the wrong track or misunderstood what is involved. It is less embarrassing to have your idea 'car parked' than not recorded at all! It is important to draw out from the group why the comment or idea should be 'car parked' at that stage. The device also ensures that ideas or comments that may be useful later on are not lost.

There are two important skills involved in the management of the information flow – the ability to:

▌ structure information – identify duplications, cluster ideas and issues into groups
▌ summarise – what the group has discussed or agreed, what point the group has reached, etc.

The key to both these skills is to move into third position (see Chapter 2) – the position that allows you to stand back from the situation and take a helicopter view. This enables you to view what is happening against the objectives and outcomes of the session. Wherever possible, you will want to encourage the group to structure the information flow themselves by asking questions such as 'What common themes are there?', 'In what ways could the information be grouped?', 'Are there any duplications?' If you are using a pre-set structure, eg as in SWOT analysis, you could do this by asking under which heading the issue should be categorised.

Summarising is also a vital part of the facilitator's role. We have already discussed, in the section on active listening and observing, the importance of summarising in one-to-one communication as a way of checking understanding, and breaking the communication down into manageable chunks. Summarising for the group fulfils much the same function:

■ It helps the group reflect on and review what they have discussed, to check for common understanding and for completeness, ie that all the relevant issues have been raised.

■ It helps to structure the discussion, by bringing a particular section of the discussion to a close and moving the group on.

■ It is particularly important in helping the group to reach agreement, by checking out what has been agreed or not, clarifying the outcomes from the discussion.

Do not take for granted the skill of managing and recording information. It can differentiate the expert facilitator, the person who is operating at the peak of his or her performance, from someone who is just ambling along in the foothills.

## After the session

The type of permanent record that is required will depend on the needs of the stakeholders in the process, ie the group and other interested parties.

In the case of discussion groups, such a record might be:

■ an exact reproduction of what was recorded during the session, eg typed-up versions of the flipcharts, or printed output where printers are attached to whiteboards, or photographs/videos of the flipchart/whiteboards, etc

■ one that is based on the outcomes from the session but which has been reorganised perhaps into a report format. In these situations it is important that the facilitator resists the urge to 'tidy up' the record too much. It is vital for the morale and motivation of the group that the record does accurately reflect what happened. It is often helpful to circulate the record to the members of the group in draft to ensure that the process that has been used to structure and format the outcomes has indeed accurately captured what happened. This part of the process depends critically on the group being clear on what the outcomes are at the end of the session – we discuss this in more detail in Chapter 6.

In the case of learning groups, the permanent records can include:

▮ the traditional pre-prepared handouts

▮ records of individuals' experiences recorded by themselves in the form of learning logs, reflection sheets, etc

▮ results of questionnaires analysing aspects of themselves, eg personality tests, leadership styles questionnaires, team roles questionnaires

▮ records of the outcomes of group experiences

▮ feedback from the facilitator and other group members.

The move from a more traditional training session to a facilitated learning session raises interesting issues about the nature of the permanent records that the learning group takes away with it. We discuss this point in more detail in Chapter 5.

We have concentrated on recording information in a written format. However, there will be occasions when it may be appropriate to use other media, for example:

▮ video cameras to record practice interviews/ presentations, etc in learning sessions

▮ tape recorders/video cameras to record general group sessions, eg focus groups.

In this chapter we have looked at core skills of active listening and observing, masterly questioning and the effective recording of information in turn, and sought to offer some useful tips and techniques. In the previous chapter we addressed the fundamental skill of building and maintaining rapport. Clearly, these are not separate and distinct skills: they operate together to begin to set up a pattern of behaviour for an excellent facilitator. We continue this theme of a pattern of behaviour in the next chapter – Behaving as a Facilitator.

## In brief

- Active listening and observing skills are key to picking up all the signals from the group – both on the content of the session/learning and on how individuals/the group are feeling about the process. It is a key aspect of building and maintaining rapport. You need to:

  - practise these skills both formally through exercises and informally through every communication opportunity

  - be aware and take positive steps to overcome the barriers to active listening and observing.

- Masterly questioning skills are a vital tool in the facilitator's toolkit. Facilitators use questions most of the time – to draw out the ideas and learning from the group. Masterly questioning involves using the right questions at the right time:

  - using open, greater response-probing, challenging, detail-probing, comparison-probing, cause and effect, clarification, redirection and closed questions

  - avoiding leading and multiple questions

  - using pauses and chaining questions, which are powerful too.

- Managing information effectively during and after the session is a key skill which is sometimes overlooked. Think about:

  - which media – eg flipcharts, bespoke systems, etc – will best meet the needs of the session

  - who should act as 'scribe' for different parts of the session – the facilitator, a second facilitator or a member of the group

- ☐  the purpose of the recording session and the process that you will be using – eg brainstorming, SWOT analysis

- ☐  checking out the information you are recording to avoid misunderstandings and filtering taking place and to ensure that ownership of the ideas, etc, remains with the group

- ☐  helping the group to structure the information

- ☐  summarising to check understanding, as a way of breaking the discussion into manageable chunks and to help the group reach agreement

- ☐  what form any permanent records of the session should take.

# 4

# Behaving as a Facilitator

In the previous two chapters we have set out the core skills required by the excellent facilitator. In this chapter we use a well-known model of behaviour to throw light on the relationship between you as the facilitator and the group with which you are working. It will also reinforce and place the core skills in a behavioural context. We hope it will help you fully to understand and make the shift to behaving as a facilitator – to walking the part, not just talking the part.

## Introduction to the model

In the early 1950s Dr Eric Berne developed a theory about personality development tied to communication which he called 'transactional analysis' (TA). It is a very useful and fascinating framework for analysing the behaviour of both ourselves and other people. You may already be familiar with this model, in which case the descriptions set out below will just help you bring them back into focus. If this model is new to you, we hope the descriptions will be sufficient to give you a flavour of what the model is about. However, you may wish to deepen your understanding by doing some further reading, as suggested at the end of this chapter.

Briefly stated, there are three of what Berne called 'ego-states' and what we call behavioural states – PARENT, ADULT, CHILD (PAC) states – and each of us is composed of, and at any time may be operating in, any one of them.

## Parent state

The PARENT in TA is the set of recordings in a person's mind of imposed, unquestioned, *external* events perceived between birth and age 5 years They are derived mostly from parents' (or parental figures') speech and behaviour – admonitions, punishments, cuddles, encouragement. Berne says they are permanent and cannot be erased, and at intervals throughout our lives they will be played back and influence our behaviour. It is sometimes described as 'Life as it is taught'.

When behaving in our PARENT state we are usually judgemental, tradition-oriented, regulatory and conventional; alternatively, we may be supportive and protective. We think, feel and do as the 'parent figure' did – with views of right and wrong, good and bad, and how we should behave, eg 'be strong', 'don't show your feelings', 'do as you're told', 'feel responsible'. The PARENT state can be broken down into two aspects: *controlling* and *nurturing* PARENT. The types of behaviour we display when we are operating in our PARENT state are:

| As a controlling parent: | As a nurturing parent: |
|---|---|
| Sets limits | Gives advice |
| Disciplines | Guides |
| Keeps traditions | Protects |
| Judges | Comforts |
| Criticises | Encourages |
| Makes rules and regulations | Nurtures |

The sort of signals we give out are:

| As a controlling parent: | As a nurturing parent: |
|---|---|
| *Words used:* | *Words used:* |
| Should, always, never, ought, must. | Let me, don't worry. |
| *Voice:* | *Voice:* |
| Ordering, directive, critical, authoritative, sneering, disgusted. | Concerned, loving, helpful, supportive, encouraging. |

*Facial expression:*
Rigid, frowning, staring, hostile.

*Facial expression:*
Smiling, nodding, proud, loving, accepting.

*Gestures, posture:*
Upright, arms folded, pointing finger, shaking head, lips tight, closed up.

*Gestures, posture:*
Pat on back, open arms, protective stance.

Often as we describe this state we vividly recall our parents or parental figures and then begin to remember times when we have behaved like them. How many times has our nearest and dearest commented 'You sound just like your mum (or dad)'?

## Child state

The CHILD in TA consists of recordings of *internal* events (feelings) experienced in the first five years of life in response to external events. Berne says that, like PARENTAL recordings, those in the CHILD are permanent and can easily be triggered by events in adult life so as to influence behaviour. When behaving in our CHILD state we think, feel, do as we did when we were small – we are *free/natural,* creative, experimental, joyful, playful – we are obedient, rebellious, insecure anxious, scared – *adaptive* so our needs are met. It is sometimes known as 'Life as it is felt'. The CHILD state can be broken down into two aspects: *natural/free* and *adapted* CHILD. The types of behaviour we display when we are operating in our CHILD state are:

**As a natural/free child:**

Natural/free
Creative

Experimental
Joyful
Playful/fun-loving

**As an adapted child:**

Obedient
Conditioned/conventional responses

Insecure
Anxious/scared
Sullen/rebellious

The sort of signals we give out are:

| As a natural child: | As an adapted child: |
|---|---|
| *Words used:* | *Words used:* |
| I want, mine, won't, scared, fun, fantastic. | I want, I wish, I'll try, please, thank you, sorry. |
| *Voice:* | *Voice:* |
| Loud, energetic, giggling, excited, playful, aggressive, swearing. | Servile, whining, defiant, sullen. |
| *Facial expression:* | *Facial expression:* |
| Relaxed, alive, wide-eyed, joyful, angry, seductive, curious. | Pouting, sad, helpless, avoiding eye contact. |
| *Gestures, posture:* | *Gestures, posture:* |
| Spontaneous, uninhibited, fidgety, lively. | Dejected, curled up, perfectly still. |

As we think about the CHILD state we start to remember ourselves as children and then remember occasions when we know we behaved in a child-like way. What is different is that those behaviours are not just general child-like behaviours but rooted in the behaviours and responses that we actually experienced as children.

## Adult state

The third state, ADULT, is the last one to develop, only beginning after about 10 months of age. It is formed from data acquired and computed through exploring, thinking out and testing ideas. We use the data stored in our PARENT and CHILD states as information with a similar standing to that which we experience in the 'real' world – comparing and testing it to make it fit other knowledge. We then store it in the ADULT, leaving the PARENT and CHILD recordings unaltered. It is sometimes known as 'Life as it is tested'. When behaving in our ADULT state we operate in the 'here and now', are rational and unemotional. We seek information, respect other people, are constructive and not dogmatic.

The ADULT in TA:

*Gathers* data from

▮ the outside world
▮ the inside, eg
   ☐ how the CHILD feels and what he or she wants
   ☐ what the PARENT says
   ☐ what the memories of past decisions stored in the ADULT have to say.

*Computes* the data:

▮ sorts out the best options from the data
▮ estimates probabilities
▮ plans the steps in the decision-making process.

The types of behaviour we display when we are operating in our ADULT state are:

Asking questions to gather data/information
Giving factual/objective information
Analytical
Rational and logical
Non-judgemental
Unemotional.

The sort of signals we send out when we are operating in the ADULT state are:

*Words used*:
When, where, what, who, why, facts, alternatives, results, reasons, check it.

*Voice*:
Even, confident, enquiring, calm, decisive, unemotional.

*Facial expression*:
Alert, open, thoughtful, attentive, responsive.

*Gestures, posture*:
Erect, open, relaxed.

## *Operating in* PARENT/ADULT/CHILD *states*

Berne says that we are all the time operating from one or other of the states – in the way we habitually think and behave in response to life's stimuli. We all operate in all the states, but we may be in some more than others. There is nothing wrong with being in a particular state: no one state is 'better' than the others. However, we may find it more helpful in achieving our outcomes to be in a particular state at a particular time – what we need is to get our state right for the current situation, constantly asking if we are in the right state for the transaction we are dealing with.

For example, when at work, being in our CHILD state in its creative, uninhibited form can be invaluable in brainstorming sessions, where you want to generate lots of ideas and step outside the usual boundaries, or at the Christmas party! However, it may not be a helpful state to operate in at the management meeting! Being in our PARENT state is useful in situations where order and rules are essential, but not when displayed as dogmatism or resistance to change. The only PAC state which it is desirable to have functioning at all times is the ADULT – which takes into account an awareness of the PARENT and CHILD states *and the situation* to determine what behaviour is appropriate in the current situation.

The recognition of PAC states and their effect on our own and others' behaviour is an invaluable tool for working with and influencing people.

## Interacting with others

When we are dealing with others, operating in particular states is likely to generate particular responses from them.

For example, a CONTROLLING PARENT is likely to 'hook' an ADAPTED CHILD (or possibly another CONTROLLING PARENT). Let's look at a specific transaction between two people. If a facilitator of a learning sessions says to you after an exercise: 'That was a very disappointing piece of work: I would have expected better from you' (from their CONTROLLING PARENT state) – what is your response likely to be? First, examine how are you feeling – it is quite likely that you are feeling a mixture of emotions. Perhaps you feel upset and worried and may respond with: 'I'm so sorry, I just could not get the hang of what you wanted – I was trying hard, really' perhaps in a rather distraught or whining voice. On the other hand you may feel rather rebellious: 'Who does she think she is, commenting like that?' You may then well respond: 'What was wrong with it?' in an angry and resentful voice. Both of these responses are from your ADAPTED CHILD state. It might just 'hook' your own CONTROLLING PARENT state so that you respond with 'You should not speak to me like that.'

None of these responses is particularly helpful if the outcome that the transactor was looking for was an improvement in performance. What would have been helpful is to have engaged in a discussion about the way in which the piece of work did not meet the appropriate standard and how it might be remedied. This type of logical, rational discussion usually occurs when both parties are in their ADULT states.

However, there may be times when operating from a CONTROLLING PARENT state is just what is required. For example, if you're facilitating a group session and despite previous interventions the group has not made the required decision and there is only a limited amount of time left, then you might say: 'We must take a decision in the next five minutes. I propose we take a show of hands.'

The transaction can work the other way round. If you operate, for example, from your ADAPTED CHILD state, saying in a group session discussing the timetable for the introduction of a new computer system 'Oh dear, I don't think I shall be able to persuade my colleagues that we can meet the deadline,' probably in a rather pathetic voice, you will usually hook some form of PARENTAL response. For example, the response may come from a NURTURING PARENT: 'Don't worry, we'll help you' or it might hook a CONTROLLING PARENT who responds: 'There's no choice: you must meet the deadline,' probably in a rather irritated manner. Neither of these responses would be very useful to you. What you need is to discuss ways of persuading your colleagues or renegotiating the deadline. Again, this is a transaction better undertaken with both parties in their ADULT states.

We are often asked whether there are ever times when it is helpful to operate from an ADAPTED CHILD state, as it sounds a rather unattractive state. The answer is definitely 'yes'. If you are really in trouble, under pressure or frightened you may want the support and protection offered by someone operating in their NURTURING PARENT state. The only problems that can arise are that people get locked into habitual transactions – you get used to always going to your manager whatever the nature of the problem or decision required, and lose your confidence to make these judgements yourself. Or your manager gets used to giving you very detailed instructions, checking up frequently to see how you are getting on, and stops expecting you to take any decisions. We saw a classic example of this locked behaviour when we did some work with a team that was experiencing difficulties – we call this the Nice but Useless Team. Everyone said how supportive the manager was, she always had an open door, wanted to know how you were and how things were going. However, they felt that sometimes she did not have her eye on the ball and the team lacked direction. The manager said what a super team she had, they were always so helpful. However, she felt under great pressure because they kept coming to her with all their minor problems and decisions and she simply did not have time to do her own work. When we described the model to them the whole team immediately identified what was happening – the manager was operating in NURTURING PARENT state and the whole team in ADAPTED CHILD state.

Someone operating in NATURAL CHILD may 'hook' a NUR-TURING PARENT who will respond lovingly and tolerantly to the probably exuberant behaviour in situations where there are no constraints, eg no work to be done or lessons to be learned against a tight deadline. In the work situation, such behaviour can 'hook' a CONTROLLING PARENT response in the person who gets fed up with other members of the group 'who are just larking around and not pulling their weight'. Alternatively such behaviour might hook another NATURAL CHILD response: 'Fantastic idea, let's try something really way out' – such behaviour can be very infectious – which can be very useful when you want the group to be acting creatively. The NATURAL CHILD state can also be a very useful learning state – particularly when you want the group to think outside their normal boxes, be willing to experiment and open their minds to new and perhaps rather radical ideas. As adults, we often learn best when we are having fun!

Someone operating in ADULT state is most likely to 'hook' an ADULT response. If someone is being very rational, reasonable and calm it is quite difficult to respond from either the PARENTAL or CHILD states. However, it is not helpful always to respond to a PARENT or CHILD stimulus with an ADULT reaction straight away. If someone is very upset or worried, our building rapport skills will tell us that we need to enter their world and understand how they are feeling before leading them out of it. So an appropriate response could be to match their voice and body language (remember the 'little goes along way' maxim) but asking questions about what is causing the problem. The very act of the person's having to think about the answers to those questions means that he or she starts to go into analysis mode and move towards a more ADULT state. A similar strategy will work well with anger.

*Table 9*

# EXERCISE ON IDENTIFYING PAC STATES

You can do this exercise individually or working in small groups.

1 Recall an incident when you were operating in one of the PAC states:

■ CONTROLLING PARENT
■ NURTURING PARENT
■ NATURAL CHILD
■ ADAPTED CHILD
■ ADULT.

2 Replay your memory of it: see what you were seeing, hear what you were hearing, feel what you were feeling.

3 Note down yourself, or if working in a group ask another group member to note down, the key words about what is happening using the following structure:

What body language, voice, words am I using?

How am I feeling?

How are other people reacting – what body language, voice, words are they using?

How do I think they are feeling?

4 Repeat the above steps for each of the ego states.

A useful exercise to help people identify the PAC states in which they are operating is to 'log' experiences of being in the different states: see Table 9 above.

Another useful and very simple exercise is to invite the group to experience operating in the different PAC states: see Table 10 opposite

This is a fun exercise, but also a very powerful one. It gives all the group members a real taste of what it is like to operate in particular PAC states and, in addition, what it is like to work in a group where the full range of

*Table 10*

## EXERCISE ON OPERATING IN PAC STATES

1 Divide the group up into fives – although it can work with larger groups as well.

2 Tell the group that they are in a meeting to discuss a proposed 'Awayday' for the group. They can put forward whatever ideas they want. Explain that they are going to be allocated a PAC state in which they must operate for a period of time as they discuss the 'Awayday'.

3 Allocate each of the five PAC states between the group and then rotate after three to five minutes. (Use a flipchart to show the allocations. Ring a bell when it is time for a change of PAC state. The timing of the change depends on how quickly each member of the group takes on the allocated PAC state.)

4 Continue until all the group members have experienced all the PAC states.

5 Afterwards, ask the group to reflect individually for five minutes on the experience – what state did they find easiest to operate in? what state did they find hardest to operate in? etc.

6 In the plenary session, ask the group to feedback their comments to the whole assembly.

PAC states is in operation. Usually, people comment about how annoying and frustrating they find the CONTROLLING PARENT and ADAPTED CHILD states when they are in action!

## Implications for facilitating groups

As we hope you have already begun to appreciate, this model has strong implications for facilitating groups. In mature groups discussing and deciding on issues, or learning new knowledge and skills, the ideal behaviour state for most of the group most of the time will be ADULT. To generate this response the facilitator him- or herself needs to operate in the ADULT state. With a more directive approach, it is likely that the facilitator will be operating for more of the time in a CONTROLLING

PARENT state and therefore generating ADAPTED CHILD responses or other CONTROLLING PARENTS from within the group, which may lead to unhelpful behaviours in the group. However, ADULT is not always the appropriate state for the facilitator to be in – there will be times when other states may be helpful.

## Helpful states for facilitating groups

### ADULT

Operating in the ADULT state, you:

▍ question effectively to explore and probe issues and draw out learning experiences

▍ provide factual and objective information as required by the group

▍ provide information on processes to help the group structure, analyse issues and make sense of learning experiences

▍ help the group to develop and use models that assist in problem-solving and learning

▍ are non-judgemental about ideas, comments – use appropriate questions and processes to encourage the group to the review them

▍ are non-judgemental about behaviours – offering feedback which gives a clear description of the behaviour that has occurred and the outcomes of that behaviour

▍ monitor the group and encourage it to review its performance and behaviours.

### NURTURING PARENT

Operating in the NURTURING PARENT state, you:

▍ provide a secure and trusting atmosphere to discuss important and sensitive issues

▍ provide a secure and trusting environment for the group to practise new skills and behaviours

▮ bring in and support struggling group members

▮ coach individuals who need particular help and support in the learning role.

These are very useful behaviours when members of the group are feeling insecure, operating in their CHILD states and need help. This may occur with immature groups who are in the early stages of their development. However, remember the cautionary tale of the Nice but Useless Team; by operating as NURTURING PARENT you will tend to generate/encourage a CHILD response and cultivate a relationship of dependency on you, so it is unhelpful to spend too long in this state.

## NATURAL CHILD

This may, on the face of it, be a surprising state to suggest a facilitator should operate in. However, operating in the NATURAL CHILD state, you:

▮ encourage the group to operate in their NATURAL CHILD states as well

▮ thereby encourage the group to be creative, willing to experiment and take risks

▮ encourage the group to have fun!

It is very useful state, for example, in brainstorming sessions – as facilitator you can take the lead in encouraging 'off the wall' suggestions by making them yourself and behaving in a very lively, lighthearted way. Clearly, it is important to choose the right time to operate in a NATURAL CHILD state. At inappropriate times it may generate a PARENTAL response from your group!

## CONTROLLING PARENT (with an immature group)

By operating in a CONTROLLING PARENT state with an immature group – one that is in the early stages of learning to work together – you:

▮ provide clear direction and focus for the group

▌ set rules and boundaries within which the group can function safely

▌ provide firm structure to the discussion and processes.

It goes without saying that operating in CONTROLLING PARENT state for too long will be counter-productive. Your resulting ADAPTIVE CHILD group at best will not be committed to the objectives, be they learning ones or those of a discussion group, or will take no ownership for the outcomes and they may well rebel!

## Unhelpful states for facilitating groups

### CONTROLLING PARENT (with a mature group)

Operating in a CONTROLLING PARENT state with a mature group, you:

▌ tell the group what needs to be discussed and how to do it

▌ tell the group what they must learn and the best way to go about it

▌ have set and 'right' ideas/views/solutions

▌ direct the group towards specific solutions/decisions

▌ are evaluative and judgemental

▌ encourage ADAPTED CHILD reactions.

As a result, members of the mature group will get frustrated and angry at being treated 'like children'. They may try to lead you into ADULT, but if you stay resolutely in your CONTROLLING PARENT state they are likely to try to break off the transaction – either by walking out themselves or getting rid of you!

### ADAPTED CHILD

Operating in an ADAPTED CHILD state, you:

▌ will look for conditioned, conventional and limited ideas

▌ will be unwilling to challenge ideas and constraints

■ will be unwilling to challenge unsatisfactory behaviours in group members, eg dominating and
blocking behaviour

■ will have low energy levels and generate a similar
response in the group

■ will be anxious and nervous about how to help the
group.

It is perhaps fairly obvious that trying to facilitate effectively from an ADAPTED CHILD state is virtually impossible. In that state you will lack the internal resources to
'manage' the group in a facilitative way. Very likely you
may resort to directive approaches to cover up your lack
of confidence.

In summary, one of the keys to successful facilitation is
flexibility of behaviour. This is the flexibility to choose
the appropriate PAC state in which to operate to best
meet the needs of the group, and when to move out of
it. The PAC model is also very useful in helping members of the group to understand the impact of their
behaviour on others, and vice versa, the impact of
others' behaviours on themselves. It provides an objective way for the group to analyse individuals' behaviours.
However, remember that all models have their limitations and, as Galagan (1993) reminds us, a model is
only one map of the world and not the territory itself.

## In brief

■ The transactional analysis (TA) model offers some
very useful insights into the impact of different
behavioural styles on the relationship between facilitator and the group and hence on the quality of the
facilitation process.

■ There are three main behaviour states – PARENT,
ADULT, CHILD (PAC). The PARENT state can be sub-
divided into CONTROLLING PARENT and NURTURING
PARENT and the CHILD state into NATURAL CHILD and

ADAPTED CHILD. We all operate in all these states at different times.

▮ Operating in a particular PAC state is likely to 'hook' specific PAC states in other people. These may be helpful or unhelpful for the facilitation process. The successful facilitator is flexible and chooses the appropriate PAC state in which to operate to best meet the needs of the group.

## Further reading

Transactional analysis was popularised in Eric Berne's book *Games People Play* (Penguin, 1968) and that of his disciple Tom Harris in *I'm OK, You're OK* (Arrow Books, 1995). For a sound and user-friendly account we would recommend you try *TA Today* (Stewart and Joines, Lifespace Publishing, 1987).

# 5 Designing Learning Sessions

## Introduction

Facilitation skills are generally regarded as a type of delivery skill – a different approach to the way you deliver the training/learning to the delegates during the training/learning session. However, we suggest that moving towards a facilitative approach to training/ learning is a much bigger change. In the previous chapters we have talked in terms of mindsets or maps of the world. Being a 'facilitator' of learning may require a change in your map of the world. As a facilitator you will:

- talk about 'learning' and avoid the use of the word 'training'
- see the learners as having great reservoirs of existing knowledge, skills and wisdom
- want and encourage the learners to have control of their own learning – it is their learning programme, not your training programme
- see your role as supporting and guiding them through the learning process
- see your expertise as particularly in learning processes, with expert subject knowledge only as required.

To operate as a facilitator in this way means taking a completely fresh look at the whole way you manage learning sessions, and therefore at their design.

We should emphasise that this chapter is not about the general design of learning sessions – there are many good books on this subject, including within the IPD's *Training Essentials* series (Hardingham, 1996). This chapter is about the key issues involved and the approaches required by adopting a facilitative approach to learning.

The key issues in the design of facilitated learning sessions are how to:

■ agree with the participants learning objectives that also meet the needs of the organisation

■ develop learning contracts that share ownership and responsibility

■ use learning exercises that build on participants' experiences

■ share decisions on learning methods with the participants

■ be flexible but yet achieve the objectives in the time-scale available.

## Designing and agreeing learning objectives

The traditional approach is that after a full training needs analysis (TNA), a training specification is prepared which sets out among other things the learning objectives required to meet the need. The TNA is usually focused on the organisation/business needs. Indeed, in our earlier book *Training Needs Analysis and Evaluation* (Bee and Bee, 1994) we emphasise the importance of there being a clear link between business need and the training delivered, and for a structured process for establishing that training is the best solution to a particular need. Then, that the training is specified very precisely to ensure that it meets the need, and that measures are in place to check that the need has been met. This process is driven from the organisational perspective rather than the individual one and often the prospective learners are not involved directly.

It might seem logical to suggest that if you are taking a facilitative approach to learning there should be a change in your approach to the TNA process – to involve the learners directly in identifying their own learning needs. Ultimately, if an organisation is seeking to achieve individual ownership of learning then this is what needs to happen. In practice, it may be difficult to have a direct dialogue with *all* the potential learners as part of a formal TNA process, although some consultation with prospective learners often takes place – perhaps by involving a typical sub-group of them in the process. The direct dialogue usually comes through performance management systems, through the questionnaires/interviews between an individual and his or her line manager which are geared to focusing on the total performance and development of an individual. However, as these individual needs are collected together and processed, the direct link between a specific individual's learning need and the eventual training offered can get lost. For example, if a learning need for a particular individual is 'to organise their work better' – they are likely to be offered a time management course of some sort. If there is a training need that is perceived to be required by a whole group, or sometimes even the whole organisation, then inevitably the learning needs of the individual will be subsumed by a generalised view of the collective need.

Of course, herein lies the crux of the matter – to meet an individual learning need, which is based on the precise gap between the performance standard set and the existing level of performance of that individual, requires an individual solution. This is where, for example, coaching and self-managed learning approaches really score. These should and can be tailored to individual needs. As soon as you enter the realm of group training/learning the dichotomy arises of trying to meet diverse individual learning needs through one learning event.

It is therefore likely that you will design your learning event against a specification that includes a set of generalised (in terms of individual needs) learning objectives. Traditionally, the participants will be advised of the learning objectives at the stage when they are nominated or choose to come on the particular event. Then at the start of the session the learning objectives are displayed as a given, with discussion usually for clarification only. As traditional trainers we have often felt slightly uneasy about this lack of individual focus and ask the participants to add some personal objectives, which we may or may not overtly try to meet.

So how do you give ownership of these general pre-set objectives to the learners? The simple answer is 'with difficulty' unless you are prepared to have the learners contribute to, and therefore possibly amend, the learning objectives. This sounds a rather revolutionary concept – after all, in the past we have concentrated on getting really well-formed learning objectives and designing our training to meet them. Surely, all our well prepared plans could turn out to be useless? The answer lies in two key factors:

▌ Having a clear aim for the learning event that the learners accept is the purpose of why they are there. For example, it could be 'to deliver a high standard of customer care to our colleagues and external customers' or 'to manage our work and ourselves effectively'. This effectively sets the *parameters and boundaries* for the learning event and prevents a major change of direction. For example, we were asked to deliver one-day workshops giving an overview of the whole training cycle for operational trainers who were about to be assessed for selection into a new restructured department. These workshops were generally very successful and the learning objectives and content were very much in line with what the learners wanted. Except for the last group, who were a group of operational trainers working in a far-flung outpost of the organisation, and to whom there had been some miscommunication about the purpose of the workshop. They came along expecting and wanting a session on delivery skills! Now, the brief for the session from the client had been very clear and the overall aim had been set as 'to describe and explain the role of the trainer in the new organisation'. Against the background of this aim we were able to explain and sell our original programme.

∎ Being prepared to be flexible – in terms of session planning and the learning methods/exercises that you use. This may seem a rather alarming concept at first – many of us will have been brought up on the idea of having well-planned sessions, which tell us exactly what we are doing and when. However, we are not suggesting that you cease to plan – rather we shall introduce you to a different sort of planning: see later in this chapter.

Remember that, within the stated aim of the learning event, it is more than likely that the learning objectives will stay much the same. However, you may find differences reflecting the learners' views on the relative importance of different areas of learning. Intuitively, we will have often reviewed and amended the learning objectives in the past in a more informal way. Most trainers will have had experiences, for example, of groups not being typical of the target audience for which the learning programme was designed. We designed a learning event aimed at helping middle and senior managers implement new disciplinary procedures. We ran a series of these programmes and towards the end the learning population changed significantly to include supervisors, whose role and needs were very different from the middle/senior managers. We, of course, tacitly amended the learning objectives and content to reflect this.

Having convinced you, we hope, that you are not setting off down a slippery slope to chaos and learning disaster, the next issue is how to involve the learners in

*Table 11*

## EXERCISE ON CONTRIBUTING TO THE LEARNING OBJECTIVES

STEP 1    Explain the purpose of the exercise: 'to create learning objectives which meet their specific learning needs within the context of the overall aim of the learning event'.

STEP 2    Put up the overall aim for the session on a flipchart. Divide the learners into small groups (of three or four) and ask them to describe what they would see, hear and feel as they were achieving the aim of the training, eg delivering a high standard of customer care. Ask the groups to feedback their experiences to the plenary group and capture the key words that are used on the flipchart(s). Put up the flipchart(s) so that they are clearly visible.

STEP 3    In the same small groups, ask the learners to reflect on their individual strengths and weaknesses in respect of meeting the overall aim; then to prioritise these strengths and weaknesses for the group, taking into account the need in terms of the numbers within the group with that particular strength/weakness and the extent of the strength or weakness. (NB This is not intended to be a scientific assessment, just a guide.) In the plenary session, assemble an overall prioritised list of strengths and weaknesses. It is important to focus on both strengths and weaknesses so that the emphasis is on building on their existing experience, knowledge and skills as well as identifying the gaps. Put the results up on flipchart(s) which are clearly displayed.

STEP 4    In the same small groups, next ask the learners to put up on the flipchart what they would like to learn from the event. In the plenary session, assemble an overall list. This is the moment then to display the proposed learning objectives and facilitate the group in amending, deleting and creating a set of learning objectives to meet their learning needs. Put these up on flipchart(s) in a very prominent place!

STEP 5    Individually, ask the learners to reflect on these group learning objectives and use a form of starring to annotate the learning objectives to indicate the relative importance for themselves, and if necessary add some individual learning objectives. Invite the people to share their individual objectives with the group. As facilitator, you will need to emphasise the importance of each individual's taking responsibility for meeting his or her learning objectives.

setting the learning objectives. We have used the type of approach to be seen in Table 11 opposite.

This exercise is very valuable not just for the purpose of involving the learners in the setting of their own learning objectives, but it also focuses them very clearly on:

■ the overall aim – what they are trying to achieve in business/organisational terms

■ what that aim actually means to them in terms of what they will see, hear and feel when achieving it

■ their own strengths and weaknesses – their own personal starting points.

It is also the vital first step in inviting the learners to take control and responsibility for their learning. We have deliberately not put timings for the above exercise because they will depend on the extent and nature of the learning, and therefore on the length of the learning event. For example, if the learning event is over three days, then the exercise could take up to two hours. For a one-day event, the room for manoeuvre is much more limited and you may choose to do an abbreviated version of 30 minutes or so – combining some of the steps. The exercise is intended only to give you a flavour of how you could approach this – the choice is yours!

## Developing learning contracts

Most of us will be familiar with the concept of learning contracts. They can range from quite formal documents that are often used in long-term training/educational programmes, to the informal ones that are developed at the beginning of workshops, etc, and which consist of a few bullet points on a flipchart, covering issues such as confidentiality, respect, timekeeping, etc. Essentially, we are talking about the latter type, however strengthening them to provide a basis, a real contract, for truly sharing control and responsibility for the learning event. As trainers, we have often mouthed the words that learners must take responsibility for their own learning, that it is their learning event rather than ours, the trainer's. However, have many of us – either the trainers or the learners – really meant it? Hasn't it always been accepted that the trainer is in control and that if the learning event was unsuccessful in any way it was largely down to the trainer – through inadequate design or poor delivery skills!

If we genuinely wish to share control and responsibility, then we have to take some positive steps to change people's perspectives of the traditional roles and responsibilities. The learning contract is a very useful vehicle for doing so. We have used the following approach successfully:

*Table 12*

## EXERCISE ON DEVELOPING LEARNING CONTRACTS

STEP 1    Define the word 'contract' as:

'a formal agreement between people or groups, which sets out the terms of the working arrangement between them and covers performance standards, behaviours and responsibilities'.

Put this up on a flipchart and ask the group what they see as the advantages and disadvantages of having such a contract for this particular learning event. Mostly people see the advantages as: everyone being clear about their responsibilities; it being useful to agree behaviours, such as time-keeping and confidentiality. Sometimes people suggest that the contract could be too constricting and stifle creativity or make the event too regimented. At this stage, allow the discussion simply to flow, and at the end suggest that what is needed is a contract that maximises the advantages and minimises the disadvantages.

STEP 2    Put up the aim of the contract as:

'to enable us as a learning group to share control and responsibility for the learning event in meeting the learning aim and objectives.'

Invite comments. Sometimes people ask what we mean by 'share responsibility' or 'control'. We tell them that they can define it how they like!

STEP 3    Set up small groups (of three or four) and ask them to propose a list
(on a flipchart) of what they want, in terms of performance/
behaviours from:
- the facilitator
- themselves as learners.
You, as facilitator, will do the same. It is helpful to allow about 15
minutes for this process.

STEP 4    The group shares its flipcharts and then you facilitate the group to
reach an agreed contract with the group. This is usually not a difficult
process because a lot of consensus generally emerges. The sorts of
statements that result are as follows:

| LEARNER BEHAVIOURS AND RESPONSIBILITIES | FACILITATOR BEHAVIOURS AND RESPONSIBILITIES |
|---|---|
| To be fully committed to the learning aim and learning objectives | To be fully committed to the learning aim and learning objectives |
| To arrive on time at the beginning of sessions | To arrive in sufficient time to ensure that the learning environment is prepared and ready |
| To stay until the agreed ending of sessions (unless there are very urgent reasons, which need to be agreed with the group) | To make clear statements about the timings of beginning and ends of sessions, breaks, exercises, etc |
| To abide by the timings of exercises unless you have negotiated extra time | To monitor and take responsibility for the time management of the sessions/exercises |
| To debate constructively and agree thelearning methods to be used against the learning objectives | To debate constructively and agree the learning methods to be used against the learning objectives |
| To participate fully and to the best of your abilities in all exercises and sessions | To explain the purpose of sessions and exercises clearly |
| To question constructively if you do not understand the purpose or content of the sessions/exercises | To facilitate the learning from each session/exercise to maximise the benefits to the individual and the group |
| To raise any issues of concern about the learning event openly with the whole group (unless they are so personal thatthey should be raised individually) | To raise any issues of concern about the learning event openly with the whole group (unless they are so personal that they should be raised individually) |

| LEARNER BEHAVIOURS AND RESPONSIBILITIES | FACILITATOR BEHAVIOURS AND RESPONSIBILITIES |
|---|---|
| To listen actively and observe others so as to fully understand what is being communicated | To listen actively and observe others so as to fully understand what is being communicated |
| To respect others' views, by not interrupting, talking over, or ignoring others | To respect others' views, by not interrupting, talking over, or ignoring others |
| To treat as confidential everything that occurs if it affects another individual | To treat as confidential everything that occurs if it affects another individual |
| To support and help each other | To support and help all learners |
| To be willing to give and receive constructive feedback | To be willing to give and receive constructive feedback |
| To take responsibility for maximising the learning from each session/ exercise to the best of one's ability, for both oneself and others | To take responsibility for maximising the learning from each session/ exercise to the best of one's ability, for individuals and the group |
| To take responsibility for monitoring the learning contract and sharing with the group if the terms are being broken. | To take responsibility for monitoring the learning contract and sharing with the group if the terms are being broken. |

Not surprisingly, the two lists should look very similar – the contract is, after all, about sharing control and responsibility.

STEP 5    Invite everyone to sign the agreed contract. This is the opportunity to say that if anyone has any doubts about the terms of the contract, he or she should voice them now. Signing the contract makes a very individual commitment to it.

STEP 6    This is another very important document – display it prominently and close to the learning aim and objectives. These two documents are the cornerstones, the solid foundations for the learning event.

There may be some areas of controversy or concern, for example:

▌ if the facilitator is required to report back on the performance of the learners. It is important that if this is an organisational requirement, perhaps for assessment purposes, then this should be made very clear from the outset when someone agrees to come on the learning event. The facilitator may need to clarify exactly what type of information will be in the reports and whether the learners will have the opportunity to see them. It goes without saying that the more open the reporting system the better. It is very difficult (perhaps impossible) to sell the concept of learners having control and responsibility for their learning if they are excluded from the reporting process.

■ how to decide whether an issue should be shared with the group or is sufficiently personal to be a matter between the facilitator and the individual learner. Usually the group is happy to leave it to the individual's discretion, but perhaps you should build into the contract the opportunity to raise the issue if people feel that they are being excluded from a discussion that should include them or the group as a whole.

The content of the contract is not unexpected or very revolutionary; however, the process concentrates everyone's mind on:

■ the concept of sharing control and responsibility
■ what that actually means in terms of their own behaviours
■ that it is important that each person sticks to the terms of the contract.

## Using learning events that build on learners' experiences

Experiential learning is not a new idea but we believe it is fundamental to the concept of facilitating learning. You may be familiar with the some of the concepts of experiential learning and the Kolb (1984) learning cycle. However, to give us all a common starting point we shall briefly set out the principles. Learning is conceived as a four-stage cycle: see Figure 1. To take a simple example:

*Figure 1*

## LEARNING CYCLE

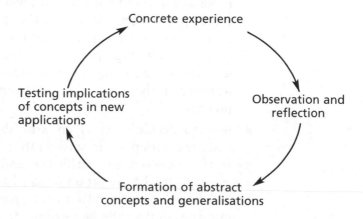

- The first stage is having a concrete experience, eg taking a walk across a field and noting that you have cold wet feet.
- In the second stage you observe and reflect on what has happened, ie you observe and feel your wet feet and reflect on the cause of it – water is getting into your shoes.
- The third stage is that you try to make sense of what has happened and formulate some idea of how to deal with the experience better, and generalise to a wider situation – eg wearing wellingtons might solve the problem.
- The final stage is to test the implications of the idea/concept in a new situation, eg you repeat your walk across the field or another field, and, of course, generate a new experience – and so the cycle starts again.

We are learning all the time; with every experience we have we are automatically processing it and acting on it, trying it out and then learning from it again. This is, of course, how we learn as babies and small children. We learn from the experience of touching a hot radiator that it is hot and hurts, and that it might be a good idea not to touch it again – and indeed not to touch other objects that look like it. As Dewey (1938) put it:

> The principle of continuity of experience means that every experience both takes up something from those which have gone before and modifies in some way the quality of those which come after . . . What he has learned in the way of knowledge and skills in one situation becomes an instrument of understanding and dealing effectively with the situations which follow. The process goes on as long as life and learning continues.

This understanding of how we learn has crucial implications for us as facilitators. Kolb (1984) puts it powerfully:

> The fact that learning is a continuous process grounded in experience has important educational implications. Put simply, it implies that all learning is relearning. How easy and tempting it is in designing a course to think of the learner's mind as being as blank as the paper on which we scratch our outline. Yet this is not the case. Everyone enters every learning situation with more or less articulate ideas about the topic in hand.

How many of us do, in reality, design our training as though our potential learners are like great barrels waiting to be filled up with the knowledge and skills we want to impart? Rather than really appreciating and designing for learners whose barrels are full of fine wine (or whatever your image of a delicious and valuable drink is!) and that our role is to help that wine mature, or blend it with some other fine wines, or top it up a little. This is, in essence, what an important part of experiential learning is all about – it is:

■ drawing out the experiences
■ helping the learner to structure and understand those experiences in the context of the particular learning objectives

▮  transforming those experiences into new knowledge and skills.

These can be experiences that have already occurred, tapping into part of that large barrel of existing fine wine; or experiences that we set up as part of the learning event, effectively where we are topping up or adding to our barrel of experiences in a planned way. We shall look at examples of both.

## *Tapping into existing experiences*

We now use this approach in all our learning events. For example, in customer care programmes we set up the following exercise at an early stage:

*Table 13*

## EXERCISE ON BEING A CUSTOMER

STEP 1    Explain the purpose of the exercise: 'to experience the world as a customer so as to identify the key aspects of customer care'.

STEP 2    Working in small groups (of three or four), first ask each learner in the group to identify:

– a situation when you experienced excellent customer care
– a situation when you experienced very poor customer care

then to relive the experience: to see what you were seeing, hear what you were hearing and feel what you were feeling. Explain that you want them fully to experience/relive that situation now. As each learner recounts their experiences, another member of the group records the key points being made. You may wish to set boundaries around the experiences, eg examples from the workplace, or examples in banks, etc, depending on whether you want to focus on more specific examples and behaviours.

STEP 3    In the plenary session, ask for examples of each type of experience in turn and, as facilitator, begin to structure those experiences, perhaps into: helpful and unhelpful behaviours, grouping similar behaviours together, grouping 'before', 'during' and 'after sales' behaviours; or using a fishbone analysis approach (see Chapter 6), each of the main ribs constituting a type of behaviour. This is where your skills as a facilitator are being used to the full. It is your role to help structure those experiences in such a way that the group can use the information and move forward.

This is a very valuable exercise because it achieves two important purposes:

▋ it starts to identify the key factors in delivering excellent customer care – the overt purpose, and in addition

▋ it causes the learners to move into second position – ie to see the world through the customer's eyes, from standing in their shoes, hearing the same messages.

We have set up similar exercises in performance management workshops, where we ask learners to relive experiences of receiving constructive feedback and destructive criticism; in presentation skills workshops, where we ask them to relive experiences of being part of the audience of excellent and poor presentations; and so on.

You may also recall that in Chapter 4, as part of introducing you to the PARENT/ADULT/CHILD model, we suggested that you carry out an exercise where you relive experiences when you have operated from a particular state, such as CONTROLLING PARENT or NATURAL CHILD, as a way of fully understanding what life is like when you are operating in that state – what you are seeing, hearing and feeling.

There may be occasions when it appears that the learners do not have any direct experience of the subject being learned – for example, learning to be a train driver or perhaps to use a particular software package. However, they will have experience of similar situations, eg driving a car or being a passenger on a train, and using other software packages. We would suggest that there is no learning arena where the learners will not have some relevant experience to build on. Your role as facilitator is to help them identify those experiences and see the link with the current learning area. This can be quite a fascinating challenge, but it ensures that you never forget that your learners are barrels full of fine wine. You just have to learn how to tap it and help it develop and mature.

The potential use of these types of exercise is enormous. A few words of caution, however – reliving some experiences can be powerful experiences in themselves and may cause distress. So, for example, if in a time management workshop you are asking someone to relive an experience where they felt under great stress, it is sensible to suggest that they do not use the worst moment of their life, but that on a scale of 1 to 10 (10 being catastrophic!) they choose an example of about 5 or 6.

Finally, another powerful example of the use of this type of exercise is to ask your learners to identify two examples of really effective learning experiences – times when they felt that they had learned a lot and got that real buzz from learning. Invite them to relive these experiences. This exercise again has two very useful outcomes:

▌ It enables learners to identify the factors that helped them to learn – very useful information both for themselves and their facilitator.

▌ It takes the learners into a state when they felt all the excitement, joy, wonder, sense of achievement arising from the process of learning – this is a very useful state to have your potential learners in!

## Setting up new experiences

We are probably more familiar with these types of exercises. These are exercises that are set up specifically to give the learner an experience that will be helpful in achieving the learning objectives – for example:

▌ Role plays – frequently used in all forms of interview training, for example for recruitment, performance management, disciplinary situations, etc; in customer care training, for example handling difficult customer situations; and in facilitation skills training such as running facilitated sessions where other learners play the group roles. Sometimes specially briefed actors are used to bring out specific learning points.

▌ Real plays – a variation on role plays where learners interact with their 'real world' colleagues in facilitated 'real life' situations, for example in performance management learning, carrying out a performance management interview with a manager's actual member of staff – but in the learning situation, with observers, etc.

▌ Skills practice (a form of role play) – for example, learners making a short presentation, or running a training session, giving first aid, using a piece of equipment.

▌ Business games/simulations – for example, where learners run a mock organisation, having experiences of making decisions about recruitment, marketing, finance etc; dealing with emergencies.

▌ Games – where the activity does not directly try to simulate the real world but, by setting up situations which are unusual and fun, for example building a Lego tower, planning the building of a pyramid, gives learners experiences that highlight generic skills and behaviours.

▌ Outdoor/adventure training – an extreme form of a game, but where the whole learning event is focused around outdoor/adventure. The concept is that by giving the learners experiences that are outside their work environment, it enables them to think and behave outside the normal constraints.

These provide an interesting range of experiential exercises. The first four are specifically aiming to give the learners as 'real' an experience as possible, or as similar an experience to that which would occur in the work environment. The key to their success is to be able to design them to replicate the real world as closely as possible. The last two types of learning methods are based on the belief that it is useful to step outside of the actual issues and look at the knowledge, skills and behaviours in a completely different context or environment. The key to their success is in identifying the appropriate experiences that will generate the knowledge, skills and behaviours being learned. The risk with these approaches is that the knowledge, skills and behaviours learned in these different contexts may be anchored in the experience itself and may not easily be transferred into the real world.

So far we have looked at the more traditional form of learning event. However, many of the new approaches to group learning have gone one stage further down the experiential route. For example:

■ Action-based learning – when the learning event is based around tackling real workplace issues and projects. As the group tackles these issues, the necessary inputs of learning are contributed by the facilitator, or sometimes by the group members themselves, as they are needed. Clearly, there are no doubts about the relevance, application and transfer of the learning to the workplace with this type of approach. However, because the learning has arisen from specific experiences only, the challenge lies in ensuring that the learning can be applied more widely.

■ Self-managed learning – where the group, often referred to as a learning set, meets on a regular basis, perhaps monthly, and each member has a certain amount of time to discuss his or her learning needs and issues with the group. The group is there to provide their knowledge and skills to help each other to identify their learning needs and devise strategies to meet them. The individual learner is then responsible for implementing these strategies and reporting back.

The great strength of experiential learning approaches is that:

> The learner is directly in touch with the realities being studied ... It involves direct encounter with the phenomenon being studied rather than merely thinking about the encounter or only considering the possibility of doing something with it.
>
> (Keeton and Tate, 1978)

This book addresses the issue of facilitating learning groups and hence this chapter focuses on learning events involving groups. However, the ultimate in experiential learning is, of course, learning in the workplace, which is often individually based:

▮ Carrying out particular projects that have been designed to expand and develop an individual's (or sometimes a group's) knowledge, skills and behaviours. They might be used to introduce the learners to a new area of the business – for example a finance professional might be given a marketing project – or to give specific experience of particular management skills, eg project management. Often, this excellent learning strategy is marred by a lack of attention to key aspects of its design It is important that the project is:

  ☐ carefully selected and designed to meet the learning need of the individuals

  ☐ organised so that the learners are supported by a 'facilitator' in terms of monitoring performance, providing feedback, drawing out the learning, dealing with issues and problems that arise, etc.

▮ Secondments that have been designed to develop the learner's knowledge, skills and behaviour through the specific experience of doing another job. This sort of approach is frequently used with graduate trainees, who are seconded to different parts of the organisation to build up an all-round knowledge of the organisation as well as develop specific professional skills, eg HR, finance, and generic skills of working as part of a team. The problem with secondments is often similar to that with projects – that not enough attention is paid to either their selection or the support needed to maximise the learning from them.

▮ Finally, but not least, tackling the normal challenges of the learner's own job. Again, the success of this as a learning strategy depends on a clear identification of the learning needs, clear identification or creation of opportunities within the job to meet those learning needs, and the facilitation of the learning through feedback and support. Ideally, these would be met by a well-designed and implemented performance management system. The key lies with the learner having available someone to facilitate their learning – it could be their line manager or some form of mentor. Many organisations are exploring the use of mentors as a way of strengthening the support that learners have in the workplace.

What makes experiential learning such an important and interesting concept is that it makes critical links between 'formal' learning through learning events, 'informal' learning through one's work and everyday life, and personal development. It is also, of course, the basis for the principle of continuous learning and development, as Kolb (1984) put it, by 'portraying learning as a continuous lifelong process'. Every moment of our lives we are having experiences and the opportunity to learn from them. What experiential learning does is highlight this process and invite us to make the most of it. Our role as facilitators is to help learners to tap into their experiences, to help them structure and make sense of them and develop new learning from them. In fact, the core of the facilitation approach is to help them move round Kolb's learning cycle and, by enabling them to understand the process, to help them to use it positively for their own development. This is giving them the double gift of:

▍ showing them that the concept of continuous/life-time learning is not a terrible burden, committing them to hours of boring study – it is about making the most of a natural process that they are using all the time

▍ helping them to take control of their own learning and development – the power to learn for themselves.

## Sharing decisions on learning methods

Again, we suspect your heart is sinking – surely an important part of your planning and preparation is carefully choosing the appropriate learning methods and designing the appropriate exercises. The answer is undoubtedly yes. What we suggest, however, is that you build in some flexibility – some alternative approaches. We suggest the following process:

1   Structure the learning event in the normal way, breaking the learning down into manageable chunks – what we shall call learning sessions.

2   For each learning session, set out, as normal, the outcomes you wish to achieve from that session linked to the learning objectives. However, be very clear and specific about those outcomes – write them down at the start of your session plan.

3   Plan your learning session in the normal way. However, positively list the alternative methods that could be used to achieve the same outcomes. Beside each method note the reasons, and in what circumstances, you might or might not choose that particular method. Prepare as normal for your preferred approach. If, in your view, there is an alternative approach that could be used as effectively, prepare for it as well.

This may appear to generate a lot more work. However, most of the process is actually the same as you would be using now. You would normally be reviewing a range of methods and be clear why you have selected a particular one. All we are suggesting is that you note down your thought processes. Also, most of us do prepare some alternative exercises – in case we run out of time and need something shorter, or we end up with some spare time, or the group is a different size from what we expect, etc.

The next stage is how you involve your learners in

deciding on the appropriate learning methods. This is quite straightforward: you share your thought processes with them just as you would do if you were explaining to another trainer/facilitator how to run the learning event. You are the expert in the learning processes; but, they are the ones who will be using them. As a facilitator you are not 'in charge', so it must be the learners' choice whether to participate. It is your job to explain/sell and agree the best approach with them. We suggest the approach laid out in Table 14.

In fact this is not very different from what you might normally do. It is customary to take the learners through the programme. However, we tend to present it as the way it is going to be done – for information – and not for debate. The advantage of the above approach is that:

▌ The learners will really understand the programme and how the different parts contribute to their achieving the learning objectives. For many learners, having a sound understanding of the overall picture helps them to make sense of the parts.

▌ Sharing the decisions on learning methods will share ownership of them with the learners – this should encourage commitment and buy-in. It will help learners' motivation to participate fully in the various exercises. Many exercises are marred by a less than enthusiastic approach to them by participants.

## Flexibility is the key

We have said a lot about the fact that being a facilitator is not just about using a set of skills but is a state of mind: of the need to adopt a map of the world that means that you see the learners as equal partners in the learning process. You believe that it is important that the learners are involved in deciding on the learning objectives and learning methods, and that they should share ownership of the whole process. However, all of this

*Table 14*

## EXERCISE ON SHARING DECISIONS ON LEARNING METHODS

STEP 1    After you have agreed the learning objectives, explain the learning plan that you have devised, using the following format:

| SESSION | OUTCOMES/ OBJECTIVES FOR SESSION | PROPOSED LEARNING METHODS TO BE USED | REASONS FOR CHOICE |
|---|---|---|---|
| ONE | To identify the key factors in delivering excellent customer care. | Group exercise – to discuss experiences of being a customer. | Everyone has had lots of experience of being a customer – the exercise will use this experience as a starting point. |
| ... | ... | ... | ... |
| FOUR | To practise the skills of dealing with challenging customers. | Role plays with observers. | It is important to have the opportunity to try out the new skills and behavioural strategies in a safe environment. You will have the opportunity to see what works for you and to get feedback on enhancing these skills. |

You might decide not to write down the reasons, but explain them orally.

STEP 2    After you have described each session, ask the learners if they have any comments on the method used. If any learner is unhappy with a particular approach – perhaps the idea of role plays – then it can be very useful to surface those concerns so that hopefully you can resolve them. If there is general consensus against a particular approach be prepared to discuss modifications or alternative ones. For example, if there is general concern about role plays as set out, then suggest perhaps coached role plays, ie where the learner carries out the role play in small chunks, with coaching and feedback as he or she goes along.

implies the need to be flexible about the way you do things – to be willing to amend the learning objectives, adopt different learning methods, etc. We are sure that as trainers we have all talked rather glibly about responding to the needs of the learners; however, to what extent in the past have we been willing to deviate from our pre-determined session plans? To do so requires us to:

▌ let go of the belief that we know best, and be willing to believe that the learners may in fact know best about their own needs

▌ be very expert in learning processes – about what methods can best achieve specific outcomes

▌ be very expert in the core skills of facilitation – of being able to build rapport with the learners so as really to understand what matters for them, actively pick up all the signals from them, and question them effectively to establish their needs and views on the learning process

▌ keep a clear vision of the overall aim and outcomes required

▌ be willing to plan and re-plan as the learning event progresses in order to the achieve the learning objectives in the time-scale

▌ be confident in our ability to explain to and persuade all the stakeholders in the learning event – client/sponsor, managers of the learners, the learners themselves – that the facilitative approach is the right one.

This last point can be very important, particularly if you are working in an organisation which has not whole-heartedly adopted the facilitative way of working. We hope that we have furnished you with the appropriate reasons to put forward – the advantages of taking such an approach and the inbuilt safeguards that minimise any risks.

Flexibility also means being prepared to deal with situations that can arise from moving towards a more learner-owned process. In the next chapter we look at some of the more common challenging situations that can occur when facilitating groups of all types. In the rest of this chapter we look at some specific situations that can and do occur in learning groups that have embraced the philosophy of shared ownership and responsibility for their learning.

## Questioning the aim

In the section on agreeing learning objectives we stated that one of the key factors in ensuring that the learning objectives that are agreed with the learners meet the organisational needs is having a clear and accepted aim. What happens when the aim is not accepted by some or all of the group?

A good example of this situation occurred in a learning event which had as its aim 'to provide participants with the necessary project management skills to run their own work projects'. On the face of it there would seem to be nothing particularly controversial about this aim, but behind it lay a plan to organise all the department's work on a project basis, with project plans, gantt charts, monitoring processes, etc. Many staff in the department either could not see any advantage in moving to this way of working or actually thought it would get in the way – adding bureaucratic procedures. In a more trainer-led environment, the usual approach is to allow a little time for the participants to let off steam and then get on with the training course. Clearly, with the learner-led approach it is not as simple as that – the learners them-selves must agree and accept that they will work with the aim.

The approach we used was to break the group down into smaller groups and ask each sub-group to propose ten advantages in moving towards project-based work-ing and as many disadvantages as they wanted to list. (It is important to give them a target for the list which they will find most difficult and where there may be resistance to seeing, in this case, any advantages.) In the plenary session we facilitated the group to come up with the top ten advantages first. We then listed all the disadvantages and got the group to prioritise them. (We used a system where the learners had five stars – they could allocate all their stars to one issue or one to each of five issues.) We suggested to the group that as part of the exercise to agree learning objectives, they build in ones that would enable them to address the five most serious disadvantages as identified by their prioritised list. All we had done was to help structure their thinking down a more constructive path.

Another example occurred in working with a group of administrative staff. The aim of their learning event was 'to provide participants with the knowledge and skills to manage their workload more effectively'. This group told us that there were no ways that they could manage their workload more effectively as they were completely dependent on the demands of the professional staff they supported. They were overworked and fed up. In their view there was no point in their being on the programme – it should be directed to the professional staff. Does this sort of reaction have a familiar ring to it? Again, in the more traditional trainer-led approach you allow them to have a few moans, do a bit of empathising and then suggest that they try out some ideas and move into the programme. This will not work with a learner-led event simply because they will not take any ownership – they will 'reluctantly' allow you to carry on, but the burden of responsibility to make it work would be on you. So what do you do? In fact, you take a similar approach to that in the first example. Divide the learners into small groups and ask them to list ten areas of their work over which they exercise some control and then to list all the areas over which they have no control. In the plenary session we facilitated, the group arrived at a list of ten areas of work over which they had control and a prioritised list of those that they felt they had no control over. This was enough for them to be willing to move on to a constructive discussion of the learning objectives.

Does this type of approach always work? The answer is that generally it does, and if it doesn't then it is likely that there are serious issues around the validity of the aim.

## Avoiding learning methods

There are some sorts of learning methods that strike terror into some learners' hearts. Role plays are a particularly good example. In the good old trainer-led days, learners might have blanched a little but then buckled down to it reluctantly. Needless to say, in these circumstances the role plays are often not as productive as they might be and it is a struggle to achieve the learning from them. In the learner-led approach, it is important to deal with these concerns so that all the learners are willing (remember the learning contract) to participate in them fully. At this stage it is helpful to introduce the concept of learning styles. You may be familiar with this, but to ensure we are all are talking the same language, here follows a short summary.

From their research, Honey and Mumford (1986) concluded that there are four main learning styles, as depicted in Table 15 overleaf.

There is a learning styles inventory that enables learners to identify their learning styles profile. This provides very useful information for them as learners and for yourself as a facilitator. In very simplistic terms, it helps identify which learners will tend to like which types of learning methods. So try the approach described in Table 16 before the discussion on learning methods.

*Table 15*

## LEARNING STYLES

| STYLE | DESCRIPTION | SOME IMPLICATIONS FOR TRAINING AND DEVELOPMENT |
|---|---|---|
| *Activists* | Learn best from experiences in association with others. They learn by trial and error – by real-life experimentation. | Prefer learning experience to involve activity. Like novelty, challenges. Dislike passive learning – lectures, detached analysis, solitary effort. |
| *Reflectors* | Like to stand back and ponder over and observe experiences from different perspectives. They like to think things through before taking action. | Learn best by drawing on own and others' experience. Like to plan, observe and reflect. Dislike being thrown in at the deep end, group activities. |
| *Theorists* | Learn best by analysing things logically. Dislike ambiguous, subjective areas where there is no clear structure or theory. | Like activities which are logically structured, allow examination of underlying theories. Give opportunities to question, allow time for review and drawing conclusions. |
| *Pragmatists* | Like trying out ideas, theories, and techniques to see if they work in practice. | Learn best by problem-solving in the real work situation. Like to see an obvious benefit. Dislike too much theory. Give plenty of opportunities to practise. Offer tips and techniques. |

*Table 16*

## EXERCISE ON UNDERSTANDING YOUR LEARNING STYLE

STEP 1    Divide the group up into smaller groups, with a mix of learning styles in each. (Ask the delegates to complete the learning inventory before the event if possible; otherwise do it there and then – it takes only about 15 or 20 minutes.) Ask the groups to consider each of the learning styles, relating it to themselves and their previous experience as learners, and note down what sorts of learning methods will be most and least attractive.

STEP 2    In the plenary session, discuss and develop the implications of the different learning styles on the sorts of learning methods used, and how they are used.

This exercise will generally show that, for example, Activists have no problems with role plays – they enjoy the activity, the challenge of being centre stage. The Pragmatists do not mind too much either – they will enjoy trying out the new skills (people often have high scores as both Activist and Pragmatist). The Reflectors and Theorists will not be too keen on role plays. However, understanding why they feel that way can be very helpful, and also provide the route through to their being willing to use it as a learning method. For the Reflectors, you will explain that there will be plenty of time for preparation and they can choose to go later so that they can observe other role plays first. For the Theorists, you will explain that there will be plenty of input/theories/models to help them plan and structure the role plays. This is often enough to make them participate willingly in the role plays.

## Managing the time

Serious concerns are often voiced about achieving the objectives within the time allowed. We discussed these in general terms in Chapter 1. The move from the more traditional approach of tightly designed learning events to those where flexibility is the name of the game, in terms of both what is being learned and how it is being learned, raises issues of time management. We suggest the following 'disciplines' to help manage facilitated learning events:

▌ In your planning of the event you will have allocated approximate times to each learning session. As you review the learning objectives and methods with the group, if any amendments are made then review the time allocated to the individual sessions – perhaps to allow for a new session to reflect a new learning objective, or a shorter session to reflect a different learning approach. Part of your expertise as a facilitator is to be skilled in assessing the time required for different learning approaches and working out the time implications of changes.

▌ Put up an outline plan with clear timings shown, perhaps on a flipchart, so that the whole group is aware of the target timetable.

▌ In your learning contract, you will probably have agreed some 'rules' regarding time-keeping after breaks, during exercises, etc. This will help ensure that time is not wasted.

▌ If some exercises or plenary sessions are taking longer – share this knowledge with the group and invite a brief re-plan.

The key to managing the time effectively is to be aware, at the earliest point, of deviation from the plan and take appropriate action. Don't be tempted to think you can make up time in the last afternoon!

### Recording information during and after the learning event

With traditional training approaches, the trainer will usually come prepared with boxes of pre-prepared handouts, manuals, exercise sheets, etc. With the more flexible approach of facilitated learning this raises issues regarding the capture and recording of information and the permanent records that learners take away with them from the session. With facilitated learning think about:

▌ using a learning log – usually in the format of a loose-leafed folder. This will include reflection sheets which learners can use to record their learning, issues for further exploration, etc, after sessions or at the end of the day. It can also be used to hold the outcomes of exercises, questionnaires, group discussions, etc.

▌ encouraging the learners to design their own feedback sheets for exercises – this allow them to use their own wording and gives a greater sense of ownership to the information collected. It also covers the situations when learning methods have been agreed that are different from those planned

▮ short, summary handouts – recording key information on procedures, models, etc. Wherever possible, encourage the learners to undertake further reading – good references, with a brief description of how each one will contribute to their learning, and perhaps some questions that can be answered as a result of the further research, using copies of articles, etc.

The emphasis at all times should be on looking for ways to encourage the learners to seek out and record information for themselves. Such information will always be more meaningful and relevant to the individual learner than any prepared general material.

In the next chapter we go on to look at some processes and techniques that can be used in the more general group sessions.

## In brief

▮ Being a facilitator of a learning session means adopting a new map of the world – seeing learning as a partnership of joint responsibility and ownership between you and learners.

▮ The key issues in the design of facilitated learning sessions are:

  ▢ agreeing learning objectives with the participants that also meet the needs of the organisation

  ▢ developing learning contracts that share ownership and responsibility

  ▢ using learning exercises that build on participants' experiences

  ▢ sharing decisions on learning methods with the participants

  ▢ being flexible, yet achieving the objectives in the time-scale available.

# 6

# Useful Processes for Facilitating Groups

## Introduction

This chapter explores useful processes for facilitating all types of groups. Although it is written specifically for those who will be facilitating groups to discuss and explore issues, resolve problems, develop new ideas, etc, the techniques and processes are equally useful in the learning situation as well. This chapter looks at the following areas:

▌ preparing to facilitate

▌ helping the group get started

▌ using tools and techniques to solve problems, generate new ideas, take decisions, get agreement

▌ reviewing, learning and moving forward.

## Preparing to facilitate

We are sure you have heard the maxim 'fail to prepare, prepare to fail'. This is a fairly obvious statement if you are going to facilitate a learning session, and we discussed the nature of this preparation in detail in Chapter 5. However, if you are going to facilitate a discussion session where you are intended to operate in a totally neutral position – perhaps as an outside consultant or an inside consultant brought in specifically for the role – it may be tempting to think there is nothing to do until the day itself. After all, you are not expected to know anything about the subject area itself. You are expected to be an expert in processes and you have them at your finger-tips. So, what else do you need to do? The answer is that there are five important ways in which you can prepare:

1   *Clarify with your client what the purpose of the session is and whether there are clear outcomes required or expected from the session(s).* Clients often have clear outcomes in mind, but sometimes they do not. For example, we were asked to facilitate a customer services management team, a group of eight people, on an 'Awayday'. We were told that the team had booked a day away as an opportunity to step back from their routine work and examine their role and their performance. They were also staying residentially the night before in order to have time to meet socially over dinner and afterwards. The brief was as general as that, although the department manager added that he was hoping that one outcome would be an action plan. A complete contrast to this rather open brief was a session that was set up for representatives from the training departments of a large decentralised organisation. This organisation was heavily into quantitative performance indicators and had decided that the training function was a little lacking in this area. (Does this sound familiar to you?) A day-long session had been set up with a clear outcome of producing a set of indicators. Then there are sessions that have an overall purpose but the outcomes of which are very general. For example, we are often asked to facilitate focus group sessions such as one with staff from an engineering servicing division which was going through a major restructuring exercise. These were short sessions – an hour-and-a-half to two hours – and the brief was to explore the issues that the staff felt were important in the way the department functioned and what changes they would like. The results of all the sessions would be brought together in a report which

would form an important input to the restructuring study.

It is perhaps fairly obvious that without a clear under-standing of what the group is trying to achieve it is difficult to prepare for the session. If the brief is very vague, as with the customer services department, at least you know in advance that at an early stage in the session the group will need to take the time to discuss the purpose and outcomes in more detail.

2    *Discuss and think about the time-scales: is it one session or several; how long is each session?* Sometimes the client will already have made the arrangements and your job is just to turn up and facilitate. In other situations the client may need advice on the best approach. The key issue in both cases is to try to ensure the time-scale and the outcomes match, ie there is an appropriate amount of time to achieve the outcomes, just as with learning groups. However, sometimes it is harder to make the judge-ment. With learning groups, if you can obtain clear information on current levels of knowledge/skills/ behaviours, and there are clear learning objectives, then from experience you can make a reasonable estimate. However, in the situation of discussion groups you may know little about the group's ability to work together to discuss these types of issues – you may not be aware of the sensitivity or strength of feeling surrounding certain issues, or the difficulty of solving certain problems. If it is possible, it is useful to explore these issues with your client. Sometimes the client may say that the group can get away for only two hours or for a morning and that the group simply has to do its best in that time. The more you facilitate a range of sessions the better you will become at judging time-scales. Our message is: give it some thought – do not just take it as given.

3    *Obtain as much background information as possible on the subject area of the discussion.* Although you are

not expected to be a subject material expert, it is helpful to understand some of the details. For example, in facilitating a team in discussing its role it is useful to have some understanding of what that role is, and to understand some of the jargon and technical terms in common use by that team. In the case of the customer services team described earlier, they used a lot of acronyms as a form of shorthand. The group will not want to stop frequently and explain points of factual detail or jargon. It may – and we emphasise the word 'may' – also be helpful to have an awareness of some of the key issues. This is not essential and there is a danger that you are pre-positioned, both consciously in the processes you have planned to use, and subconsciously in what you are expecting to hear and respond to during the session. Often much of this information will be available from documents. You are positively *not* expected to be an expert; however, you will generally be expected to be a knowledgeable layperson. It is not always an easy balance to get right. For example, being too aware of the issues may cloud your objectivity and neutrality – and always bear in mind from where or whom you are getting the information.

4  *Find out as much as possible about the make-up of the group.* For example:

   ▌ Individuals' roles/reasons for being part the group – are they a work team, such as the customer services team, or are they representatives of different teams and on the group to represent a particular point of view, eg in the case of the representatives from the different training departments of a large organisation producing performance indicators? Or are they there to provide expertise or experience in a specific area, eg perhaps as the marketing and finance experts on a new product launch project?

   ▌ The level of knowledge/skill of the individual

group members – does everyone have a similar starting point for the purpose of the discussion? If not, it can be helpful to explore ways of bringing the group up to a common basic standard. For example, in the group of training managers described above, a paper was sent out in advance of the session explaining the basis and structure of the performance indicators used.

▌ The nature of the hierarchical/organisational relationships of the members – eg are there direct managerial relationships within the group? Is one of the group members considerably more senior than the rest, etc? This can clearly affect the group dynamics, and it is helpful to know in advance.

5    *Consider the types of processes that might be helpful to draw out and analyse the issues, generate solutions, etc.* (We cover the processes in detail later in the chapter.) It is well worth while having an outline plan of action and rough timetable for the session. However, do *not* be committed to it. With true facilitated sessions, the group will decide on the processes used and the time-scales. You will have a strong input on the process side of the session, but not the final say. It is important to be open-minded about process, otherwise you may find yourself pushing a particular approach – and then guess who will own that process and the outcomes from it! When reviewing the types of process that you think might be useful for that particular session, a valuable tip is to check on whether the organisation is using any particular process at that time. There is often a process that is 'flavour of the month' and it is very likely that the group will want to use it. It is not helpful if your understanding of the process is less than that of the rest of the group. This happened to us once when we were training a group of auditors in facilitation skills. Each of them ran a practice session, and in one of the first of these sessions the

learner facilitator used a process we had never come across. It did not work well and we were hampered in our feedback by not knowing whether it was an inappropriate process to have used in that situation, or whether it was used badly. In theory, of course, you get the group/individual to explain the process, but sometimes they will not be able to explain the process or model fully, and for more complex models you need time to think them through.

A rather controversial issue in terms of preparation is whether or not it is helpful to have any knowledge of the interpersonal relationships within the group, eg who hates working with whom, or alternatively the potential for cliques forming. On the positive side, often you will not have a lot of time to get to know the group and advance warning of potential problem areas can save time and trouble. However, it can also get in the way – these will always, by definition, be someone else's subjective judgements. They might not always be quite right and they might prevent you from objectively observing what is going on in terms of the group dynamics. Sometimes you will be given this information whether you want it or not! Our advice is to keep it at the back of your mind but not to act on it unless you identify corroborating evidence. This also applies to comments on individual group members, eg he or she tends to dominate or is rather quiet; he or she is rather aggressive or tends to over-react.

If you are an internal consultant, or indeed someone who is quite close to the group, you will be party to quite a lot of the information that might be considered unhelpful – knowledge of the issues, of the individuals involved – and which may affect your ability to operate fully as a facilitator. As this information is based on your own experiences rather than others' views, it is harder to put to one side – it forms part of your map of the world. If you want to operate as a true facilitator then you need to be very disciplined in your handling of the session –

more conscious than a completely external facilitator of how you are reacting to the situation and the people involved. We wrote in Chapter 2 about the concept of taking up positions – first, second and third positions. Taking up third position – the helicopter view – and doing a quick review of whether you are letting your map of the world and filters affect how you are behaving can be a useful self-check.

## Helping the group to get started

Often a major challenge in facilitating group sessions to resolve issues, generate ideas, etc, is that you may be working with a group that has not worked together before, and often against a very tight time-scale. You may have only a few hours to get the group started and then operating effectively. The whole process of how teams learn to work together has been well researched. A popular model is that of there being four stages in the development of a group – which we extend to five – consisting of:

■ forming – the stage where the group is operating as individuals and will often keep the discussion at a superficial level as they begin to find out about each other

■ storming – the stage that is characterised by a lot of turbulence and conflict, as group members flex their muscles and start to push at the boundaries of group tolerance. It is considered a key stage. Groups will often try to avoid it and go on to the next stage; however, inevitably they will return to it later!

■ norming – the stage when the group begins to establish norms of behaviour, often referred to as the group 'processes'

■ performing – the stage when the group is operating at peak effectiveness

■ mourning – the stage when the group is closing down and moving on to other activities.

To find out more details of this model see Bee and Bee (1997).

So how do you attempt to telescope this process? In fact you may not be able to do so with some groups. The worst scenario is where there is no experience of working together in that particular group and individuals have little experience of working as part of *ad hoc* groups. Some organisations use a lot of *ad hoc* groups/project teams to run their business and train their staff to operate as part of such teams. In these situations the group members will be skilled at working as members of a group and will slip into the discussion of the subject area of the session like well-oiled machines. In other groups, the facilitator will need to manage the development process.

There are five key activities for turning your group from a machine made up of a lot of ill-fitting parts, all pulling in different directions, rubbing against each other and generally clanking and rasping, into that sleek, smooth-running machine that purrs along. These are:

▌ getting the environment right

▌ making the introductions

▌ establishing ground rules of behaviour

▌ clarifying and focusing the group on the objectives of the session

▌ planning the session.

### Getting the environment right

As part of our preparation for facilitating learning groups, we usually consider the physical environment in some detail – what size of main training room we shall need, whether we shall need any additional syndicate rooms, what might be the appropriate layout, etc. With discussion groups – perhaps because they are meeting together for only a short time and they are seen as an extension of normal working activities – the same attention is not given to the environment in which the group will work. This is a pity, because just as with the learning groups the environment can have either a serious negative effect or a really positive influence. The key factors are to try to ensure that the space used:

▋ is quiet – it is not helpful to have to contend with road noise, or the building works associated with putting in the new network system, or the video of the learning session going on next door, or the ventilation system, or a noisy showroom the other side of a flimsy wall, etc

▋ is free from interruptions – ideally, there are no telephones, the room is not being used as a short cut through to a neighbouring office (you think we are joking!)

▋ is large enough for the purpose – will allow for small group work if you need it or there are additional rooms available for this; there is enough wall space to display flipcharts; or it is simply comfortable enough to spend two or three or more hours in

▋ is light (natural daylight is a real plus), well ventilated, at the right temperature – or, even better, able to be regulated

▋ is laid out appropriately, or, even better, with flexibility to change the layout if necessary.

The traditional layout tends to be tables in the form of an open 'U', with the facilitator at the front with a table, an overhead projector, flipcharts, etc. A surprisingly powerful way to change the 'emotional' environment and the energy of the group is to remove the tables. We all talk, perhaps rather glibly, about tables acting as a barrier. However, you really appreciate that they do so if you start a learning group or general discussion group with tables and then remove them. Often, the participants are rather reluctant – they say they like the tables to rest their papers on (so provide clipboards) or they just feel more comfortable with tables – after all, they are usually used to having a desk as their own private space and they feel more vulnerable or exposed without it. We frequently start out with the traditional layout and at an appropriate moment we make the change. Within a very short time, maybe only five or ten minutes, the nature of the discussion will change – people start to be more honest: they will talk more about how they feel, and quieter members of the group will start to join in; the group becomes more aware of each other as individuals.

The less formal layout also enables and encourages people to move around. As a facilitator, it is very helpful to join the group physically from time to time – perhaps when a member of the group is reporting back from small group work, or when you have asked a member of the group to take over as facilitator so that you can contribute fully. This serves several purposes:

▌ it emphasises that you, as the facilitator, are part of the group – not 'in charge' of the group

▌ it enables you to experience the world as a member of the group – on a very basic level, for example, it will help you judge whether your flipcharts are readable; at a deeper level it will help you build rapport, get into second position, with the group

▌ it acts as a role model for moving around.

It can be very helpful to encourage people to change their positions – people can get locked into particular standpoints or views on an issue, or have a mental block on a particular learning issue, and simply changing position physically can sometimes unblock the thought processes. Also, sometimes unhelpful sub-groups can form as a result of people sitting together.

We have been talking here about the physical environment – the next sections are about getting the emotional/social environment right as well.

## Making the introductions

We all know about the need for introductions – so that the group starts to learn a little about each member and individuals begin to feel more comfortable as part of that group. However, in addition the introductions stage can be a very useful way of encouraging the participants to think creatively and step outside their usual way of doing and thinking about things. In the situation of discussion groups there are a number of factors that will influence your approach:

▋ the extent to which the group members know each other already. Clearly, with a work group, eg the customer services team described earlier, the need for introductions is quite different from a group in which the members may not have even met before.

▋ the length of the discussion session. If you have only a couple of hours, then it would be inappropriate to have a lengthy introductions stage.

▋ the culture of the organisation. With learning sessions, participants come along (mostly!) because they expect and want to learn new ways of doing things. Usually, they will be more open at the outset to perhaps a more innovative approach to making their introductions, such as using games and metaphors. This may not be the case in discussion groups – participants often see the session as an extension of their normal working activities and expect to behave as they do normally in their work environment.

▋ the types of participant. Although it is unwise to make generalisations, you will often find that the more senior the participants the more difficult it is to break the ice and get the group operating as a group. They may be more unwilling to expose their vulnerabilities and take risks, and the issue of personal agendas becomes more important. Also, individuals who are not used to working in discussion groups, for example those in operational jobs, may find the initial stages harder.

All the above factors could suggest that you need to keep your introductory stage short and perhaps take a more traditional approach. However, weighed off on the other side of the scale is the need to start the group development process. You will need to make a judgement on the most appropriate approach. Set out below are a range of suggested ideas for the introductory stage.

**A**    Ask each group member to provide the following information:

   – their name

   – their job title/department/organisation

   – what they want to achieve from the session

   – what they believe they can contribute to the session.

This is a straightforward and simple approach. If the group members all know each other, then you can exclude the name and job title, etc. For your purposes as facilitator you can ask them just to write the information on name boards. It is helpful to have a pre-prepared flipchart with the questions on them, with some eye-catching symbols, eg

WHAT DO YOU WANT TO ACHIEVE FROM THE SESSION? (stick man looking into the distance)

WHAT CAN YOU CONTRIBUTE? (open hand)

This type of approach is seen as relatively 'normal' – the questions seem sensible in the context. However, they are encouraging the group members to start to talk about their expectations and to focus specifically on what they can contribute.

**B**    For groups that know each other well, the introductions can focus on the theme of the session. For example, with one group which was a departmental team that had been restructured, we asked the group members to describe how they viewed/felt about the team using the metaphor of types of cars.

The results turned out to be quite fascinating and caused enormous amusement, which was helpful as the atmosphere had started out quite tense. The team had been through a stressful period. The manager of the team saw the team in very optimistic terms – as a shiny, high-powered racing car. The rest of the team had varying images – from a cheerful much-loved old banger to a boring Ford Escort (apologies to Ford Escort owners – not our views!). It emphasised right at the start the range of perspectives and provided a really useful starting block from which to launch the whole session. Perhaps best of all it injected some humour into a session that was likely to raise sensitive issues. By using a metaphor it helped the group to be honest about how they saw and felt about the department at an early stage, which helped the subsequent discussions. Metaphors are very useful devices to start individuals and groups thinking creatively.

C    In learning groups, using metaphors can be a very powerful way to start off the learning session. For example, we have asked group members to describe themselves using the metaphor of an animal. It is often helpful to get them started if you as the facilitator first introduce yourself in this way. In time management sessions, one of us often uses the metaphor of a cat and the way cats lie stretched out sinuously, basking in the warmth of the sun, and purring happily – clearly just taking enormous pleasure from that moment in time. We make the point that we wish we could be more like cats in this respect and live more in the present rather than forever be thinking about and planning the future. In another learning group, which was looking at training evaluation, we asked them to draw a picture of how they visualised training evaluation in their organisation at that time. Many of them saw it in terms of an enormous mountain to climb, but more positively with the summit bathed in sunshine! It can be helpful to ask the group to work in pairs to help the creative process develop.

What you are trying to do is to use the introduction stage as a form of ice-breaker – to get:

I    all the group members to speak at an early point

I    the group members to start to understand where each is coming from – both in terms of their formal positions and their approach to issues, ie their maps of the world

I    the group to become comfortable, ie move through the 'forming' stage

I    the group to begin to think creatively.

### Establishing ground rules of behaviour

In the previous chapter we discussed the merits and content of what we referred to as a learning contract for the learning group. That contract was about the group agreeing to key aspects of the way they wanted to learn together. The ground rules for discussion groups are much the same, although they tend to be simpler. We talked earlier about the stages of development for groups and teams – by asking the group to agree ground rules you arc moving the group artificially into the norming stage. Therein can lie the problem: the group may not feel ready to discuss, let alone agree, any norms of behaviour. They may even feel uncomfortable discussing them. Also, some groups may not see the need for ground rules at all – they believe they are competent people who are used to working in groups. They do not need to waste time on this sort of thing, they want to get on and discuss the real issues! At the other end of the spectrum, in some organisations the concept of ground rules of behaviour is well established, and indeed you will find them pre-printed and pinned up in all the meeting rooms.

So, as ever, the watchword is flexibility. For some groups, it may not be appropriate to raise the ground rules at the outset, but as behavioural issues arise you may begin to suggest that the group might find it helpful to agree some guidelines. The term 'ground rules' may not always be helpful – in some groups you may choose to talk about 'useful ways of working' or 'helpful and unhelpful behaviours'. Some group members may not understand quite what you mean by ground rules of behaviours, so consider asking the members of the group individually to take three minutes to write down three behaviours they really like in group working and three behaviours they dislike. On other occasions you can simply brainstorm them out. However, an important stage is to ensure the whole group understands what each rule means and agrees to it. An example of a typical set of ground rules is set out in Table 17.

The set of ground rules below are expressed in fairly businesslike language – in the real situation you use the words offered by the participants, eg 'don't talk in sub-

*Table 17*

## GROUND RULES

| DO: | DON'T: |
|---|---|
| ▮ ask questions when you don't understand something | ▮ talk over/interrupt other people |
| ▮ listen to what others have to say | ▮ leave your mobile phone on/make phonecalls during the session |
| ▮ respect others' views and feelings | ▮ talk in sub-groups (unless asked to) |
| ▮ be honest | ▮ put people down, eg rubbish their ideas |
| ▮ be prepared to disagree but always give reasons for your disagreement | ▮ hold back when you want to make a contribution |
| ▮ be a good time-keeper – coming back from breaks, in small group working, etc | |

groups' might come out as 'don't chat with your mates' while the group is working.

Finally, make sure that the ground rules are written out in large clear lettering (usually on a flipchart) and put up in a prominent place!

## Clarifying and focusing the group on the objectives

This is a vital stage in the process. It is essential that the whole group is crystal clear about the objectives and outcomes for the session. In the section on preparation we emphasised the importance of getting as much clarification as possible prior to the session. However, sometimes the brief will be vague and therefore there will be a need for the objectives and outcomes to be firmed up at the session. Also, be prepared to find out that the group wants to amend or sometimes set completely new objectives and outcomes. The cardinal rule to remember is that the group must fully own the objectives – they must not be your objectives, or your interpretation of their objectives. Your role is to ensure that they are well defined and expressed in a format that every member of the group understands. It is useful to use the traditional mnemonic of SMART to check out with the group that the objectives are specified in a way that will be most helpful to the group – ie that the objectives are:

Specific: What specifically is the group trying to achieve? For example, in the case of the customer services department discussing their role, the group decided that the specific outcomes it wanted to achieve were:

– a structured analysis of the problems and opportunities facing the department

– a set of performance standards for the whole department

– an action plan for the department for the next six months.

In the case of the group of trainers, the outcomes

were quite clear: to produce four key performance indicators that would enable the training function's performance to be measured. If a group has been charged with looking for solutions to a specific problem, or with coming up with ideas, it is essential to check whether the group is expected to come up with 'the solution' or 'the idea' or a set of options for putting forward to another forum.

**M**easurable: How will the group know that they have achieved the objective? In the case of the two examples above, there are tangible outcomes in terms of whether an action plan or performance standards have been produced. However, it will sometimes be useful to be even more specific and define, for example, what an action plan will consist of and be clear what a performance standard or target will look like. In other cases, for example, the focus groups set up to explore issues and problems, it is not always possible to visualise the final outcome. However, what can be helpful is perhaps to agree the extent of the coverage to ensure that all areas are discussed, such as systems, procedures, skill levels, etc.

**A**greed: The group agrees the objectives – it is worth checking each objective formally and asking for some sign of assent from every member of the group.

**R**ealistic: Does the group have the resources it needs, eg knowledge, skills to achieve the objectives? This is a very important check – there is nothing more frustrating than realising part-way through a session that a key bit of information is missing or a key person who should be involved has been omitted. If there are resources missing it does not necessarily mean that the session should be aborted; it may be possible to obtain the missing information, or the group may decide that it will move forward in the knowledge of the missing resource and seek either to compensate for it or simply acknowledge that the outcomes have been reached without that particular resource.

**T**ime-bounded: Is it clear how much time the group has to achieve the objectives? For example, by when must the final outcome be delivered? By the end of this session, by two weeks after this session, is there a possibility of additional sessions, etc?

Do not seek to rush this stage. Sometimes, if a group feels under the strain of a tight time-scale or wants to get on to other work, then there will be pressure to 'get on with the job'. However, in our experience such groups will almost inevitably find they have to return to this stage at a later point and may find that they have wasted a lot of time in between – rather like the storming stage in the group's development. In fact, this stage often generates the storming phase as the group battles its way to agreement on the objectives. If there is *not* a lot of debate about the objectives, then we start to worry.

### Planning the session

'What? Not more to do before you get on to the real work!' we hear you cry; we see you grimace; we feel your frustration. The answer is yes, but take heart – this is a relatively quick stage and we assure you that as facilitator you will be really glad to have gone through it. A major role for the facilitator is to try to help the group achieve the objectives in the time-scale allotted. This can be an almost impossible task unless you and the group have agreed milestones along the way. For example, focus groups should agree a subdivision of the time for the coverage of each of the identified areas – systems, procedures, skill levels, etc. In the case of the group of trainers who had a day to agree key performance targets for the training function, there was quite a detailed plan drawn up for the process that was going to be used. For example, the group broke down into sub-groups, each exploring a different type of training. There was a time set for the groups to report back, and then for the plenary session, and then for the next stage, and so on.

There is nothing worse than facilitating a group that has had a really productive session generating lots of solutions to a problem and then finding that there are only ten minutes left to evaluate the solutions and prioritise them. We exaggerate to make the point, but we suspect that there will be many readers who will recognise this situation, having experienced it either as a member of a group or, even worse, as the facilitator. Not only is it likely that the evaluation and prioritisation will be inadequate, but the group ends up feeling very frustrated that this key stage has been rushed, and as a result, much of the good work done previously has been wasted.

So our message is: plan the session with your group and then use all your skills to keep the group on target. Sometimes all that is necessary is to remind the group when it should be moving on to the next stage, for example by saying 'We have five minutes left to specify the problem.' On other occasions the group may decide that it needs more time on a particular stage and your role then is to help the group re-plan. Again, just as with the ground rules and the objectives, it is helpful to have the plan put up in a prominent position in the room where all group members can see it. Often, you will not need to intervene formally – just looking at the plan will be enough to get at least one member of the group to seek to move the group on. If the group is really deeply engrossed then it may be necessary to intervene – standing up and walking over to the plan will make the point powerfully.

## Using tools and techniques to solve problems, generate new ideas, take decisions

A key role for the facilitator is to help the group to structure their discussion by using appropriate models, tools and techniques. The facilitator will be expected to be an expert in these 'technical' processes. In the section on preparation we suggested that you began to think about what might be the appropriate process to use in the specific situation you are being asked to facilitate. It is important that you feel confident about when to use a particular model or technique, and how to use it. You will need to be able to explain the process clearly to the group and then help the group to apply it to their issue/problem. However, remember that although looking after the process side of the session is your role, the group must own the process that they use. You can make suggestions, but will need to be prepared to run with what the group decides it wants to do. It is not always easy to manage a process with which you are not familiar, so, as we suggested in the preparation stage, it is very worth while doing your research before the session and identifying if there are any particular models that are popular in that organisation at that time.

There are many general problem-solving models available. Set out below is a seven-step model that we use as a standard approach. This model provides a structure for the problem-solving session and within it we use some tools and techniques for tackling specific stages. The tools and techniques we shall describe are:

■ SWOT (Strengths, Weaknesses, Opportunities, Threats) analysis/PEST (Political, Economic, Social, Technological) analysis

■ Fishbone analysis

■ Force-field analysis

■ Brainstorming.

These are described in detail in Appendices B to E (pages 169–180).

### Seven-step problem-solving model

1    Define the problem clearly. It is vital to start with a clear description and understanding of the current situation. The group needs to establish:

■ what is happening *specifically* – what they are seeing, hearing and feeling that indicates there is a problem

■ at least one recent, concrete *example* of the problem/issue

■ what are the *costs* of the situation in the widest sense and who/which groups are affected

■ who actually *owns* the problem/issue

■ where the impetus for *change* is coming from.

It can be helpful to use a specific model to analyse the situation, such as the SWOT and PEST models described in Appendix B, Fishbone analysis described in Appendix C or Force-field analysis described in Appendix D.

2   Focus on the target. Groups that make the most progress have a clear vision of the desired outcome and direct their efforts towards this vision. Groups that focus on desired outcomes achieve more than groups that focus only on the problem itself. The following steps can help group members develop a 'target':

■ express the target *positively* – what you want to achieve, not what you want to stop happening, eg 'deliver high-quality customer service' rather than 'reduce customer complaints'

■ *visualise* success/the outcome – what you will see, hear and feel

■ ask who else *shares this vision*, who else would like to see this outcome happen and how to involve them in the process

■ identify how achievement of the target will contribute to your *objectives/purpose/mission* – to ensure relevance and congruence to the wider vision.

3   Generate solutions. Encourage people to think widely and creatively for solutions using techniques such as brainstorming – see Appendix E.

4   Evaluate the solutions. This is the stage at which

your facilitation skills become very important in helping the group:

■ *clarify* ideas/solutions, remove duplications

■ '*cluster*' the ideas/solutions – ask the group which ideas/solutions are related, then group them with an appropriate label

■ identify the *criteria* by which the solutions will be evaluated – eg cost, time, need for training – and then methodically evaluate each of the solutions against the criteria. Some of perhaps the more unusual solutions may drop out an early stage. However, do not underestimate the value of, or discard too soon, what seem like bizarre solutions – they may actually be the right ones or spark off a train of thought leading to the right one.

5    Agree (one or more) solutions, depending on your objectives. This may be straightforward in that the *best* solution or solutions are quite clear from the evaluation process of Step 4. However, in the complex world of today this is often not the case – it may come down to judgement. It is at this point that it is important to have agreement on how decisions are to be reached in these situations:

■ By consensus, ie everyone agrees to support the decision as the best way forward, even though it might not be their preferred solution. On the positive side it should ensure everyone's commitment, but on the negative side it may lead to safe/non-controversial solutions rather than the optimum ones. Also, it can be very time consuming. An important part of the process of achieving consensus is to explore the differences between the various solutions and consider 'chunking up' to a level where agreement is possible and then working back from there.

■ By voting, allocating stars or a show of hands – the solution supported by the majority is adopted. Variations on this can be used – the most sophisticated is probably the single transferable vote system. The voting approach has the merits of being fair and being seen to be fair. However, it can be divisive if team members are seen to oppose each other or are seen to be voting in support of their friends/functional colleagues.

6    Agree how the decision is to be communicated and implemented:

■    Who needs to be informed?

■    What information do they need, eg a report to the management team, memos to people involved?

■    Is a detailed plan required for implementation?

7    Check with the whole group for understanding of what has been agreed. Check for commitment – is everyone prepared to proceed with the solution? Actually ask people to commit to it – they may do so, but with some reservations. Check that those reservations will not hinder their part of the implementation. Be prepared on how to handle lack of commitment at this stage – probe what is stopping commitment, etc. There may be occasions when it will not be possible to reach full agreement and it may be necessary to record the dissent in a formal way – perhaps using the mechanism of a minority report.

If you are unfamiliar with or inexperienced in using a particular technique, then it can be helpful to carry out a mock run-through, using the process on the specific issue as part of your preparation. It will give you the opportunity to reflect on any problem areas, for example what may be the best generic categories to use in your Fishbone diagram, what might be a zany contribution to the brainstorming session to get the group thinking creatively, some examples of driving and restraining forces if you are proposing to use Force-field analysis.

Finally, we leave you with the remainder of the quote in Galagan (1993), which we first mentioned in Chapter 2, in which she quotes a warning:

> They [the models] are maps to the territory and not the territory itself. In fact, the more powerful they are to make things clear, the more they can blind people in areas not represented in the model.

Models, process tools and techniques can make an immensely useful contribution to helping the group to structure and analyse its thinking. However, whichever you use will inevitably encourage the group to view the problem/issue/opportunity through that particular filter. It is very important at the end of any session, when using a particular model or technique, to invite the group to step back from the model/technique and review the outcomes from a common sense or model-free point of view.

## Reviewing, learning and moving forward

This is a stage that is often overlooked – the problem is solved, the new ideas generated, now the group can pack its bags and go home. This is a pity, because this is the stage when the group can undertake some really useful learning, about such issues as:

- how well they performed individually as part of that group
- how well the group performed as a whole
- the usefulness of the different models and techniques used.

Reviewing what happened can also be very therapeutic for the group:

- It can provide the opportunity to celebrate what went well – this is very important as a way of reinforcing the processes and behaviours that achieved the results.
- If there were significant problems – perhaps in terms

of the way individuals worked together, or in meeting the time-scales – it is an opportunity to stand back and analyse objectively what occurred. If this process does not take place, then there is a danger that group members will leave feeling frustrated and unhappy, that unhelpful behaviours will not have been tackled, and there may be an unwillingness to work as part of that group again or in similar group sessions.

## Reviewing the process

We would emphasise that this stage concentrates on the *process* – not on reviewing the outcomes. A line needs to be drawn – the outcomes part of the session has been completed and this stage is concentrating solely on reviewing the process of how the group reached these outcomes. We often use questionnaires such as the one in Table 18, and ask the group members to complete these individually – this can often take 10 or 15 minutes. We also complete a similar questionnaire ourselves, as facilitators. We then invite the group members to discuss the issues, taking one question/issue at a time. It is important to emphasise that the purpose of the review is to learn (not to vent their frustration or refight any battles from the session!). In the plenary session, it is helpful to draw out the list of learning points – under the headings of:

▮ as a group member
▮ as a facilitator.

You may be surprised, and indeed feel that we must be masochists, to have the two headings – thinking that the emphasis should be on learning about how to work as part of the group. However, it is very important to have the two headings because:

▮ it makes a statement that you yourself are expecting to learn as the facilitator, and are seeking feedback to help you learn
▮ as facilitator you are part of the group – but your role

is sufficiently distinct for there to be possibly different learning points

▌ all the group members may act as facilitators
themselves in different situations or may become
facilitators.

It also brings us full circle to the point we made in Chapter
1: in the most mature groups everyone is a facilitator.

As a final stage in the review process, invite the group to
record on their questionnaire the learning points that
are most relevant and meaningful for themselves – these
may be from the list derived from the plenary session or
from their own individual reflections.

You can take as little or as long as you like on the review
process. If there are time constraints then you may decide
to go for a simpler approach – perhaps to get the group
members to list the five key aspects they liked about what
happened and the five key aspects they disliked and what
they would wish to do differently. The plenary session can
either be reflective and discursive or short and punchy.
However, our advice is to go through some form of
review process. In organisations that are using the facilitative approach as part of a more major culture shift, the
review process becomes even more vital. It is part of the
organisation's developing a learning culture.

In our experience, although initially some group members start off thinking that such a review may be a waste
of time – 'too much navel-gazing' – they all become
very involved in the discussion and feel that they have
learned a lot. This is often the time when the quiet
members of the group come into their own – they want
either to explain why they found it difficult to participate, or to explain that they participated as much as they
wanted. These group members often have particularly
interesting perspectives on what happened as they have
sometimes operated almost as observers for periods in
the session. For the more dominant members of the

*Table 18*

# REVIEW QUESTIONNAIRE

---

### REVIEWING THE PROCESS – WHAT HAVE YOU LEARNED?

**Section A**

**Please reflect on how you and the group have worked together. Complete this questionnaire honestly. It is for your own private use. However, we shall ask you to share your views with the group.**

**How clear were YOU/the whole group about the objectives of the exercise?** How was the process helped or hindered by this?

**How do you feel about YOUR contribution to the session that has just taken place?** Were you able to say all you wanted to say? How did that influence what happened in the group? Describe how satisfied you were with your participation level/influence. Was working in this group a good experience for you or not? Why was this?

**How did the GROUP perform (content)?** Did the group achieve its objectives within the time-scale allowed? What affected the team's performance? Why was this?

**How did the GROUP perform (personal/interpersonal process)?** How involved were the members of the group – did any group members dominate the group activity/hardly participate at all? What effect did this have on group performance? Did anyone make comments that were particularly helpful to/not well received by the group? What were these comments?

**How did the GROUP perform (technical process)?** What models and processes were used? How helpful or not were they to the group in achieving its objectives?

**How well do you think the FACILITATOR performed?** What did the facilitator do that helped or hindered the group in its performance of the task? What other comments do you have on the performance of the facilitator?

**How do YOU feel at the moment?** What are you particularly pleased about? What could you have done differently? What will you do differently in future sessions?

**Section B**

**This section is for completion after the plenary session as a record and celebration of the learning you have gained by working as part of the group.**

**What are the key learning points from being a group member?**

**What are the key learning points from being a facilitator?**

group it can encourage reflection on their approach. For you, as the facilitator, it provides feedback that is worth its weight in gold. We go on to discuss reviewing your own skills as a facilitator in more depth in the last chapter – Facilitating your Own Development.

As facilitators of learning sessions, we are familiar with the type of self-complete questionnaires, often referred to as 'happy sheets', used at the end of learning sessions. However, these are usually completed individually and are not discussed within the group – they focus on the individual's learning in terms of the achievement of the learning objectives and on the 'trainer's' skills and use a lot of rating scales. There is often little attention paid to the processes used and the way the group learned together. They sometimes appear to be used as vehicles to 'beat up' the trainer rather than as learning tools – there is not sufficient depth of information to gain real insights into what has happened. There are considerable benefits to designing a questionnaire similar to that above and taking the time to review the processes with the learning group.

In the next chapter, we go on to look at a model that is particularly useful for reviewing the way individuals operate within group sessions, and suggest some helpful techniques for approaching challenging situations.

## In brief

- It is important to prepare, in order to:
  - clarify the purpose of the session and the expected outcomes
  - think about the time-scales required
  - obtain background information on the subject area
  - find out about the make-up of the group.
- A major challenge is to help the group get started, by:
  - getting the physical environment right
  - making the introductions
  - establishing ground rules of behaviour

- clarifying and focusing the group on the objectives of the session
- planning the session.

▮ A key role for the facilitator is to help the group to structure their discussion by using appropriate models, tools and techniques, eg

- a problem-solving model
- SWOT/PEST analysis
- Force-field analysis
- Fishbone analysis
- Brainstorming.

▮ A stage that is often overlooked is that of reviewing what happened, in order to learn and move forward. The group can undertake some really useful learning about such issues as:

- how well they performed individually as part of that group
- how well the group performed as a whole
- the usefulness of the different models and techniques used.

Reviewing what happened can also be very therapeutic for the group. Consider using questionnaires and discussing the results with the group.

## Further reading

ROBSON M. *Problem Solving in Groups.* Aldershot, Gower, 1993.

# 7

# Reviewing Group Processes and Dealing with Challenging Situations

## Introduction

In the previous chapter we were concentrating on the more technical processes – the tools and techniques that help the group to structure and analyse the problem, and formulate a solution. In this chapter we focus on the personal and interpersonal processes: how the individual is responding and dealing with a situation and how the individuals within the group are reacting with each other and with the facilitator.

Research (Rackham and Morgan, 1977) identified different types of behaviour that were used regularly by people in group sessions/meetings. Some of these behaviours were positive and helped the business of the session to progress; others were negative in that they hindered the progress of the group towards meeting its objectives. Some of the behaviours are particularly helpful for the facilitator of the sessions and others are more helpful for the group members.

Broadly speaking, the behaviours fall into four distinct categories:

- initiating behaviours
- reacting behaviours
- clarifying behaviours
- process behaviours.

These behaviours are described below in the context of the facilitator's role and in terms of the way in which they are used by group members.

We also address some of the challenging situations that the facilitator and the group might face.

## Helpful and unhelpful behaviours

*Table 19*

### INITIATING BEHAVIOURS

| BEHAVIOUR | DESCRIPTION | USE BY FACILITATOR | USE BY GROUP MEMBERS |
|---|---|---|---|
| *Making content suggestions* | These are suggestions which put forward: <br>■ a new concept, idea, line of thought<br>■ a new perspective on the current idea.<br><br>For example, in a discussion on reducing the number of customer complaints, the suggestion might be made to 'look at the procedures for after-sales care', or in the middle of a discussion on customer care training, that 'the issue might lie with the managerial training rather than with shop-floor training'. | This behaviour is not used a great deal by the facilitator in general group sessions – the facilitator's role is to encourage others to make these suggestions by using questioning skills.<br><br>In learning groups, again the facilitator will be seeking to draw out the new learning ideas from the group. | This is a very helpful behaviour. It is very important that there are sufficient content suggestions to keep the discussion and learning moving forward and to ensure all aspects of issues are covered. |
| *Making process suggestions* | These are suggestions relating to the way in which the group manages its work, eg setting ground rules, using techniques such as brainstorming or SWOT analysis, and to the learning methods used. | This is key behaviour for facilitators. A major part of their role is to ensure that appropriate processes are being used to maximise individuals'/group's effectiveness and learning. | It is very helpful to have process suggestions made by the group members. It is more likely that the group will commit to, and operate, processes for which they feel a sense of ownership. |

| | | | |
|---|---|---|---|
| *Building on suggestions* | A behaviour that extends or builds on others' ideas or suggestions. For example, in response to the content suggestion on managerial training, someone would respond with a question: 'What aspects of managerial training are you thinking about?' or a comment: 'Yes, let's look at what training we give to our first-line supervisors first.' | An important behaviour for the facilitator will be to build on *process* suggestions made by the group members. The facilitator will avoid directly building on content suggestions – the facilitator's role is to encourage others to build on the suggestions by using questioning skills. This can be very important for sometimes key ideas will be overlooked as the group moves forward too quickly on to a new area of discussion. This may happen to the ideas of quieter and less assertive members of the group. | This is a key behaviour for group members. It is very important for ideas and approaches to be explored and developed before the group moves on to a new area of discussion. Otherwise some important ideas can be lost. |

*Table 20*

## REACTING BEHAVIOURS

| BEHAVIOUR | DESCRIPTION | USE BY FACILITATOR | USE BY GROUP MEMBERS |
|---|---|---|---|
| *Agreeing/ supporting* | This is a conscious, open and direct declaration of agreement or support for the ideas and/or suggestions of another member of the group. For example: 'Yes, if we do that, everyone has a chance to get their issues discussed' or 'That's a good idea, | This is not a behaviour used a great deal by the facilitator in general group sessions – he or she must try to remain neutral and draw out the group's response. In learning sessions, from time to time, it may be helpful for the | This can be a very helpful behaviour. It helps the group move towards overall agreement and consensus on issues, and cements learning. It is also very supportive towards individuals. |

| | | | |
|---|---|---|---|
| | it will make a worthwhile con- tribution to saving costs' | facilitator to agree and support some com- ment on aspects of the learning and its process. However, it will always be helpful to seek out the group's views first. | |
| *Disagreeing* | A clear and *honest* statement of dis- agreement *giving reasons*. For example: 'I don't think that change to the pro- cedure will work because it will not give sufficient time for the despatch department to ...' or 'I don't feel it will be effective to use that strategy in my negotiation with my boss because our relationship is so distant.' | As with the previous behaviour, this is not used a great deal by the facilitator – it is better to remain neutral and draw out the group's response. This can be an important role for the facilitator with immature groups, where group members may feel uncomfortable disagreeing with each other. The facilitator can help by explaining that disagreement is as important as agree- ment, and by empha- sising the importance of giving clear reasons for the disagreement. It is also useful to point out that, in disagreeing in a constructive manner, you are commenting on the idea/issue not on the person proposing it. | As with agreeing/ supporting, this is a very helpful behaviour in moving the group towards decision- making and taking on board learning concepts. In immature groups, group members may feel uncomfortable in disagreeing with each other and need to be encouraged to do so. Also, the way that the point of disagreement is made is crucial: that reasons are given and *how* it is expressed in terms of voice, eg calm rather than irritated, and in terms of body language – looking at, but not eye- balling, the individual you are disagreeing with, etc. |

| *Blocking/ difficulty- stating* | Blocking an idea/ suggesting or stating a difficulty *without giving a reason*. For example, 'It won't work.' 'That will cause havoc.' Blocking can be verbal, as in these examples, but it can also be non-verbal such as breaking off eye contact with the speaker and engaging another group member with their eyes, so inviting them to speak. A very common form of blocking is to interrupt/talk over the speaker. | It probably goes with-out saying that this is very unhelpful behavi-our for any facilitator! The facilitator needs to be on the lookout for this type of behaviour in others and be ready to deal with it. It is useful if the ground rules of the behaviour/ learning contract covers it, as you can then simply refer to these. Otherwise, try question-ing to encourage the blocker to be more constructive, eg 'What are the reasons why it won't work?' For dealing with inter-rupting/talking-over see later in the chapter. | It is equally and obviously unhelpful behaviour from group members. Sometimes the behaviour happens through thought-lessness – it is a quick, instinctive reaction to an idea – and the individual will respond to questioning about the reasons for the blocking statement. Sometimes it is more deliberate, as a member of the group tries to block a particular proposal or a specific individual's ideas. |
| :-- | :-- | :-- | :-- |
| *Defending/ attacking* | This is defensive behaviour which seeks to strengthen your own position or diminish the ideas of another member of the group by attack-ing their contribution, eg 'That's typical of you: you never give me the information in sufficient time to do anything with it!' or 'We would have completed the exercise if you had given us a proper briefing!' | Again, it probably goes without saying that this is very unhelpful behaviour for a facilitator! The facilitator needs to be alert to this type of behaviour in others and be ready to deal with it. Yet again, it is useful if the ground rules of behaviour cover this type of behaviour as you can simply refer to these. See later in the chapter for other strategies to help in this situation. | This is equally and obviously unhelpful behaviour from group members. It can often result from existing patterns of behaviour that were established long before the group met on this par-ticular occasion. It can be very destructive behaviour. |

*Table 21*

# CLARIFYING BEHAVIOURS

| BEHAVIOUR | DESCRIPTION | USE BY FACILITATOR | USE BY GROUP MEMBERS |
|---|---|---|---|
| *Checking understanding* | A behaviour which seeks to establish whether you have understood what someone else has said, eg 'Tom, when you said you wanted more time, did you mean for the planning stage?' | A key role for the facilitator is to clarify points and ensure the group has a common understanding of issues and areas of learning. | It is also very helpful behaviour for group members. A mature group that is operating at peak effectiveness will display a lot of this type of behaviour. |
| *Summarising* | Gathering together the discussion to date in a succinct way, so that all members of the group can go forward with a clear and common understanding of what has been said, agreed or learned. It is important that no new ideas are included and that the summarising is factual and does not include the summariser's own opinions. | This is another key behaviour for the facilitator. It is an important technique for keeping the group on track and focused on the objectives. It is also a key behaviour in helping the group to structure their learning experiences. | This is also a helpful behaviour for group members, but is more likely to be undertaken by the person in the facilitator role. |
| *Seeking information* | Seeking facts and opinions, drawing out learning from others, using a range of questioning skills. | Another important role for the facilitator is to use his or her questioning skills to open up issues, probe, explore learning experiences, etc. | This is also a helpful behaviour from group members. |

| | | | |
|---|---|---|---|
| *Giving information* | Offering facts, opinions and clarification to others. | In general group sessions, the facilitator is an expert in the processes – not the content. To maintain neutrality the facilitator should always avoid offering opinions. However, he or she may need to input factual information from time to time if it is not available from within the group. This will be a more frequent behaviour in learning groups. | It is important for group members to contribute information, particularly from their areas of expertise and based on their experiences. |
| *Disclosure* | Displaying vulnerability by freely admitting mistakes, sharing feelings. | It sometimes can be useful for the facilitator to share with the group how he or she feels about what is happening in the group/process. For example, to say: 'I am concerned that we are losing sight of the objective of . . .' Or 'I feel that the process I suggested is not helping to move the discussion forward. How do you feel about it?' | This type of behaviour can be helpful at the appropriate time. For example, a group member may say 'I'm sorry, I do not understand what you all have been talking about for the last 10 minutes.' However, it can be used to avoid issues and conflict to the detriment of the group objectives. For example, to say 'I just do not feel equipped to comment on the proposal or give any feedback' is not helpful. |

*Table 22*

# PROCESS BEHAVIOURS

NB: Process behaviours in this model relate to the way the *group processes* work.

| BEHAVIOUR | DESCRIPTION | USE BY FACILITATOR | USE BY GROUP MEMBERS |
|---|---|---|---|
| *Bringing in* | Encourages the in-volvement of another person in the dis-cussion by directing comments or questions at them. For example, saying: 'Jane, we would value your comments on . . .' or 'Simon, what do you think was the key learning point?' | A key role of the facilitator is to en-courage participation by all group members. The facilitator will be monitoring the group the whole time and in particular will be looking out for group members who are not participating. | This is very helpful and supportive behaviour by group members. It can be rather artificial and intrusive for the facilitator to be intervening, and may come more naturally from within the group. |
| *Shutting out* | Excluding another person from the discussion, often by ignoring someone's contribution, inter-rupting or answering a question directed at someone else. | This is clearly very un-helpful behaviour for a facilitator! It is very destructive behaviour if it occurs in a group and the facilitator will want to take action quickly when it does. It is difficult to deal with, and usually the easiest way is to refer to the ground rules/ learning contract. For other strategies see later in this chapter. | This is a very un-helpful behaviour. Sometimes it is done unconsciously because someone simply does not rate another member's views very highly. They may not be aware how obviously they are displaying this lack of respect. On other occasions it will be a deliberate attempt to dominate the discussion and/or individual members of the group. |

The above model is a very useful way of monitoring individual and group behaviour. For groups that will be working together over a period of time it can be very helpful to introduce them to the model. The approach we take is to put simplified versions of Tables 19 to 22 on to OHP slides leaving the last two columns blank, and then to invite the group to comment on whether the behaviours are helpful or unhelpful. It is an excellent way of establishing some very important ground rules of behaviour for the group, and also of clarifying the role of the facilitator in general group sessions. It can also make it easier for you and other group members to comment on the unhelpful behaviours, as you have established a 'language' for describing them. Sometimes a group will become so comfortable with using the model that someone just has to say 'blocking' to nip in the bud a piece of poor behaviour. It will certainly increase awareness of both helpful and unhelpful behaviours.

The model can also provide a very useful structure for a group to review how it is working together. Sometimes we are asked to come in as consultants to help a group to improve its performance. It may be a work team that is finding its regular meetings unproductive, or a project team that wants some assistance in reaching peak performance quickly. Often we observe the group over a couple of sessions using the structure of behaviours set out earlier, and record the frequency of behaviours displayed by the individual members of the group, with some examples of particular key behaviours. We then present the results to the group. It is quite fascinating how using this model can readily identify the problem areas. For example, with one group there was very little building on suggestions and a lot of blocking behaviours. As a result the group tended not to follow up or conclude on useful ideas. Describing the patterns of behaviours enables groups both readily to identify the causes of unproductive sessions and to plan the action that needs to be taken.

## Dealing with challenging situations

However skilled and experienced the facilitator, and however mature the group, there will be occasions when a member or members of the group find themselves at odds with what is going on. Whatever the reason, it is important that the facilitator has a range of strategies for dealing with these situations. While we would resist the suggestion that there might be standard 'recipes' for dealing with standard 'challenging situations', it is important that facilitators are able to respond in an appropriate way. In this way, the energy and expertise of the group members are maintained and channelled into the session objectives rather than into unproductive activities.

Dealing effectively with these situations helps to:

▌ maintain the group environment as a place where individuals can be open, frank and honest with their contributions

▌ harness the full potential of the group

▌ maintain group motivation and morale by staying within accepted rules/norms of behaviour.

The best method of dealing with situations is to anticipate them by staying in touch with group behaviour by:

▌ monitoring energy levels and maintaining the middle ground between boredom and overload

▌ being aware of signs of confusion or lack of understanding, particularly of group processes

▌ identifying signs of group member avoidance, withdrawal or moving into 'comfort zone'

▌ staying alert for unacceptable intra-group behaviour which might frustrate the facilitation process.

## Some useful strategies

The strategies involve a combination of the key facilitation skills of building and maintaining rapport, active listening and observing, and masterly questioning.

### Lack of involvement of the whole group

▮ Go round the group asking each member in turn what he or she thinks about the issue under consideration, causing each member to speak; start with something relatively unthreatening and build from there.

▮ Describe the behaviour you are experiencing, the effect this is having, and make a process suggestion to get things moving, eg 'Things seem to have gone a bit quiet. We seem to have stalled. Would it help if we had a summary as to where we were at?'

▮ Be comfortable with silence yourself: legitimise it with the group, eg 'Well there seems to be a lot of thinking going on. Let's take a five-minute thinking break.'

▮ Use safer, less threatening areas for discussion, if possible, until the group feels more confident/mature.

### Lack of involvement of individual(s)

▮ Involve the individual at a safer, less threatening level, so allowing him or her to develop the confidence needed to get involved and/or challenge the real issues. For example, ask direct questions of the individual in areas where you know he or she has expertise.

▮ Confront the issue (gently) with the individual concerned, eg 'Sally, you seem to be quietly thinking about the issues: is there something you would like to say about . . .?'

▮ Find out if the non-involvement is due to a process issue which you can clarify, eg the person does not understand the process of brainstorming or how a learning exercise is to be run.

▮ If the problem is just one or two individuals, talk to them privately during a break and explain the value of the contributions they can make.

## Avoidance of issues

■ Describe to the individual or the group exactly what you see, without interpretation, so that they can see the consequences of their non-involvement or avoidance, by gently asking for an explanation of what you have observed, eg 'Chris, whenever we get on to the subject of managing diversity you go very quiet or raise a completely different issue. Is there some sort of a problem with managing diversity?'

■ If just one or two individuals are involved, talk to them privately during a break and explore the reasons for their behaviour.

## Cynicism

■ Encourage the cynic(s) to get their cynicism off their chest and express their feelings to the group.

■ Accept an individual cynical remark as a legitimate contribution. Thank the person, seek clarification and work through the consequences openly. If there is any validity in what has been said, accept this and use the contribution. Often the cynic is the person who has an interesting perspective on the real issues!

■ Ask the rest of the group for their views on the issue. Peer group response is often the most powerful way for dealing with unhelpful cynicism. On the other hand, if the views are shared more widely, it may be important to bring them to the surface and deal with the issues – it is unlikely that the group will progress until this happens.

■ Respond to cynical views with facts and information (maintaining your neutrality, possibly by asking the appropriate questions to generate the information from other members of the group).

■ Remember that cynicism often comes from the ADAPTED CHILD state – try not to let it 'hook' your CONTROLLING PARENT: lead them into ADULT using the strategies above.

## Blocking and shutting out (interruptions/talking over)

I Remind participants of the contract, the ground rules they entered into at the beginning of the facilitation process; be firm with this *discipline* if the behaviour continues, explaining the problems of people not being allowed to speak without being interrupted, explaining the need to balance their contributions with the need to listen to the contributions of others.

I Acknowledge the interruption and offer to deal with it later when the timing might be more appropriate.

I Try your non-verbal gestures, facial expression, etc, to head off the interrupter.

I With typical blocking statements like 'It won't work' or 'It can't be done that way', explore the reasons for the statement. For example, say 'What makes you think the new procedure won't work?' or 'What specific problems do you foresee in implementing the new system?'

## Irrelevant contributions

I First, be careful; who is to say that the contribution is irrelevant before it has been tested? It is just possible the individual has seen a unique breakthrough idea or an unusual and perceptive aspect of the learning process, so check it out. For example, ask 'Joan, where does what you have just said fit in with our objective?' or 'David, that is an interesting comment – how does that relate to the ... model?'

I If in doubt about the relevance, work with the individual, by probing, to try to establish the relevance of what he or she is saying.

I Be quick to refocus the group on the objective(s) if the contribution is irrelevant.

## Anger

I Acknowledge their anger and empathise with them, even when you feel that their anger is unjustified, eg

'I understand that you feel angry ... why do you think the report is phrased in that way?'

∎ Try to identify the source and direction of their anger, using probing questions.

∎ Reflect back the content of what they have said in more neutral and unemotional language. For example, if they say 'Clearly, nobody was interested in or valued my feedback', reflect back with 'I appreciate that you were disappointed that your comments were not included in the report.' Use your voice to match the emotion, but at a lower energy level.

∎ If possible, work through the reasons why they feel as they do, dealing with the source of the anger if you can.

∎ Remember that anger is coming from either the CONTROLLING PARENT or very often the ADAPTED CHILD state. Lead them back to the ADULT state – questioning is a very powerful tool here.

## Lack of tolerance

∎ Set out for the group member precisely what you are seeing and hearing, without any interpretation, so giving him or her the opportunity to see how he or she is coming across. For example, 'Pat, I notice that every time someone in the group uses the words 'politically correct' you shake your head and close your eyes. Is there something you want to share with us about this issue?'

∎ Encourage the individual to raise his or her awareness of the intolerance, and understand the consequences of the behaviour he or she is demonstrating, by asking appropriate questions, eg 'Pat, what effect do you think it has when you read your notes while Dee is speaking?'

∎ Remind the group of the ground rules for behaviour.

## Individuals who talk at length and without focus

∎ If the contribution is sound but is stopping other

group members making a contribution, thank them for their valuable contribution and suggest that it would be useful to get others' perspectives now before they move on.

▍ If the group member appears to have lost focus, say 'Lyn, it would be helpful if you could explain how your comments relate to the objectives.'

▍ Remind the group of the ground rules for giving people time and space to contribute.

## Individuals who resist consensus

▍ Use your probing skills to identify clearly and specifically the areas of disagreement so that these can be discussed.

▍ 'Chunk up' – seek to find a level of agreement that the individual can buy into, and work from there. For example, if the group was discussing approaches to cost-cutting and was finding it difficult to reach agreement on specific costs to be cut, you would 'chunk up' to a level where they could all agree – perhaps on the level of cost savings required and how they should be apportioned across different areas, eg distribution, marketing, etc, and then work back down to the detail.

▍ Describe, without interpretation, what you are seeing or hearing and the consequences for the group if consensus is not reached.

These are just a sample of situations and examples of strategies to use. By being in rapport with the group and by actively listening to and observing individuals within the group, you will identify when there may be the need for the sort of process interventions described above. By identifying the PARENT/ADULT/CHILD states of the 'challenging' person you will also more readily determine the appropriate intervention to make.

## In brief

▪ Using a model of helpful and unhelpful behaviours can provide a beneficial basis:
  ☐ for ensuring that the group works productively together
  ☐ for reviewing the group's processes.

▪ There is a range of strategies that the facilitator might consider when dealing with challenging situations, such as lack of involvement of the whole group or individuals, avoidance of issues, cynicism, blocking and shutting-out behaviours, irrelevant contributions, anger, lack of tolerance, individuals' talking at length and without focus, and resistance to consensus.

# 8
# Facilitating Your Own Development

We hope that we have convinced you of two important principles:

■ We never stop learning, and the key to effective learning is understanding the process of learning.

> Human beings are unique among all living organisms in that their primary adaptive specialisation lies not in some particular form or skill or fits in an ecological niche, but rather in identification with the process of adaptation itself – in the process of learning. We are thus the learning species. (Kolb, 1984)

■ Using a facilitative approach to learning and working with groups helps to support and enhance the learning process, and hence personal development.

These principles apply particularly powerfully to your development as a facilitator. Being a facilitator requires a very high level of communication skills:

■ the ability to establish and maintain rapport with the group/individuals

■ being able to pick up all the signals that provide the vital information on how well the group/individuals are working

■ excellent questioning skills to draw out the learning/solutions from the group/individuals

■ the ability to sift and sort information to help structure the learning and problem-solving process.

Being a facilitator requires developing expertise in the processes of facilitation:

▌ the technical processes to do with learning methods, problem-solving, etc

▌ the group processes to do with helping the group to work together effectively to achieve its objectives.

Finally, being a facilitator means seeing yourself, as Berry (1993) puts it, as some sort of a medieval alchemist whose goal is to turn base metal into gold – experimenting with processes to achieve this aim. It is about maximising individuals' contributions to group working and their potential for learning by empowering them to take control, responsibility and ownership for their own efforts.

You never stop improving these skills. From every experience you have of operating as a facilitator, working as part of a group, observing group situations or simply in everyday communication situations, you learn about what works and what does not work, and in what circumstances. However, if in addition you deploy your skills of structuring the feedback you get from these experiences, you can maximise this learning. The sources of feedback are:

▌ yourself

▌ other members of the group

▌ observers, where they exist.

In Chapter 6 we discussed a process for structuring the feedback from group members (and which could be used in a similar way for observers). Here we are going to concentrate on structuring self-feedback. We suggest that you develop a series of questions that cause you to examine the application of your skills and the resulting outcomes (see Table 23, for example).

*Table 23*

# SELF-FEEDBACK QUESTIONS

**Process skills**

 1  How adequate was my planning for the learning/problem-solving session?

 2  How comfortable was the group with the learning objectives/objectives for the session? (Review the process you used for agreeing the objectives.)

 3  How appropriate were the learning objectives to the aim(s) of the session?

 4  How adequate were the learning contract/ground rules of behaviour that were established by the group? (Review the process you used to arrive at these.)

 5  How appropriate were the technical processes – eg models, learning methods – used? (Review each technical process.)

 6  How well did I build and maintain rapport with the group/individuals? (List examples of strong rapport and when rapport broke down – analyse what happened.)

 7  How well did I pick up the verbal and non-verbal signals from the group? (List examples of useful signals picked up and those missed, and what were the implications.)

 8  How effectively did I use my questioning skills? (List examples of particularly effective and less effective questions.)

 9  How effectively was information sorted and recorded?

10  How well timed was the session?

11  How neutral was I in the process? (To what extent did I impose my own ideas and ways of doing things on the group?)

12  How effective was the review and close down of the group? (Review the process and the learning outcomes.)

**Outcomes**

13  How well were the learning objectives achieved? (Address each in turn.)

14  To what extent has the aim been achieved?

15  How was responsibility and ownership shared between me and the group?

16  How did the group/individuals feel at the end of the session?

17  What did the group/individuals learn from working as part of that group?

**Key learning points**

18  Reflecting on the answers to the above questions, what are the key learning points for me? (Reinforce the positive points and express areas of improvement constructively.)

**Follow-up action**

19  What further action do I need to take to support the achievement of the aim and outcomes? (These may have been agreed during the group session or may have occurred to you as a result of reflecting on the process and outcomes. For example, you may have agreed to finalise and distribute a record of the session, or decided that on reflection an individual may benefit from further coaching, or noted that issues have arisen regarding the achievement of the aim that it would be helpful for you to follow up with the appropriate people.)

20  What action do I need to take to continue my development as a facilitator? (Would I benefit from training or coaching in aspects of my facilitation skills? Would I find it helpful to receive more feedback? Are there key areas that I will concentrate on during the next session when I am the facilitator?

It is important to review and record what went well, as well as the areas where you felt that you could have done better. This review should be a celebration of success as well as an opportunity to learn.

We see our facilitation skills as a tree – the roots are the core skills and behaviours that we discuss in Chapters 2, 3 and 4; these must be strong and healthy for the tree to grow and develop. Just as our tree needs sun and rain to grow, so do we need experiences to try out our facilitation skills and gain feedback from them. Just as our tree extracts the nutrients from the soil using the sun and rain, so we extract the learning from our experiences. We use these to develop straight and substantial branches – the processes we use, covered in Chapters 5, 6 and 7.

We visualise our tree as an oak of about 40 years old – it is well established, with a strong root system and a fine network of branches, and it has a good coverage of shiny green leaves that continuously wave and rustle in the wind as they seek out the sun and the rain. We look forward to its growing into a fully mature oak – one of those splendid parkland trees! We hope that you, too, will enjoy the experience of becoming an expert facilitator – create your own vision or metaphor for what this means to you. The individuals and groups that you will work with will take the knowledge and skills you share with them as a role model, so you will also be shaping a veritable forest of your own 'facilitation' trees!

## In brief

- You never stop improving your skills as a facilitator. With every experience you have as a facilitator – working as part of a group, etc – you are continually learning.

- You can maximise this learning by seeking feedback – from other members of the group, observers and, in particular, yourself. Consider developing a set of questions that causes you to reflect on your skills and behaviours as a facilitator.

- Visualise yourself developing as a facilitator – perhaps growing from a sapling or partly mature tree into one of those really fine substantial trees, or perhaps as a fledgling learning to fly and enjoying the freedom and fun of soaring through the skies.

# Appendix A: Different Media for Recording Information

| MEDIUM | ADVANTAGES/ DISADVANTAGES | TIPS |
|--------|----------------------------|------|
| FLIPCHART | ▌ cheap to buy or hire<br>▌ easy to move from place to place and within a room<br>▌ large capacity for recording information<br>▌ flexible in terms of being able to tear off sheets and display material around the room<br>▌ provides a permanent record<br>▌ relatively inflexible in that once information is recorded it cannot easily be amended. | ▌ consider using more than one flipchart – it is often helpful to have several areas for recording information<br>▌ think very hard about where you locate the flipchart(s), so that they provide maximum visibility for the group but easy accessibility for the facilitator – you don't want to be tripping over them all the time<br>▌ identify suitable locations in the room for displaying sheets once completed<br>▌ identify how you are going to secure the sheets, eg using ready-made rails (make sure you know how to use them: there is definitely a knack with them – we speak from bitter experience of struggling with them ourselves), Blue-Tack or drawing-pins<br>▌ make sure that you have an adequate supply of paper and flipchart pens in a range of colours<br>▌ take into account their inflexibility in terms of erasing/rearranging material by: |

|  |  |  | – planning the structure of how you are going to record the information<br>– leaving plenty of space to allow you to fill in and add bits<br>▮ be careful where you position yourself to write on the flipchart so as not to block the visibility of the chart<br>▮ concentrate on developing the technique of writing on the charts without turning your back on the group – it is possible by standing sideways-on<br>▮ practise writing to ensure, in terms of size of lettering, etc, that the material is fully visible to all the group. |
|---|---|---|---|
| WHITE-BOARDS |  | ▮ often supplied as part of the fixtures of rooms<br>▮ some flexibility of positioning if they are the type that run on rails, but not as flexible in this respect as the flipcharts as they are always on a wall, and the fixed variety are completely inflexible<br>▮ very flexible in terms of being able to erase and amend information<br>▮ limited capacity<br>▮ no permanent record. | ▮ make sure that the whiteboard is clean<br>▮ check that you have the appropriate pens – they will be marked as suitable for whiteboards – some pens are not erasable (except with some difficulty)<br>▮ ensure that you have an eraser<br>▮ use only where you know that you will be able to record all the information you need on the whiteboard and that you do not require a permanent record<br>▮ be careful where you position yourself to write on the whiteboard so as not to block the visibility of the chart<br>▮ concentrate on developing the technique of writing on the board without turning your back on the group – it is possible by standing sideways-on<br>▮ practise writing to ensure, in terms of size of lettering, etc, that the material is fully visible to all the group. |

| | | |
|---|---|---|
| ELECTRONIC WHITEBOARDS | ▮ these have the same advantages and dis-advantages as white-boards except it is possible to produce a permanent record; the record is produced on A4 paper, which can be photocopied for circulation. | ▮ tips as above, except there is the added flexibility of providing a permanent record<br>▮ use when it is helpful to have a permanent record. |
| OVERHEAD PROJECTOR SLIDES/STRIP | ▮ included for com-pleteness, but is not often used for recording information during a session, although it can be useful in specific situations, eg doing a worked example<br>▮ relatively small area of space visible at one time<br>▮ material can be erased, but in practice is not very flexible for grouping information and adding bits<br>▮ no permanent record is available during the session but you can photocopy the slides for use after the session<br>▮ often used for pre-senting information and it can be helpful to use a different system for recording information from the group to emphasise the change of owner-ship of the information. | ▮ most useful for doing complex worked examples where you are engaging the group in the process, eg working out critical paths on project network, or doing a costing exercise<br>▮ check the best position to prevent blocking the screen as you are writing<br>▮ be clear on the process to be used because it is not easy to backtrack and amend (neatly!)<br>▮ check pens to be used – non-permanent and of appropriate thickness – 'fine' is often best for this type of work. |
| COMPUTER-ASSISTED PRESENTATION SYSTEMS | ▮ most commonly used for pre-prepared pre-sentations, not often used for recording information | ▮ need to be skilled to use the system effectively (or have a skilled 'scribe')<br>▮ can be used as a second stage – perhaps using |

| | | |
|---|---|---|
| | ▪ are highly flexible in allowing for rearrange-ment of information<br>▪ can provide a well-designed and typed permanent record<br>▪ need careful management of the lighting environment<br>▪ it is difficult to facili-tate and operate the keyboard – you really need a separate 'scribe'. | flipcharts for brainstorming the ideas, then transferring to this system to structure and evaluate them. |
| BESPOKE SYSTEMS | ▪ these are usually designed for a specific situation, although some facilitators have developed their own systems, eg using large boards covered in coloured paper to which large cards for comments/ideas, etc can be attached<br>▪ such a system allows for easy groupings of ideas/comments, additions, deletions – permitting a high degree of flexibility<br>▪ unlike using standard Post-it notes, these cards are very visible<br>▪ can be free-standing or designed for wall mounting, so can provide a permanent record through the session<br>▪ can be photographed to provide a per-manent record for use after the session<br>▪ can be bulky to carry around. | ▪ these types of systems can be very useful for problem-solving and developing ideas and initiatives<br>▪ be imaginative with use of colour<br>▪ encourage participants to write brief comments/details in large and legible writing to ensure visibility<br>▪ plan where the boards will be located during and after use. |

# Appendix B: SWOT Analysis/PEST Analysis

This is a very useful process for analysing the current position of an organisation or part of an organisation. The process structures the analysis under the four headings of:

## Strengths/weaknesses

This looks at the *internal* strengths/weaknesses of the organisation in terms of such areas as:

- human resources – numbers, skills, motivation, etc
- physical assets – buildings, equipment, etc
- technology – IT, procedures
- organisational structure/culture
- product – range, branding
- finance – strength of profit-and-loss account, balance sheet, cash flow.

## Opportunities/threats

This looks at the *external* opportunities and threats posed by the outside environment in terms of such areas as:

- the economic situation, eg changes in interest rates, the strength of the £
- the competitors, eg what are are current competitors doing, are new competitors coming into the market?

▌ technological change, eg how will new developments in technology affect the organisation?

▌ government policy/legislation, eg the impact of new policy/legislation such as on health and safety, working hours, food hygiene, animal welfare, etc

▌ social change, eg type of leisure pursuits, demographic changes such as an ageing population.

This can be adapted to audit the current state of a particular department or team. In this case the strengths/weaknesses focus on the team and its contribution to the whole organisation, and the opportunities/threats can be both external to the team but within the organisation and external to the organisation as a whole – see the following example.

*Example: Department/team X*

| STRENGTHS | WEAKNESSES |
|---|---|
| Enthusiastic/motivated staff | Fire-fighting/no time for strategic thinking |
| Expertise – product/job knowledge | Processes/procedures – need review |
| Low staff turnover (can be a weakness as well) | Outdated IT |
| | Poor junior/supervisory management skills |
| Getting things done/crisis management | Lack of empowerment of front-line staff |
| Honest/straightforward approach | Lack of internal profile |
| |    – ability to influence business |
| |    – understanding of work of the department |
| |    – not change-oriented |
| | Lack of analytical/planning activities/skills |
| | Geographical dispersion of staff/offices |
| | Lack of proactivity |
| | Lack of political acumen |

| OPPORTUNITIES | THREATS |
|---|---|
| Expansion of company | Budget/staff cuts |
| Development of new products/services | Take-over bid for company |
| New technology | Proposed merger with department Y |
| Training to develop R&D skills | Increasing quality standards required |
| Business process engineering (could be a threat!) | by customers |
| Organisational cultural initiative on customer service | |

Another common model used to analyse organisational performance is PEST:

▐ **P**olitical

▐ **E**conomic

▐ **S**ocial

▐ **T**echnological.

The PEST model can be either used on its own or combined with a SWOT analysis, using each of the four factors as a structure for looking at the strengths, weaknesses, opportunities and threats in turn.

# Appendix C: Fishbone Analysis

The name derives from the finished diagram, which looks like the skeleton of a fish. It is a very useful way of clearly distinguishing between cause and effect, and indeed these diagrams are sometimes called cause-and-effect diagrams or Ishikawa diagrams (after their Japanese orginator). They encourage the group to look at a wide range of causes rather than focusing on a few obvious ones. The process is as follows:

STEP 1  Write the *effect* on the far right-hand side of the flipchart or whiteboard. (A whiteboard is easier to use because there may be quite a lot of amending and re-sorting of the information.) It is very important to express the effect in terms as specific as possible. So, for example, if the effect was 'high turnover of staff', you may need to discuss with the group whether they want to explore the causes of turnover of all staff, or of specific categories only, such as supervisory staff or computer technicians. The more general the effect the more general will be the causes.

STEP 2  Draw in the main bones of the fish, labelling each with a generic area of cause, eg

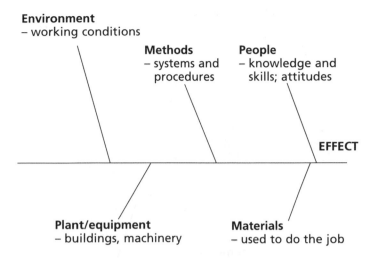

**Environment**
– working conditions

**Methods**
– systems and
  procedures

**People**
– knowledge and
  skills; attitudes

**EFFECT**

**Plant/equipment**
– buildings, machinery

**Materials**
– used to do the job

You can use whatever generic areas are most suited to the issue or organisation. For example, if you are discussing staff turnover you may decide that 'plant/ equipment' is not a useful heading and you may wish to subdivide the 'systems and procedures' heading into 'HR systems and procedures' and 'other systems and procedures'. For example, it may be appropriate to use the headings from an organisation's quality model.

Step 3  Brainstorm the list of causes (see Appendix E for details of how to set up a brainstorming session). Whoever is recording will need to try to list the causes in the appropriate part of the diagram – on the appropriate rib. If the ideas are coming thick and fast, all the recorder may be able to do is write them down somewhere and be prepared to re-categorise them at the end of the brainstorming session. Also, some causes on the same rib may be linked and it is helpful to have a sub-rib. For example, take the rib, 'people' in the effect 'customer complaints':

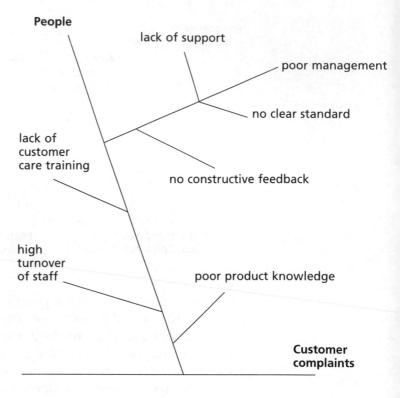

**People**

lack of support

poor management

no clear standard

lack of
customer
care training

no constructive feedback

high
turnover
of staff

poor product knowledge

**Customer
complaints**

STEP 4    Give the group some time to step back from
the process: perhaps five to ten minutes of
quiet thought, or over a cup of coffee. Ask
the group to review the diagram for:

- completeness – have all the causes been
identified?

- criticality – which are the key causes? The
Pareto principle tells us that 80 per cent of
the effect is likely to result from 20 per cent
of the causes.

STEP 5    Add any missing causes and identify the critical causes by circling them on the diagram.

# Appendix D: Force-field Analysis

Force-field Analysis was developed by Kurt Lewin. It encourages the group to visualise the problem in terms of a balance between two opposing sets of forces:

■ the driving forces – which are pushing to make the problem or current situation better

■ the restraining forces – which are pushing to make the problem or current situation worse.

STEP 1    Set out on a flipchart the following:

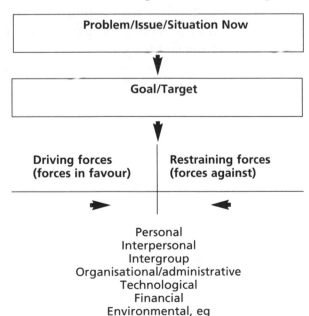

STEP 2:    Fill in the Problem/Issue/Situation Now and Goal/Target boxes.

STEP 3:    Make a list of all the forces that might restrain or oppose a solution/change. Rank them in order of the forces that are the strongest and therefore might be most difficult to overcome. List them on the right-hand side of the chart. It is often helpful to indicate the strength of the restraining force by drawing an arrow under each force, the length representing the degree of opposition that might be encountered.

STEP 4:    Then make a list of the driving forces – those that encourage and facilitate change. Rank them and depict them, as in Step 3, on the left-hand side of the chart. The aim is to capitalise on those that will make the greatest contribution    to    resolving    the problem/bringing about the desired change.

NB It can be helpful to use the brainstorming technique (see Appendix E) to generate the list of the driving and restraining forces.

*Example 1*

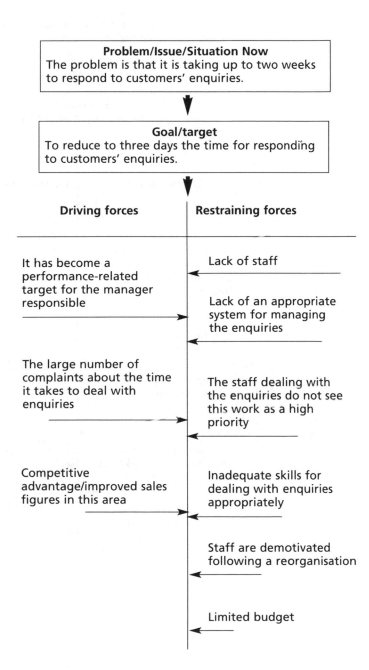

**Problem/Issue/Situation Now**
The problem is that it is taking up to two weeks to respond to customers' enquiries.

**Goal/target**
To reduce to three days the time for responding to customers' enquiries.

| Driving forces | Restraining forces |
|---|---|

It has become a performance-related target for the manager responsible

Lack of staff

Lack of an appropriate system for managing the enquiries

The large number of complaints about the time it takes to deal with enquiries

The staff dealing with the enquiries do not see this work as a high priority

Competitive advantage/improved sales figures in this area

Inadequate skills for dealing with enquiries appropriately

Staff are demotivated following a reorganisation

Limited budget

*Example 2*

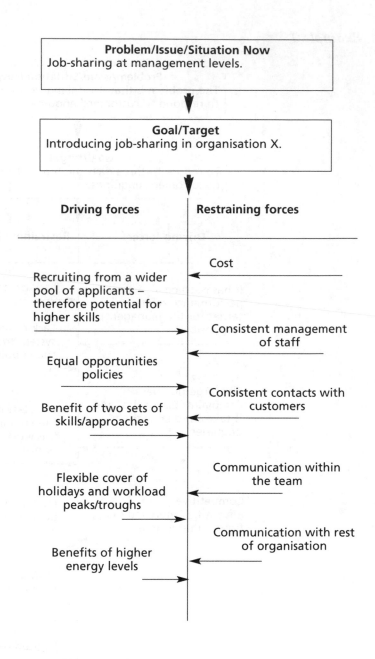

**Problem/Issue/Situation Now**
Job-sharing at management levels.

**Goal/Target**
Introducing job-sharing in organisation X.

**Driving forces**                     **Restraining forces**

                                        Cost

Recruiting from a wider
pool of applicants –
therefore potential for
higher skills

                                        Consistent management
                                        of staff

Equal opportunities
policies

                                        Consistent contacts with
                                        customers

Benefit of two sets of
skills/approaches

                                        Communication within
                                        the team

Flexible cover of
holidays and workload
peaks/troughs

                                        Communication with rest
                                        of organisation

Benefits of higher
energy levels

# Appendix E: Brainstorming

STEP 1: Introduce the purpose of brainstorming: eg 'to encourage creative thinking and generate ideas'.

Set a time-scale – this will depend on the nature of the problem, but is usually short, eg between five and 20 minutes. A tight time restraint encourages a rapid pace and raises the energy levels.

Select a recorder and set up a flipchart to record the ideas.

STEP 2    Clarify and write the focus of the brainstorming session on the top of the flipchart.

STEP 3    Review the ground rules:

■ go for quantity – as many and as bizarre as possible

■ piggyback – if someone else's idea triggers a slight variation for you, call it out

■ no evaluation – all ideas are accepted and valuable, no judgement of ideas or comments on them are allowed at this time

■ everyone to participate – start with each team member contributing in sequence, but allow people to pass and butt in (see piggy-backing, above) – if a lot of people pass, open it up

▍ encourage the team to have fun – to laugh *with* the wild ideas not *at* them

▍ record all ideas visibly

▍ stop immediately at the end of the allotted time.

# References

BATESON G. (1972) *Steps to an Ecology of Mind*. London, Ballantine.

BEE F. *and* Bee R. (1994) *Training Needs Analysis and Evaluation*. London, Institute of Personnel and Development.

BEE R. *and* BEE F. (1997) *Project Management: The people challenge*. London. Institute of Personnel and Development.

BENTLEY T. (1994) 'Facilitation'. *Training Officer*. Vol. 30, No. 6, July–August. pp 184–186.

BERRY (1993) 'Changing perspectives on skills development'. *Journal of European Industrial Training*. Vol. 17, No. 3. pp 23–32

BOON M. (1998) Unpublished material from conference 'Getting a Return on Development', IPD, Central London Board.

DEWY J. (1938) *Experience and Education*. Kappa Delta Pi.

GALAGAN P. A. (1993) 'Helping groups learn'. *Training and Development*. October. pp 57–61.

HANDY (1989) *The Age of Unreason*, London, Business Books.

HARDINGHAM A. (1996) *Designing Training*. London. Institute of Personnel and Development.

HART (1992) *Faultless Facilitation*. London, Kogan Page.

HONEY P *and* MUMFORD A. (1986) *The Manual of Learning Styles*. Maidenhead, Honey.

KEETON M. *and* TATE P. (1978) *Learning by Experience: What, why, how.* San Francisco, Calif., Jossey-Bass.

KOLB D. A. (1984) *Experiential Learning.* New York, Prentice-Hall.

LONG R. F. (1992) 'The journey to strategic facilitation'. *Journal of European Industrial Training.* Vol. 16, No. 6. pp 22–31.

MCGREGOR D. (1961) *The Human Side of Enterprise.* Maidenhead, McGraw-Hill.

MCDERMOTT I. (1996) Unpublished training material. International Training Seminars.

MEHRABIAN A. *and* FERRIS L. (1967) 'Inference of attitudes from non-verbal communication in two channels'. *The Journal of Counselling Psychology.* Vol. 31. pp 248–252.

RACKHAM N. *and* MORGAN T. R. G. (1977) *Behaviour Analysis in Training.* Maidenhead, McGraw-Hill.

URWICK (1947) *The Elements of Administration.* London, Pitman.

# Index